Classes and Cultures
1780-1945

Richard Brown

Published by Authoring History

http://richardjohnbr1066.wordpress.com/
https://sites.google.com/site/lookingathistory/

First published in 2011; second edition, 2022

ISBN: 9798412430898

Front Cover: Honoré Daumier (1808-1879), *'En dehors de la boutique du marchand d'estampes'* (Outside the print seller's shop), 1860-1863.

Contents

Acknowledgements

One of the constant things about research and writing History is that it is ever-changing, a paradox given the finality of the past. I remember being told by an aged and eminent historian five decades ago that 'historians are like good wine; they mature with age'. The genesis of this book lies long in my past. In fact, its origins go back to when I first began teaching in the early 1970s. Much of my work at university focused on medieval history; I had only taken one course in modern history. It was a shock to the system, though hardly a surprise, when I found that most of my teaching would be modern and I quickly had to familiarise myself with the Industrial Revolution and its consequences. I spent most of the succeeding decades teaching the subject at GCSE and Advanced Level with growing confidence and enjoyment. Though I retained my interest in medieval history, it was evident that this was not what I would spend much time teaching.

I have always enjoyed teaching and much of that enjoyment came from teaching the fundamentals of being a historian and from my students' overwhelmingly positive reactions. Their often irreverent comments made teaching what it should always be, a joint search for understanding and knowledge in an environment that is encouraging and entertaining. They will never know how grateful I was and remain for their willingness to engage with my ideas and the ideas of other historians and writers and how far they have influenced the persistently evolving nature of this work that was first drafted fifty years ago and has been revisited and revised in subsequent years. For those of us who remember when teaching was once more than simply getting students through examinations or reaching targets, the mutual enjoyment of discovering the past and understanding its histories is something I still savour.

Series Preface

British Society 1780-1945 consists of five books that seek to explain the major social developments that occurred during the late-eighteenth, and nineteenth centuries and, unlike the first edition of this series, extends into the first half of the twentieth century. *British Society 1780-1945* consists of five volumes:

Volume 1: Economy, Population and Transport
Volume 2: Classes and Cultures
Volume 3: Work, Health and Poverty
Volume 4: Education and Crime
Volume 5: Religion and Government

The second volume examines the nature of social classes and cultures from the late-eighteenth century to the mid-twentieth century. The book first looks at the ways in which contemporaries and historians have viewed classes and how a 'class' society developed as the result of economic change. The remaining three chapters follow the conventional three class definition and consider the working-classes, middle-classes and upper-classes. Particular regard is placed on the changing role of working-class and middle-class women and how their economic, social and cultural roles changed when faced with massive economic dislocation and male-dominated outlooks.

Series Prologue

If forced to find a metaphor for writing about Victorian and Edwardian social history I should prefer something like Penelope's web—a garment endlessly woven by day and unpicked again by night.[1]

Reading David Cannadine's study of nineteenth century Britain—*Victorious Century: The United Kingdom, 1800-1906*—I was struck by his comments in the preface that he, like me, was 'lucky enough to grow up in what were in many ways the final years of the 'long' nineteenth century—namely the 1950s.'[2] The United Kingdom was still, or at least thought of itself as, a formidable international power with both a large navy and global empire. Textiles, coal-mining, steel manufacture and engineering—many in coal-powered factories—remained Britain's traditional staple industries, the creation of the industrial revolution in the late-eighteenth century.

In the 1780s, the bulk of Britain's population still lived in the countryside and most industry was located within rural environments. Industrial growth drew in the surplus population from other regions into towns and cities. By the middle of the nineteenth century, half the population lived in the countryside, but by the end it was only a third. Britain had become an industrialised and urbanised society and the rural world became increasingly that of a declining minority. D. H. Lawrence (1885-1930), who grew up in the Nottinghamshire coalfield at the end of the nineteenth century, described the development of the landscape at the start of his novel, *Sons and Lovers* published in 1913. At this time, despite the building of these new mines, the mines and villages were still surrounded by the countryside, like 'black studs on the countryside, linked by a loop of fine chain, the railway'.[3] The decades between the 1860s and the end of the Second World War in 1945 transformed Britain swiftly and profoundly. British society became urbanised and suburbanised, secularised, democratised; general assumptions about social relationships and politically legitimate behaviour shifted from vertical hierarchical community groupings to stratified classes: in a word, it became 'modern'.[4]

These dramatic economic and industrial changes were caused by equally dramatic changes in population in terms of growth and especially in population distribution. Wealth creation associated with industrial growth allowed the maintenance of a larger population while the concentration of new industries in certain areas saw widespread population movements. Massive social change rarely occurs uneventfully and the growth and shifts in population were

[1] Harris, Jose, *Private Lives, Public Spirit: A Social History of Britain, 1870-1914*, (Oxford University Press), 1992, (Penguin), 1993, p. 251.
[2] Cannadine, David, *Victorious Century: The United Kingdom, 1800-1906*, (Allen Lane), 2017, p. xvii.
[3] Lawrence, D. H., *Sons and Lovers*, 2 Vols. (B. Tauchnitz), 1929, Vol. 1, p. 4.
[4] Shannon, Richard, *The Crisis of Imperialism, 1865-1915*, (Paladin), 1974, p. 11.

accompanied by a wide range of problems as demands for housing, sewerage, water, food, labour and leisure all expanded. Britain was becoming an urbanised and industrial society with all the problems, as well as benefits that this entailed. Rather than this being a source of pride or optimism, contemporary middle-class observers feared that the city was becoming a place of 'dreadful delight'. Manchester was 'Coke Town', London the 'modern Babylon'. At a physical level, urbanisation compounded existing social problems of sanitation, disease, and housing and gave rise to new ones that contemporaries linked to crime, prostitution and poverty. Cities were seen as sites of moral corruption and violence inhabited by criminals, drug addicts, prostitutes, homosexuals and immigrants. But some Victorians saw cities as places of excitement and many took advantage of the growing leisure opportunities on offer. Others went 'slumming', exploring working-class districts, slums and rookeries either in pursuit of excitement or to offer charity.

By 1914–and this had not fundamentally changed by 1945–Britain had become a society in which individuals' class determined their life expectations and this was mirrored in which carriages people used on the railways and in accommodation on ocean liners. Wealthier passengers were separated from the poorer for the whole journey. The very wealthy passengers paid the most for their tickets and stayed in first-class accommodation. Less wealthy middle-classes and upper-working-class paid less and stayed in second-class accommodation. The poor third-class passengers paid the least for their tickets and stayed in third-class or what used to be called 'steerage'. On the *Titanic*, Decks A-D were reserved for the first-class passengers with second-class passengers on Decks D-G. Third-class passengers were on Deck G near the ship's engines. Each class of passenger had their own entrance to the ship and could sit on their designated decks to relax. This was put in place to stop the different classes from mixing. The only time that people from all social classes came together was during the church service held in the first-class quarters on Sunday. In terms of accommodation, food and facilities available on the liner, there was also a clear class division. In third-class, there were only two baths to share between the 710 passengers while the first-class suites had their own bathing facilities. When the *Titanic* sank in April 1912, a far higher proportion of third-class passengers perished than those in first- or second-classes.[5]

The ship became a metaphor for the problems and tensions facing society. Everyone found ammunition in the fate of the *Titanic* and put their own spin on it: suffragists and their opponents; radicals, reformers, and capitalists; critics of technology and modern life; racists and xenophobes and champions of racial and ethnic equality; editorial writers, preachers and poets. Fundamentalists saw the iceberg as divine punishment for worldly pride and self-indulgence.[6]

---

[5] Biel, Steven, *Down with the Old Canoe: A Cultural History of the Titanic Disaster*, (W. W. Norton & Co.), 1996.
[6] See, for instance, 'Morals of the Disaster', *Sheffield Daily Telegraph*, 18 April 1912,

Protestant sermons used the *Titanic* to condemn the budding consumer society and working-class ballads made the ship emblematic of the foolishness and greed of the rich. Yet early accounts of the disaster focused largely, and with little evidence of the heroism of well-to-do passengers like John Jacob Astor IV (1864-1912), who put 'women and children first' in the lifeboats[7] and anti-suffragist agitators used this as evidence that women were too weak to be allowed the vote. This myth of first-class heroism was used to trumpet a good deal of racist cant about heroic Anglo-Saxon manhood, at the expense of foreigners, Black people and lower-class *Titanic* passengers, who were often depicted in early accounts as cowards though others chose to celebrate the noble workers who went down with the ship.

The economic and social changes of the late-Victorian and Edwardian years contributed to crisis but it is unclear what the crisis represented. Darwinism had shaken Christianity and problems in the economy, the revelation of enduring poverty and the alteration of the social structure called many Victorian ideas into doubt. To many men and women, especially younger people Victorian ideas and values no longer seemed satisfying. Consequently, the years between 1870 and 1914 were filled with exploration and speculation as people searched for new ordering principles. Fundamental assumptions about the economic and social systems came under attack and new ones emerged.[8] Britain's experience in the First World War was its first taste of 'total war' when around six million British people had direct experience of trench warfare while most of the civilian population became involved in the war effort in some way. The emotional trauma suffered by many men who were conscripted to serve in the Armed Forces. There was widespread bereavement because of the death of family and friends.[9] Many upper and middle-class women gained new experience from taking up paid employment for the first time.[10] After two decades of economic and political crisis and widespread unemployment, the Second World War replaced the horror of the trenches with the horror of the Blitz. This meant change and upheaval though this was more evident after 1945

---

p. 6, an early discussion of the issue of lifeboats, and 'Ethics of the Great Tragedy', *Pall Mall Gazette*, 23 April 1912, p. 1, discusses 'in the catastrophe of the Titanic the symbol of our present life'.

[7] 'The Age of Chivalry', *Pall Mall Gazette*, 18 April 1912, p. 4, 'Suffragettes and Male Chivalry. Strange Opinions', *Pall Mall Gazette*, 18 April 1912, p. 4, reporting on an article published in *Le Figaro*.

[8] Reynolds, David, *The Long Shadow: The Great War and the Twentieth Century*, (Simon & Schuster), 2013, considers the long-term transformative effects of the war.

[9] Seldon, Anthony, and Walsh, David, *Public Schools and the Great War*, (Pen & Sword Military), 2013, examines its impact on public schools. Of those public schoolboys who fought in the war, a fifth were killed.

[10] Molinari, Véronique, 'Le droit de vote accordé aux femmes britanniques à l'issue de la Première Guerre mondiale: une récompense pour les services rendus?', *La revue LISA*, vol. 6, (4), (2008), pp. 71-87.

than after 1918. There is, however, a debate about the nature and extent of the change produced by the war. This centres on whether the war is seen as the cause of fundamental change or whether, alternatively, it can be seen as a catalyst that accelerated existing political, social and economic trends.

There are many parallels between Britain today and Britain during the 'long' nineteenth century. Both societies were coping with sustained population growth and the tensions this creates between different ethnic groups. Today's concern over unfettered immigration from the European Union and especially 'economic migrants' from beyond Europe was one of the reasons why people decided in the 2016 referendum to opt narrowly for 'Brexit'. In the nineteenth century, there was unease over Irish immigration and, after 1880, from the influx of poor Jewish refugees especially from Eastern Europe and Russia. Poverty, housing shortages and exploitation in the workplace remain issues today as they were over a century ago. Our current obsession with the environment was paralleled by the Victorians who sought, and failed, to take remedial action necessary to counter the social impact of industrial change and urban growth. Education, crime and the nature of leisure are equally issues on which the attitudes of Victorians have much in common with our anxieties today over educational standards, knife-crime and binge-drinking, for them it would have been the garrotting panic of the early 1860s and Fenian and anarchist terrorism. The surveillance society of the nineteenth century was the pervasive presence of the bobby on his beat whereas today we are saturated with CCTV and speed cameras. Debates over the role of government and the extent to which it should impinge on people's lives remain as important and unresolved to us as they were to our ancestors. The origins of the 'nanny state' lie in the debate in the early 1850s over whether Britain should or should not be compelled to be vaccinated or bathed into health. We are still as psychotically fixated with our position in society as Victorian working men and women and those from the middle- and upper-classes. Belief and unbelief remain controversial whether the tensions between Anglicans and Nonconformists or 'Catholic aggression' in the nineteenth century or today's debates over female and gay priests, Islamic jihad or why creationism should not be part of the school curriculum.

Preoccupations with how to manage the problems created by economic and demographic change were unresolved by 1945. There may have been some improvements in people's quality of life but these were often small and unevenly distributed. For most people, life remained a constant battle for survival to keep above the poverty line especially for the young and the old. The 'arithmetic of woe' was all-pervasive. Only through demanding work, self-help and a modicum of luck could most people maintain any semblance of quality in their lives. The fear of poverty and yet the recognition that poverty was inevitable at some stage in the individual's life was ever-present. Today, in an increasingly digitalised society, it is not difficult to find similar circumstances. Poverty has not been eliminated; in fact, if anything, in the last two decades it has worsened with growing concerns about a 'benefit culture', 'fuel poverty', the problems associated with an increasingly ageing population and the economic crisis of 'credit-crunch Britain' and fear of austerity and recession and the growth of food banks as the only way many people can avoid starvation and even then not all the time. We now have free access to schooling and medical care but this has not necessarily resulted in a more meritocratic or necessarily a healthier society. Thirty-five years of the National Curriculum have not made students better educated or better prepared for their 'place' in the global labour market. We still have a large number of students leaving schools with minimum standards of literacy and numeracy despite a progressive rise in the school-leaving age. The National Health Service and advances in medical technology mean people can be cured of diseases that would have killed them in Victorian Britain but we are now plagued with rising levels of obesity and alcohol-related diseases. People from poorer backgrounds, whatever of the plaudits of government, remain disadvantaged. The poor it appears are getting poorer and the rich richer, a return to something like the 'two nations' of Disraeli's England. In many respects, the social and political agenda thrust on to the Victorians remains unresolved. Statements about a 'broken society' that periodically punctuate contemporary political debate would have been familiar to many Victorian social commentators.

1 Classes

The old society, then was a finely graded hierarchy of great subtlety and discrimination, in which men were acutely aware of their exact relation to those immediately above and below them, but only vaguely conscious except at the very top of their connections with those on their own level.... There was one horizontal cleavage of great import, that between the 'gentleman' and the 'common people', but it could scarcely be defined in economic terms.[1]

All societies are, to some extent, stratified or divided into different social groups. They may be functional, defined by their contribution to society as a whole or may be in competition with each other for social control or wealth. They may share common 'values', have a common 'national identity' or form part of a pluralistic society in which different 'values' coexist with varying degrees of consensus or conflict. They have different names like 'castes' or 'ranks' or 'classes'. British society between 1780 and 1945 has been called a 'class society' but there are some differences between historians about its precise meaning or whether it is meaningful at all. Were there two classes or three or five or any classes at all? Were there common values? It is important to have some understanding of the 'wholeness' of society, whether nationally or within a given community because it was this that people were reacting against or attempting to preserve. The diversities of individual lived experiences must be given meaning not in isolation but within their web of social relationships.

A paternalist society?[2]

Society in the 1780s remain paternalist and hierarchical, one of mutual and reciprocal obligation. What mattered was not what was later parodied as 'forelock tugging' but the often sympathetic and active participation by the elites in the lives of the rest of society. There was an expectation of reciprocity, a common outlook and recognition of interests and, if necessary, sheer coercion to maintain civil stability in a hierarchical social structure. The Christian faith and moral code were a common possession of all of society and rank, station, duty and decorum were central social values. For paternalists, society should be authoritative, though tempered by adhesion to the Common Law and ancient 'liberties'. It should be hierarchical and 'organic' in nature with people knowing their appointed place within a defined 'social order'. Finally, it should be 'pluralistic' with different hierarchical 'interests'--for instance, the landed interest or the West Indian interest--making up the organic whole.[2] Within this structure,

---

[1] Perkin, H., *The Origins of Modern English Society 1780-1880*, (Routledge), 1969, 2nd ed., (Routledge), 2002, p. 24.
[2] Roberts, David, *Paternalism in Early Victorian England*, (Croom Helm), 1979,

paternalists had certain duties and held certain assumptions. There was a duty to rule, a direct result of wealth and power that followed from this and an obligation to help the poor, not passively but with active assistance. Paternalists also believed in the duty of 'guidance', of firm moral superintendence that governed relationships at all levels of society and continued to play an important role even in innovative areas of the economy.[3] Apprenticeship, for instance, was more than an induction into craft skills; it was incorporation into the social experience or common wisdom of the working community. Practices, norms and attitudes were, as a result, reproduced through successive generations within an accepted framework of traditional customs and rights based on a vague notion of 'the moral economy'.[4]

Patronage was central to the paternalist ethic and it retained its importance throughout the nineteenth, twentieth and into the twenty-first century though its nature has changed.[5] It was a key feature of an unequal face-to-face society in the late-eighteenth century, crossing social barriers and bringing together possibly hostile groups. Patronage involved a 'lopsided' relationship between individuals, a patron and a client of unequal status, wealth and influence. It could be called a 'package deal' of reciprocal advantage to the individuals involved. At one level, it was a formal process where an individual has the authority, power or right or in his 'gift' to appoint another individual to a particular position. It is true that by the 1830s these 'politically useful' forms of patronage such as jobs for electors and rewards for political supporters had largely decayed but to assume that there was a general decline in patronage is to fundamentally misconceive the issue.[6] Patronage remained central to the Church of England with prime ministers still exercising considerable influence over episcopal appointments[7] and in the Arts.[8] The nineteenth century is often

---

pp. 2-10.

[3] Revill, George, '"Railway Derby": occupational community, paternalism and corporate culture, 1850-90', *Urban History*, Vol. 28, (2001), pp. 378-404, and Revill, George, 'Liberalism and paternalism: politics and corporate culture in "Railway Derby", 1865-75'. *Social History*, Vol. 24, (1999), pp. 196-214, provide a valuable case study.

[4] Thompson, E. P., 'The Moral Economy of the Crowd in the Eighteenth Century', *Past & Present*, Vol. 50, (1971), pp. 76-136, reprinted in his *Customs in Common*, (Merlin Press), 1991, pp. 185-259, with 'The Moral Economy Reviewed', pp. 259-351.

[5] Bourne, J. M., *Patronage and Society in Nineteenth-Century England*, (Edward Arnold), 1986, is an essential study.

[6] Harling, Philip, *The waning of 'Old Corruption': the politics of economical reform in Britain, 1779-1846*, (Oxford University Press), 1996.

[7] See, for instance, Gibson, William T., '"A Great Excitement": Gladstone and church patronage, 1860-1894', *Anglican and Episcopal History*, Vol. 68, (1999),

seen as an age in which professionalism replaced patronage in British political and social life but this is too stark a distinction. Careers were opened up to talent and merit as the upwardly-mobile middle-classes gained entry into the old preserves of the aristocracy and gentry.[9] Fewer places were 'reserved' just because they were within the gift and bequest of those with wealth and property. Elections and examinations, especially after 1850, made steady inroads into elitism and merit was substituted for manipulation and management. But patronage remained an important feature of British society and gained important footholds in Britain's growing empire.

Many of the political, social and economic changes of the first half of the nineteenth century, however, increased the amount of patronage that was available. There was a dramatic growth in the number of 'administratively necessary' offices.[10] The prison, factory, health and schools Inspectorates were all staffed, at least initially, through patronage. This was paralleled in local government where 'efficient' patronage was used by rival elites within communities as an extension of party politics. It did not reach the level of the American system where 'to the winner belong the spoils' and the winning party gave government jobs to its supporters, friends and relatives, something reformed from the 1860s onwards. Finally, offices may have been filled by personal nomination but individuals had to possess some basic competence. This notion of 'merit' received wider application after the Northcote-Trevelyan Report of 1854, though patronage comfortably withstood much of the onslaught of merit until the 1870s.[11] Only the northern urban middle-classes were indifferent

---

pp. 372-396, Disraeli's church patronage, 1868-1880', *Anglican and Episcopal History*, Vol. 62, (1992), pp. 197-210, and 'The Tories and church patronage: 1812-1830', *Journal of Ecclesiastical History*, Vol. 41, (1990), pp. 266-274.

[8] See, Morrison, John, 'Victorian municipal patronage: the foundation and management of Glasgow Corporation Galleries 1854-1888', *Journal of the History of Collections*, Vol. 8, (1996), pp. 93-102, and Wolff, Janet, and Arscott, Caroline, '"Cultivated Capital": patronage and art in nineteenth-century Manchester and Leeds', in Marsden, Gordon, (ed.), *Victorian values: personalities and perspectives in nineteenth-century society*, (Longman), 1998, pp. 29-41.

[9] Wooldridge, Adrian, *The Aristocracy of Talent: How Meritocracy Made the Modern World*, (Allen Lane), 2021, pp. 144-174, 234-255.

[10] This is evident in Clifton, G. C., *Professionalism, patronage and public service in Victorian London: the staff of the Metropolitan Board of Works, 1856-1889*, (Athlone Press), 1992, and Porter, Dale H., and Clifton, G. C., 'Patronage, professional values and Victorian public works: engineering and contracting the Thames embankment', *Victorian Studies*, Vol. 31, (1988), pp. 319-349.

[11] This was particularly evident in the Indian Civil Service: Compton, J. M., 'Open Competition and the Indian Civil Service, 1854-1876', *English Historical Review*, Vol. 83, (1968), pp. 265-284, and Moore, R. J., 'The abolition of

to patronage though it was still evident in, for instance, the promotion of science.[12] The bulk of the middle-classes were located in the genteel world of the professions and of propertyless independent incomes, far less entrepreneurial and competitive than their industrial equivalents. As long as common areas and values existed, patronage continued to have broad application and utility.

In many respect more importantly, patronage also operated (and still operates) at a less formal level in the 'old boy network', predominantly though not exclusively male in character until after 1945.[13] It is an informal network linking members of a social class or education or profession or organisation within wider networks of kinship and friendship in order to provide connections and information and favours especially in business or politics. It functions as an uncharted, invisible system that excluded from membership less powerful men and women. The phrase 'It's not what you know, it's whom you know' is associated with this tradition. A young doctor who becomes the protégé of an older physician or clique is in a more advantageous position for advancement and upward mobility than those who do not have this support. Among those born in the 1840s, approximately 20 per cent listed in *Who's Who* had attended one of the Clarendon public schools. Even today, the alumni of the nine Clarendon schools are 94 times more likely to reach the British elite than those who attended any other school. Alumni of elite schools also retain a striking capacity to enter the elite even without passing through other prestigious institutions, such as Oxford, Cambridge or private members clubs.[14] This network was reinforced by the round of balls, parties and sporting events that formed the social elite's calendar and defined the character of the class as a whole. The country lifestyle of hunting, shooting and fishing, the social calendar of county society and the system of titles and honours cast a cloak of tradition over new forms of economic power. The continuation of the old-boy network is a major reason for the preservation of traditional elites in British society and why social mobility into the upper echelons of

---

patronage in the Indian Civil Service and the closure of Haileybury College', *Historical Journal*, Vol. 7, (1964), pp. 246-257.
[12] Cardwell, D. S. L., 'The patronage of science in nineteenth-century Manchester', in Turner, Gerard L'Estrange, (ed.), *The patronage of science in the nineteenth century*, (Noordhoff International Publishing), 1976, pp. 95-113.
[13] Reeves, Aaron, Friedman, Sam, Rahal, Charles and Flemmen, Magne, 'The Decline and Persistence of the Old Bay: Private Schools and Elite Recruitment 1897-2016', *American Sociological Review*, Vol. 82 (2017), pp. 1167-1187, https://doi.org/10.1177/0003122417735742
[14] Rubinstein W. D., Education and the Social Origins of British Elites, 1880-1970', *Past & Present*, Vol. 112, (1986), pp. 163-207, Rubinstein W. D., 'The Social Origins and Career Patterns of Oxford and Cambridge Matriculants, 1840-1900', *Historical Research*, Vol. 82, (2008), pp. 715-730.

society is restricted.

Changing views of classes

During the late-eighteenth and early-nineteenth centuries, social values that had existed unaltered for several hundred years began to be challenged. From the 1780s, writers tried to make sense of a Britain of increasing contrasts. British society before the economic changes, and in many areas after it, was based on face-to-face, often daily, contact between individuals of different social status who recognised their 'place' or 'station' in life and the duties and responsibilities this imposed on them. Social control was based on recognition of social status, be it political power, economic wealth or social and cultural development. Population growth, the expansion of towns and the move from a rural to urban economy splintered this ordered structure. The poet Robert Southey (1774-1843) wrote in 1829, 'The bond of attachment is broken'.[15] Changing religious observance broke the 'bond of dependency' between squire, parson and labourer. The aristocracy and gentry gradually 'cut' their lives off from those of their labouring workers. The layout of country houses and gardens that evolved from the mid-seventeenth century demonstrated a move towards domestic privacy.[16] Client relationships became less important as 'masterless' labour became more mobile and centred in urban communities.

Urbanisation arose beyond the paternal framework. People moved to towns because they saw them as 'free' from the constraints of rural society as well as furnishing economic opportunities. Those who threw themselves into city life did not see themselves as victims. William Aitken (1814?-1869) described his fellow Manchester Chartists as 'sons of freedom' and saw city life as liberating, not oppressive. It is not surprising that people flooded into those 'dark satanic mills' and few ever returned to that 'green and pleasant land'. The middle-class perception of cities and large towns was very different. For them, cities and towns had a foggy,

---

[15] Southey, Robert, *Sir Thomas More: or, Colloquies on the Progress and Prospects of Society*, 2 Vols. (John Murray), 1829, Vol. 2, p. 135.

[16] See, for instance, Pollock, Linda A., 'Living on the stage of the world: the concept of privacy among the elite of early modern England ', in Wilson, Adrian, (ed.), *Rethinking social history: English society, 1570-1920 and its interpretation*, (Manchester University Press), 1993, pp. 78-96, Meldrum, Tim, 'Domestic service, privacy and the 18th century metropolitan household', *Urban History*, Vol. 26, (1999), pp. 27-39, and Taylor, William M., 'Visualising comfort: aspect, prospect, and controlling privacy in *The Gentleman's House* (1864)', in Taylor, William M., (ed.), *The geography of law: landscape, identity and regulation*, (Hart Publishing), 2006, pp. 65-83. Floud, Roderick, *The Economic History of the English Garden*, (Allen Lane), 2019, provides analysis of the cost and nature of the expansion of gardens after 1720.

malarial landscape, a place where revolutionary tempers might suddenly erupt to overthrow society and where rookeries were the dominion of menacing criminality. This reflected their fear of the streets, aversion to crowds and anxiety about the soulless character of society. In addition, after 1850 and in the larger communities well before, towns and cities ceased to be face-to-face societies and became places of anonymity. In London, for instance, the green spaces between its constituent villages were quickly absorbed into the inexorable sprawl of the city. Samuel Wilberforce (1805-1873), the Bishop of Oxford, said in a talk on 'the London we live in' in 1864:

> He looked out of the bedroom windows of the little inn in which he was staying at the surging crowd which passed and re-passed beneath him; and he could have screamed for someone who knew him.... This feeling of isolation in the midst of a vast crowd was absolutely painful.[17]

An 'abdication on the part of the governors' had been recognised as early as the 1810s even though it was Thomas Carlyle (1795-1881) who popularised it in the 1840s.[18] The changing focus of the economy away from land towards manufacturing and service industries led to a gradual decline in the economic power of the paternalist landed elite and the statutory fabric of state paternalism was gradually dismantled. Paternalism was grounded in reciprocal obligations like 'just wages' and 'fair prices', many of which were given a statutory basis in Tudor and Stuart legislation. From the 1770s, this legislation was either allowed to lapse or deliberately repealed. The principles of 'the free market' would not accommodate the protectionism inherent in paternalism. The question is whether the caring landlord ever existed in reality and how far there was an actual 'abdication' or whether it was simply thought so by those fighting to retain older values in the face of social and economic change. There is no doubt that society changed but to see this solely in terms of a shift from paternalistic solidarity to unbridled individualism is too stark. Nineteenth century society had elements of both, but despite this, there persisted a widespread belief that there had been a shift from a paternalist to a capitalist society.

Harold Perkin (1926-2004) characterised the late-eighteenth and early-nineteenth century as a 'one-class society'.[19] Only the aristocratic elite could, he maintained, be seen as a 'class'. This view of a unitary

---

[17] Cit., Waller, P. J., *Town, City and Nation, England 1850-1914*, (Oxford University Press), 1983, p. 49.

[18] Ibid., Perkin, H., *The Origins of Modern English Society 1780-1880*, pp. 183-196, discusses this issue.

[19] Ibid., Perkin, H., *The Origins of Modern English Society 1780-1880*, pp. 36-38.

11

capitalist ruling class certainly did not exist by 1830. Karl Marx (1819-1883) saw the British ruling class as an 'antiquated compromise' in which, while the aristocracy 'ruled officially', the bourgeoisie ruled 'over all the various spheres of civil society in reality'.[20] The aristocracy, that Marx thought had 'signed its own death warrant' as a result of the Crimean War (1853-1856), proved much more resilient in maintaining a strong presence in the Cabinet, Parliament and the Civil Service. The proprietary fortunes and power of the large landowners remained virtually intact until the end of the century and the relatively amicable blending of aristocratic landowners and wealthy industrialists remains one of the striking features of British society in the latter half of the century.

The complexities of classes

Class identity was surprisingly strong in nineteenth century Britain, reinforced through networks of collective mutuality and associational culture. The social cost of economic and demographic change was borne by the working-classes. There had always been a gulf between rich and poor but what altered was the way in which that division was regarded across society. An alternative to the vertical relationships of a paternalistic hierarchical society lay in the horizontal solidarities of 'class'.[21] Richard Dennis sums up the problem of class in the following way:

> Evidently the road to class analysis crosses a minefield with a sniper behind every bush...it may not be possible to please all the people all of the time...[22]

There are, however, problems in whether to use class in a singular or plural form. Some argue that it is misleading and unnecessary to adopt the plural form simply to acknowledge strata of workers differentiated by income, occupations, region or some other variable. This view neglects the gap between skilled, semi-skilled and unskilled workers within the working-classes between whom there were considerable cultural as well as economic differences or between the humble clerk and merchant bankers and financiers within the middle-classes.

There are differences over the meaning of 'class' or whether it is

---

[20] Marx, Karl, 'The Crisis in England and the British Constitution', in Marx, K., and Engels, F., *On Britain*, (Moscow State Publishing House), 1953, pp. 410-411.

[21] The literature on 'class' is immense but theoretical perspectives can be found in Calvert, P., *The Concept of Class*, (Hutchinson), 1983, Giddens, A., *The Class Structure of Advanced Societies*, (Hutchinson), 1973, and especially Neale, R. S., (ed.), *History and Class: essential readings in theory and interpretation*, (Basil Blackwell), 1984.

[22] Dennis, R., *English Industrial Cities in the Nineteenth Century: A Social Geography*, (Cambridge University Press), 1984, pp. 187-188.

meaningful at all?[23] Many contemporaries interpreted early Victorian society in terms of two classes. Benjamin Disraeli (1804-1881) popularised the idea of 'two nations', the rich and the poor.[24] Elizabeth Gaskell (1810-1865) wrote of Manchester that she had 'never lived in a place before where there were two sets of people always running each other down.'[25] Tory Radicals were not alone in using the two-class model. Friedrich Engels (1820-1895) referred to the working-class in the singular and offered a model dominated by two classes, the bourgeoisie and the proletariat, in which other classes existed but were growing increasingly less important.[26] Left-wing historians, E. P. Thompson (1924-1993) and John

---

[23] Neale, R. S., *Class in British History 1680-1850*, (Basil Blackwell), 1983, and Neale, R. S., *Class and Ideology in the Nineteenth Century*, (Routledge), 1972, the useful bibliographical essay by Morris, R. J., *Class and Class Consciousness in the Industrial Revolution*, (Macmillan), 1980, and his 'The industrial revolution: Class and Common Interest', *History Today*, Vol. 33, (5), (1983), pp. 31-35, are good starting points for the period before 1850. See also, Briggs, A., 'The language of 'class' in early-nineteenth century England ', in Briggs, A., and Saville, J., (eds.), *Essays in labour history in memory of G. D. H. Cole*, revised edition, (Macmillan), 1967, pp. 43-73, and Jones, G. Steadman, *Languages of Class*, (Cambridge University Press), 1983. Joyce, Patrick, *Visions of the People: Industrial England and the question of class 1840-1914*, (Cambridge University Press), 1991, takes the question of language further and questions the veracity of a view of society grounded simply in 'class'. Prothero, I., *Artisans and Politics in Early Nineteenth-Century London*, (Dawson), 1979, Smith, D., *Conflict and Compromise: Class Formation in English Society 1830-1914*, (Routledge), 1982, and Calhoun, C., *The Question of Class Struggle*, (Basil Blackwell), 1982. Reid, Alastair J., *Social Classes and Social Relations in Britain 1850-1914*, (Macmillan), 1992, is the best and briefest starting-point for this period. Benson, J., *The Working-class in Britain 1850-1939*, (Longman), 1989, is a sound general survey. McKibbin, R., *The Ideologies of Class: Social Relations in Britain 1880-1950*, (Oxford University Press), 1990, is an excellent study. Perkin, H., *The Rise of Professional Society: England since 1880*, (Routledge), 1989 2nd, ed., (Routledge), 2002, extends his earlier work in a masterful study. Meacham, Standish, *A Life Apart: The English Working-class 1890-1914*, (Thames & Hudson), 1977, and Bourne, Joanna, *Working-class Cultures in Britain 1890-1960*, (Routledge), 1994, are excellent.
[24] See Disraeli, Benjamin, *Sybil or The Two Nations*, (B. Tauchnitz), 1845.
[25] Gaskell, Elizabeth, *North and South*, (B. Tauchnitz), 1855, p. 48.
[26] Engels, F., *Die Lage der arbeitenden Klasse in England*, (Otto Wigand), 1845, translated into English as *The Condition of the Working-class in England*, New York, 1887, London, 1891; various editions including W. O. Henderson and W. H. Chaloner, (Blackwell), 1958, Victor Kiernan, (Penguin), 1987, and Tristram Hunt, (Penguin), 2009. McLellan, D., *Engels*, (Fontana), 1977, Carver, T., *Engels*, (Oxford University Press), 1981, and Hunt, Tristram, *The Frock-coated Communist: The Revolutionary Life of Friedrich Engels*, (Allen Lane), 2009, provide valuable critiques.

Foster (1940-), have also used this model. [27]

For Edward Thompson, class experience was the result of the productive relations into which people entered. The essence of class lay not in income or work but in class-consciousness, the product of contemporary perceptions of capital and labour, exploiter and exploited. But Thompson enlarged the horizons of working-class history to include not simply trade unions, real wages and popular political traditions but the broader cultural experience of working people. His was a cultural and experiential view of class as much as an economic one. Class, Thompson stated, 'is defined by men as they live their own history, and, in the end, this is its only definition.'[28] Class was the outcome of the inherited or shared, active and conscious experiences of working people. His was not an economically determinist view of class but one in which workers' voices and wills and feelings led them towards collective identity, struggle and action. For Thompson, no consciousness, no class. *The Making* has been extensively debated in the decades since it was published especially by those who privileged radical language over Thompson's collective action.[29]

John Foster's study of Oldham, South Shields and Northampton found that 12,000 workers sold their labour to 70 capitalist families.[30] The working-class, Foster argues, went through three stages of developing consciousness. Initially it was 'labour conscious'. Consumer prices ceased to be a major concern and shifted to the levels of their own wages.[31] Then it became 'class conscious' where attempts to resolve industrial and economic problems, initially by a vanguard of skilled workers, became

---

[27] Foster. J., *Class Struggle and the Industrial Revolution: early industrial capitalism in three English towns*, (Weidenfeld), 1974.

[28] Thompson, E. P., *The Making of the English Working Class*, (Gollancz), 1963, p. 11.

[29] Palmer, Bryan, *The Making of E. P. Thompson: Marxism, Humanism and History*, (University of Toronto Press), 1981, Kaye, H. J., *The British Marxist Historians*, (Polity), 1984, pp. 167-220, and Kaye, H. J., and McClelland, D., (eds.), *E. P. Thompson: Critical Perspectives*, (Polity), 1990. See also, Palmer, Bryan D., et al, 'E. P. Thompson's The Making of the English Working Class at Fifty', *Labour/Le Travail*, Vol. 71, (2013), pp. 149-192, Fieldhouse, Roger, and Taylor, Richard, (eds.), *E. P. Thompson and English radicalism*, (Manchester University Press), 2013, and Burton, Antoinette, and Fortado, Stephanie, (eds.), *Histories of a Radical Book: E. P. Thompson and The Making of the English Working Class*, (Berghahn), 2021, pp. 1-6, 85-100.

[30] Foster's view of the *petit bourgeoisie* and his attempts to explain it away have been criticised by historians such as R. S. Neale who interpose a 'middling' class between the middle and working-classes in his 'five-class model': Neale, R. S., 'Class and class-consciousness in early-nineteenth century England: three classes or five?', *Victorian Studies*, Vol. 12, (1968-9), pp. 5-32.

[31] Ibid., Foster. J., *Class Struggle and the Industrial Revolution: early industrial capitalism in three English towns*, pp. 47-72.

politicised.[32] Political reform was seen as a necessity for the resolution of economic problems: only a Parliament elected on the People's Charter would be prepared to legislate in favour of working-class concerns. Foster suggests that the movement was a victim of its own success and that the bourgeoisie was alerted to the threat of the potentially revolutionary masses and adopted a policy of economic liberalisation by conceding some proletarian demands specifically mentioning the Ten Hour Act 1847 and the offer of household suffrage in 1849. This, he maintained, marked a major tactical victory and led to a 'liberalised consciousness' by which the bourgeoisie, aided by growing economic prosperity after 1850, was able to attach important sections of the working population—a labour aristocracy—to its consensus ideology grounded in individualism and 'respectability'.[33] Skilled workers had previously formed the revolutionary vanguard but became reformist in attitude, accepting economic realities to get the best deal they possibly could though individual and collective bargaining.

The model assumes that change was based on conflict or 'class war' between competing classes for economic dominance. It recognises other social groups but subsumes them within the two-class perspective. It acknowledges that although there may have been a significant degree of ideological homogeneity in the vibrant and volatile social magma of the industrial factory towns, this was less evident in rural areas and the older urban areas where class consciousness was less well formed and where older patterns of social interaction retained their importance. Diversity of experience within the working population led to diversity of responses.[34]

Others saw things differently. Most contemporary and modern analysts have followed a three-class model. David Ricardo (1772-1823), the economist, identified three economic classes based on rent, capital and wages broadly 'upper', 'middle' and 'working' classes. The journalist Henry Mayhew (1812-1887) went further dividing society in the late 1840s into 'those who will work, those who cannot work, those who will not work and those who need not work'.[35] Contemporary attitudes have been

---

[32] Ibid., Foster. J., *Class Struggle and the Industrial Revolution: early industrial capitalism in three English towns*, pp. 73-125.

[33] Ibid., Foster. J., *Class Struggle and the Industrial Revolution: early industrial capitalism in three English towns*, pp. 203-249.

[34] For critiques of Foster see Thompson, E. P., *Times Higher Education Supplement*, 8 March 1974, Saville, John, *The Socialist Register*, 1974, pp. 226-240, Stedman Jones, Gareth, *New Left Review*, March-April 1975, and Gray, Robert, *Marxism Today*, December 1977, pp. 367-371. See also, Kent, Christopher, 'Victorian social history: post-Thompson, post-Foucault, postmodern', *Victorian Studies*, Vol. 40, (1), (1996), pp. 97-133.

[35] Mayhew, Henry, *London Labour and the London Poor: A Cyclopaedia of the Condition and Earnings of Those That Will Work, Those That Cannot Work, and Those That Will Not Work*, 4 Vols. (Griffin, Bohn and Co.), 1861.

complicated by lack of agreement among historians on when a 'class system' came into being and how far the older values survived into the Victorian period. Perkin argued that, as the result of industrialisation, urbanisation and religion–the 'midwife' of class–a class society emerged between 1789 and 1833 or, more precisely between 1815 and 1820. Class was characterised:

...by class feeling, that is, by the existence of vertical antagonism between a small number of horizontal groups, each based on a common source of income.[36]

The paternalist view of society was not, however, ended by these class antagonisms and potential conflicts of emergent class society were contained by reforming existing institutions. For Perkin, compromise was a central reason for the endurance of older social values and structures and that only an 'immature' class society was characterised by violence. Each class developed its own 'ideal' and, by 1850, he believed, three can be clearly seen: the entrepreneurial ideal of the middle-classes, a working-class ideal and an aristocratic ideal based respectively on profits, wages and rent. The 'struggle between ideals' was:

...not so much that the ruling class imposes its ideal upon the rest, but that the class that manages to impose its ideal upon the rest becomes the ruling class.[37]

The mature class society that emerged by the 1850s was, despite the differences that existed between classes, not marked by overt conflict but by tacit agreement and coexistence under the successful entrepreneurial ideal. The same destination reached by Foster but by a different route.

Between 1880 and 1914, class society reached its zenith.[38] The rich, both large landowners and capitalists, consolidated into a new plutocracy that had already begun to emerge in the 1850s. The middle-classes, increasingly graduated in income and status, expressed their social position physically in their dress, furnishings and housing and in their geographical segregation from one another and the rest of society in carefully differentiated suburbs. Working-classes families were also able to distinguish themselves from their peers by better Sunday if not every-day dress and by better furnished houses in marginally superior areas. Only the very poor, the 'residuum' as Charles Booth (1840-1916) called them, had no choice at all and were consigned to the slums. They were the most

---

[36] Ibid., Perkin, H., *The Origins of Modern English Society 1780-1880*, p. 37.

[37] Ibid., Perkin, H., *The Origins of Modern English Society 1780-1880*, pp. 218-270, for discussion on the 'struggle between ideals'.

[38] Perkin, H., *The Rise of Professional Society: England since 1880*, (Routledge), 1990, pp. 27-63.

segregated class of all because everyone else shunned them and their homes.[39]

Between the constitutional crisis from 1909 to 1911 and the General Strike in 1926, class society in Britain underwent a profound crisis as the relatively peaceful co-existence between classes broke down. The classes of capital and labour clashed and government became reluctantly involved, by no means wholly on the side of capital. Fear of social revolution was raised before 1914 with threats from Suffragettes over votes for women and Irish Nationalists and Ulstermen over the future status of Ireland and from more aggressive mass trade unionism. This was further complicated by the outbreak of war in 1914 and its consequences especially revolution in Russia, Germany, Austria-Hungary and Turkey. The war ruthlessly laid bare the failings and deficiencies of society, the economy and the political system that were not resolved in the inter-war years.[40]

The decades since the publication of Edward Thompson's *The Making of the English Working Class* in 1963 has done little to clarify the situation. Even if he is right that 'class happens', answers to the central questions of 'when?', 'how?' and 'why?' have been surprisingly inconclusive.[41] The postmodernist debates of the late 1980s and early 1990s demolished, at least temporarily, any notion of grand narratives as a means of explaining agency and change reducing it to part of the 'linguistic turn'. Marxist writers and labour historians maintain the hegemonic status of class while others have suggested that work and religion united people in large numbers but that class as a unifying force bringing large numbers of people together never really existed.[42] Nevertheless, despite the importance of class and political development within the realm of social movements, history remained largely untouched by semantic niggling and methodological extremes of the deconstructionist arguments.[43] The debate

---

[39] Ibid., Perkin, H., *The Rise of Professional Society: England since 1880*, pp. 171-217. See also, Welshman, John, *Underclass: A history of the excluded since 1880*, (Quadrille), 2013.

[40] Ibid., Perkin, H., *The Rise of Professional Society: England since 1880*, pp. 218-285.

[41] Neale, R. S., *Class in British History 1680-1850*, (Basil Blackwell), 1983, and *Class and Ideology in the Nineteenth Century*, (Routledge), 1972, the useful bibliographical essay by Morris, Richard, *Class and Class Consciousness in the Industrial Revolution*, (Macmillan), 1980, and his 'Class and Common Interest', *History Today*, Vol. 33, (1983), pp. 31-35, remain sound starting points for the period before 1850. Corfield, Penelope, (ed.), *Language, History and Class*, (Basil Blackwell), 1991, is also an excellent collection of papers.

[42] See, for instance, Joyce, Patrick, *Work, Society and Politics*, (Harvester Press), 1980, and Joyce, Patrick, (ed.), *The Historical Meaning of Work*, (Cambridge University Press), 1987.

[43] Croll, Andy, 'The impact of postmodernism on modern British social history',

did, however, result in a gradual shift away from class as the only significant explanation of working-class action and towards a recognition that the working-classes shared diverse identities—gender, age, religion, race and ethnicity and location—that also played their part in defining who the working-classes were.

Classes are not and never were monolithic blocks of identical individuals. Class helped working people describe themselves in relation to society they experienced as well as to society as a whole. It provided identity for workers no longer bound by paternalist values as well as consciousness of that class identity. It responded to growing population, greater social mobility, urban growth and new patterns of work based in the factory or workshop. When the working-classes came into existence remains unclear. For some workers, popular radicalism and conservatism in the 1790s marked its beginnings while for others it was the radicalism between 1815 and 1821 that gave class substance. What people did, where they lived and significant divisions within the working-classes between skilled, semi-skilled and unskilled, working men and women and rural and industrial workers were perhaps more important in defining how workers viewed class than an overarching sense of 'classness'. It was the diversity of their lived experience as much as their unity of purpose that marked the working-classes in the century between 1840 and 1940.

There were other ways in which individuals were differentiated in society by 1830 that transcended, but contributed to, the 'paternalist-class' debate: religion, gender and race. In 1780, the language of religion was part of a common culture but by 1850, this situation was under sizable attack from the increasingly pluralistic nature of religious observance and experience. Three aspects of religious life can be identified. At one level, religion is made up of a quest for individual truth and salvation. Faith, belief and piety were seen by many as important features of people's lives. At the level of organised religion, Christianity was an institution and religion a social and moral force providing a generally agreed framework for the 'Christian life'. Very few people in 1780 denied all religious ties and belonged, at least nominally, to a Church or sect. Finally, a non-denominational heritage that transcended sectarian boundaries infused social and personal relationships. Churches, chapels and cathedrals provided visible symbolism of its history and heritage. The Bible was a constant presence in people's minds and hearts and biblical quotations, language and images provided a common mental landscape. It is the 'associational' dimension of religiosity that is of particular importance. In broad terms the social appeal of the churches in 1800 can be compared to

in Berger, Stefan, (ed.), *Labour and Social History: Historiographical Reviews and Agendas*, *Mitteilungsblatt des Instituts für Soziale Bewegungen*, Vol. 27, (2002), pp. 137-152.

a 'sandwich'. The Church of England formed the top and bottom slices: the aristocratic elite and some from the working-classes. The meat in the sandwich consisted of middle-class and working-class Nonconformists. Roman Catholicism took up a similar position to the Church of England. Catholic Irish immigrants stood outside this because of their religion, language and cultural attitudes. In practice, however, social responses to religion were less clear-cut. Methodism penetrated into working-class areas in both town and country and there was an extension of Anglican activity among the middle-classes. But the *Religious Census* 1851 showed, formal religious observance had already declined.

The most obvious means of differentiating people within society was on the basis of gender. In 1780, men of all social classes discriminated against women legally, morally, economically and politically. Society clearly differentiated between the worlds of men and women. Status and power lay with the former. Women's work commanded a woman's rate, even when they were involved in the same processes as men.[44] In manufacturing occupations, with the exception of textiles, women generally earned about half the average weekly earnings of men. New methods of wage payment introduced in the late-nineteenth and early-twentieth centuries reinforced the idea of a woman's rate. Women were more often paid piece rate than men and found their rates lowered or they earned 'too much'. Wages were always low with piece rates producing incomes ranging from 5s to 15s a week. Non-manual workers generally earned a higher percentage of the average male earnings: women shop assistants earned about 65 per cent as much as men in 1900 and women teachers 75 per cent their male colleagues. In all-female occupations, women did worst of all. Nineteenth century nurses were often paid little more than domestic servants.[45] Indeed their pay was actually reduced to encourage middle-class applicants who did not need the money. Middle-class parents were roundly condemned by feminists for allowing their daughters to work for pocket money because they considered it to be more respectable and genteel. Theirs was voluntary rather than real work.

The proportion of women in industry declined from the 1890s, except in unskilled and some semi-skilled work but their role in higher professional, shop and clerical work increased. The introduction of the telephone and typewriter from the 1870s saw the army of male clerks replaced by female office workers. The revolution in retailing provided additional employment for women and by 1911 one-third of all shop

[44] Brown, Richard, *Sex, Work and Politics: Women in Britain, 1780-1945*, (Authoring History), 2014.
[45] Sweet, Helen M., 'Establishing Connections, Restoring Relationships: Exploring the Historiography of Nursing in Britain', *Gender & History*, Vol. 19, (2007), pp. 565-580.

assistants were female. The number of women in commerce and many industries increased between 1891 and 1911, but the proportion of women in paid employment hardly changed and remained around 35 per cent. But the characteristics of female employment changed substantially. Before 1914, domestic service was still the overwhelming source of employment for women and girls, though the clothing and textile trades employed more women than men. Women, however, were also beginning to infiltrate the lower grade clerical and service occupations. In 1901, 13 per cent of clerks were women, but by 1911 this had risen to 21 per cent, though the higher clerical grades remained almost exclusively male. Nevertheless, the employment status of women remained inferior to that of men: in 1911, 52.1 per cent of women occupied semi-skilled or unskilled jobs compared to 40.6 per cent of men.

People could also be distinguished by race. Welsh migrants in Liverpool, for instance, were bound together by strong cultural and linguistic ties despite their relative lack of residential concentration. Families travelled long distances to worship together in Welsh-speaking Calvinistic chapels, Welsh newspapers circulated in the city and the National Eisteddfod was held there on occasions. To be 'successful' in the nineteenth century meant being 'English', culturally if not by nationality and to become part of the ruling elite meant adopting the cultural values and practices of the Establishment politically, socially, linguistically and religiously. This opened a cultural gap between those who ruled and those who were governed and excluded from political power.

Society in the 1780s was multifaceted. Class, paternalism, community, race, sex and religion each played their part in a process of self-definition and group identity. Attitudes resulted from circumstances, opportunities and fears created by an economy in which there were elements of continuity as well as change. Social attitudes, behaviour and work patterns were closely linked to support for the social hierarchy. Power was converted into moral authority and this ensured the stability of a social hierarchy threatened by change. Deference remained strong because family, work patterns and communities did little to dissuade and much to promote it. No one criterion, whether class or paternalism or dependency, can explain the complexities of society between 1780 and 1945.

2: The Working-Classes

The industrial revolution was not simply a transition from an agricultural and domestic economy to one eventually dominated by factory regimes but rather a restructuring of economy and society. Where people lived and the spaces they occupied played a critical part in how they defined their own senses of class. Their communities involved family and kin, houses and streets, churches and chapels and pubs, places of work, cultural opportunities and social and political organisations that acted and reacted upon individuals and groups developing, defining and redefining their identities. Communities were not simply defined in territorial terms but often by the diverse experiences of social interaction between similar and dissimilar attitudes, beliefs and interests. They were an amalgam of competing and contradictory and consensual and conflicting networks of people, places and spaces that made up localities, regions and nations.[1]

The labouring population made up the bulk of society consisting of those who earned their wages largely through manual work,[2] what medieval historians called, 'the submerged nine-tenths' and later writers termed 'the lower orders'. This remained the case in 1945. The working-class may have been, as Edward Thompson suggested, 'present at its own making' but it was not until after 1840 that most Britons saw themselves as working-class and were treated as such by politicians and press. After 1945, the working-classes became 'the people', whose interests were equated with those of Britain itself. There were, nonetheless, wide differences within workplaces and communities. The working-classes were marked by divisions and sub-divisions on the basis of skills, wages, gender, levels of control and so on. People worked in rural or urban environments and in agriculture, manufacturing or in the growing service sector in which a growing non-manual 'blue-collar', working-class emerged. Some were skilled, others semi-skilled but most were unskilled. Work determined two fundamental elements of their existence: the ways in which workers spent most of their waking hours and the amounts of money they had to their disposal.[3]

---

[1] Britain was the first country to introduce an explicit class hierarchy to organise occupational census data when the Registrar-General prepared a summary of occupations designed to represent 'social grades' in the Annual Report for 1911--published in 1913--and used the data in the *Census Tables on the Fertility of Marriage Census.*

[2] Rule, J., *The Labouring Classes in Early Industrial England 1750-1850,* (Longman), 1986, Benson, J., *The Working-Class in Britain 1850-1939,* (Longman), 1989, Savage, M., and Miles, A., *The remaking of the British working class, 1840-1940,* (Routledge), 1994, Brown, K. D., *The English Labour Movement 1700-1951,* (Gill and Macmillan), 1982, and August, Andrew, *The British Working Class 1832-1940,* (Longman), 2007, are good starting points.

[3] Joyce, Patrick, 'Work' in Thompson, F. M. L., (ed.), *The Cambridge Social History of Britain 1750-1950: Vol. 2, People and their environment,* (Cambridge University

Work also determined most other aspects of working-class life: the standards of living they enjoyed; standards of health; the types of housing they lived in; the nature of their families' and neighbourhoods' lives; the ways in which leisure time was spent and the social, religious, political and other values they promoted.[4]

Changing nature of work

The swing away from domestic forms of production can be roughly explained by three developments: the growth of population, the extension of enclosure with its consequent reduction in demand for rural labour and the advent of mechanised production boosting productivity and fostering the growth of new towns and cities. The result was a shift in the nature of the labour market, something evident in censuses from 1841.[5] Ploughmen gave way to copper-plate printers; professional photographers flourished as executioners fell. Snuffer makers–the handheld device for putting out candles–were extinguished as gaslights arrived, the amanuensis–who wrote letters for the illiterate–and abecedarian–freelance teachers of the alphabet–became obsolete with compulsory education. Sportsmen appeared with John Wisden (1826-1884) recorded in 1861 as a cricketer. Professional footballers disguised themselves as 'billiard players', so as not to breach the amateur rules of their sport. In 1851, Charlotte Bronte (1816-1855), by then author of *Jane Eyre* and *Shirley*, entered her occupation as 'none' and while up to 400,000 women engaged in prostitution in the nineteenth century, only seven fearless Cornish girls in Falmouth were shameless enough to declare it. In 1911, in political protest over female suffrage, several women described their profession as 'domestic slaves' for the family.[6]

Press), 1990, pp. 131-194.

[4] Ibid., Benson, John, *The Working-class in Britain 1850-1939*, pp. 9-38, is the best introduction to this issue. Joyce, Patrick, (ed.), *The Historical Meanings of Work*, (Cambridge University Press), 1987, is an excellent collection having a seminal introduction by the editor.

[5] Hopkins, E., 'Working hours and conditions during the industrial revolution: a reappraisal', *Economic History Review*, 2nd series, Vol. 35, (1982), pp. 52-66, and Reid, D. A., 'The decline of Saint Monday 1776-1876', *Past & Present*, Vol. 71, (1976), pp. 76-101, and 'Weddings, weekdays, work and leisure in urban England 1791-1911: the decline of Saint Monday revisited', *Past & Present*, Vol. 153, (1996), pp. 135-163, and Schwarz, L., 'Custom, wages and workload in England during industrialization', *Past & Present*, Vol. 197, (2007), pp. 143-175, cover important topics. Voth, H. J., *Time and work in England 1750-1830*, (Oxford University Press), 2000, asks whether working hours in England increased as a result of the Industrial Revolution while Steedman, Carolyn, *An Everyday Life of the English Working Class: Work, Self and Sociability in the Early Nineteenth Century*, (Cambridge University Press), 2013, suggests that historians have overstated the importance of work to the working man's understanding of himself as a creature of time, place and society.

[6] Liddington, Jill, *Vanishing for the Vote: Suffrage, Citizenship and the Battle for the Census*, (Manchester University Press), 2014.

The enclosure of common lands from the 1770s had a profound impact on the livelihood of rural workers and their families who had customary rights to use common land for grazing, gleaning and so on. What is often misunderstood is that 'common land' did not 'belong to' the local community, like all land it belonged to private owners, and it was not equally accessible to people in communities—it applied only those 'commoners' who had customary rights to use 'the common'. The need for food security during the French Wars led to substantial investment in arable farming sustained by high food prices. It was customary for rural labourers, in demand until 1815 to be hired for a year, to enter service in another household and to live with another family, receiving food, clothes, board and a small annual wage in return for work, only living out when they wished to marry.

The spread of enclosure especially in southern England thrust rural labourers on to the labour market in a search for work that was made the more acute by falling arable farm prices and wages between 1815 and 1835 and by a growing labour surplus.[7] The depressed conditions in arable farming led to a greater reliance for many workers on earnings and on relief provided through the Poor Law. The result of the growth in labour supply and agricultural depression was the collapse of farm service in the south and east of the country with farmers employing labourers when they were needed. Wages remained low and but variable from one area to another.[8] In the North wages were higher because of the affluence of mixed and pastoral areas compared to the wheat-growing counties of southern England and from competition for labour from industrial towns where wages were generally higher. In 1851, James Caird (1816-1892) found that farmer workers were paid from 13-14s per week in the West Riding, Lancashire and Cumberland but only 7-8s per week in southern counties like Cambridgeshire, Berkshire, and Suffolk.[9] Counties close to London such as Sussex, Essex and Hertfordshire also had higher rural wages of 9-10s per week.

Within rural communities there was an important hierarchy based upon levels of skills that paralleled levels of wages. Bird-scarers, generally children, were at the base of this hierarchy while ploughmen were at the top. Only the better-educated shepherds had greater status within their communities.[10] Rural

---

[7] Richardson, T. L., 'Agricultural labourers' wages and the cost of living in Essex, 1790-1840: a contribution to the standard of living debate', in Holderness, B. A., and Turner, M. E., (eds.), *Land, labour and agriculture, 1700-1920: essays for Gordon Mingay*, (Hambledon), 1991, pp. 69-90.
[8] Clark, Gregory, 'Farm wages and living standards in the industrial revolution: England, 1670-1869', *Economic History Review*, Vol. 54, (2001), pp. 477-505, provides a valuable longitudinal study.
[9] Caird, James, *English Agriculture in 1850-51*, (Longman, Brown, Green and Longmans), 1852, pp. 511-519.
[10] Armstrong, A., *Farmworkers: a Social and Economic History 1770-1980*, (Batsford), 1988, and Snell, K., *Annals of the Labouring Poor: Social Change and Agrarian England 1660-1900*, (Cambridge University Press), 1984, are excellent on rural

industrial workers were usually rather better off. In the south Pennines, the survival of a dual farming-weaving economy gave some protection against poverty though, as the textile industry became more mechanised and factory-based, the distress of rural textile workers became more acute.[11] In these rural parts of the north-east, labourers left the land for manufacturing towns and independent small landowners and tenant farmers had to pay higher wages to keep labour. This led to many farms employing no labour relying on family members to cultivate and gather crops and manage sheep flocks. The effects of rural poverty can be seen in malnutrition and associated ill-health.[12] A survey of 1863 showed that most English rural labourers relied heavily on a diet of bread and potatoes, with meat consumption varying from season to season and area to area. Men were generally better fed than the rest of the family.[13] Even so, the food supply in the countryside was rather better than that available to the urban poor: it was fresher and there were chances to supplement it from gleaning, fishing or poaching or from the cottage garden.

A similar hierarchy of skill existed in industrial Britain and the distinction between skilled and unskilled labourers was one of enduring importance. Artisans formed an 'aristocracy of labour', well paid and, though not immune to adverse economic conditions, relatively secure in traditional trades where they acquired their skills through apprenticeship. They differed from factory workers in having the skills needed to complete an entire product, for instance in cabinet-making or book-binding, rather than one stage of a product. Initially, they were untouched by mass production and as late as 1850, there were as many artisans as factory workers. The creation of new skills saw the gradual creation of new skilled elites: foremen, overseers, mechanics and technicians as well as managers. Artisans guarded their skills and high standards of workmanship against the threat of mass production and 'dilution' from cheaper workers. Semi-skilled and unskilled manual labour was exposed to economic conditions and to unemployment or under-employment. Men were generally able to restrict women to the lower-paid margins of manufacturing. In the textile industries, for instance, men dominated new technologies such as the self-acting spinning 'mule' perfected in the early 1820s. The 'sweated trades' or the growing demands for domestic servants, low skill, low pay, long hours, was the destination for many working women.[14]

---

conditions.

[11] Chartres, John, 'Rural industry and manufacturing', in Collins, E. J. T., (ed.), *The Agrarian History of England and Wales, Vol. 7: 1850-1914, part 2*, (Cambridge University Press), 2000, pp. 1101-1149.

[12] See contemporary analysis in Denton, John Bailey, *The Agricultural Labourer*, (Stanford), 1868, pp. 35-44, Wilson, Arthur Fox, *Earnings of Agricultural Labourers by Great Britain Board of Trade*, (HMSO), 1900.

[13] Burnett, John, 'Country Diet', in Mingay, G. E., (ed.), *The Victorian Countryside*, (Routledge), 1981, Vol. 2, pp. 554-565, provides a summary.

[14] Honeyman, Karina, *Women, Gender and Industrialisation in England, 1700-1870*,

The development of factory-based textile production had a profound effect on outwork, the other source of earned income for rural workers. Different parts of the country were associated with different products with lace-making round Nottingham, stocking-knitting in Leicester, spinning and weaving of cotton and wool in Lancashire and Yorkshire. The growth of the mills damaged the status and security of very skilled branches of outwork. People in rural households were thrown into poverty if such work contracted and, even when in work earned miserably low rates of pay. The fate of the handloom weavers, stocking-frame knitters and silk weavers in the 1830s and 1840s, all reflected the impact of technological change on the distribution of work.[15] Textiles were not the only industry to experience such structural changes. Mechanisation had an impact on a wide variety of employment across town and country and the position of skilled workers was undermined while the demand for new skills grew

Apprenticeship and dilution

Urban workers had always been more reliant on cash wages than had their rural counterparts. Pre-industrial towns were largely commercial and market centres rather than places of manufacture and employment was more specialised than elsewhere. The service sector was important with lawyers, accountants, bankers and merchants. In 1841, Dunstable, with a population of just over 2,500 people had an accountant, three solicitors, six teachers, four doctors and an auctioneer. Small units of production by artisans operating in a domestic setting provided local services and goods rather than commodities for export or the mass market. They were frequently controlled by craft guilds that policed recruitment and training and the quality of products and established the vocabulary of the rights of 'legal' or 'society' men who worked in 'legal' shops that infused craft unions into the nineteenth century. The position of the skilled urban artisan increasingly under threat from semi-skilled and less well-trained workers after 1800.[16]

The Statute of Artificers 1563 provided a legal framework of craft regulations but these had fallen into disuse long before its apprenticeship clauses were finally repealed in 1811.[17] As this legislation only covered trades that

---

(Macmillan), 2000, and Gleadle, Kathryn, *British Women in the Nineteenth Century*, (Palgrave), 2001, are good, short introductions to the background of the subject. Burnette, Joyce, *Gender, Work and Wages in Industrial Revolution Britain*, (Cambridge University Press), 2008, is an important revisionist study that considers gender and wages in relation to market forces.

[15] See Bythell, Duncan, *The Handloom Weavers*, (Cambridge University Press), 1969, and *The Sweated Trades: Outworks in Nineteenth-Century Britain*, (Batsford), 1978, for a detailed discussion of this issue.

[16] Sheeran, George, 'Conflicting images: portrayals of the factory and the country in the nineteenth century', in *Rural and urban encounters in the nineteenth and twentieth centuries: regional perspectives,* (Conference of Regional and Local Historians), 2004, pp. 23-40.

[17] Lane, Joan, *Apprenticeship in England, 1600-1914*, (UCL Press), 1996, and Wallis,

existed in 1563, it was not surprising that different patterns of training developed to accommodate the new trades established during industrialisation. Under the old system of apprenticeship, the pupil was formally indentured normally at age ten–or seven for the navy–and joined a master's house traditionally for seven years before being recognised as a journeyman qualified to practice the trade. It was also usual for journeymen to 'live in' entitling him to bed, board and wages in return to work, only moving out on marriage. Often journeymen 'tramped' the country in search of work in part to extend their experience and knowledge of their trade but also to escape increasingly uncertain employment prospects in their immediate locality.[18] To become a master the journeyman had to produce his 'masterpiece', demonstrating his mastery of the skills of the specific trade as well as having the capital necessary to establish his own workshop.

From the early-nineteenth century, fewer apprentices were completing their indentures and journeymen's wages were falling, signs employers were no longer bothered about hiring only men who had served their time. Apprenticeship did not disappear after the 1814 repeal but altered significantly to become a free contract with no restriction on its length or on the number of apprentices allowed in any one workplace. This led to a dilution in the labour force and a blurring of the boundaries between 'society' and 'non-society' men, a situation made worse by the mechanisation of production that required fewer skills than handwork.[19]

The nature of training for skilled work changed; apprenticeships were shortened and concentrated on specific skills rather than on an understanding of all aspects of production. Lads collaborated with journeymen rather than being attached to a master's household with various adverse results. The new system bore heavily on apprentices' families, who frequently still paid for indentures while the apprentice lived at home and could expect little or no wages for his

---

Patrick, 'Apprenticeship and Training in Pre-modern England', *Journal of Economic History*, Vol. 68, (2008), pp. 832-861, provide background. Gowing, Laura, *Ingenious Trade: Women and Work in Seventeenth-Century London*, (Cambridge University Press), 2021, places female apprenticeship at the centre of women's work.

[18] See Hobsbawm, E. J., 'The tramping artisan' in his *Labouring Men*, (Weidenfeld and Nicolson), 1964, pp. 34-63, and ibid., Thompson, E. P., *The Making of the English Working-class*, and 'Time, Work-Discipline and Industrial Capitalism', *Past & Present*, Vol. 38, (1967), pp. 56-97, reprinted in *Customs in Common*, (Merlin Press), 1991, pp. 352-403.

[19] Humphries, Jane, 'English Apprenticeship: A Neglected Factor in the First Industrial Revolution', in David, Paul A., and Thomas, Mark, (eds.), *The economic future in historical perspective*, (Oxford University Press), 2001, pp. 73-102. Rose, Mary B., 'Social policy and business; parish apprenticeship and the early factory system, 1750-1834', *Business History*, Vol. 31, (1989), pp. 5-32, Lane, J., 'Apprenticeship in Warwickshire cotton mills, 1790-1830', *Textile History*, Vol. 10, (1979), pp. 161-174, and a valuable comparative study Elbaum, Bernard, 'Why apprenticeship persisted in Britain but not in the United States', *Journal of Economic History*, Vol. 49, (1989), pp. 337-349.

efforts until his time was served. The old, stipulated ratios between journeymen and boys were increasingly ignored and apprentices became a cheap alternative for adult labour further depressing the adult labour market. This was resented by the journeymen expected to train recruits, souring relations and often making training uncooperative. Many were dismissed as soon as they were old enough to command an adult rate, a practice more common during economic downturns.[20] Abuse of apprenticeship triggered sporadic industrial disputes as skilled workers tried to protect their position and to prevent their trades being flooded by excess labour. The independence of their 'aristocratic' status was upheld through the rhetoric of custom and the invention of 'traditions' to sanction and legitimise current practices. This excluded employers and market calculations from the opaque world of custom, tradition, craft mystery and skill, a separate culture upheld by secrecy, theatrical ceremony and, when necessary, ritualised violence. By these means skilled workers defended their position at the 'frontier of control'.

Negotiation, strikes and machine breaking were strategies used by workers, to put pressure on employers.[21] They often combined a defence of traditional forms of manufacture in which threats of direct action were used as a tool to negotiate with refractory employers. Croppers–highly paid workers whose skills lay in neatly cutting the nap from cloth using iron shears weighing up to 60lbs– felt they must make a stand against industrial change. When a crude machine was invented on which an unskilled man and a boy could do in a day what it took a skilled cropper a week, they took direct action. This intensified already existing anger among artisans and textile workers at the shift by employers from skilled workers to cheaper efficiency of mass production. What emerged was a powerful protest from a men who felt they must make a stand against industrial capitalism. The spectre of the factory haunted these skilled working men. The rhythm of industrial life in Yorkshire was being transformed.[22] Skills had no

---

[20] Honeyman, Katrina, *Child workers in England, 1780-1820: parish apprentices and the making of the early industrial labour force*, (Ashgate), 2007, Steinberg, Marc W., 'Unfree Labor, Apprenticeship and the Rise of the Victorian Hull Fishing Industry: An Example of the Importance of Law and the Local State in British Economic Change', *International Review of Social History*, Vol. 51, (2006), pp. 243-276, and Reinarz, Jonathan, 'Learning By Brewing: Apprenticeship and the English Brewing Industry in the Late Victorian and Early Edwardian Period', in Munck, Bert De, Kaplan, Steven L., and Soly, Hugo, (eds.), *Learning on the shop floor: historical perspectives on apprenticeship*, (Berghahn Books), 2007, pp. 111-130, and 'Fit for management: apprenticeship and the English brewing industry, 1870-1914', *Business History*, Vol. 43, (2001), pp. 33-53.
[21] Randall, Adrian, *Before the Luddites: Custom, Community and Machinery in the English Woollen Industry, 1776-1809*, (Cambridge University Press), 2003, Horn, Jeff, 'Machine-breaking in England and France during the Age of Revolution', *Labour/Le Travail*, Vol. 55 (2005), pp. 143-166.
[22] Crump, W. B., *The Leeds woollen industry, 1780-1820*, (Thoresby Society), 1931,

value and individual liberties were ceded to employers who expected people to work for long hours in appalling conditions. Work was no longer performed just at home to the sound of the spinning wheel and handloom but in vast 'manufactories' to the rhythm of the time-clock and the factory whistle.[23] Luddites were forced underground and into violence by the repressive attitudes of a political establishment that refused to allow working men to meet together and to organise.[24] In 1826, there was a wave of machine breaking in Lancashire, in part caused by the introduction of Richard Roberts' (1789-1864) improved technology that was more extensive than in 1812.[25] Twenty-one factories were attacked and 1,000 looms destroyed.[26] Three years later, power looms were targeted by Manchester's working-classes. Machine breaking was important in the Swing riots particularly in 1830 when, in more than 1,500 incidents, a large proportion of England's threshing machines were smashed but there were also attacks on industrial machinery.[27] An attack on Beck's steam factory in Coventry in 1831[28] saw an end to machine breaking and the working-classes abandoned it as a means of resolving work-related disputes at least in industrial Britain as workers turned to more effective and less destructive forms of political activism.[29]

Jenkins, D. T., *The West Riding Wool Textile Industry, 1770-1835: a study of fixed capital formation*, (Pasold Research Fund), 1975, Caunce, Stephen, 'Complexity, community structure and competitive advantage within the Yorkshire woollen industry, c.1700-1850', *Business History*, Vol. 39, (4), (1997), pp. 26-43.

[23] Voth, H. J., *Time and Work in England 1750-1830*, (Oxford University Press), 2000, Schwarz, L., 'Custom, wages and workload in England during industrialization', *Past & Present*, Vol. 197, (2007), pp. 143-176.

[24] Thomis, Malcolm, *The Luddites: Machine-breaking in Regency England*, (David & Charles), 1970, remains valuable. See also Binfield, Kevin, (ed.), *Writings of the Luddites*, (John Hopkins University Press), 2004, pp. 1-68, and Vincent, Julien, Bourdeau, Vincent, and Jarrige, François, *Les Luddites: Bris de machines, économie politique et histoire*, (Maisons-Alfort), 2006, pp. 17-54.

[25] Walsh, David, 'The Lancashire 'Rising' of 1826', *Albion*, Vol. 26, (4), (1994), pp. 601-621.

[26] 'Serious Riots in Blackburn and the Neighbourhood', *Lancaster Gazette*, 26 April 1826, p. 2, 'Serious Disturbances in Lancashire', *Lancaster Gazette*, 6 May 1826, p. 3, provide detailed accounts.

[27] For the 1816 East Anglia riots, see Peacock, A. J., *Bread or Blood: a study of the agrarian riots in East Anglia in 1816*, (Gollancz), 1965, and for 1830 Hobsbawm, E. J., and Rudé, George, *Captain Swing*, (Penguin), 1973, and the revisionist study, Griffin, Carl J., *The Rural War: Captain Swing and the Politics and Protest*, (Manchester University Press), 2012; Randall, Adrian, ''The Luddism of the Poor': *Captain Swing*, Machine breaking and Popular Protest', *Southern History*, Vol. 32, (2010), pp. 41-61.

[28] 'Incendiary Fires', *Manchester Times*, 12 November 1831, p. 7.

[29] Dunbabin, J. P. D., *Rural Discontent in Nineteenth Century Britain*, (Faber), 1975, and Archer, John E., *"By a flash and a scare": incendiarism, animal maiming and poaching in East Anglia, 1815-1870*, (Oxford University Press), 1990, on arson as a form of rural protest.

Reduced to wage-earning and without rights to the materials and product of their labour, skilled workers fought to retain control over the 'labour process' and to defend their workplace autonomy against the new labour disciplines favoured by political economists and employers.[30] In South Wales, for instance, a strike in 1822 marked the emergence of the colliers' clandestine organisation known as the 'Scotch Cattle'. First reports of a secret society among Monmouthshire iron-workers appeared in the early 1810s and it played an ill-defined role in the strikes of 1816, 1818 and 1819. There may have been links between the trade society and the Scotch Cattle movement since both defended workers' rights and attempted to control the output of the iron and coal industries and the recruitment and training of workmen.[31] Even in new forms of work organisations, workers often succeeded in safeguarding their status despite 'deskilling' technology and increased division of labour.[32] But in defending or reconstructing skilled status, their actions were divisive: not just a line drawn against employers but also unfair or unskilled competition in the labour market.[33] Skills as property became skills as patriarchy that left women defenceless against their increasingly marginalised labour. In lace-making, for instance, boys worked as threaders and could move into the adult men's jobs as twisters. By contrast, girls worked as bobbins winders but this did not lead to jobs with greater skills. At the same time, new mechanised processes enabled cheaper forms of bulk production. As a result, the market became saturated with semi-skilled workers, who knew something of the trade but did not possess the full range of skills expected of the qualified man. Henry Mayhew, chronicling London's labour market in the 1840s, contrasted the position of the 'honourable' tradesman with the 'slop' workers whose wages and products undercut old, recognised prices and reduced job security long assumed to belong to the man with an established craft.[34]

---

[30] That this was often unsuccessful is explored in Green, David R., *From artisans to paupers: economic change and poverty in London, 1790-1870*, (Scolar & Ashgate), 1995. See also, Levene, Alysa, '"Honesty, sobriety and diligence": master-apprentice relations in eighteenth- and nineteenth-century England', *Social History*, Vol. 33, (2008), pp. 183-200.

[31] Jones, David, J. V., 'The Scotch Cattle and their Black Domain', in Jones, David, J. V., *Before Rebecca: Popular Protest in Wales 1793-1835*, (Allen Lane), 1975, pp. 86-112, Jones, E. J., ''Scotch cattle' and early trade unionism in Wales', in Minchinton, W. E., (ed.), *Industrial South Wales, 1750-1914: Essays in Welsh Economic History*, (Augustus M. Kelley), 1969, pp. 209-217.

[32] Knox, William, 'Apprenticeship and De-skilling in Britain 1850-1914', *International Review of Social History*, Vol. 31, (2), (1986), pp. 166-184.

[33] See, for instance, Brodie, Marc, 'Artisans and dossers: the 1886 West End riots and the East End casual poor', *London Journal*, Vol. 24, (1999), pp. 34-50.

[34] Mayhew, Henry, *London Labour and the London Poor*, 4 Vols. (Griffin, Bohn, and Company), 1861-1862, and Thompson, E. P., and Yeo, E., (eds.), *The Unknown Mayhew: Selections from the Morning Chronicle 1849-50*, (Penguin), 1971, provide evidence for the 1850s and should be used in conjunction with Mayhew, Henry, *The*

The most obvious impact of industrialisation was found in the more intense and strictly disciplined nature of work in those industries transformed by the new technology: textiles, coal-mining, metal-processing and engineering. Pauper child labour was used to man early mills because the regularity of work was alien to an adult population used to a greater degree of autonomy in conducting their working lives.[35] Higher wages available in factories provided insufficient compensation for this loss of 'freedom'. Impoverished handloom weavers would send their daughters to work on the power looms but resisted the prospect themselves. Hours in the early factories were probably no longer than those in the domestic trades but what made them unacceptable was the mind-numbing tedium of the work involved, the loss of public feast days and holidays and, for middle-class commentators, the physical consequences of long hours and the appalling conditions in the factory towns.

Changes in labour market conditions during the nineteenth century made it difficult to make clear distinctions between the employed, the unemployed, the underemployed, self-employed and the economically inactive. Subcontracting was rife, notably in the clothing trade where middlemen 'sweated' domestic women to earn a profit. The 'slop' end of the fashion and furnishing trades competed frantically for such orders as were available at almost any price. Casualism became more visible towards 1900 as cities grew. Short-term engagements and casual employment were particularly associated with the docks and the construction industries. The casual labour of the old East End was trapped within an economy of declining trades and conditions of employment deteriorated. By the early 1870s, London's shipbuilding had slumped beyond the point of recovery and by the 1880s most heavy engineering, iron founding and metal work had gone the same way.[36] Competition from provincial furniture, clothing and footwear factories could only be met by reducing labour costs and this led to the increasing importance of metropolitan sweated trades.

By 1900, many philanthropic and social reformers were calling for a revival of apprenticeship schemes that, they argued, were the most efficacious way of providing training and a skilled workforce.[37] They were also seen as an antidote

---

Morning Chronicle Survey of Labour and the Poor, 1849-50, 6 Vols. (Caliban), 1980. Humpherys, Anne, *Travels into the Poor Man's Country: The Work of Henry Mayhew*, (University of Georgia Press), 1977, is a valuable study.

[35] Honeyman, Katrina, 'The Poor Law, the Parish Apprentice, and the Textile Industries in the North of England, 1780-1830', *Northern History*, Vol. 44, (2007), pp. 115-140.

[36] Rankin, Stuart, (ed.), *Shipbuilding on the Thames and Thames-Built Ships: a symposium for researchers and authors held on Saturday 2 September 2000: supported by London Borough of Southwark, Department of Education & Leisure and the Greenwich Maritime Institute to mark the 130th anniversary year of the launch of "Lothair", last large vessel built in Rotherhithe, 1870*, (Rotherhithe & Bermondsey Local History Group), 2000.

[37] Cowman, Krista, *Apprenticeships in Britain c. 1890-1920. An overview based on contemporary evidence*, unpublished paper, November 2014.

to more exploitative forms of child labour and to those jobs that promised comparatively high wages for youngsters just out of school but provided no training or long-term security. Many of these jobs, such as errand, van or messenger boys or unskilled factory work often ended with dismissal at 18 or 19 when they were replaced by cheaper school leavers. By then, they were regarded as too old for training and so drifted into unskilled, low-paid jobs or unemployment or into the criminal justice system. In 1909, the Majority Report of the Royal Commission on the Poor Laws concluded that the appeal of 'occupations which offer no opportunity of promotion to employment for men are disastrous.' This reinforced a shift in opinion feeding demands for a more systematic approaching to the training of young workers to guard against 'blind alley jobs and the growing number of unskilled workers.

Diversities of work

Between 1801 and 1841, the population of Dunstable doubled from slightly fewer than 1,300 people to nearly 2,600. Nearly 60 per cent of its population was female largely because they worked temporarily in the straw industry either as plaiters or hat makers during the hat-making 'season' (that included the date for the census). A shift in Dunstable's economy had already begun with the decline of the overnight coach trade because of improved roads and the growth of the straw industry. The opening of the London-Birmingham railway led to the sudden end of the coaching trade in 1839 causing temporary crisis according to local historian William Henry Derbyshire who lived through the changes:

> A period of great depression ensued, upon the extinction of the traffic of the road, which continued for some years; but after a while, the business men of the town, directed their whole attention to the extension and development of the Straw trade, which had existed in Dunstable for more than 200 years, although it had hitherto been carried on to a very limited extent...[38]

Evidence from *Pigot's Directory for Bedfordshire* for 1839 and the 1841 Census suggest the depression proved short-lived and the town's economy quickly recovered and, unlike other areas of Britain that were experiencing depressed conditions in 1841, the hat trade proved resistant to declining sales until 1843. Dunstable was typical of small market towns with its vibrant retail trade, established traditional crafts, growing professional services and close links with the surrounding countryside. It was not an isolated, parochial community but with its links to London straw manufacturers and the imminent arrival of the railway, also an outward looking town.

Of the nearly 1,029 people—40 per cent of its population—where the census specifies occupations, 2.62 per cent fell into the 'professional' category, 13.51 per cent were in 'intermediate' occupations, 22.25 per cent were in 'skilled' jobs,

---

[38] Derbyshire, W. H., *The History of Dunstable*, 2nd ed., (James Tibbett), 1882, p. 97.

54.90 per cent in 'partially skilled' occupations and the remaining 6.90 per cent in 'unskilled' work. With no upper-class living in the community, economic and political direction for the town was provided by the middle-classes, For instance, there were an accountant and solicitor, local clergy and those involved in teaching and those with intermediate occupation, small independent skilled manufacturers, skilled artisans with apprentices and more important food providers. Those with skilled jobs made up almost a quarter of the occupied population and included fourteen bakers, fourteen butchers, two confectioners, four dealers, three fishmongers, one fruiterer, seven grocers (plus one woman grocer), four innkeepers, two maltsters and in traditional trades nine blacksmiths, one cabinet maker, one chair maker, one chimney sweep, one clockmaker, one cooper, five cordwainers, two gun makers, one gunlocksmith, one rope maker, three saddlers (plus a woman saddler), four sawyers, five wheelwrights and a whitesmith.[39]

Those in partially skilled occupations were dominated by women workers in the hat trade and in domestic service while most men were agricultural labourers. In the straw industry, there were three male bleachers and eleven male blockers or bonnet blockers—more skilled work--two male straw plaiters, one male straw bonnet sewer, one male straw hat maker, one male straw hatter, five female bonnet makers, 174 bonnet sewers, three female straw bonnet makers, 23 female straw bonnet sewers, one female straw hat maker, one female straw hatter, thirty six straw plaiters, four female straw sewers and one female thread binder. The final category of unskilled work consisted entirely of men, most of whom were classified as general 'labourers'. There was under-registration of child labour in the 1841 census but 10 per cent of those registered as 'occupied' were between the ages of nine and fourteen—29 out of 277—most worked in the straw trade as plaiters with a few in domestic service and two apprentices. Child labour mirrored the employment of adults in Dunstable in 1841 in farming, domestic service and especially the hat industry.

At the base of urban society were casual workers who formed a residual labour force that was often entered on initial migration to a town when no other work was available. Such work as hawking and street trading, scavenging, street entertainment, prostitution and casual labouring and much domestic work fell into this category. Below this was vagrancy and poor relief. Casual trades were largely concentrated in large cities, especially London, and though numbers fluctuated, 'general' labourers were a feature of most communities. Very low and irregular incomes condemned families to rooms in slums, but in London they would emerge from the rookeries of St. Giles to sell their goods in the City or in middle-class residential districts. Large numbers of street traders in prosperous middle-class areas caused antagonism and sometimes fear so that the police were often called to control street trading activities helping to

---

[39] Brown, Richard, *People and Places: Britain 1780-1950*, (Authoring History), 2017, pp. 221-262.

reinforce middle-class stereotypes of a dirty and dangerous sub-class that should be confined to the slums.

Above the casual street traders were unskilled mainly casual occupations in which workers were hired for a few hours at a time and then laid off for long periods without notice. These included labourers in the building trades, in sugar houses and other factories, carters, shipyard workers and especially dockers. All towns had such workers but they were especially important in port cities such as London, Liverpool, Bristol and Glasgow and in industries like coal mining or clothing that had a partly seasonal market. Precise numbers involved in this work cannot be ascertained. In Liverpool, over 22 per cent of the employed labour in 1871 were general, dock or warehouse labourers, many casual. When in work Liverpool dockers earned high weekly wages, ranging from 27s for quay porters to 42s for a stevedore but few maintained such earnings for any length of time and in a bad week earned only a few shillings.[40] Conditions changed little between 1780 and 1945. These workers were frequently in debt and regularly pawned clothes. In good times they would eat meat or fish but normally their diet was largely bread, margarine and tea. Illness or industrial injury–common in dangerous dockland working conditions–led to financial disaster even with the introduction of workmen's compensation legislation from 1897. Casual workers needed to live close to their workplace since employment was often allocated on a first-come, first-served basis. Liverpool dockers mostly lived close to the docks limiting their housing choices to old, insanitary but affordable housing.[41]

Factories provided more regular employment after 1830, as did public services as railway companies and many commercial organisations. Skilled manual labour was privileged: a Lancashire cotton spinner earned 27-30s per week in 1835 and an iron foundry worker up to 40s.[42] In coal mining, skilled underground workers earned good wages and in key jobs such as shot-firing, putting, hewing and shaft sinking usually had regular employment although this often meant moving from colliery to colliery or between coalfields. Textile towns like Manchester, Bradford and Leeds and metal and engineering centres such as Sheffield and the Black Country tended to suffer less poverty than cities like Glasgow, Cardiff, Liverpool or London. Skilled engineering trades were amongst the earliest to unionise, along with artisans and craftsmen, particularly in London

---

[40] 'Life at the Docks, By a Dock Labourer', *Liverpool Mercury*, 25, 26, 27 December 1882, Douglass, D. J., *A History of the Liverpool Waterfront, 1850-1890: The Struggle for Organisation*, (Fonthill Media), 2013.

[41] Palmer, Sarah, 'The Labour Process in the 19th Century Port of London: Some New Perspectives', *Environments Portuaires*, (Presses universitaires de Rouen et du Havre), 2018, https://books.openedition.org/purh/7753?lang=en, Taplin, E. L., 'Dock Labour at Liverpool: Occupational Structure and Working Conditions in the late Nineteenth Century', *Transactions of the Historic Society of Lancashire and Cheshire*, Vol. 127, (1978), pp. 133-154.

[42] Boot, H. M., 'How skilled were Lancashire cotton factory workers in 1833?', *Economic History Review*, 2nd series, Vol. 48, (1995), pp. 283-303.

and northern industrial towns.[43] Protecting their interests jealously, despite dilution in their position, they commanded higher wages and regular work. This gave many advantages: renting a decent terraced house in the suburbs avoiding the squalor of Victorian slums but with a long walk to work or, later in the century, the use of the cheap 'workmen's trains'.

Although contemporaries placed considerable emphasis on the development of large-scale factory manufacture, domestic production and small workshops dominated the economy until the mid-nineteenth century. A major restructuring of the British economy after 1890 brought significant changes in the working conditions and operation of the labour market. Women played an increasingly important role in the workforce, new technology and machinery created different jobs demanding new and often less individually crafted skills. Older workers, particularly in heavy industries, often found it difficult to adjust to new work practices, for instance, the use of assembly lines in the motor and electrical industries developed in the inter-war years. The years between 1890 and 1945 retained many of the work patterns from the nineteenth century but, after 1918, textiles, iron and steel and coal found their positions and employment challenged by adverse global conditions.

Did standards of living rise or fall between 1780 and 1850?

Many contemporaries regarded poverty as a persistent feature of society, since only by feeling its pinch could the labouring poor be inspired to work. It was not poverty as such but pauperism or destitution that was regarded as a social problem. The attitude of early Victorians combined fatalism, 'For ye have the poor always with you' and moralism, destitution was the result of individual weakness of character.[44] *Fraser's Magazine* in 1849 commented:

> So far from rags and filth being the indications of poverty, they are in the large majority of cases, signs of gin drinking, carelessness and recklessness.[45]

Such people, if massed together in sufficient numbers, were seen as a social menace and a threat to political order.

From the 1790s the politics of poverty played a significance role in the timing, location and nature of how working people responded to economic change and calls for radical political reform. Although wages were important in shaping individuals' behaviour, it was the broader notion of standards of living that proved critical. The difficulty is that discussion of living standards is

---

[43] On the emergence of trade unions, see Rule, John, (ed.), *British Trade Unions 1750-1850: The Formative Years*, (Longman), 1988, and Reid, Alistair, J., *United We Stand: A History of Britain's Trade Unions*, (Allen Lane), 2004.

[44] *St Matthew*, Chapter 26: verses 8-11.

[45] 'Work and Wages', *Fraser's Magazine for Town and Country*, Vol. 40, (1849), p. 528.

confused by a range of methodological problems.[46] What is the meaning of living standards? Is it a qualitative or quantitative concept or both? Industrialisation occurred largely before national offices were established dedicated to the gathering and processing of social and economic data. This means that historians often rely on educated guesswork. What evidence can be used? Although we have data of variable quality on food prices, it is incomplete for rents and manufactured foods other than clothing. Statistics, one of the main fuels in the debate, obscure the diversity and harshness of working-class experience. Should historians be using 'actual' wages or 'real' wages as the basis for their arguments?[47] These issues gave rise to a debate between optimists and pessimists, especially about the decades before 1850 over, not simply whether living standards fell or rose, but over what living standards and the whole revolutionary economic experience means.[48] Pessimists saw Britain through the spectrum of Charles Dickens' (1812-1870) Coketown or William Blake's (1757-1827) 'dark, satanic mills' with capitalists squeezing more surplus value out of the working-classes. Optimists saw Britain as the birthplace of a consumer revolution that made more and more goods available to ordinary people. Many contemporaries believed that industrialisation saw a deterioration or little improvement in the lives of ordinary workers. They were mistaken and today, the debate is less about whether industrialisation made people better off but about when. By the 1970s, most economists were on the side of the optimists, a position bolstered by sophisticated econometric and statistical techniques and neo-classical economic theory and a broadening of the debate to encompass 'quality of life'. This proved short-lived with a revival of the pessimist case in the 1990s. Nonetheless, the debate remains far from resolved but there is an

---

[46] Rubinstein, W. D., *Wealth and Inequality in Britain*, (Faber), 1986, and Kaelbe, H., *Industrialisation and Social Inequality in Nineteenth Century Europe*, (Berg), 1986, provide useful analysis of the issues. Floud, R., Wachter, K., and Gregory, A., *Height, Health and History: Nutritional status in the United Kingdom 1750-1980*, (Cambridge University Press), 1990, a major contribution to the debate. Crafts, N. F. R., 'Some dimensions of the 'quality of life' during the British industrial revolution', *Economic History Review*, Vol. 50, (1997), pp. 617-639, is valuable. Humphries, Jane, 'Standard of Living, Quality of Life', in Williams, Chris, (ed.), *A Companion to Nineteenth-Century Britain*, (Blackwell Publishers), 2004, pp. 287-304, summarises the debate.

[47] Crafts, N. F. R., and Mills, Terence C., 'Trends in real wages in Britain, 1750-1913', *Explorations in Economic History*, Vol. 31, (1994), pp. 176-194, and Feinstein, C. H., 'Pessimism perpetuated: real wages and the standard of living in Britain during and after the Industrial Revolution', *Journal of Economic History*, Vol. 58, (1998), pp. 625-658, and 'What really happened to real wages?: trends in wages, prices, and productivity in the United Kingdom, 1880-1913', *Economic History Review*, second series, Vol. 43, (1990), pp. 329-355.

[48] Weaver, Stewart, 'The Bleak Age: J. H. Clapham, the Hammonds and the standard of living in Victorian Britain', in Taylor, Miles, and Wolff, Michael, (eds.), *The Victorians since 1901: histories, representations and revisions*, (Manchester University Press), 2004, pp. 29-43.

increasing emphasis on the regionality and diversity of living standards. The issue is not less about whether the standards of living of the working-classes as a whole rose or fell but which parts of the country are being discussed or which jobs within those different parts of the country are being explored.[49]

Industrialisation and urban growth increased the diversity, quantity and regularity of work that was available. Descriptions of earning a living in pre-industrial, rural and industrial areas show that in the absence of industry, most workers were under-employed and lived in a state of chronic poverty. Even skilled workers—such as shoemakers, blacksmiths and carpenters—were rarely able to make a good living from their trade as few of their neighbours had the means to pay for their services. Of necessity, skilled workers often turned to agriculture to make ends meet, contributing to the low living standards suffered by those working solely on the land. Industrialisation provided employment opportunities that were unavailable in pre-industrial Britain. Factories needed workers but so too did the coal mines that provided the fuel that powered industrial growth. Machines had to be maintained, warehouses organised and raw materials and finished goods transported to markets. Urban growth created demand for labour in building, furniture-making, the manufacture of clothes and shoes and the making of bread. In the British Isles in the 1300s, the population of about 3.5 million consumed 7 million loaves of bread—weighing 1 kilogram each—a day such was its centrality to people's diet. By the 1820s, 17 million loaves were baked daily but by 1945, with the exception of during wartime, bread was no longer the primary food—though it remained important—and bakers no longer occupied a central place in the country's culture. Demand for labour meant that many industrial workers were employed throughout the year and this helped to pull many out of the grinding poverty of rural labourers.

The impossibility of measuring happiness forces economists and historians to equate standards of living with monetary measures such as real wages or real income. 'Real wages' are usually defined as money income adjusted for the cost of living but not for well-being such as health, longevity, pollution, unemployment, conditions of women and children, urban crowding and the leisure time. Although there have been attempts to capture various dimensions of well-being, real wages per person remains the most influential indicator. From the 1750s, real wages stagnated or grew slowly and this lasted through the price peak of 1812-1813 and the distress of the post-war years between 1815 and 1821. Slow growth in consumption and real wages was largely a consequence of slow growth in the economy as a whole. In London this downward trend was not reversed until the 1820s, though it was not until the

---

[49] Griffin, Emma, *A Short History of the British Industrial Revolution*, (Macmillan), 2010, pp. 144-161, is a good summary of current thinking; see also her 'Diets, Hunger and Living Standards during the British Industrial Revolution', *Past & Present*, Vol. 239, (1), (2018), pp. 71-111 and *Bread Winner: An Intimate History of the Victorian Economy*, (Yale University Press), 2020.

1840s that the levels of the 1740s were regained and exceeded. The national index compiled by Lindert and Williamson shows that growth in real incomes between 1781 and 1819 was slow but that after 1819 their figures are far more optimistic suggesting that real wages nearly doubled between 1820 and 1850.[50] By 1830, the worst excesses of the pessimist scenario seem were at an end and real wages for the bulk of the working population were rising, though whether their optimistic assessment is entirely valid is questionable. Feinstein produced an alternative and more pessimistic series of real wages based on a different price index suggesting that real wages rose more slowly.[51] His main conclusion is that over the 75 years from 1778-1782 to 1853-1857 the increase in real weekly earnings, allowing for unemployment and short-time working, was less than 30 per cent. Wage earners' average real incomes were broadly stagnant for 50 years until the early 1830. If we add in the effects of unemployment, poor harvests, war, pollution, urban crowding and other social problems and especially the effects of the intense depression in the economy between 1837 and 1843, the modest rise in average income could well have been accompanied by a fall in the standards of living of the working-classes. For Feinstein, real wages only increased by about half that suggested by Lindert and Williamson between 1771 and the 1850s. Growing population and Irish immigration produced an abundant surplus of labour and this constrained significant rises in real wages until the labour market began to contract in the mid-1850s and 1860s. By 1850, there had been little or no improvement in real wages and, though life expectancy had increased, it was not until the 1870s that real gains were made.

Wages were higher in English cities than in the countryside but rents were higher and the quality of life lower. What proportion of the rise in urban wages reflected compensation for worsening urban squalor rather than true increases in real incomes? Williamson—using methods developed to measure the ill-effects of twentieth century cities—found that between 8 and 30 per cent of the higher urban wages compensated for the inferior quality of life in cities.[52] Brown found that much of the rise in real wages in the factory districts could be seen as compensation for poor working and living conditions.[53] Another criticism of

---

[50] Lindert, Peter, and Williamson, Jeffrey, 'English Workers' Living Standards during the Industrial Revolution: A New Look', *Economic History Review*, Vol. 36, (1), (1983), pp. 1-25. Crafts, N. F. R., 'English workers' real wages during the industrial revolution: some remaining problems'; with reply by Peter Lindert and Jeffrey Williamson, *Journal of Economic History*, Vol. 45, (1985), pp. 139-153.

[51] Feinstein, Charles H., 'Pessimism perpetuated: real wages and the standard of living in Britain during and after the Industrial Revolution', *Journal of Economic History*, Vol. 58, (1998), pp. 625-658.

[52] Williamson, Jeffrey G., *Did British Capitalism Breed Inequality?* (Allen and Unwin), 1985, pp. 7-33.

[53] Brown, John C., 'The Condition of England and the Standard of Living: Cotton Textiles in the Northwest, 1806-1850', *Journal of Economic History*, Vol. 50, (1990), pp. 591-615.

Lindert's and Williamson's findings is that their results were for workers who earned wages and that we do not know what happened to people who worked at home or were self-employed. Because the consumption per person of tea and sugar, thought of as luxury goods at the time, failed to rise along with real wages, Mokyr has suggested that workers who were not in the Lindert-Williamson sample may have suffered sufficiently deteriorating real incomes to offset rising wage income; in other words, the average person was no better off. Mokyr's explanation could also explain a lag between industrialisation and the diffusion of its benefits.[54] The problem with this discussion is that it is speculative, indicating what might have been the case.

So, what did people earn? Crafts estimated that British income per person (in 1970 U.S. dollars) rose from about $400 in 1760 to $430 in 1800 and $500 by 1830 and then jumped to $800 in 1860.[55] This indicated slow growth lasting from 1760 to 1830 followed by higher growth beginning sometime between 1830 and 1860. For this doubling of real wages not to have made the lowest paid better off, the share of income going to the lowest 65 per cent of the population would have had to fall by half for them to be worse off after the economic growth. It did not. In 1760, the lowest 65 per cent in Britain received about 29 per cent of total income; in 1860, their share was only down to 25 per cent. So the lowest 65 per cent were substantially better off with an increase in average real income of more than 70 per cent. The estimates of real income imply that a mildly optimistic conclusion on living standards is justified for the century after 1760. Feinstein also concluded that there was a 'moderate' rate of improvement in real earnings between 1781 and 1855. From the 1780s to 1815, average nominal wages kept largely in step with the cost of living and thus there was almost no increase in average real wages. After 1815, there was slow progress but by 1855 average real wages were only 30 per cent ahead of those in the early 1780s. Earnings fell back during the cyclical depression between 1838 and 1842. 'It was only from the late 1850s that the average British worker enjoyed substantial and sustained advances in real wages.'[56] In the 1760s most high-wage counties were in the south-east. By 1850, they were in the Midlands and North: in Lancashire wages were more than a third higher than in Buckinghamshire, a differential that continued until the end of the century.[57] This North-South divide[58] and wage payments must be assessed in the context of family income

---

[54] Mokyr, Joel, (ed.), *The British Industrial Revolution: An Economic Perspective*, (Westview Press), 1999 and ibid., Mokyr, Joel, *The Enlightened Economy*, pp. 449-472. See also, Mokyr, Joel, *A Culture of Growth: The Origins of the Modern Economy*, (Princeton University Press), 2016.

[55] Crafts, Nicholas F. R., *British Economic Growth During the Industrial Revolution*, (Oxford University Press), 1985.

[56] Ibid., Feinstein, Charles H., 'Pessimism perpetuated: real wages and the standard of living in Britain during and after the Industrial Revolution', p. 643.

[57] Solomon, Guy S., *The living standards of Tyneside coal miners, 1836-1862*, M.Sc., Thesis, University of York, 2014.

and the higher cost of living for the working-classes, a hardship aggravated by the family poverty cycle and the devastating impact of recurrent short-term crises.[59]

The long period of slow economic growth makes pessimistic conclusions about shorter periods plausible. For instance, did the working-classes become worse off during the early years of England's industrialisation between 1760 and 1830, when Crafts' estimates show real income per person growing at only about 0.3 per cent annually? Growth at such a slow rate made a worsening in the living standards of the working-classes possible. Most economists agree that the distribution of income became more unequal between 1790 and 1840 but adding in the effects of unemployment, poor harvests, war, disease and urban overcrowding, the modest rise in average income could well have been accompanied by a fall in the working-classes' standards of living. Other evidence supports the conclusion of slow improvement in living standards during the years of the industrial revolution. Crafts and Harley emphasised the limited extent of modernisation in England for much of the century of the industrial revolution whilst Feinstein found only a small rise in consumption until 1819 with a rapid rise subsequently.[60]

Analysis of standards of living hides important structural changes in the composition of working-class family income before 1850.[61] The assumption on which the figures were based, especially the dominance of money-wages and of the male breadwinner, lack validity until 1850 by which time workers had been deprived of traditional perks and rights and the working-class family had been forced to redefine gender roles and functions.[62] The imposition of monetary forms of wage payment marked a fundamental change in employers' attitudes to property and labour. What had previously been accepted as a customary right now became crime: employers could no longer allow workers to appropriate any part of the materials or product of their labour, no matter how small. What

---

[58] On this issue, see Baker, Alan R. H., and Billinge, Mark, (eds.), *Geographies of England: the North-South divide, material and imagined*, (Cambridge University Press), 2004.

[59] Harison, Casey, 'The standard of living of English and French workers, 1750-1850', in Rider, Christine, and Thompson, Michael, (eds.), *The industrial revolution in comparative perspective*, (Krieger), 2000, pp. 165-178, provides a useful comparative study.

[60] Crafts, Nicholas F. R., and Harley, C. Knick, 'Output Growth and the British Industrial Revolution: A Restatement of the Crafts-Harley View', *Economic History Review*, Vol. 45, (1992), pp. 703-730.

[61] Voth, Hans-Joachim, Living standards and the urban environment', in Floud, Roderick, and Johnson, Paul A., (eds.), *The Cambridge economic history of modern Britain, Volume 1: industrialisation, 1700-1860*, (Cambridge University Press), 2004, pp. 268-294.

[62] Horrell, Sara, and Humphries, Jane, 'The origins and expansion of the male breadwinner family: the case of nineteenth-century Britain', *International Review of Social History, Supplement*, Vol. 5, (1997), pp. 25-64, summarises the debates.

was at stake for workers was not simply a traditional source of 'extra' income, but the maintenance of some independence in the workplace, control over their products and the labour process. Age was probably the most important factor in determining output and earnings. In the 1830s, the youngest and fittest handloom weavers earned 25 per cent more wages at the same time as a weaker person could earn on the same machine. Throughout the trades, the elderly or rather the prematurely old were often forced to give up the better-paid tasks as they were affected by various forms of occupational disorder. For instance, the Sheffield fork-grinding industry killed off a quarter of its workforce every five years.[63] Differences in output and earnings were kept to a minimum where group solidarity and trade societies were strong, but these forms of mutual protection did not apply to the so-called 'dishonourable' trades or in the over-stocked outwork industries. Here, in the absence of day rates or 'legal', union-backed piece prices, opportunistic middlemen and commercially minded masters were able to exploit cheap, unskilled labour through the piece-rate system. Even in 'honourable' trades, few workers were fortunate enough to enjoy full-time work throughout the year.

The focus on the adult male 'breadwinner' has diverted attention away from the notion of the family income. Earnings in this period were assessed in family not individual, terms with the family often functioning as a unit of production. Research into household budgets escapes the narrowness of real wage studies and offers the possibility of analysing welfare at the level of the individual but this is hampered by the scarcity and poor quality of the surviving evidence. By 1830, however, prospects for women and hence family earnings deteriorated considerably. The first victims of technological or structural unemployment were women who encountered a new prejudice and sexual division of labour and the harsh economic costs of the new male breadwinner ideal.[64] Traditionally, manufacturing skill had been largely associated with men and this had created a sense of male solidarity that extended beyond the workplace into community and home. Men's struggles to maintain their skilled place in the workforce against machinery and the encroachment of unskilled women was an important part of their efforts to maintain their social status within communities and their families. This justified keeping women away from the new technology, as in a petition from the Staffordshire potters in 1845:

---

[63] Williams, Naomi, 'The reporting and classification of causes of death in mid-nineteenth-century England: the example of Sheffield', *Historical Methods*, Vol. 29, (1996), pp. 58-71.
[64] Horrell, Sara, and Humphries, Jane, 'Women's labour force participation and the transition to the male-breadwinner family, 1790-1865', *Economic History Review*, Vol. 48 (1995), pp. 89-117, and '"The exploitation of little children": child labour and the family economy in the industrial revolution', *Explorations in Economic History*, Vol. 32, (1995), pp. 485-516.

To maidens, mothers and wives we say machinery is your deadliest enemy...It will destroy your natural claims to home and domestic duties....[65]

It also limited men's incomes, as cotton spinner pleaded in 1824:

The women, in nine cases out of ten, have only themselves to support, while the men generally have families...The women can afford their labour for less than men.... Keep them at home to look after their families.[66]

Sexual segregation was enforced in textile mills where women were denied access to the best-paid skilled jobs. Skill was a male preserve in the modern factory, protected by trade union organisation and internal subcontracting that gave mule spinners a role for which women were deemed ineligible. Textile mills apart,[67] mechanisation and the factory system brought few new opportunities for women: female employment was derisory in iron and steel, railways, chemicals and the expanding heavy industries. Legislation in 1842 restricted female work in the mines.[68] Sexual segregation was by no means restricted to the factory and occurred wherever men were confronted with changes in the location or process of work. In rural England, for instance, female participation was limited to haymaking and weeding corn by 1830 but there were important regional differences. Wives and daughters of migrant Scottish labourers astonished farmers in East Anglia in the 1880s by doing work that had been done exclusively by men there for almost a century.[69] New tools also played a part in the diminishing role of women with the scythe replacing the sickle.

---

[65] Cit., Drake, Barbara, *Women in Trade Unions*, (Labour Research Department), 1920, reprinted, (Virago), 1984, p. 6.

[66] *Manchester Guardian*, 20 November 1824, p. 3.

[67] There were severe limitations on women's roles in textiles; see, Valverde, Mariana, '"Giving the female a domestic turn": the social, legal and moral regulation of women's work in British cotton mills, 1820-1850', *Journal of Social History*, Vol. 21, (1987-8), pp. 619-634.

[68] John, Angela V., *By the sweat of their brow: women workers at Victorian coal mines*, (Croom Helm), 1980.

[69] Verdon, Nicola, *Rural women workers in nineteenth-century England: gender, work and wages*, (Boydell), 2002, and *Working the Land: A History of the Farmworker in England from 1850 to the Present Day*, (Palgrave Macmillan), 2017, provide an overview while Ulyatt, Donna J., *Rural women and work: Lincolnshire c.1800-1875*, (Anderson Blake Books), 2005, and MacKay, John, 'Married women and work in nineteenth-century Lancashire: the evidence of the 1851 and 1861 census reports', in Goose, Nigel, (ed.), *Women's work in industrial England: regional and local perspectives*, (Local Population Studies), 2007, pp. 164-181, provide valuable case studies. See also, Sharpe, Pamela, 'The female labour market in English agriculture during the Industrial Revolution: expansion or contraction?', in ibid., Goose, Nigel, (ed.), *Women's work in industrial England: regional and local perspectives*, pp. 51-75.

The family income suffered as a result but most men for economic reasons welcomed the new sexual specialisation. They were increasingly vulnerable to seasonal unemployment with the expansion of production that was less labour intensive and they were determined to restrict cheap female competition.[70] Yet in many cases, the wife's contribution to the family income remained crucial but the force of growing opposition to women working confined their employment to the lowest paid 'dishonourable' and sweated trades.[71] Their cheap labour was exploited to reinforce still further male hostility towards 'unfair' competition. Relations between the sexes in the London tailoring trades were at crisis point in the early 1830s when Owenite Socialists championed the rights of women to work and called on the London tailors union to adopt a policy of 'equalisation' in order to unite all the workforce. The resulting strike was a disastrous failure and led to further marginalisation of female workers in the trades.[72]

Domesticity was the best of a narrow range of options for working-class married women but for those employed in the sweated trades, it was a cruelly illusive ideal. Until their children were old enough to contribute to the family income, there was no release from the double burden of unpaid housework and ill-paid waged work. Unable not to work, married women were driven lower and lower into the sweated trades or prostitution by the forces of social convention that condemned but continued to exploit their labour. The middle-classes deplored the 'unnatural' behaviour of young working mothers and condemned them for leaving their children with incompetent child-minders. However, only a quarter of female mill workers were married and of those with children utmost care was taken to ensure that a close relative, lodger or neighbour looked after them. Less than two per cent of all infant children in industrial Lancashire were left to the mercies of professional child minders.

Expenditure on basic needs for working-class families was significantly higher than for the middle and upper-classes.[73] Food was by far the most important item in agricultural areas and there was little discernible improvement

---

[70] Clark, Gregory, 'Farm wages and living standards in the industrial revolution: England, 1670-1869', *Economic History Review*, Vol. 54, (2001), pp. 477-505, provides a valuable longitudinal study.

[71] Blackburn, Sheila, *A fair day's wage for a fair day's work?: sweated labour and the origins of minimum wage legislation in Britain*, (Ashgate), 2007, Blackburn, Sheila, '"Between the devil of cheap labour competition and the deep sea of family poverty?": sweated labour in time and place, 1840-1914', *Labour History Review*, Vol. 71, (2006), pp. 99-121, and Blackburn, Sheila, '"Princesses and sweated-wage slaves go well together": images of British sweated workers, 1843-1914', *International Labor and Working-Class History*, Vol. 61, (2002), pp. 24-44.

[72] Schmiechen, J. A., *Sweated industries and sweated labour: the London clothing trades: 1860-1914*, (Taylor & Francis), 1984.

[73] Horrell, S., and Humphries, J., 'Old questions, new data, and alternative perspectives: families' living standards in the industrial revolution', *Journal of Economic History*, Vol. 52, (1992), pp. 849-880.

in diet between the 1790s and 1850. The agricultural labourers' families surveyed by Davies and Eden between 1787 and 1796 were spending 75 per cent of their income on food.[74] Nearly two-thirds of food spending (62 per cent) was devoted to bread, over half of all income (52.5 per cent) was spent on bread alone. Whereas farm-workers in the 1840s were spending 75 per cent of their income on food, miners were spending less, 58 per cent, and only 40 per cent of their food expenditure was on bread. The total proportion of their income devoted to bread was about 25 per cent, less than half the proportion paid by agricultural labourers. Among the factory workers, 60 per cent of income was spent on food, and of this 36 per cent was spent on bread. The overall proportion of family income that was spent on bread was 23 per cent. There were clear differences between the diets of agricultural and industrial families in part the result of the higher wages paid to mining and manufacturing families leading to a more varied and higher animal protein-based diet. [75]

The distribution of food within families was not equitable with women and children receiving smaller shares compared with men. Contemporary working-class autobiographies suggest that in mining and manufacturing families, 18 per cent of writers had experienced hunger but this rises to 42 per cent in agricultural families. Working people bought poor quality food in small quantities for immediate consumption and rarely received value for money. Food was often obtained from the Saturday night markets where dealers were able to off-load their otherwise unsaleable produce: Engels (1820-1895) commented that 'the workers get what is too bad for the property-holding class.'[76] They were often dependent on credit and had to pay the higher prices of the obliging small shopkeepers. Provisions were dearer still where workers were victims of the truck system and the poor quality, adulterated foods of the 'Tommy shops'.[77] Despite stringent legislation from 1831, the truck system remained common practice into the 1850s in south Staffordshire and in much of rural East Anglia where gang masters supplied subcontract labour at the cheapest daily rates.[78]

---

[74] Davies, David (1742-1819), *The Case of the Labourers in Husbandry Stated and Considered*, (R. Cruttwell), 1795; Eden, Frederick Morton (1766-1809), *The State of the Poor: A History of the Labouring Classes in England, with Parochial Reports*, 3 Vols. (J. Davis), 1797.

[75] Ibid., Griffin, Emma, 'Diets, Hunger and Living Standards during the British Industrial Revolution'.

[76] Ibid., Engels, Frederick, *The condition of the working class in England*, p. 104.

[77] On the operation of the truck system see, Hilton, G. W., 'The British truck system in the 19th century', *Journal of Political Economy*, Vol. 65, (1957), pp. 237-256, and Hilton, G. W., *The truck system, including a history of the British Truck Acts, 1465-1960*, (W. Heffer), 1960.

[78] Verdon, Nicola, 'The employment of women and children in agriculture: a reassessment of agricultural gangs in nineteenth-century Norfolk', *Agricultural History Review*, Vol. 49, (2001), pp. 41-55.

Other historians have suggested that unmeasured effects of environmental decay offset any gains in well-being because of rising wages. The physical nature of people reflects important aspects of their well-being and height is thought to reflect nutritional status, an aggregate measure of the effects of food intake, environment and disease. Floud, Wachter and Gregory in their study of armed forces recruitment records argued that, although there was a secular increase in average heights over the past two centuries, the stature of people born between 1825 and 1860 declined.[79] This decline has been attributed chiefly to an increase in urban living. If average height can be taken as an index of human well-being, the evidence suggests a decline during a period in which real wages rose. Rural dwellers were the tallest occupation group during the nineteenth century, despite being the most poorly paid. Evidence of regional differences is embedded in every analysis of living standards but have had surprisingly little impact on the historical narrative that remains wedded to the notion of pessimism rather than difference.

As with food, those at the lower end of the housing market received scant value for money.[80] Housing accounted for anything up to a third of a labourer's wages compared to about a sixth of the income of the middle-classes. The nuclear family, the sacred cow of English social history, was too expensive for families who lived with kin or in lodgings for the first few years of marriage. Foster found that the proportion of families living with relatives ranged from a third in Northampton to over two-thirds in South Shields while in Preston in 1851, lodgers were present in 23 per cent of all households.[81] Many urban workers were also subject to the 'house trucking' system where housing was dependent on their employers, an extension of the 'tied' cottage system of rural England. For working-class teenagers, clothes and accessories were the first call on income after they had paid their contribution to the family income. Many poor families, however, relied on cast-off, second-hand or stolen goods.[82] Clothes could be easily pawned or fenced and there are many recorded cases of petty theft: in Manchester there was an average of 210 reports a year in the 1830s of clothing stolen from hedges or lines. Extra income was often spent on clothes since they were easily pawnable as well as providing immediate enjoyment.[83]

---

[79] Floud, R., Wachter, K.W., & Gregory, A., *Height, Health and History: Nutritional Status in the United Kingdom, 1750-1980*, (Cambridge University Press), 1990.

[80] Williams, Samantha, 'Poor relief, labourers' households and living standards in rural England c.1770-1834: a Bedfordshire case study', *Economic History Review*, Vol. 58, (2005), pp. 485-519.

[81] Ibid., Foster. J., *Class Struggle and the Industrial Revolution: early industrial capitalism in three English towns*, pp. 125-131.

[82] Richmond, Vivienne, *Clothing the Poor in Nineteenth-Century England*, (Cambridge University Press), 2013, pp. 52-92, Worth, Rachel, *Clothing and Landscape in Victorian England: Working-Class Dress and Rural Life*, (I.B. Tauris), 2018, pp. 48-69.

[83] Tebbutt, Melanie, *Making Ends Meet: Pawnbroking and Working-Class Credit*, (Leicester University Press), 1983, and Hudson, K, *Pawnbroking: an aspect of British*

Variations in standards of living, wages and working conditions were as great in towns as in the countryside. Average urban wages were certainly higher by the mid-nineteenth century but so were rent and food so that urban dwellers were not necessarily better off than their rural counterparts. Women's wages were invariably well below those of men and families dependent on a sole female wage earner were among the poorest of the urban population. Jobs promising a regular weekly wage, with little cyclical unemployment, were rare, highly prized and jealously guarded. Unemployment was the norm for most workers and was a major factor in the urban labour market and in turn had a significant impact on standards of living, quality of housing and the residential areas to which people could aspire. Wages, prices and rent were central to working-class fears providing a common point of reference for all those who laboured whether in the fields, the factories or in the home and distinguished them from the interests of other classes in society. They gave an added potency to other areas where working people felt things in common. They were politically excluded; they saw themselves as subject to a corrupting state and venal administrators that exploited their political weakness but they also regarded themselves as true patriots and as 'the People' who sought to restore a mythic and democratic view of a constitution no longer under the 'Norman Yoke'.[84] From the early 1830s, working people developed a growing awareness of their particular situations and this created a common sense of political purpose.

Skills, work and management, 1850-1914

Factories employing large numbers of workers in the North, especially in Lancashire and the West Riding attracted attention from contemporaries and were regarded as typical of the manufacturing economy in the nineteenth century. By 1850, combined spinning and weaving cotton factories in England averaged 310 workers and this increased to 429 by 1890. In Scotland, cotton factories had 216 workers in 1850 and 304 by 1867. In 1863, Armstrong's engineering and ordnance works on Tyneside had 3,800 workers and in the 1840s the Dowlais ironworks in South Wales employed 5,000 people. These large concerns were, however, not typical. In 1838, woollen and worsted mills in the West Riding averaged between 45 and 76 hands and by 1870 still employed only 70 workers. In 1851, more than 80 per cent of industrial firms in Scotland employed less than 20 operatives. In London, in manufacturing trades such as tailoring and cabinet-making work was sub-contracted to small workshops while in Birmingham small enterprises and workshops drove economic growth.

---

social history, (Bodley Head Ltd.), 1982.
[84] Hill, Christopher, *Puritanism and Revolution*, (Secker & Warburg), 1958, pp. 50-112, considers 'The Norman Yoke'. *Le joug normand: La conquête normande et son interprétation dans l'historiographie et la pensée politique anglaises*, (Université de Caen), 2004, pp. 15-55, provides a more recent perspective.

Growing competition and dynamic markets were not accompanied by a shift towards newer technologies and their application was uneven and slow. Only 22 per cent of silk-looms were powered in 1870 and hand spinning mules were still widely used in the 1880s.

Handwork remained important throughout the nineteenth century as employers in the clothing and furniture industries faced pressures to reduce costs in highly competitive markets. Manufacturers sub-contracted to small masters who hired home workers often at cheap piece rates for very long hours. This more complex division of labour undermined skilled craft workers. For instance, subcontracting in London cabinet-making in the 1830s and 1840s saw workers specialising in one aspect of the trade—such as sawing, turning, fret-cutting, or polishing. Highly skilled workers, largely adult males, faced a further threat from the use of low-paid child or female labour. Factory legislation in 1833, 1842, 1844 and 1847 restricted the hours of work of children and young people in textiles and mining and this was extended to other industries in the 1860s and 1870s while compulsory elementary schooling further reduced opportunities for child labour. Although women were increasingly marginalised in the economy, it was often in employers' interests to replace male with cheaper female labour. In 1861, the Courtauld silk factory employed 900 women and only 189 men and in the straw hat trade most workers were women with men confined to the more skilled areas of production such as hat blocking.

New forms of production, even if they did not involve new technology, placed skilled workers under considerable pressure. Craft-like control persisted in amended form in the mid-Victorian factory, a privilege enjoyed by a new 'aristocracy of labour'. Foster argues that these workers derived their enhanced status from a change in employer strategy. Skilled workers were incorporated into a new authority structure designed to strengthen discipline and increase productivity. The introduction of the 'piece master' system in the engineering factories brought skilled engineers into active involvement in management as group leaders and technical supervisors. In cotton factories, spinners retained skilled status as a crucial group after the introduction of the self-acting mule in the 1820s. These male workers intensified the labour of juvenile and female time-paid assistants, an effective adaptation of traditional gender and family roles to the factory environment.[85] There is some disagreement over the extent to which their position was secure. Stedman Jones insists that real control had already passed to employers with the restructuring of industry on 'modern' lines.[86] Skilled workers sought to preserve their status and differentials through the

[85] Ibid., Foster. J., *Class Struggle and the Industrial Revolution: early industrial capitalism in three English towns*, pp. 224-238.

[86] Jones, Gareth Stedman, *Outcast London: a study in the relationship between classes in Victorian society*, (Oxford University Press), 1971, pp. 19-51. See his critique of Foster 'Class Struggle and the Industrial Revolution', in his *Languages of Class*, (Cambridge University Press), 1983, pp. 25-74.

goodwill of their employers. In the absence of technical expertise, employers were often forced to concede considerable autonomy to skilled workers though they generally derived some benefit from the arrangement. In cotton spinning, a skilled hand was needed to adjust the quadrant nut and oversee variations in the yarn on self-acting mules. Allowing mule spinners to hire their own piercers relieved employers of direct responsibility for labour recruitment and discipline but it also helped to preserve their status by controlling access to the trade. Apprenticeship operated in a similar way, providing employers with a skilled workforce trained at worker expense. This pragmatic compromise between skilled workers and employers was usually negotiated informally and locally. Capital made production possible, but the actual details of production, workers insisted was their responsibility.

Where no independence was allowed, workers were often reluctant to enter employment whatever wages it offered. Domestic service, a comparatively well-paid occupation largely unaffected by cyclical unemployment, was shunned by working-class girls in factory districts and urban areas. Lancashire marriage registers show that servants tended to marry husbands from a lower social-economic status than their peers, an indication of the stigma attached to service in an area where other female employment was readily available.[87] The middle-classes in these factory districts relied on rural migrants for domestic servants and some obtained cheap live-in servants from local workhouses.[88] Factory employment offered women some independence but they seldom held the most well-paid and responsible jobs especially supervisory tasks that carried skilled status and workplace authority. Male preserves were jealously protected by 'closed' trade unionism. Women were denied access to the well-paid spinning sector not because they were physically incapable of operating self-acting mules but lacked the necessary technical skills and experience.[89] They had been excluded from the spinning factories in the 1810s and 1820s when the use of 'doubled' mules put a premium on male physical strength. Without recent practical experience, women became the victims of discontinuity in the

---

[87] Anderson, Michael, 'What can the mid-Victorian censuses tell us about variations in married women's employment?', *Local Population Studies*, Vol. 62, (1999), pp. 9-30.

[88] Horn, Pamela, *The rise and fall of the Victorian servant*, revised edition, (Sutton Publishing), 2004, Higgs, Edward, 'The tabulation of occupations in the nineteenth-century census with special reference to domestic servants', in Goose, Nigel, (ed.), *Women's work in industrial England: regional and local perspectives*, (Local Population Studies Society), 2007, pp. 250-259, Drake, Michael, 'Aspects of domestic service in Great Britain and Ireland, 1841-1911', *Family & Community History*, Vol. 2, (1999), pp. 119-128, and Jamieson, Lynn, 'Rural and urban women in domestic service', in Gordon, Eleanor, and Breitenbach, Esther, (eds.), *The world is ill-divided: women's work in Scotland in the nineteenth and early twentieth centuries*, (John Donald), 1990, pp. 136-157.

[89] Freifeld, Mary, 'Technological change and the "self-acting" mule: a study of skill and the sexual division of labour', *Social History*, Vol. 11, (1986), pp. 319-343.

transmission of craft skills and knowledge from one generation to another. The cult of domesticity sought to limit female paid employment to the brief period before marriage hindering the acquisition of workplace skills. In some parts of Lancashire, married women went out to work in substantial numbers, but not in its spinning belt where the well-paid spinners and engineers feared a loss of status should their wives return to paid employment.

The earliest uses of the term 'aristocracy of labour' referred to hierarchies within certain crafts, like coach-making, in the 1830s and 1840s and the labour aristocracy described in the third quarter of the century may represent the expansion of these groups under the favourable conditions of the mid-Victorian boom. There is no doubt of the cultural importance of traditions drawn from artisan cultures of the 1830s and earlier or of the economic importance of apprenticed skills drawn from these older trades. However, there were newer trades, especially associated with engineering, shipbuilding and the rapid expansion of capital goods that altered the make-up of the working-classes. In 1870, George Potter (1832-1893), a prominent unionist and radical journalist wrote:

> The working man belonging to the upper-class of his order is a member of the aristocracy of the working-classes. He is a man of some culture, is well read in politics and social history.... His self-respect is also well developed. [90]

His view of the 'aristocracy of the working-classes', distinguished from other workers by their way of life, values and attitudes and seen as a moderating influence on the politics of popular protest, is scattered widely through contemporary accounts of the working-classes in the third quarter of the nineteenth century.[91] The notion of a labour aristocracy is not only an economic

---

[90] *The Reformer*, 5 November 1870.

[91] Harrison, Royden, and Zeitlin, Jonathan, (eds.), *Divisions of labour: Skilled workers and technological change in nineteenth century England*, (Harvester), 1977, and More, Charles, *Skill and the English working class, 1870-1914*, (Taylor & Francis), 1980, provide the context. Gray, Robert, *The Aristocracy of Labour in Nineteenth-century Britain c.1850-1914*, (Macmillan), 1981, is an excellent summary of early research on the subject but needs to be read in conjunction with the relevant sections of Reid, Alastair J., *Social Classes and Social Relations in Britain 1850-1914*, (Cambridge University Press), 1995, and Lummis, Trevor, *The Labour Aristocracy, 1851-1914*, (Scolar), 1994. See also, Shepherd, M. A., 'The origins and incidence of the term "labour aristocracy"', *Bulletin of the Society for the Study of Labour History*, Vol. 37, (1978), pp. 51-67, Moorhouse, H. F., 'The Marxist theory of the labour aristocracy', *Social History*, Vol. 3, (1978), pp. 61-82, and 'The significance of the labour aristocracy ', *Social History*, Vol. 6, (1981), pp. 229-233, and Reid, Alastair J., 'Politics and economics in the formation of the British working class: a response to H. F. Moorhouse', *Social History*, Vol. 3, (1978), pp. 347-361, and McLennan, Gregor, 'The labour aristocracy and 'incorporation': notes on some terms in the social history of the working class', *Social History*, Vol. 6, (1981), pp. 71-81.

concept. Working-class behaviour and experience was not confined to the workplace and the basis for a cohesive upper stratum within the working-classes existed within communities. Labour aristocracy was not simply about 'control' in the workplace but about culture and community, values and life-styles and above all status and this set them apart from the less advantaged sections of the working-classes.[92]

Engineering is often regarded as central to the formation of a labour aristocracy.[93] The expansion of the industry was associated with the expansion of skilled employment, much of it highly paid. Skilled engineering workers had been under pressure in the 1840s culminating in the lock-out of 1852. Thereafter, the pace of technical change slackened, at least until the 1890s and there was a spread of techniques from their narrow base in Lancashire and the West Riding. The industry was heavily dependent on the skilled labour of turners and fitters. Management's authority was limited by craft custom and foremen retained their trade affiliations, often belonging to the same craft unions and were only gradually transformed into a distinct supervisory stratum. There were attempts by some employers to respond to new competitive challenges from the 1870s and introduce further technical change, but these developments were more marked in some regions than others and the entrenched position of apprentice-trained craftsmen remained intact in many engineering centres.[94] Building is often cited as a classic case of a 'traditional' sector growing to provide the infrastructure of an industrial-urban society.[95] But, by 1900, wood-working and stone-cutting machines, new materials like concrete and steel as well as acute depression were undermining craft controls. The piecemeal application of machines was typical of the changes occurring in labour-intensive crafts in the second half of the century, with effects on the pace of work, the versatility and initiative of skilled labour and the possibility of 'dilution'. The position of building craftsmen in the labour aristocracy depended on their ability to maintain trade boundaries in the face of these pressures.[96]

Skilled workers had the resources, bargaining position and craft traditions

---

[92] Kerswell, Timothy, 'A Conceptual History of the Labour Aristocracy: A Critical Review', *Socialism and Democracy*, Vol. 33, (1), (2019), pp. 70-87.

[93] Musson, A. E., The Engineering Industry' in Church, Roy, (ed.), *The Dynamics of Victorian Business: Problems and Perspectives to the 1870s*, (Routledge), 1980, pp. 87-106, and Saul, S. B., 'The Mechanical Engineering Industries in Britain, 1860-1914', in Supple, Barry, (ed.), *Essays in British Business History*, (Oxford University Press), 1977, pp. 31-48.

[94] Zeitlin, Jonathan, 'Engineers and compositors: a comparison', in ibid., Harrison, Royden, and Zeitlin, Jonathan, (eds.), *Division of labour: Skilled workers and technological change in nineteenth-century Britain*, pp. 185-250.

[95] Cooney, E. W., 'The Building Industry', in ibid., Church, Roy, (ed.), *The Dynamics of Victorian Business: Problems and Perspectives to the 1870s*, pp. 142-160.

[96] See Crossick, Geoffrey, 'The labour aristocracy and its values: a study of mid-Victorian Kentish London', *Victorian Studies*, Vol. 19, (1976), pp. 301-328.

that supported unionism.[97] Between 1850 and 1870, trade unions grew from 250,000 to 500,000 members though they still formed a small proportion of the total working-class population of 20 million. Unions were legal from 1825 but an adequate legal standing was not established until 1875 and in the previous half century they had been subject to intimidation and prosecution. Industrial action was common as, for instance, in 1842. The Preston lock-out of 1853-1854 saw conflict between employers and workers in an attempt to reverse the 10 per cent wage cuts made during the depression in 1847.[98] Cotton workers, who sort the restoration of their wages in the more buoyant economic conditions of the early 1850s, were starved back to work after twenty-eight weeks, a decisive defeat. By contrast, in Stockport and Blackburn workers won a 10 per cent increase. This marked a turning-point in strategy as union leaders cultivated an image of moderation and respectability to secure recognition from reluctant employers who accepted unions and their negotiating rights on the strict understanding that union officials would 'police' the agreement.[99] Although union recognition elsewhere was delayed until the 1880s, Blackburn weavers pointed the way towards modern collective bargaining. In already unionised industries, similar conciliation and arbitration schemes enjoyed considerable success in the late 1860s and early 1870s. They were first introduced in the Nottingham hosiery industry and were of mutual benefit to unions and employers, an institutional expression of the mid-Victorian compromise in labour relations.[100] New sliding wage-scales were welcomed in coal and iron trades where wage disputes had broken many unions: conciliation boards now automatically adjusted wages to product price.[101] Some of the other schemes clearly favoured employers. In the building trade, for instance, employers took advantage of mutual negotiation to reassert and redefine managerial powers curtailing the autonomous regulation of the trade.[102]

---

[97] Musson, A. E., 'Class struggle and the labour aristocracy, 1830-1860', *Social History*, Vol. 1, (3), (1976), pp. 335-356.

[98] Dutton, H. I., and King, J. E., '*Ten Per Cent and no surrender': the Preston strike, 1853-1854*, (Cambridge University Press), 1981.

[99] Beattie, Derek, *Blackburn: the development of a Lancashire cotton town*, (Ryburn), 1992, provides the context but see also, Daumas, Jean-Claude, et al, 'Trade unionism in textiles towns and areas', in Robert, Jean-Louis, Prost, Antoine, and Wrigley, Chris, (eds.), *The emergence of European trade unionism*, (Ashgate), 2004, pp. 56-57, 64-65 and 70-73.

[100] Church, R. A., 'Technological change and the Hosiery Board of Conciliation and Arbitration, 1860-84', *Yorkshire Bulletin of Economic & Social Research*, Vol. 15, (1963), pp. 52-60.

[101] Loftus, Donna, 'Industrial conciliation, class co-operation and the urban landscape in mid-Victorian England ', in Morris, R. J., and Trainor, R. H., (eds.), *Urban governance: Britain and beyond since 1750*, (Ashgate), 2000, pp. 182-197, and Porter, J. H., 'Wage bargaining under conciliation agreements, 1860-1914', *Economic History Review*, second series, Vol. 23, (1970), pp. 460-475.

[102] Price, Richard, *Masters, Unions, and Men: Work control in building and the rise of*

After 1850, these unions were elitist and moderate in character excluding women and unskilled workers from their trades. Organisations of skilled workers grew from the early 1850s and their leaders made significant alliances with middle-class Liberals. Their focus was on the specific needs of skilled workers and, although there were attempts to move beyond sectional concerns and form national union organisation across trades these received little support. The London Compositors nonetheless supported the builders' unions in their strike in 1859 and sent funds to striking cork cutters. In Scotland, unions organised local trades councils to support the organisation of skilled workers. There were often differences over industrial action between the national leadership, which preferred to avoid them if possible, and district committees that took a more confrontational view. For instance, when the Manchester District Committee of the Amalgamated Society of Engineers printed placards attacking piece work, the union authorities instructed them to remove them. The district committee refused. Union leaders put on a moderate face to offset hostility by the public and in Parliament but it had to balance this with questions of wages, control and even union recognition that motivated the continued militancy of local rank and file members.

Culture and community in the factory became the concern of 'scientific management', an approach significantly more sophisticated than the paternalism of the 1850s and 1860s. The working environment improved as employers implemented new factory legislation extending the range of welfare programmes, but other initiatives were less benevolent. From the 1880s, pioneer forms of scientific management[103] promoted by Frederick W. Taylor (1856-1915), an American mechanical engineer, provided new managerial techniques to raise productivity and curb the power of organised labour and were pursued as international competition increased and prices fell.[104] In Taylor's view, the task of factory management was to determine the best way for the worker to do the job, to provide the proper tools and training, and to provide incentives for good performance. He broke each job down into its individual motions, analysed these to determine which were essential and timed workers with a stopwatch. With effective time and motion—Taylor's lasting contribution to management

labour, 1830-1914, (Cambridge University Press), 1980, pp. 94-197, looks at the development of industrial relations from the late 1860s.
[103] Kreis, Steven, *The diffusion of an idea: a history of scientific management in Britain, 1890-1945*, Ph.D., Thesis, University of Missouri, 1990, Whitson, Kevin, *Scientific Management Practice in Britain, A History*, Ph.D., Thesis, University of Warwick, 1995.
[104] 'Taylorism' originated in the United States and stood for the logical development of the division of labour. The various aspects of manufacture were found and then applied to an assembly line structure. See, Taylor, Frederick Winslow, *The principles of scientific management*, (Harper & Brothers), 1911, and Hounshell, David A., *From the American System to Mass Production, 1800-1932: The Development of Manufacturing Technology in the United States*, (JHU Press), 1985.

studies--the worker became far more productive. Lenin (1870-1924) initially decried it as a 'scientific' system of sweating' more work from labourers though after the Revolution in 1917 he took a more positive view.[105] What Taylor preached was the substitution of reason for habit, a new way of looking at familiar things.

This was not entirely new to British industry and there is evidence of a form of scientific management operating in the Boulton and Watt Foundry in 1795.[106] The extent of Taylor's influence in Britain and when this occurred is contested. Some accounts suggest that it was apparent in work practices before 1914; for others it was a product of the First World War or even of developments in the 1930s. What is clear is that new work methods were applied with less zeal and more compromises in Britain than in the United States and that while Taylorism became the accepted managerial ideology, management practice remained largely unaffected by it. The design and planning of production processes became a managerial prerogative, a task undertaken by new production engineers, while shop-floor operatives were kept under constant surveillance by foremen. This challenged the skilled workers' belief that they had autonomy in their spheres of production. Supervision was accompanied by new methods of payment and incentive schemes such as bonus systems. Employers wished to take advantage of technological developments of the 'second industrial revolution': semi-automatic machines, standardised and interchangeable parts and the increasing use of semi-skilled labour on tasks previously the preserve of a skilled elite.[107] Scientific management threatened to undermine skilled status and craft organisations but, in the British context at least, they proved highly resilient.

The failure to root out craft practice and the reluctance of employers to sacrifice social and industrial peace for the promise of scientific management have been attributed to the social nature of British capitalism, its early industrial institutions and a non-interventionist state unable to challenge an unenterprising culture. British decline followed from the institutional rigidities formed in the first half of the nineteenth century especially the aristocratic ruling class culture of British capitalism that was hostile to production values. Britain did not develop a professional service class capable of supporting scientific management but surrendered shop floor control to trade union shop stewards aided by the growing strength of the Labour Party and the emergency conditions of two world wars. For instance, failure to integrate spinning, weaving and marketing, fierce competition, rigid wage lists and the conservatism of vested interests led to

---

[105] Signed 'W', *Pravda*, No. 60, 13 March 1913.

[106] Demidowicz, George, *The Soho Manufactory, Mint and Foundry, West Midlands: Where Boulton, Watt and Murdoch made History*, (Liverpool University Press), 2022.

[107] See, Zeitlin, Jonathan, 'The meaning of managerial prerogative: industrial relations and the organisation of work in British engineering, 1880-1939', in Harvey, Charles E., and Turner, John, (eds.), *Labour and business in modern Britain*, (Frank Cass), 1989, pp. 32-47.

continued technical backwardness in cotton production. Unlike the United States, transition from iron to steel took place without changing either the structure of small-scale producers and competitive firms or trade union organisation and collective bargaining. The institutions of the labour movement, trade unions, TUC and Labour Party may have quickly allied with progressives and modernisers in the scientific management camp. There was shop floor resistance but this institutional opposition limited its scope and deprived it of important sources of organisation and support.

The results of attempts to reorganise production varied from industry to industry. Craft organisation remained stronger where employers were hindered by market forces, inelasticity of product demand or its perishable nature. Hand compositors in the newspaper industry gained control of the 'hot type' linotype machines for their own exclusive 'craft' use, a privilege extracted from employers in the competitive market for a perishable product and retained a monopoly until the shift of production from Fleet Street to Wapping in the 1970s.[108] Some employers decided against reorganisation when faced by threats of craft resistance, a sensible, if short-term, solution for family-owned firms making satisfactory profits. Also the product market for British-made capital goods was highly individualised, a significant obstacle to the introduction of standardised mass production techniques. Ships, machines and railway engines were constructed to fulfil the individual needs of customers. It was not until the bicycle boom of the mid-1890s that a broad-based demand for a product with standardised parts emerged and at this point engineering employers began to introduce American-style machine tools and lathes.[109]

Mechanisation was implemented in the midst of workplace conflict, as employers combined in a national organisation, the Engineering Employers Federation[110] to reverse the gains secured by the Amalgamated Society of Engineers during the craft militancy of the 1889-1892 boom.[111] In the lock-out of 1897, the EEF[112] insisted on their absolute right to manage but their victory

---

[108] See, Duffy, Patrick, *The skilled compositor, 1850-1914: an aristocrat among working men*, (Ashgate), 2000.

[109] Powell, Christopher G., *The British building industry since 1800: an economic history*, second edition, (Spon), 1996, pp. 74-98. Skingsley, T. A., 'Technical training and education in the English printing industry: a study of late 19th century attitudes', *Journal of the Printing Historical Society*, Vol. 13, (1978-9), pp. 1-25; Vol. 14, (1979-80), pp. 1-58.

[110] Zeitlin, Jonathan, 'The internal politics of employer organization: the Engineering Employers' Federation, 1896-1939', in Tolliday, Steven, and Zeitlin, Jonathan, (eds.), *The Power to Manage?: Employers and Industrial Relations in Comparative Historical Perspective*, (Routledge), 1991, pp. 46-70, especially pp. 47-55.

[111] Burgess, K., 'New Unionism for old? The Amalgamated Society of Engineers in Britain', in Mommsen, W. J., and Husung, H.-G., (eds.), *The development of trade unionism in Great Britain and Germany, 1880-1914*, (German Historical Institute, Harper-Collins), 1985, pp. 166-184.

did not mean the crushing of the union or a thorough transformation of the division of labour. The aim of employers was to boost output and reduce labour costs without major capital spending. Throughout the 1890s, there were similar disputes in other major industries as employers reasserted their authority in pursuit of lower costs and more efficient use of labour.[113] Between 1892 and 1897, 13.2 million days were lost through disputes compared to 2.3 million between 1899 and 1907 when new systems of national collective bargaining, similar to those in engineering, took effect.[114] Conflict was particularly intense in the coalfields.[115] Collective bargaining arrangements, the outcome of national strikes and lock-outs in the 1890s, recognised and confirmed the role and functions of craft trade unions, while making clear the power and prerogatives of employer authority.

The workplace relationships of the 1850s and 1860s were reconstructed in different forms. Skilled workers had to resolve whether they could or should retain their exclusive status. Some workers were prepared to shed some of their exclusivism to strengthen their position against modernising employers. The aristocratic boilermakers set the example preventing a major reorganisation of steel ship production by a flexible union policy that kept the boundaries of membership under constant review. When the need arose, semi-skilled workers were granted membership, an important step towards the establishment of a closed shop. Attitudes to unskilled workers also depended on circumstances: some were admitted, others were not. This redefinition of their boundaries of exclusion to admit previously prohibited groups of workers proved highly effective in allowing skilled workers to retain their aristocratic status in the new conditions of late-Victorian Britain. It helps to explain why the Cabinet-Makers' Association succeeded while the older Friendly Society of Operative Cabinet-Makers shrivelled into narrow craft restrictionism.[116] Old-fashioned prejudice was most difficult to abandon where gender was concerned. Craft organisation in the Potteries remained narrow and sectional, powerless to prevent displacement as cheap female labour was put to work on new machines.[117] The

---

[112] 'The Engineering Dispute', *Northern Whig*, 28 July 1897, p. 8, 'The Engineering Dispute', *Morning Post*, 24 December 1897, p. 3.

[113] This is evident in Smith, D. N., 'Managerial strategies, working conditions and the origins of unionism: the case of the tramway and omnibus industry, 1870-91', *Journal of Transport History*, third series, Vol. 8, (1987), pp. 30-51, and Lester, V. Markham, 'The employers' liability/workmen's compensation debate of the 1890s revisited', *Historical Journal*, Vol. 44, (2001), pp. 471-495.

[114] Cronin, James E., 'Strikes 1870-1914', in Wrigley, Chris, (ed.), *A history of British industrial relations, Vol. 1: 1875-1914*, (Harvester), 1982, pp. 74-98.

[115] Church, Roy A., and Outram, Quentin, *Strikes and Solidarity: Coalfield Conflict in Britain, 1889-1966*, (Cambridge University Press), 2002, pp. 38-58, 95-112.

[116] Betjemann, Peter, 'Craft and the Limits of Skill: Handicrafts Revivalism and the Problem of Technique', *Journal of Design History*, Vol. 21, (2008), 183-193.

[117] Anderson, G., 'Some aspects of the labour market in Britain 1870-1914', in Ibid.,

persistence of exclusive status reflecting the interplay between 'genuine skill'--a necessary exercise of dexterity, judgment and knowledge--and 'socially constructed skill'–status upheld by organisational control.[118]

Managerial control was exerted over technical expertise previously located on the shop-floor. A distinction emerged between planning and execution, the implementation of which depended on supervisory workers, trained technicians who owed their position to knowledge acquired at night school. Shop-floor skills were increasingly limited and specialised despite the continued existence of apprenticeship that passed on knowledge of the trade. Formal, indentured arrangements in the older crafts steadily declined but apprenticeship expanded in several growing industries such as building and printing where there was agreement between employers and workers over training methods.[119] With greater specialisation of work and skill, apprentice labour was quickly turned to profit by employers, a source of cheap labour that, as earlier in the century, undermined the position of adult men in the labour market.[120]

Despite the persistence of skill differentials, the working-classes became more homogeneous in late-Victorian England. The proportion of the occupied population engaged in farming fell from 15 per cent in 1871 to 7.5 per cent in 1901 as rural migrants entered the most rapidly expanding sections of the domestic economy, transport and mining marking a major shift from worse to better paid jobs and from less to more regular employment. Small units continued to proliferate in some sectors of the economy but the factory finally emerged as the predominant form of organisation even in the sweated and shoemaking trades leaving poor outworkers stranded in old centres of small-scale 'sweated' workshop production.[121]

Diversities and standards of living, 1850-1914

Improved standards of living during the mid-Victorian period owed more to greater stability in employment than a marked increase in wages.[122]   The

---

Wrigley, Chris, (ed.), *A history of British industrial relations, Vol. 1: 1875-1914*, pp. 1-19.

[118] Griffiths, Trevor, *The Lancashire working classes: c.1880-1930*, (Oxford University Press), 2001, is an excellent case-study.

[119] Powell, Christopher G., *The British building industry since 1800: an economic history*, second edition, (Spon), 1996, pp. 74-98. Skingsley, T. A., 'Technical training and education in the English printing industry: a study of late 19th century attitudes', *Journal of the Printing Historical Society*, Vol. 13, (1978-9), pp. 1-25; Vol. 14, (1979-80), pp. 1-58.

[120] See, for instance, Wilcox, Martin, 'Opportunity or Exploitation? Apprenticeship in the British Trawl Fisheries, 1850-1936', *Genealogists' Magazine*, Vol. 28, (2004), pp. 135-149.

[121] See, Gazeley, Ian, 'Manual work and pay, 1900-70', in Crafts, Nicholas F. R., Gazeley, Ian, and Newell, Andrew, (eds.), *Work and pay in twentieth-century Britain*, (Oxford University Press), 2007, pp. 55-79.

economy was characterised by high, relatively stable prices and high levels of consumption.[123] This was, however, punctuated by inflation between 1853 and 1855 and 1870 and 1873. Food prices rose less than most other prices resulting in marked increases in the consumption of tea, sugar and other 'luxuries'. In dietary terms, there was no significant advance in the standard of living until the falling prices of the 1880s.[124] Brewing apart, food production and retailing remained a largely unrevolutionised industry until 1900. Real wages kept pace with food price rises, but rents proved increasingly expensive with sharp increases in the mid-1860s. For some workers substantial and lasting advances in real wages did not occur until the late 1860s. The real wages of Black Country miners actually fell by a third during the mid-1850s and did not recover fully until 1869, after which there was a major advance carrying real wages to 30-40 per cent above levels in 1850.[125] Earnings in cotton exhibited a similar chronology with relatively modest advances in the 1850s followed by major advances after 1865: between 1860 and 1874, weavers' wages rose by 20 per cent and spinners by between 30 and 50 per cent.[126]

In this period, skilled workers earned twice those who were unskilled and they were less exposed to unemployment. For skilled unionists in the metal, engineering and shipbuilding industries, there were only two occasions, in 1858 and 1868, when the unemployment rates reached double figures. For agricultural labourers, the mid-Victorian boom brought no real improvement in standards of living and ironically, when improvement occurred in the 1870s and 1880s, it was against the backdrop of falling farming profitability.[127] In 1874, civil

---

[122] Church, Roy, *The Great Victorian Boom, 1850-1873*, (Macmillan), 1975, summarises the research position in the mid-1970s. Levi, Leone, *Wages and Earnings of the Working Classes*, (John Murray), 1867, provides a valuable study of wages in the mid-1860s.

[123] Boyer, George R., *The Winding Road to the Welfare State. Economic Insecurity and Social Welfare in Britain*, (Princeton University Press), 2019, pp. 75-105, examines living standards 1861-1908.

[124] See, Clayton, Paul, and Rowbotham, Judith, 'An unsuitable and degraded diet? Part one: public health lessons from the mid-Victorian working class diet', *Journal of the Royal Society of Medicine*, Vol. 101, (6), (2008), pp. 282-289, 'An unsuitable and degraded diet? Part two: realities of the mid-Victorian diet', *Journal of the Royal Society of Medicine*, Vol. 101, (7), (2008), pp. 350-357, and 'An unsuitable and degraded diet? Part three: Victorian consumption patterns and their health benefits', *Journal of the Royal Society of Medicine*, Vol. 101, (9), (2008), pp. 454-462.

[125] Mitchell, B R., *Economic Development of the British Coal Industry 1800-1914*, (Cambridge University Press), 1984, pp. 197, 214, 242, 244.

[126] Hunt, E. H., *Regional wage variations in Britain, 1850-1914*, (Oxford University Press), 1973.

[127] See, for instance, Williams, L. J., and Jones, D., 'The wages of agricultural labourers in the nineteenth century: the evidence from Glamorgan', *Bulletin of the Board of Celtic Studies*, Vol. 29, (1982), pp. 749-761, and Horn, Pamela, 'Northamptonshire agricultural labourers in the 1870s', *Northamptonshire Past & Present*, Vol. 4, (1971),

servant, banker and Conservative politician George Trout Bartley (1842-1910) suggested that three out of four people in a typical village required public relief at some stage in their lives.[128] In some industrial areas there was a similar lack of material advance. In the Black Country, only the skilled building trades enjoyed an increase in real wages despite peak production in local coal and iron industries. On Merseyside, wage rates for skilled and unskilled workers remained stable until eroded by high food prices in the early 1870s. Women workers in sweated trades and casual employment gained least during the mid-Victorian period, though there is some evidence for improvement in day rates for charring and washing in the 1870s. This was not the case for women involved in straw plaiting facing cheap imports from the Far East and changing fashion away from straw to other fabrics for hats. Bedfordshire's 20,701 female plaiters in 1871 were reduced to 485 by 1901 working for substantially reduced wages.[129]

Friendly societies were also common in rural areas and unskilled agricultural labourers were prominent members. In 1801, for instance, there were 123 Societies in Somerset and 30 in Wiltshire, increasing to 565 and 271 respectively by 1855.[130] Friendly societies were increasingly male in membership, though there were three 'female' clubs in the villages of Cheddar, Wrington and Shipham in the 1790s and by 1850 almost one in ten women was a member. Membership fluctuated with economic conditions and level of agricultural wages demonstrating the insecure status of its poorer members. This was evident in the large Hampshire Friendly Society where drop-out rates averaged about six per cent per year in the second half of the century. Urban studies suggest that divisions within the working-classes were reflected in membership of different societies. In Bristol, there was a division between the Odd Fellows with the highest subscription, the Foresters and then the Shepherds with more unskilled workers.[131] Despite greater stability of employment and a belated increase in earnings, few working-class families rose above economic insecurity and bouts of periodic poverty. At critical moments in the family cycle even the differential enjoyed by skilled workers proved inadequate to prevent considerable hardship. This was very severe at times of general distress when a downturn in the trade cycle or a harsh winter led to short-time working and unemployment.

Workers in the East End were hit hard by the crisis of 1866-1868, the result of an unlucky coincidence of conditions. The shipbuilding industry was dependent on government favour and foreign orders but this collapsed after the banking failures of 1866, a financial panic that brought an end to the boom in

---

pp. 371-377.

[128] Bartley, George, *The Seven Ages of a Village Pauper*, (Chapman and Hall), 1874, pp. 2-5.

[129] Dony, John, *A History of the Straw Industry*, (Gibbs, Bamforth & Co., Luton), 1942, pp. 123-141, 163-170.

[130] Fuller, M. D., *West Country Friendly Societies*, (Oakwood Press), 1964, p. 25.

[131] Gorsky, M., 'Mutual aid and civil society: friendly societies in nineteenth century Bristol', *Urban History*, Vol. 25, (1998), pp. 302-322.

railway and building construction.[132] The winter of 1866-1867 was extremely harsh and was accompanied by high food prices and the return of cholera adding to the hardship.[133] The overall effect was to amplify the casual labour problem. This can also be seen particularly in the Lancashire Cotton Famine of 1861-1865, a protracted period of distress and unemployment.[134] This was sparked by the blockade of the southern American ports by Federal Navy cutting supplies of raw cotton to Europe, including Lancashire and Scotland. Lancashire mills had four month supply of cotton stockpiled and had enough time to stockpile another month.[135] The impact did not hit immediately but without raw further materials, production had stopped by October 1861. Mill closures, mass unemployment and poverty struck northern Britain leading to soup kitchens being opened in early 1862.[136] During the winter of 1862-1863, 49 per cent of all operatives in the 28 Poor Law Unions of the cotton district were unemployed with a further 35 per cent on short-time. The persistence of such mass unemployment was unparalleled. In Ashton, the worst hit town where there was little industrial diversification, 60 per cent of the operatives remained unemployed as late as November 1864, while in Salford the unemployment rate stood at 24 per cent. After 1865, Lancashire operatives began to benefit from the mid-Victorian boom but others were less fortunate.

Unemployment on this scale had a disastrous impact on standards of living and posed considerable problems for Poor Law and philanthropic relief agencies once workers had exhausted their savings. The Poor Law and the

---

[132] Baxter, Richard, *The Panic of 1866 and its Lessons on the Currency Act*, (Longman, Green and Co.), 1866, Turner, John D., *Banking in Crisis: The Rise and Fall in British Banking Stability, 1800 to the Present*, (Cambridge University Press), 2014, pp. 53-54, 63.

[133] 'Monthly Report', *Birmingham Daily Gazette*, 3 January 1867, p. 7, detailed weather patterns during 1866 reporting the revival of cholera 'in a virulent form' from mid-July reaching its peak during the second week in August. See also, 'Cold and Cholera', *Belfast Morning News*, 21 January 1867, p. 3.

[134] Arnold, R. A., Sir, *The History of the Cotton Famine: From the Fall of Sumter to the passing of the Public Works Act*, (Saunders, Otley and Co.), 1864, Henderson, W. O., *The Lancashire Cotton Famine, 1861-1865*, (Manchester University Press), 1934, and Farnie, Douglas A., 'The cotton famine in Great Britain', in Ratcliffe, B. M., (ed.), *Great Britain and her World 1750-1914: Essays in honour of W. O. Henderson*, (Manchester University Press), 1975, pp. 153-178.

[135] For the impact of the famine see, Holcroft, Fred, *The Lancashire cotton famine around Leigh*, (Leigh Local History Society), 2003, Peters, Lorraine, 'Paisley and the cotton famine of 1862-1863', *Scottish Economic & Social History*, Vol. 21, (2001), pp. 121-139, Henderson, W.O., 'The cotton famine in Scotland and the relief of distress, 1862-64', *Scottish Historical Review*, Vol. 30, (1951), pp. 154-164, and Hall, Rosalind, 'A poor cotton weaver: poverty and the cotton famine in Clitheroe', *Social History*, Vol. 28, (2003), pp. 227-250.

[136] The Famine was not confined to Lancashire: for instance, 'The Cotton Famine— Distress in Down and Antrim', *Belfast News-Letter*, 1 January 1863, p. 3.

charities were unsuited to the needs of unemployed factory workers.[137] They had already come under scrutiny following events in London during the harsh winter of 1860-1861 when the temperature remained below freezing for a month causing severe privation for the casual work force.[138] Across the East End, the Poor Law system simply broke down as the number of paupers increased from about 96,000 to over 135,000.[139] To meet this crisis charitable funds were distributed without investigation, an exercise condemned in John Hollingshead's (1827-1904) investigative journalism as indiscriminate 'stray charity'.[140] The Poor Law Board, already under investigation by the Parliamentary Select Committee, was determined to prevent similar problems by insisting on the strict compliance with the Outdoor Relief Regulation Order. However, local Guardians refused to force the respectable unemployed to perform demeaning work tasks in the company of idle and dissolute paupers. They paid out small weekly allowances of between 1s and 2s per head on the assumption that this meagre non-pauperising sum would be augmented from other sources, short-time earnings, income from other members of the family or charitable aid.

Residential segregation was not entirely a nineteenth century innovation. It had existed before 1780 mainly at house-to-house levels while individual streets and districts in small towns were more commonly socially mixed in character. Tenements in Glasgow were largely an instance of one-class housing but with different levels of status and income within the working-classes on different floors. Engels suggested that there was a separation and segregation of classes in Manchester and other industrial towns in the 1840s that gave a clear-cut definition of urban dwelling.[141] Generally segregation has been viewed negatively as the move by those who could afford it to more attractive districts leaving the working-class residuum trapped in unpleasant and unhealthy areas. A more positive view suggests that clustering groups with similar aspirations and income levels within small neighbourhoods encouraged a sense of community. Within communities, there were important differences in the size and quality of working-class housing and there was residential segregation within the working-classes often with strong occupational differentiation. For instance, dwellings for railwaymen, bus and tram workers and dockers could be easily distinguished from the superior districts and housing favoured by skilled craftsmen. In the

---

[137] Tanner, Andrea, 'The casual poor and the City of London Poor Law Union, 1837-1869', *Historical Journal*, Vol. 42, (1999), pp. 183-206.

[138] 'The Weather and the Parks', *London Evening Standard*, 12 January 1861, p. 6, 'The Wind and Weather', *London Evening Standard*, 14 January 1861, p. 8. The Serpentine was iced over and 'had been crowded by 3000 persons during the day' with '2,000 sliders and skaters on the lake in Kensington Park.'

[139] 'Parliamentary Committee. Poor Relief', *London Evening Standard*, 9 March 1861, p. 8, suggests that the system function effectively only because of contributions from the public and that the poor law rates would not have been sufficient on their own.

[140] Hollingshead, John, *Ragged London in 1861*, (Smith, Elder & Co.), 1861, p. 244.

[141] Ibid., Engels, F., *The Condition of the Working-class in England*, p. 79.

1880s, middle-class visitors and researchers saw slums as uniformly awful, yet their residents quickly sorted themselves into the deserving and disreputable. The residential pattern that matured after 1850 and which, to a degree, lasted until the devastating blitz in the 1940s, had many frontiers between classes. Sometime it was marked by a physical feature like a railway line—people came from the wrong side of the track--or the invisible line between the right and wrong side of a street. This was especially the case in the line between classes with marginal differences in income...the lower middle-class and the upper-working-class. The lower middle-class tended not to have incomes any higher than those of skilled workers and family incomes were often lower as it was not done for wives to go to work. Yet their housing and that of the upper-working class was very similar: terrace houses with a front parlour and back extensions housing a scullery and extra first floor bedroom and outside privies until the 1890s. Lower middle-class houses may have been more decorated with a larger amount of lace curtains but the differences between the two classes' housing was not readily apparent.

Working-class real wages rose dramatically from the mid-1870s to the mid-1890s, while unemployment remained close to the levels of the mid-Victorian boom.[142] Money wages were not decisive in improving living standards but the dramatic fall in food prices that accounted for much of the working-class budget. Prices tumbled by over 40 per cent resulting in the most substantial and sustained increase of real wages in the nineteenth century. Allowing for unemployment, real wages of average urban workers were 60 per cent higher in 1900 than in 1860.[143] The seaside holiday represented escape from the city and was not something initiated by the middle-classes and imitated by the working-classes.[144] Escape to the sea by workers came before of railways. The major increase in demand—linked to rising real wages--was in the late-nineteenth century and it was only then that the seaside holiday became a recognisable part of urban popular culture. A week at the seaside that many working-class Lancastrians had come to enjoy by the 1880s was unusual and elsewhere the norm was the day trip. Demand grew with the number of visitors to Blackpool

---

[142] Saul, S. B., *The Myth of the Great Depression 1873-1896*, (Macmillan), second edition, 1988, summarises research.

[143] Ibid., Feinstein, C. H., 'What really happened to real wages?: trends in wages, prices, and productivity in the United Kingdom, 1880-1913', and Feinstein, C. H., 'New estimates of average earnings in the United Kingdom, 1880-1913', *Economic History Review*, Vol. 43, (1990), pp. 595-632, and Gourvish, T. R., 'The standard of living 1890-1914', in O'Day, Alan (ed.), *The Edwardian age: conflict and stability 1900-1914*, (Macmillan), 1979, pp. 13-34.

[144] Walton, John K., 'The demand for working-class seaside holidays in Victorian England', *Economic History Review*, 2nd series, Vol. 34, (1981), pp. 249-265, and 'The seaside and the holiday crowd', in Toulmin, Vanessa, Russell, Patrick, and Popple, Simon, (eds.), *The lost world of Mitchell and Kenyon: Edwardian Britain on film*, (BFI Publishing), 2004, pp.158-168.

rising from 1 million in 1883 to 2 million ten years later and to 4 million by 1914.[145]

There was considerable diversity in living standards. All workers endured economic fluctuations of one kind or another, not least in the troughs in the economy in 1878-1879, 1884-1887 and 1892-1893, but their severity diverged markedly. Shipbuilding felt the full impact of the world trade depression as there was an oversupply of ships in the early 1870s and mothballing vessels was not an option during the depression. Over 20 per cent of boilermakers and shipbuilders earned 40s or more in the early-twentieth century, the income available for consumption was substantially less than these wages suggest. At times of full employment, skilled workers paid off debts incurred during the last spell of unemployment and saved for the next interruption in earnings. Workers in the building trades were subject to a different rhythm, longer than the five to seven year trade and investment cycle experienced in capital goods industries. Swings in the building industry lasted twenty years or more: from a peak in 1876, earnings and work levels were reduced until the mid-1890s, the start of the next boom that reached a double peak in 1898 and 1903. During booms, fully employed builders' labourers were economically independent and were able to live above the poverty line without supplementary income. Within the long cycles, building activity remained at the mercy of the weather, with a seasonal trough from November to February pushing those without savings back into poverty.

Winter was a slack season in many other trades, bringing hardship to the casually employed in the docks, on the streets and in the sweatshops. This was mostly evident when trade was depressed and in 1886 led the unemployed to riot. There had been agitation amongst the unemployed during the severe depression of 1879 and each winter from 1883 to 1887 when economic distress was at its worst. For the first time unemployment became a political issue seen as distinct from poverty and deserving of public sympathy and remedial action by the state. The recently formed Social Democratic Federation had organised meetings of the unemployed from 1884 but serious rioting did not begin until February 1886 when virtually all work in building and at the docks stopped. A meeting of around 20,000 unemployed men in Trafalgar Square on 8 February– addressed by the Fair Trade League calling for protective tariffs and relief work– was interrupted by the SDF demanding more revolutionary socialist measures. Scuffles broke out between the two groups that degenerated into more general rioting that initially shook the West End of London and lasted for the following three days.[146] Tensions continued for the rest of 1886 with unemployed camping

---

[145] Walton, John K., 'Resorts and Regions: Blackpool, Southport, Lancashire and Beyond', in Brown, Alyson, (ed.), *Historical perspectives on Social Identities*, (Cambridge Scholars), 2006, pp. 7-22.

[146] Brodie, Marc, 'Artisans and Dossers: The 1886 West End Riots and the East End Casual Poor', *The London Journal*, Vol. 14, (2), (1999), pp. 34-50. See also, *Hansard*,

out in Trafalgar Square and St. James' Park. The government, slow to act, was prodded into action by the propertied classes the following year and on 13 November 1887– 'Bloody Sunday'–the Square was cleared by the police and two squadrons of Life Guards.[147] The following Sunday there was a further demonstration that saw the death of Alfred Linnell (1846-1887), a young clerk. The authorities found work for 895 unemployed in one day when the news of the riots in London reached Glasgow.

Charles Booth's (1840-1916) survey found that it was the irregularity of work rather than low rates of pay that accounted for working-class impoverishment.[148] Working in the clothing trade was still seasonal and sweated. Female workers in the cheap 'slop' end of the market in London worked no more than two and a half days a week at a daily rate of 2s 6d to 4s for machinists and 1s 6d to 3s 6d for button-holers. Wages were higher in the West End bespoke trade. Up to 30s per week was paid during brisk periods especially during the 'season' but milliners and dressmakers and tailoresses were frequently driven into prostitution during the slack season returning to the shops with the advent of the new season's trade. Morals, contemporaries observed, fluctuated with trade.[149]

Unemployment

It is difficult to superimpose twenty-first century notions of unemployment on the mid-nineteenth century labour market.[150] There are no statistics, national or otherwise. Patterns of work were diverse between different industries and trades but also within the same industry in different parts of the country.[151] The enormous variation in the nature of waged work is not the only difficulty. Industrialisation separated work from home and this reduced wage-earning capacity of married women who were limited by household duties. The age limits of the working population were determined simply by physical capacity. Statutory attempts to impose restrictions on the use of child labour in the 1830s

House, of Lords, Debates, 18 February 1886, cc 556-577.

[147] Creighton, Sean, 'From Revolution to New Unionism: The Impact of 'Bloody Sunday' on the Development of John Burns' Politics', in Flett, Keith, *A History of Riots*, (Cambridge Scholars Publishing), 2015, pp. 11-39, Solomon, Vlad, *State Surveillance, Political Policing and Counter-Terrorism in Britain 1880-1914*, (Boydell Press), 2021, pp. 99-111..

[148] For Booth's residuum, see, Welshman, John, *Underclass: A History of the Excluded, 1880-2000*, (Continuum International Publishing Group), 2006, pp. 1-44.

[149] The phrase originated in Sherwell, Arthur, *Life in West London*, (Methuen), 1897, p. 146.

[150] Ibid., Boyer, George R., *The Winding Road to the Welfare State. Economic Insecurity and Social Welfare in Britain*, pp. 106-133, 169-216.

[151] On this issue see, Whiteside, Noel, *Bad Times: Unemployment in British Social and Political History*, (Faber), 1991, and Burnett, John, *Idle hands: experience of unemployment, 1790-1990*, (Routledge), 1994.

and 1840s initially proved unsuccessful. Both employers and parents colluded in their evasion, the former because child labour was cheap and more easily disciplined; the latter because children's earnings were vital in the constant battle against poverty.[152] Larger families tended to be poorer families and family size grew during the first half of the century. The introduction of compulsory schooling 1880 was far more effective in eliminating such practices than anything that went before.

Victorian England did not recognise a common age of retirement from working life that was determined by the requirements of the job and the physical capacity of the worker.[153] Work was overwhelmingly manual and premium was placed on physical strength and stamina that faded with age, especially when accompanied by a poor diet consequent on low earnings and as a result, the age at which workers 'retired' varied considerably. In the 1840s, Engels noted how miners' working conditions bred chronic illness and whose job required a high level of physical fitness, were forced to stop work at 35-45 and rarely lived beyond the age of 50.[154] At the same time, Mayhew documented the case of a 70 year old London needlewoman who was refused help by the relieving officer because she was considered fit to earn her own living.[155] In all branches of the labour market, advancing years saw reduced earnings and irregular work and, if death did not intervene, eventual reliance on children, charity or the poor law.

To avoid the punitive poor law, those desperate for work crowded the casual labour markets found in Britain's major ports, urban building sites and gasworks, where the heavy nature of the work, the competition for jobs and daily fluctuations in the demand for labour meant that secure employment was nearly impossible. Here, good character, skill and regular work habits counted for nothing in the daily round of hiring and firing. Casual labour was widely

---

[152] For the debate on the effectiveness of enforcement see, Peacock, A. E., 'The successful prosecution of the Factory Acts, 1833-55', *Economic History Review*, second series, Vol. 37, (1984), pp. 197-210, Nardinelli, C., 'The successful prosecution of the Factory Acts: a suggested explanation', *Economic History Review*, second series, Vol. 38, (1985), pp. 428-430, and Bartrip, Peter W. J., 'Success or failure? The prosecution of the early Factory Acts', *Economic History Review*, second series, Vol. 38, (1985), pp. 423-427.

[153] See, for example, Goose, Nigel, 'Farm service, seasonal unemployment and casual labour in mid nineteenth-century England', *Agricultural History Review*, Vol. 54, (2006), pp. 274-303, focuses of Hertfordshire.

[154] Ibid., Engels, Frederick, *The condition of the working class in England*, pp. 247-262.

[155] Ibid., Mayhew, Henry, *London Labour and the London Poor: The Condition and Earnings of Those that will work, cannot work, and will not work*, Vol. 1, p. 404. Millinery and dressmaking constituted the higher end of female work with the needle; they were 'respectable' occupations for young women from middle-class or lower middle-class families. The number of women involved in dressmaking alone in the early 1840s was estimated to be 15,000: House of Commons, *Reports from Commissioners: Children's Employment, Trade and Manufactures, Sessional Papers*, Vol. XIV, (1843), p. 555.

recognised as a major source of inefficiency since large numbers of casuals were incapable of regular work, of social and moral degeneration–poverty bred criminality, sickness and incapacity–and this posed a major threat to Britain's industrial and imperial dominance. Under-employment bred unemployability: if treated like a pauper, the unemployed regular man would eventually behave like one, ending up as another casual labourer incapable of holding down a permanent job.

The only way to break this cycle, reformers argued, was to protect the regular man and distinguish his treatment from that of the pauper, the habitual casual, the vagrant, the drunkard and the petty criminal: the sources of 'the social problem'. The solution lay not in the provision of municipal public works as this merely added the chance of another short-term job and exacerbated problems of casualism and irregularity. Instead, inter-linked labour exchanges should rationalise the labour market: to remove the inefficient, the idle, the vagrant and habitually irregular workers and to concentrate work in the hands of the most efficient, thereby improving industrial and commercial performance. This strategy underpinned the reforms introduced by Liberal governments in Britain: the Labour Exchanges Act in 1908, the National Insurance Act of 1911 and the introduction of old age pensions from 1 January 1909.

No respectable worker or his family would turn to the poor law in time of distress except when absolutely essential to survival.[156] By 1850, 'pauper' carried a social stigma second only to that of the convicted criminal. This helps to explain the huge expansion of clubs, societies and associations that collected contributions from working people in order to help them cope in the event of a crisis.[157] Insurance against unemployment was less common and was largely confined to skilled men in printing, construction, engineering, metal-working, shipbuilding and some of the older crafts in leather-working, bookbinding and furniture-making. It operated through trade unions and was principally designed to prevent union men being forced to work below the recognised rate when desperate for want of work. In other sectors of the economy, notably mining and textiles, unions negotiated work-sharing schemes as an alternative form of protection against the threat of recession. The negotiation of working practices was designed to protect jobs as well as maintain wages.[158]

---

[156] Boot, H. M., 'Unemployment and Poor Law relief in Manchester, 1845-1850', *Social History*, Vol. 15, (1990), pp. 217-228, provides a valuable local study.

[157] Fisk, Audrey, *Mutual self-help in southern England, 1850-1912*, (Foresters Heritage Trust), 2006, and Cordery, Simon, *British friendly societies, 1750-1914*, (Palgrave Macmillan), 2003, Gorsky, Martin, 'Friendly society health insurance in nineteenth-century England', in Gorsky, Martin, and Sheard, Sally, (eds.), *Financing medicine: the British experience since 1750*, (Routledge), 2006, pp. 147-164, and Alborn, Timothy L., 'Senses of belonging: the politics of working-class insurance in Britain, 1880-1914', *Journal of Modern History*, Vol. 73, (2001), pp. 561-602.

[158] Hatton, Timothy J., 'Unemployment and the labour market, 1870-1939', in Ibid., Floud, Roderick, and Johnson, Paul A., (eds.), *The Cambridge economic history of*

By 1906, unions that did provide help for those out of work covered about 1 million workers but did not distinguish very clearly between those idle due to strikes and those unemployed because of a depression in trade. Debts were regarded as 'misfortunes' and debtors as 'unfortunate', not a reflection of moral failings. For most of the workforce, there was no automatic support to fall back on when recession struck and, in trying to maintain their self-esteem, resorted to various things. Credit played a major role within all classes but especially working-class families and loans were obtained from money-menders or relatives and neighbours and local traders on the understanding that debts would be repaid when times were not so hard.[159] This was a system of 'mutual lending' reflecting the nature of economic activity as a fundamentally social activity embedded in historically specific cultural norms and expectations.[160] Local pawnshops were a familiar resort of many who pledged items on Monday and redeemed them on Friday when (and if) the wages arrived.[161] The unemployment of the husband frequently pushed the wife into taking in more washing, more cleaning, child-minding and sewing and, in the last resort, into prostitution in order to supplement dwindling family resources. Working-class households survived on a precarious structure of credit that tended to collapse when employment was scarce, debts mounted, the rent was unpaid and creditors at the door. By various strategies, the families of unskilled labourers 'got by' most of the time, but without any security outside the informal help of family or friends. The only other option for the unemployed was migration from depressed to more prosperous areas within Britain or emigration to colonies such as Canada, New Zealand and South Africa where labour was still scarce. Emigration, whether assisted[162] or not, was an option for the young and skilled since colonies were not prepared to be used as a dumping ground for Britain's surplus labour and colonial governments had as little desire for British paupers as for British convicts.[163]

---

modern Britain, Vol. 2: economic maturity, 1860-1939, pp. 344-373, and Boyer, George R., and Hatton, Timothy J., 'New estimates of British unemployment, 1870-1913', *Journal of Economic History*, Vol. 62, (2002), pp. 643-675.

[159] Finn, Margot, *The Character of Credit. Personal Debt in English Culture, 1740-1914*, (Cambridge University Press), 2003.

[160] Dr Ben Griffin, review of *The Character of Credit. Personal Debt in English Culture, 1740–1914*, (review no. 435), https://reviews.history.ac.uk/review/435 Date accessed: 28 December 2021.

[161] Dickens, Charles, 'The Pawnbroker's Shop', Sketches by Boz. (Chapman and Hall), 1839, pp. 138-144.

[162] Howells, Gary, '"On account of their disreputable characters": parish-assisted emigration from rural England, 1834-1860', *History*, Vol. 88, (2003), pp. 587-605, considers Bedfordshire, Norfolk and Northamptonshire. See also, Haines, R., 'Nineteenth century government-assisted immigrants from the United Kingdom to Australia: schemes, regulations and arrivals 1831-1900, and some vital statistics 1834-1860', *Flinders Occasional Papers in Economic History*, Vol. 3, (1995), pp. 1-171.

By the late-nineteenth century, urban growth concentrated unemployment and underemployment in an unprecedented fashion and made social distress more visible. With the migration of the middle-classes and the skilled working-classes to the suburbs, those unable to find regular employment were left behind, forming the backbone of an 'inner city' problem. The new visibility of disorganisation in the labour market, at a time of German and American economic expansion, the extension of the vote to most working men in 1884, the growth of trade and labour organisation and the inability of traditional institutions to cope with the situation combined to promote the unemployment question as a key issue in national politics for the first time.[164] It took over twenty years to convert emergency intervention into permanent government policy.[165]

Working-class women in the economy

Between 1780 and 1945, there were significant and radical changes in many areas of British economic and social life. A critical question is whether there were parallel changes in the world of women's work.[166] In the late-eighteenth century, the main employment available to women in Britain were in agriculture, domestic service, dressmaking and textile manufacture. After 1860, however, young women began to enter previously all-male areas like medicine, pharmacy, librarianship, the civil service, clerical work and hairdressing, or areas previously restricted to older women like nursing, retail work and primary school teaching. There was a sexual division of labour and, for the most part, women did 'women's work' defined by often far lower wages than men.

Women had a reproductive rather than a productive role and as reproductive work was unpaid, society regarded it as having no economic value. This was translated into the labour market and a gender hierarchy of labour developed whereby women's work was given a lower social and economic value than that of men. The sexual division of labour split the unity of the working-

---

[163] See, for instance, Richards, Eric, 'How Did Poor People Emigrate from the British Isles to Australia in the Nineteenth Century?' *Journal of British Studies*, Vol. 32, (1993), pp. 250-279, and Gray, Peter, '"Shovelling out your paupers": the British state and Irish famine migration 1846-50', *Patterns of Prejudice*, Vol. 33, (4), (1999), pp. 47-66.

[164] On this issue, see, Harris, José, *Unemployment and Politics: A study in English social policy, 1886-1914*, (Oxford University Press), 1972, Davidson, Roger, *Whitehall and the Labour Problem in late-Victorian and Edwardian Britain: A study in official statistics and social control*, (Routledge), 1985, and Walters, William, *Unemployment and Government: Genealogies of the Social*, (Cambridge University Press), 2000, pp. 12-53.

[165] Gazeley, Ian, and Newell, Andrew, 'Unemployment', in ibid., Crafts, Nicholas F. R., Gazeley, Ian, and Newell, Andrew, (eds.), *Work and pay in twentieth-century Britain*, pp. 225-263.

[166] I have explored this issue in greater detail in my *The Woman Question: Sex, Work and Politics, 1780-1945*, 3rd ed., (Authoring History), 2021.

classes by gender and often the enmity between the two groups was seen in trade union activity.[167] Women were also regarded as a cheap reserve pool of labour that could be brought in and out of the workforce to suit the requirements of capital and/or the state. Finally, the Industrial Revolution led to a decisive separation between home and work. Often in pre-industrial society women were engaged in production at home. The way femininity was defined in the first half of the nineteenth century blinded most employers in the new industries to the suitability of young female labour. Industrialisation shifted large areas of production into factories or workshops and many women became factory workers or 'sweated labour'.[168] Cheap labour is a fundamental element of the capitalist mode of production and female labour was and is cheap labour. By introducing machinery and low-paid women into factories, manufacturers sought to break down many specialist tasks into a series of mechanical operations and so keep wages low. Many women were tied to the home yet needed money to support themselves and their family. Some form of outwork or homework was often their only option.

Many aspects of women's work were controversial. Women, single, married or widowed had always worked.[169] However, by the mid-nineteenth century, working wives and mothers were regarded especially by middle-class commentators as unnatural, immoral and inadequate homemakers and parents. These criticisms arose from contemporary assumptions about women's work and about the inherent nature of women themselves. It is clear that the upper- and middle-class critics of working-class women did not object to work as such. Most objections arose from the location of work and when women worked away from their own, or someone else's home what contemporaries regarded as their proper sphere. Many women saw paid work, not as an alternative to housework, but as letting them fulfil their duty as wives, mothers and homemakers. In

---

[167] See, Pedersen, J. S., 'Victorian liberal feminism and the 'idea' of work', in Cowman, Krista, and Jackson, Louise A., (eds.), *Women and work culture: Britain c. 1850- 1950*, (Ashgate), 2005, pp. 27-47.

[168] Hewitt, Margaret, *Wives and Mothers in Victorian Industry*, (Greenwood Press), 1958, is useful for information. Ibid., Bythell, D., *The Sweated Trades: Outwork in Nineteenth Century Britain*, is the standard work while Pennington, Shelley, and Westover, Belinda, *A Hidden Workforce: Homeworkers in England 1850-1985*, (Macmillan), 1989, examines a specific area.

[169] Useful studies of working women writing and speaking for themselves include: Burnett, John, (ed.), *Useful Toil: Autobiographies of Work People from the 1820s to the 1920s*, (Routledge), 1994, Chew, Doris Nield, *Ada Nield Chew: The Life and Writings of a Working Woman*, (Virago), 1982, Black, Clementina, *Married Women's Work Being the Report of an Enquiry undertaken by the Women's Industrial Council*, (G. Bell and Sons, Ltd.), 1915, especially for rural work and charwomen and Reeves, Maud Pember, *Round About a Pound a Week*, (G. Bell and Sons, Ltd.), 1913, (Virago), 1979, a survey of families living on an income of 18-26 shillings a week in Lambeth, south London carried out by the Fabian Society's Women's Group.

general, however, working-class women did not regard full-time paid work as something they would undertake all their adult lives. Married women who were compelled to work for financial reasons rarely continued working when the crisis had over. It was poverty that drove many working-class women into wage-earning work and it was widespread poverty that helps to explain men's defensive attitude against women's work. Hunt wrote of the period 1850-1914:

> Men believed that a limited amount of work was available and suspected that allowing women to share work would cause some families to be without pay as a consequence of other families taking more than their fair share.[170]

This confusion between private and public spheres can be seen in a variety of ways such as women taking in lodgers or selling food from their back kitchens or acting as a domestic servant. For instance, in Dunstable in the 1841 Census, there were 332 lodgers out of a total population of 2,582 people. All were female and most worked in the seasonal straw plaiting or hatting industry providing important income for householders. For working-class women, there could be no clear distinction between the public and private spheres, whatever they would have ideally liked.

Women's work

The notions of 'a woman's job' and 'a woman's rate' were regarded by employers, trade unions and by women workers themselves as a 'natural' experience until the mid-twentieth century. Its consequence was low pay and a sexual division of labour leading to segregation. Patterns of sexual segregation were by no means fixed throughout the country. Brick-making was a woman's trade in the Black Country where men worked in ironworks and coalpits. In Lancashire where women worked in cotton and where openings for men were scarce, it was a male preserve. It was, however, rare not to see a clear dividing line between women and men's jobs within occupations and between women and men's processes with women working in lower grade occupations for lower wages.[171]

Women's work commanded a woman's rate, even when they were involved in the same processes as men. What is difficult to explain is the persistence of low paid, sexually segregated and poorly organised work as the norm for women. The historiography of attempts to resolve this issue began

---

[170] Hunt, E. H., *British Labour History 1815-1914*, (Weidenfeld), 1981, p. 24.

[171] Bradley, Harriet, *Men's Work, Women's Work*, (Polity), 1989, is a useful survey and critique of the sexual division of labour and contains case studies of a variety of occupations. Chinn, Carl, *They Worked all their Lives: Women of the Urban Poor in England 1880-1939*, (Manchester University Press), 1988, and Snell, K. D. M., *Annals of the Labouring Poor*, (Cambridge University Press), 1985, provide an urban and rural perspective. See also, Malcolmson, Patricia, *English Laundresses: A Social History*, (Illinois University Press), 1978.

with a natural view of a sexual division of labour in which sex discrimination was an accepted part of life.[172] Early commentators on the problem, such as Sidney Webb, concluded women's inferior earnings were due to natural causes: women's productive power was usually inferior to men's both in quantity and quality.[173] This was linked to the notion that low pay was individual female choice because of their commitment to marriage, childbearing and childcare. Women were not prepared to invest in training programmes or apprenticeships, sought work close to their home, had interrupted career patterns and were prone to absenteeism. This model treated the possibility of sex discrimination as a residual factor and ignored the systemic processes that trapped women as a group rather than as individuals within certain grades and kinds of work. Modern economic and social theorists reject the notion of a sexual division of labour as natural and a matter of choice.[174] They argue for a dual labour market in which primary workers were assured a stable career with rising wages while secondary workers were often unskilled or possessed highly transferable skills, and who came to be seen as unstable workers. A large proportion of the latter were women.

By 1900, in manufacturing occupations, women generally earned about half the average weekly wages of men. Only in textiles did women earn significantly above half of male earnings. New methods of wage payment introduced in the late-nineteenth and early-twentieth centuries reinforced the idea of a woman's rate. Women were more often paid by piece rate than men and had their rates lowered to prevent them earning 'too much'. Non-manual workers generally earned a higher percentage of the average male earnings: women shop assistants earned about 65 per cent and women teachers 75 per cent of their male colleagues. In all-female occupations, women often did worst of all. Nurses were often paid little more than domestic servants.[175] Indeed their pay was actually lowered to encourage middle-class applicants who did not need the money. Middle-class parents were condemned by feminists for allowing their daughters to work for pocket money because it was considered more respectable and genteel. Theirs was voluntary rather than real work.

---

[172] Pujol, Michèle A., *Feminism and Anti-Feminism in Early Economic Thought*, (Edward Elgar Publishing Ltd.), 1992, pp. 51-74, examines the approach of economists and feminists to the question of equal pay from 1890 to 1914.

[173] Webb, Sidney, 'Differences in wages paid to men and women', *Women's Trade Union Review*, No. 3, October 1891, pp. 2-7, and more extensively in 'The Alleged Differences in the Wages Paid to Men and to Women for Similar Work', *Economic Journal*, Vol. 1, (4), (1891), pp. 635-662, and Fawcett, Millicent Garrett, 'Mr Sidney Webb's Article on Women's Wages', *Economic Journal*, Vol. 2, (5), (1892), pp. 173-176.

[174] Jacobsen, Joyce P., *The Economics of Gender*, (Wiley-Blackwell), 2007, pp. 187-247, provides a modern analysis of women's wage levels.

[175] Sweet, Helen M., 'Establishing Connections, Restoring Relationships: Exploring the Historiography of Nursing in Britain', *Gender & History*, Vol. 19, (2007), pp. 565-580.

Both employers and male trade unionists denied women access to the means of acquiring real skills through apprenticeships. After 1850, although trade unions were established among skilled and better paid workers, women were excluded. The aim of trade unionism, according to Henry Broadhurst (1840-1911), secretary of the TUC, speaking in 1875, was:

> ...to bring about a condition...where wives and daughters would be in their proper sphere at home, instead of being dragged into competition for livelihood against the great and strong men of the world.[176]

Not only was unequal pay accepted as a norm, but women's work was tolerated only where it did not compete with men's work. This pattern of male dominance and control at work was linked to power dynamics within the family. When the workplace was separated from the home, male dominance over pre-industrial work and the practice of sexually segregating tasks was carried over into the factory. The frontier between men's and women's work was defended in the face of technological change--which threatened to blur the distinction between sexual boundaries--through union exclusiveness and the control skilled men managed to exert over apprenticeship and via their power to subcontract work. The conclusions reached as to what was suitable work for women differed from area to area and between social classes but male workers, employers, government and women workers themselves largely shared it.

Women worked full-time or part-time either outside the home in a workshop or factory or on the land or worked in their own homes or in other people's. However, a very large numbers of women worked full-time in the home for no wages at all. A contrast was made between 'real' work and work in the home which, since it has never been paid, was somehow assumed not to be 'real' work at all and consequently had become devalued in the eyes of many men and women. They had been, for instance, spinners, dressmakers, straw-plaiters and lace-makers and had combined this with housekeeping and child rearing. These activities did not arouse the controversy that accompanied the public appearance of wage-earning working women because of industrialisation, in Lancashire, West Yorkshire and the Potteries. Working wives, mothers and unmarried women were often criticised as unnatural, unfeminine, immoral and inadequate homemakers and parents. They were also attacked by male workers who feared loss of work but who wrote petitions full of apparent concern for women and their children. Men also believed that a finite amount of work was available and that letting women work would cause some families not having sufficient income as a result of other families taking more than their fair share.

Was Pinchbeck right?

---

[176] TUC, *Congress Report*, 1875, p.14.

To what extent were changes in the nature of work, especially the development of the factory system, significant in allowing women into the labour market as independent wage earners?[177] Favourably reviewed when published in 1930, it was not until the 1980s that Pinchbeck's *Women Workers in the Industrial Revolution* earned its status as a 'classic text'. Rendall claims that 'Pinchbeck's work is still of great importance, and remains a 'major survey of the impact of industrialisation on women workers in Britain.'[178] Many works on women's history start from Pinchbeck. Bythell, for instance, contrasts her optimistic view of women's opportunities to Alice Clark's (1874-1934) view that capitalism had a negative effect on middle-class women who were confined to an idle domestic existence managing servants while lower-class women were forced to take poorly paid jobs and Eric Richards' equally pessimistic view.[179]

Pinchbeck (1898-1982) argued that economic changes between 1750 and 1850 transformed women's employment opportunities making them better off. Women initially suffered from fewer employment opportunities but after 1800, there was an increase in the availability of work outside the home, improving women's status and conditions and acting as a vital element in the development of the notion of the 'family wage'. Pinchbeck saw the opportunity to specialise in housework as a privilege and the withdrawal of some married women from the labour force as an improvement. Noting that many women lost their economic independence, she considered the gains to be sufficient to make up for this loss. Noting the departure of farmers' wives from productive employment, she claimed:

---

[177] The classic works are Pinchbeck, Ivy, *Women Workers in the Industrial Revolution*, (Routledge), 1930, reprinted (Virago), 1985, Clark, Alice, *Working Life of Women in the Seventeenth Century*, (G. Routledge & Sons), 1919, and Drake, Barbara, *Women in Trade Unions*, (G. Allen & Unwin), 1920. For working women, see Steinbach, *Women in England, 1760-1914: A Social History*, (Orion), 2004, Honeyman, Katrina, *Women, Gender and Industrialization in England, 1700-1870*, (Macmillan), 2000, Sharpe, Pamela, *Adapting to Capitalism: Working Women in the English Economy, 1700-1850*, (Palgrave), 2000, Roberts, E., *Women's Work 1840-1940*, (Macmillan), 1987, Richards, E., 'Women in the British Economy since 1700', *History*, Vol. 59, (1974), pp. 337-357, and Rose, S., *Limited Livelihoods: Class and Gender in Nineteenth Century England*, (Routledge), 1992. Burnette, Joyce, *Gender, Work and Wages in Industrial Revolution Britain*, (Cambridge University Press), 2008, is an important revisionist study. John, A. V., (ed.), *Unequal Opportunities: Women's Employment in England 1800-1950*, (Basil Blackwell), 1986, is a useful collection of papers.
[178] Rendall, Jane, *Women in an Industrializing Society: England 1750-1880*, (Blackwell), 1991, p. 7.
[179] Bythell, Duncan, 'Women in the Work Force', in O'Brien, Patrick, and Quinault, Roland, (eds.), *The Industrial Revolution and British Society*, (Cambridge University Press), 1993, pp. 31-54.

In the change she sacrificed her former economic independence according to the extent to which she ceased to manage her household and contributed to the wealth of her family, but for her, the new conditions meant an advance in the social scale and did not entail any material hardship.[180]

For Pinchbeck, the move toward a 'family wage' let men support their families allowing wives to leave the labour force and this was a clear advance.

Women who remained in the labour force were better off by 1850. Pinchbeck noted that, while contemporaries thought factory conditions were poor, conditions were actually better than those in alternative employments in domestic industry. Women entering factories did not leave behind ideal conditions but domestic industries with low pay and poor working conditions. These new opportunities for waged labour in factories and workshops saw women paid wages as individuals rather than to the household head challenging the dominant patriarchy. They also offered women a degree of economic autonomy or suggested that power relations within the home might be re-negotiated. Pinchbeck concluded:

...the Industrial Revolution has on the whole proved beneficial to women. It has resulted in greater leisure for women in the home and has relieved them from the drudgery and monotony that characterised much of the hand labour previously performed in connection with industrial work under the domestic system. For the woman workers outside the home, it has resulted in better conditions, a greater variety of openings and an improved status.[181]

Pinchbeck relied on non-quantitative sources to describe patterns and trends in women's work and subsequent historians using statistical analysis generally agree with her descriptions. Horrell and Humphries argue that during the first half of the nineteenth century, there was a downward trend in female participation leading them to conclude that 'Sixty-five years on we find that our evidence largely supports Pinchbeck's views.'[182] Snell concludes that farmers hired fewer workers as annual servants in the early-nineteenth century, supporting Pinchbeck's assertion that 'the custom of employing annual servants who lived in the farm declined in favour of day labourers who were responsible for their own board and lodging'.[183] He also confirmed Pinchbeck's observation that women were apprenticed to a wide variety of trades.[184] Investigating the

---

[180] Ibid., Pinchbeck, Ivy, *Women Workers in the Industrial Revolution*, p. 42.

[181] Ibid., Pinchbeck, Ivy, *Women Workers in the Industrial Revolution*, p. 4.

[182] Horrell, Sara, and Humphries, Jane, 'Women's Labour Force Participation and the Transition to the Male-breadwinner Family, 1790-1865', *Economic History Review*, Vol. 48 (1995), pp. 89-117, at p. 113.

[183] Ibid., Pinchbeck, Ivy, *Women Workers in the Industrial Revolution*, p. 37.

[184] Ibid., Snell, K., *Annals of the Labouring Poor: Social Change and Agrarian England 1660-1900*, pp. 270-319.

employment of day-labourers, Burnette found that the patterns of agricultural female employment at a farm near Sheffield coincided with what Pinchbeck described: decline between 1815 and 1834 followed by increasing female employment.[185]

Traditionally, manufacturing skill had been largely associated with men and this had created a sense of male solidarity that extended beyond the workplace into community and home. Steam and later electrical power reduced the need for physical strength that had been used to justify male hegemony in certain trades. Despite this, male exclusiveness explains why changes in social attitudes to women's employment had remained largely unaltered by 1850. Men struggled to maintain their skilled place in the workforce against machinery and the encroachment of unskilled women was an important part of their efforts to maintain their social status within the community and their families. This patriarchal ideology was used to justify keeping women away from the new technology. These contemporary criticisms of working women were based on an ideological consideration of a proper women's sphere, not on their working conditions. With the exception of skilled artisans, whose status generally ensured an income sufficient to support a wife and family, most women in the working-classes worked not merely to 'top up' the family budget but to ensure basic levels of family subsistence.

The relationship between gender and technology was very complex. Where new technologies were introduced, they reinforced the gendered division of labour because new machinery was worked by men, whose labour was deemed to be skilled, and the existing machinery was worked by women, whose labour was regarded as unskilled. However, manufacturers were reluctant to invest in costly new technologies in areas where there was a cheap female labour force. New technology resulted in de-skilling in the long term for men as well as women. The disappearance of guilds encouraged increased use of women's labour but industrialisation did not transform existing sexual divisions of labour. Women's work was focused on a few trades typified by their links to housework. The challenge to the patriarchal nature of production produced by early industrialisation was short lived because progressively more men were forced by economic necessity into waged labour and the gendered nature of production in the family economy was refreshed by new technologies and new locations for workplaces.

Pinchbeck has not been without her critics. Rendall argues that her view that the Industrial Revolution made women better off was 'unduly optimistic' and other historians saw this period as one when women lost rather than gained.[186] The notion that the Industrial Revolution increased the participation of women

---

[185] Burnette, Joyce, 'Labourers at the Oakes: Changes in the Demand for Female Day-Labourers at a Farm near Sheffield during the Agricultural Revolution', *Journal of Economic History*, Vol. 59, (1999), pp. 41-67.

[186] Ibid., Rendall, Jane, *Women in an Industrializing Society: England 1750-1880*, p. 7.

in general outside the home is difficult to sustain. Davidoff and Hall noted that 'the loss of opportunities to earn increased the dominance of marriage as the only survival route for middle-class women.'[187] Levels of female activity varied according to area and occupation. In the north-eastern coalfields, women ceased to work underground in the eighteenth century and none in Staffordshire, Shropshire, Leicestershire and Derbyshire for some time before it was banned in the Mines Act of 1842.[188] The wives and daughters of migrant Scottish farmers astonished farmers in East Anglia in the 1880s by doing work that had been done exclusively by men for almost a century. But few women had sufficient income to make themselves independent of either their parents or husbands. Contemporaries may have been impressed by the 'freedom' of the lasses of the mill towns who secured a reputation for flashy dressing and an undeserved one for sexual promiscuity but they were atypical. In 1851, domestic service accounted for 37.3 per cent of female occupations aged 15 or over, textiles 18.5 per cent, dressmaking 18 per cent and farming 7.7 per cent. Most were in the home where constraints on emancipation were very real and where women's wages were at a level that was assumed to be supplementary.[189]

Identifying participation

The 1851 Census suggests that just over a quarter of the female population–some 2.8 million out of 10.6 million--were at work and that women made up 30.2 per cent of the country's labour force.[190] These figures imply that female participation in the labour force was low but they are misleading.[191] More women were actually employed than are listed in the census, possibly by as much as a third. Domestic service, the textile trade and the clothing trades accounted for 80 per cent of all women in recorded occupations in 1851. By

[187] Davidoff, Leonore and Hall, Catherine, *Family fortunes: men and women of the English middle class 1780-1850*, (Hutchinson), 1987, p. 273.
[188] John, A. V., *By the Sweat of their Brow: Woman Workers at Victorian Coalmines*, (Croom Helm), 1980, pp. 19-35.
[189] Mark-Lawson, Jane, and Witz, Anne, 'From 'family labour' to 'family wages'? The case of women's labour in nineteenth-century coalmining', *Social History*, Vol. 13, (1988), pp. 151-174, and Horrell, Sara, and Humphries, Jane, 'The Origins and Expansion of the Male Breadwinner Family: The Case of Nineteenth-Century Britain', in Janssens, Angélique, (ed.), *The Rise and Decline of the Male Breadwinner Family?* (Cambridge University Press), 1998, pp. 25-64.
[190] Mitchell, B. R., *Abstract of British Historical Statistics*, (Cambridge University Press), 1962, p. 60.
[191] Enumerators did not always clearly distinguish between the terms 'housekeeper' and 'housewife': see, Higgs, Edward, 'Domestic Service and Household Production', in John, Angela V., (ed.), *Unequal Opportunities: Women's Employment in England 1800-1950*, (Basil Blackwell), 1986, pp. 125-150, and John, Angela V., 'Women, Occupations and Work in the Nineteenth Century Censuses', *History Workshop*, Vol. 23, (1987), pp. 59-80.

contrast, the number of women in agriculture halved between 1851 and 1881 and there was a new and expanding category of professional occupations and subordinate offices. Other occupations employed few women, though at a regional level there were still significant numbers in the metal trades, in food and drink manufacture and also in printing and stationery work.

The proportion of the female labour force remained remarkably constant between the 1870s and the 1910s. There were very few activities where women made up three out of every ten workers involved and viewed nationally four activities accounted for almost ninety per cent of women's work.[192] In 1881, four main occupations accounted for 76 per cent of employed working-class women and this changed only slightly before 1914. Broken down by region and occupation, it is apparent that participation rates varied considerably over the country. The proportion was over a third in Bedfordshire and Buckinghamshire, Lancashire, Nottingham and Leicestershire but fell to less than one-fifth in Durham, Northumberland, Lincolnshire, Cambridgeshire, Monmouth and Kent. Such disparities were not simply reflections of a particular age-structure because women's participation in work varied greatly even for the 15-24 age-group whose members were mostly unmarried and therefore notionally available for work.

Pinchbeck argued that women's employment as day labourers on farms increased from the late-eighteenth century during the French wars, declined during the post-war depression, rose again after 1834 and then declined steadily after 1850. Verdon concluded that Pinchback's paradigm holds up well in some instances, for instance, in the west of England but not in others showing again the diversities of experiences in Britain.[193] Agriculture accounted for 12 per cent of women workers in the 1840s but had already ceased to be a major employer of women by 1881. There had been a decline in the first half of the century but this was regional in nature with, for instance, a decline in Norfolk but not in Yorkshire. After 1850, farm records indicate a decline in female workers. The fall in the number of women involved after 1861 reflects growing mechanisation but the census figures neglect the seasonal nature of much of the work and many of the women employed by farmers were not listed as employed in the censuses.[194] In nineteenth century England, women worked on farms at many different tasks and frequently did laborious, repetitive work in the fields. In the 1860s, this labour was defined as unfeminine by the middle-classes and women involved were frequently described as unsexed and immoral. Working-class radicals adopted this imagery to demand a male breadwinning wage when they fought

---

[192] Bailey, Timothy J., and Roy E., 'Women's work in census and survey, 1911-1931', *Economic History Review*, second series, Vol. 54, (2001), pp. 87-107

[193] Verdon, Nicola, *Rural women workers in nineteenth-century England: gender, work and wages*, (Boydell), 2002, is essential.

[194] Miller, C., 'The Hidden Workforce: Female Fieldworkers in Gloucestershire, 1870-1901', *Southern History*, Vol. 6, (1984), pp. 139-161.

their employers. However, the women also directly challenged their employers' authority and were frequently at odds with the development of that new male working-class respectability that stressed women's role as wives and mothers. Sayer looks at the resistances of the field women and the response to their action by the radical, mainstream and feminist press of the second half of the nineteenth century and highlights the complex relationship between class and gender.[195] Increasing numbers of young rural women went into domestic service, where they were better paid, £12-£15 per year rather than £10 as a fieldworker and were also given board and lodgings.

Domestic service was mainly an urban occupations and the most common occupation for working-class girls and women but was a largely 'hidden' occupation during the eighteenth and nineteenth centuries.[196] It was not subject to investigation by Royal Commissions or to protective regulations and was largely ignored by social reformers, trade unions and women's organisations. Between 1851 and 1871, there was an increase in the numbers employed from 9.8 to 12.8 per cent of the total female population in England and Wales. After 1871, there was a decline down to 11.1 per cent by 1911. In the 1860s a third of London's female workforce were domestic servants. It has been frequently stated that domestic servants were usually country girls who has few alternative forms of work and certainly many country girls did follow this route. The vast majority of domestic servants had a heavy workload but they did not all share the same social status. All servants were impacted by the social status of their employers and within a household there were considerable differences in power and influence between, for instance, the housekeeper and the kitchen maid and there were also male and female status hierarchies involved.[197] By 1900, there were increasing complaints about the shortage of servants from members of the middle- and upper-classes. It was not simply a matter of wages since the demand

---

[195] Sayer, Karen 'Field-faring women: the resistance of women who worked in the fields of nineteenth-century England ', *Women's History Review*, Vol. 2, (2), (1993), pp. 185-198.

[196] Manning, Anne, *Lives of Good Servants*, (G. Routledge & Company), 1857, provides some good contemporary case studies. Hill, Bridget, *Servants: English Domestics in the Eighteenth Century*, (Oxford University Press), 1996, pp. 22-43, 93-114, Steedman, Carolyn, *Labours Lost: Domestic Service and the Making of Modern England*, (Cambridge University Press), 2009, considers domestic service in late-eighteenth century England, McBride, Theresa, *The Domestic Revolution: The Modernization of Household Service in England and France 1820-1920,* (Croom Helm), 1976, is a valuable comparative work. Horn, Pamela, *The Rise and Fall of the Victorian Servant*, (Gill & Macmillan), 1975, is an important work on the subject. Higgs, Edward, *Domestic Servants and Households in Rochdale: 1851-1871*, (Garland Publishing Company), 1986, (Routledge), 2016 a valuable study of aspects of domestic service in the area of Rochdale.

[197] Higgs, E., 'Domestic Servants and Households in Victorian England', *Social History,* Vol. 8, (1983), pp. 203-210.

for servants saw them increase steadily during the second half of the nineteenth century. The wages still appeared to be low: average annual wages for 1907 were £19 10s for general servants and £26 8s for parlour maids. Despite this, an increasing number of women regarded the wages as insufficient compensation for the hard physical effort and lack of independence. There was also a growth in alternative employment. While town girls preferred to have different work to domestic service, for country girls it remained an easily available and acceptable occupation.

Textile workers increased in number throughout the period especially in the cotton industry in England.[198] This expansion was accompanied by the steady decline of the Scottish cotton industry as it became more concentrated in Lancashire. In the Lancashire industry women had more equality with men than in most other industries. The only major process from which they were excluded was mule-spinning. Women were also excluded from being tacklers or overlookers, the person in charge of a group of weavers. Women weavers were paid well compared with most other women workers. Oral evidence suggests that they earned more than unskilled men in other areas of employment and a good woman weaver could earn as much as her male counterpart. In most mills it was not the case and aggregated figures show that women weavers earned less than men.[199]

For women working in urban trades conditions declined after 1830 and the sweated trades expanded. The drive towards increasing mass production in urban trades forced male skilled craftsmen to defend their position as their livelihood was threatened. The outcome for most women workers in these trades could only be exclusion from skilled work and employment in subdivided or unskilled work at lower, often very low, wages. In the printing industry, women were effectively excluded by 1880. By contrast women bookbinders preserved their skill and status, though also their low wages relative to skilled men, until changes in the 1880s. By the 1850s, except in large cities like Manchester and Leeds, homework had disappeared from the North of England. In the Midlands and the South, however, the pattern was very different. For instance, many women in Birmingham made nails and chains in sheds attached to their homes; Northampton women made boots and shoes. One of the largest concentrations of homeworkers was in London where women worked in the various garment trades, a situation aided by the marketing of the sewing machine after 1851.

Home-based work was a major part of pre-industrial and industrial family economies and cottages trades such as straw-plaiting, glove-making, and fine embroidery persisted during the nineteenth century. Others trades such as

---

[198] Humphries, Jane, and Schneider, Benjamin, 'Spinning the Industrial Revolution', *Economic History Review*, Vol. 72, (1), (2019), pp. 126-155.
[199] Hannam, June B., *The Employment of Working-Class Women in Leeds, 1880-1914*, Ph. D., Thesis, University of Sheffield, 1984, pp. 46-90.

hosiery and shoemaking became factory-based in the 1870s and 1880s. Work could be done at all hours under any conditions. New home-based trades emerged using the pool of cheap female workers such as matchbox making, artificial flowers, umbrella making, tennis ball making, as well as all types of clothing. Regulation of women's work outside the home contained in factory legislation also led to an increase in industrial work inside the home. Most work used piece rates; it was subcontracted with no security of employment; wages were low and continued to fall during nineteenth century. Some home working was simple, repetitive work, often involving children while other work involved high levels of often unacknowledged skill.[200]

Poor working wages formed the strongest link between poverty and prostitution.[201] Petty theft was more profitable than petty manufacturing and in turn prostitution was more profitable than either. In the nineteenth century, many people used 'prostitute' to refer to women who were living with men outside marriage or women who had had illegitimate children, or women who perhaps had relations with men but for pleasure rather than money. At least half the 50,000 women estimated by a police magistrate in London in 1791 consisted of unmarried women living with a partner, while only 20,000 referred to what we would today call sex workers. For most working-class women, prostitution was casual and seasonal work depending on their financial situation and the demand that existed for their services.

In trying to assess the number of women working during this period, we run up against a number of confusing problems. The change of work-base from the home to the factory or workshop led to changing, though never fully clarified definitions of the meaning of 'work', 'employment' and 'occupation'. In effect, 'work' became shorthand for waged work. Yet formal employment was a minority theme in the social history of working-class women in this period. When the 1881 Census omitted unpaid household work as a category of gainful employment, there was a dramatic drop in the female work rate figure from around 98 per cent (and almost the same as the work rate for men) to 42 per cent. In reality, working-class women worked in large numbers and often for a considerable proportion of their lives in both paid and unpaid position. This, despite the howls of middle-class protest raised periodically in Parliament and the press against their involvement in the world of work with their consequent neglect of husband, family and home.

The First World War hastened the collapse of traditional women's work especially domestic service. Women's employment rates increased from 23.6

[200] See ibid., Bythell, Duncan *The Sweated Trades: Outworks in Nineteenth-Century Britain*, for a detailed discussion of this issue.
[201] Walkowitz, Judith, *Prostitution and Victorian Society: Women, Class and the State*, (Cambridge University Press), 1980, and MacHugh, Paul, *Prostitution and Victorian Social Reform*, (Croom Helm), 1980, deal specifically with the debate on the Contagious Diseases Acts. Fisher, Trevor, *Prostitution and the Victorians*, (Alan Sutton), 1997 is a useful collection of sources.

per cent of the working age population in 1914 to between 37.7 and 46.7 per cent in 1918.[202] Young women who once went into service preferred the freedom, better pay and conditions of the work they did during the war. They worked in assembly industries making labour-saving goods that middle-class women bought. However, many of the women employed in wartime industries were demobilised and forced back into domestic service. By 1921, government grants given to the Central Committee on Women's Training and Unemployment were tied exclusively to domestic service training.[203] In 1922, the new Insurance Act stipulated that applicants were to accept any job which they were capable of doing and had no right to work with pay and conditions comparable to their previous employment. Consequently, women were forced back into domestic service through legislation and economic expediency.

New opportunities

There was an important shift to white-blouse work after 1871. The numbers of women, many from the working-classes, engaged in such work as teaching, retail, office work and nursing increased by 161 per cent between 1881 and 1911 while those working in manufacturing industries and domestic service increased by only 24 per cent. Also the growth of the non-manual sector was far more rapid for women than for men and, to some extent, this opened up routes of social mobility for working-class girls. This did not involve a leap into middle-class status but it did provide increased element of respectability to employment. It is the division between manual and non-manual occupations that increasingly became the fundamental division in women's work rather than the, always tenuous, division between working- and middle-classes.

Clerical and office work offered increasing opportunities for non-manual work for middle- and upper-working-class women and in 1914 they accounted for about 20 per cent of clerical workers.[204] Between 1861 and 1911, the number of male clerks increased fivefold while the number of women clerks

---

[202] Ledgard, Gail, *The Invisible Workforce of the First World War: An Examination of Female Woollen Workers and Their Community in Huddersfield and the Colne Valley*, Ph. D., Thesis, University of Huddersfield, 2018.

[203] Lewis, J., *Women in England, 1870-1950: Sexual Divisions and Social Change*, (Wheatsheaf Books), 1984, pp.190-191.

[204] Bridger, Anne, *A Century of Women's Employment in Clerical Occupations: 1850-1950. With particular reference to the role of the Society for Promoting the Employment of Women*, Ph. D., Thesis, University of Gloucestershire, 2003, pp. 97-144, Jordan, Ellen, 'The Lady Clerks at the Prudential: The Beginnings of Vertical Segregation by Sex in Clerical Work in Nineteenth-Century Britain', *Gender & History*, Vol. 8, (1), (1996), pp. 65-81, Zimmeck, M., 'Jobs for the Girls: The Expansion of Clerical Work for Women 1850-1914', in ibid., John, A. (ed.), *Unequal Opportunities: Women's Employment in England 1800-1918*, pp. 152-177, Anderson, Gregory, (ed.), *The White-Blouse Revolution: Female Office Workers since 1870*, (Manchester University Press), 1988, pp. 1-47.

rose by 400 per cent. Women's clerical work was a deskilling of the high-status male confidential clerk of the late-eighteenth and nineteenth centuries. G. K Chesterton summed up attitudes when he wrote in mid-1910:

Ten thousand women marched through the streets of London saying, 'We will not be dictated to' and then went off to become stenographers.[205]

Expansion of large commercial firms and the growth of insurance, banking and communications all provided more jobs for women.[206] Typing and shorthand were presumed to be particularly suited to women. A similar rise can be found in shop-work where automatic dismissal often followed marriage giving employers constant access to younger and cheaper labour. It also upheld the notion of the separate spheres whereby the paid labour of a married woman was equated with a husband's failure in fulfilling his role in the conjugal bargain.

Although a 'consumer revolution' can be traced to the century before 1750 when there was a large and rapid increase in the consumption of goods such as tableware, curtains, pictures and cutlery, it was only after 1850 that clothing, personal and household possessions became important ways for both working- and middle-classes to show their status within their respective communities. Mass production of goods, improved transport facilities and more sophisticated sales techniques brought consumerism to the masses on a scale previously unimaginable. Changing fashions and designs stimulated demand and new forms of marketing and retailing made products cheaply and easily available to the consumer. This was evident in the growth of urban and village shops, the use of shop window displays, the development of urban department stores from the 1880s and the extension of advertising in newspaper and on billboard.[207] Until the 1850s women were largely invisible on the shop floor. Wives or housekeepers may have helped out behind the counter but working in shops remained a large male preserve. Society hostess and journalist Mary Lady Jeune (1845-1931) commented:

An afternoon's shopping was a solemn and dreary affair when one was received at the door by a solemn gentleman in black, who in due time delivered one over to another gentleman in black and perhaps again to a third, who found one a chair, and in sepulchral tone of voice uttered some magic words, such as, 'Silk, Mr Smith,' or 'Velvet, Mr A,' and then departed to seek another victim. [208]

---

[205] Cit., Ker, Ian, *G. K. Chesterton: A Biography*, (Oxford University Press), 2011, p. 270.

[206] Davies, M., *Woman's Place Is at the Typewriter: Office Work and Office Workers 1870-1930*, (Temple University Press), 1982.

[207] Adburgham, Alison, Shops *and Shopkeeping 1800-1914: Where and in what manner the well-dressed Englishwoman bought her clothes*, (George Allen and Unwin), 1964, and Cohen, Deborah, *Household Gods: The British and Their Possessions*, (Yale University Press), 2006, consider the consumer revolution in the nineteenth century.

During the second half of the nineteenth century, the workforce recruited into retailing expanded because of increasing demands for commodities such as clothing. There were 500,000 shop-girls by 1900. Some lived away from home in hostels, often provided by the stores. Hostels built specifically for low-waged single working women emerged from 1900 and by 1910 there were about 60 lodging houses for lower-middle and middle-class working women in London. The shortage of male workers, the spread of the department store and the activities of the Society for Promoting the Employment of Women (SPEW) turned women into the handmaidens of Victorian consumer culture.[209] Serving a predominantly middle-class clientele calling for attention to appearance and manners, it was occasionally championed as a suitable profession for genteel women. Shop girls and boys were recruited primarily from the working- and lower-middle-classes, fashionable consumers in their own right. They were encouraged by their employers to mimic the appearance and manners of their clientele as this was assumed to be good for business.[210]

The growth in shop work stimulated concern about working conditions leading to further legislation. amongst shop-workers, hours were notoriously long and remained so. One woman working at Selfridges in 1909 claimed she was 'the lowest form of animal life'. During busy periods employees were expected to be ready to receive customers in the store from 8am until 10pm, often not getting home until after midnight after restocking the shelves for the following day's trading. After fifty years of effort to curtail hours, a House of Lords Select Committee in 1901 could only confirm that many shops were working 80 or 90 hours a week. Pressure from the Shop-Assistants Twelve Hours' Labour League, founded in 1881, and from the Early Closing Association did result in some improvement but the shift towards a legislative solution was only very partially successful. The Shop Hours Regulation Act 1886 limited the hours of work of persons under eighteen years to seventy-four hours a week. The Shop Hours Act 1904 empowered local authorities to fix shop closing hours where two-thirds of the shops agreed. The 1911 Shops Act introduced a weekly half-day holiday for all staff and said that shops should have at least one early closing day. The Shops Act 1912 consolidated existing laws regulating employment in shops.

Women and unionism

---

[208] Jeune, Mary Lady, 'The Ethics of Shopping', *The Fortnightly Review*, Vol. 57, (January 1895), pp. 123-132, writing of the 1870s.

[209] Cox, Pamela and Hobley, Annabel, *Shopgirls: The True Story of Life Behind the Counter*, (Hutchinson), 2014.

[210] Hosgood, Christopher P., '"Mercantile Monasteries": Shops and Shop Assistants and Shop Life in Late-Victorian and Edwardian Britain', *Journal of British Studies*, Vol. 38, (3), (1999), pp. 322-352.

By 1900 it is possible to see the sexual division of labour clearly in operation. Women were clustered into a few low paid industries--where the great majority of employees were female--and in domestic service. Outworkers and domestic servants were isolated and divided workers and were to remain outside any co-operative protection or trade unionism. Feminist activity largely concentrated on the reality of the working woman's situation and on the needs that created it rather than on theoretical arguments in favour or against women's work of this kind. It was largely practical concern with the organisation of benefit societies and unions, with working conditions or wages, with the evils and miseries of outwork that motivated organisation within the working-classes. Interested middle-class women ran many of these organisations, though there was also significant working-class input.

Trade unions in this period were male-dominated and most had the interests of male trade unionists at heart.[211] They felt threatened by the way in which female labour was being used to undercut male wages and to 'dilute' male craft skills. Their reaction did not help women workers but does not explain the lowly place of women in the labour market. It is not surprising therefore that the male dominated, skilled unions in the decades after 1850 showed a studied indifference if not downright hostility to women workers.[212] Any attempts to organise women in this period came from outside the labour movement, often through the work of philanthropic women. The most notable example was the formation of the Women's Protective and Provident League (WPPL) by Emma Paterson (1848-1886)[213] the wife of a cabinet maker, in 1874 at a time when men's unions were enjoying some success, both in membership and in establishing their legality.[214] The WPPL was not a trade union but a

---

[211] Drake, B., *Women in Trade Unions*, (Labour Research Department), 1920, reprinted (Virago), 1984, is the classic starting-point on this subject. See also, Soldon, Norbert C., *Women in British Trade Unions 1874-1976*, (Gill & Macmillan), 1978, Gordon, Eleanor, *Women and the Labour Movement in Scotland 1850-1914*, (Oxford University Press), 1991, that focuses on the jute industry in Dundee and Lown, Judy, *With Free and Graceful Step? Women and industrialisation in nineteenth century England*, (Polity), 1987. See also, Taylor, Anne, *Annie Besant: A biography*, (Oxford University Press), 1992, and Pécastaing-Boissière, Muriel, *Annie Besant (1847-1933) La lute et la quête*, (Adyar), 2015, *Annie Besant (1847-1933) Struggles and Quest*, revised ed., (Theosophical Society in England), 2017, now the best study. Harrison, Barbara, *Not only the 'dangerous trades': women's work and health in Britain, 1880-1914*, (Taylor & Francis), 1996.

[212] Rose, Sonya O., 'Gender antagonism and class conflict: Exclusionary strategies of male trade unionists in nineteenth-century Britain', *Social History*, Vol. 13, (1988), pp. 191-208.

[213] Goldman, Harold, *Emma Paterson: she led woman into a man's world*, (Lawrence and Wishart), 1974.

[214] 'News of the Day', *Birmingham Daily Post*, 2 September 1874, p. 4, 'Trades Unions for Women', *Reynolds's Newspaper*, 6 September 1874, p. 3, 'Women's Trade Union', *London Standard*, 14 September 1874, p. 3.

means for pooling funds, expertise and experience. It offered sickness benefits and a host of related activities. It has been criticised for offering welfare instead of militancy and it was certainly far more of a propaganda and educational body. Its initial gains were no more than modest. Its overall membership fluctuated wildly, though in 1884 there were less than a thousand women in its unions. Even so, the League had succeeded, albeit temporarily, in organising London trades from boot and umbrella makers, tailoresses and laundresses to feather and flower workers and box makers. Its activities extended beyond London to other industrial centres like Dewsbury and Leicester.

Between 1874 and 1886, over thirty associations were formed using a model constitution devised by the League. Most of these societies were small, weak and short-lived and it is debatable whether they were 'trade unions' since their stated aim was to 'to promote an entente cordiale between the labourer, the employer and the consumer.' Strike action was condemned as 'rash and mistaken', and emphasis was placed on friendly society benefits. The only matter of real controversy was the League's opposition to protective legislation for women on the grounds that it restricted women's choice of employment and earning capacity. The lasting achievement of the League was to get the first women delegates to the TUC, among whom was Emma Paterson. However, the League's position on the question of equal pay was not very robust. As they put it in 1884:

> We have always declared against attempts to introduce women into trades at rates of wages far below those previously paid to men for similar work. We have therefore never joined in, or expressed approval of, the abuse heaped by certain middle-class papers and economists on workmen who have struck against unfair competition of this kind. [215]

In 1888 Clementina Black (1853-1922), a delegate from the Women's Trades Council, moved the first TUC equal pay resolution.

An exception was, however, made in the case of the Kidderminster Carpet Weavers strike of 1884 in which the male carpet weavers withdrew their labour in protest against the use of women who were taken on to weave velvet; a new product in the town. [216] The WPPL thought that in this case, and in contrast to their usual policy, the men should be condemned because the women were not doing similar work and were therefore not offering any competition. On Emma

---

[215] *Women's Union Journal*, Vol. 9, (98), March 1884.
[216] On the Kidderminster strike, 'The Strike at Kidderminster', *Birmingham Daily Post*, 27 February 1884, pp. 4, 8, 'The Kidderminster Trade Dispute', *Birmingham Daily Post*, 11 April 1884, p. 5, 'The Settlement of the Kidderminster Trade Dispute', *Birmingham Daily Post*, 12 April 1884, p. 5. See also, Palmer, Gladys L., *Union Tactics and Economic* Change, (University of Pennsylvania Press), 1932, pp. 138-145, Rose, Sonya O., *Limited Livelihoods: Gender and Class in Nineteenth Century England*, (University of California Press), 1993, pp. 113-120.

Paterson's death in 1886, control of the WPPL passed to Lady Emilie Dilke (1840-1906). Many of its former moderate policies were abandoned under her leadership and a more militant approach adopted. The name was changed to the Women's Trade Union and Provident League in 1889 and to the Women's Trade Union League two years later. It sought more secure funding with the introduction of a scheme of affiliation for unions with a female membership and also sought to broaden its appeal outside London and by 1891, had seventeen London unions and six provincial affiliates. During the brief period of 'new unionism' in the late 1880s and early 1890s when unskilled labour became politicised, the Women's Industrial Council (WIC) and a score of women's unions were established.[217] The late-nineteenth century saw significant industrial action by women as they campaigned for better wages and working conditions: for instance, Bryant and May's match girl strike of 1888[218] but also the Dewsbury textile workers in 1875,[219] the Aberdeen jute workers in 1884, Dundee jute workers in 1885 and Bristol confectionery workers.[220]

Despite the success of the match girl strike, a host of disincentives stood in the way of the successful unionisation of women. Male unions were barely acceptable and faced problems of recruitment and sustaining membership. The economic competition that women posed as a cheaper labour supply further resolved men not in unionising women but in deterring their role in the workplace. The 1890s saw both a growth of women's trade union membership and the creation of several new women's organisations. The Women's Trade Union Association (WTUA) was founded in 1889 by women dissatisfied with the stance of the Women's Trade Union League, amongst them Clementina Black, Amie Hicks (1839-1917), Clara James (1866-1954) and Florence

---

[217] Ibid., Drake, B., *Women in Trade Unions*, pp. 26-43, Mappen, E., *Helping women at Work: The Women's Industrial Council 1889-1914*, (Hutchinson), 1985.

[218] Bartrip. P. W. J., *The Home Office and the Dangerous Trades. Regulating Occupational Disease in Victorian and Edwardian Britain*, (Rodopi), 2002, pp. 171-232, looks at the occupational hazards of match-making, Beer, R., *Matchgirls' Strike 1888: the struggle against sweated labour in London's East End*, (National Museum of Labour History), 1988, Raw, Louise, *Striking a Light: The Truth About the Match Girls Strike and the Women Behind it*, (Hambledon Continuum), 2009, Beaver, Patrick, *The match makers*, (Melland), 1985, Satre, Lowell J., 'After the match girls' strike: Bryant and May in the 1890s', *Victorian Studies*, Vol. 26, (1982), pp. 7-31, Thornton, Danielle, 'Striking a Light: the Bryant and May matchwomen and their place in history', *Women's History Review*, Vol. 20, (2), (2011), pp. 341-342, and Raw, Louise, 'Striking a light: Bryant & May revisited', in Davis, Mary, (ed.), *Class and Gender in British Labour History: Renewing the Debate (or starting it?)*, (Merlin Press), 2011, pp. 150-170.

[219] Reynolds, Melanie, ''A man who won't back a woman is no man at all': the 1875 heavy woollen dispute and the narrative of women's trade unionism', *Labour History Review*, Vol. 71, (2), (2006), pp. 187-198

[220] Gordon, Eleanor, *Women and the Labour Movement in Scotland, 1850-1914*, (Oxford University Press), considers disputes in the jute industry.

Balgarnie (1856-1928). Its aims differed little from the parent body and it was to be a short-lived venture merging in 1897 with the Women's Industrial Council then three years old.[221] Unionism was strong in the textile and especially cotton industry where women often outnumbered male operatives. It is a reflection of this era of separate female unions that in 1870, 58,000 women were members of trade unions. In 1896, that has risen to 118,000, a figure representing some 7.8 per cent of all union members. By 1906 there were 167,000 female unionists and this had risen to nearly 358,000 in 1914.[222]

Attention shifted to the sweated trades, those trades often carried on in domestic workshops or in a house, where hours were notoriously long and wages low.[223] The appointment of a Select Committee of the House of Lords in 1888 reporting on the sweated trades and a Royal Commission in 1892 on labour conditions generally did little more than collect valuable information on both sweated and non-sweated trades. Factory legislation in 1891 and 1901 did not improve working conditions for women other than prohibiting employers from employing women for four weeks after childbirth. Sweated trades continued to arouse concern, particularly after a large influx of immigrant labour into clothing, cabinet-making and boot and shoe-making during the 1880s and 1890s in the 'sweatshops' of East London. The premises in which these trades were carried on were often decaying slum dwellings. Legislation in 1891 required lists of out-workers to be kept by factory occupiers or owners and in 1895 these lists were sent to the local Factory Inspectors twice yearly. In practice little changed: lists were partial and Local Authorities did not have the resources to follow them up. Following the appointment of a Select Committee to examine the problem of sweating in 1907 and its critical report in 1908, legislation was passed in 1909.[224] The Sweated Industries Act (sometimes called the Trades Board Act) required wage boards to establish and enforce minimum rates of pay for workers in four

---

[221] Ibid., Mappen, E., *Helping Women at Work: The Women's Industrial Council 1889-1914.*

[222] Ibid., Drake, B., *Women in Trade Unions*, table 1, p. 237. Hunt, Cathy, 'Sex versus Class in Two British Trade Unions in the Early Twentieth Century, *Journal of Women's History*, Vol. 24, (2012), pp. 86-110.

[223] Blackburn, Sheila C., '"The inspector can check a workroom is insanitary by means of his own eyes and nose': rethinking the sweatshop in Victorian and Edwardian Britain', in ibid., Davis, Mary (ed.), *Class and Gender in British Labour History*, pp. 76-95.

[224] Blackburn, Sheila C., 'Ideology and social policy: the origins of the Trade Boards Act', *Historical Journal*, Vol. 34, (1991), pp. 43-64, '"Princesses and Sweated-Wage Slaves Go Well Together": Images of British Sweated Workers, 1843–1914', *International Labor and Working-Class History*, Vol. 61, (2002), pp. 24-44 and *A fair day's wage for a fair day's work?: sweated labour and the origins of minimum wage legislation in Britain*, (Ashgate), 2007, and Melling, Joseph, 'Welfare capitalism and the origins of welfare states: British industry, workplace welfare and social reform, c.1870-1914', *Social History*, Vol. 17, (1992), pp. 453-478.

of the most exploited industries: chain-making, box-making, lace-making and the production of ready-made clothing. This legislation was gender neutral and covered homeworkers as well as factory hands but included only the lowest paying industries and less than a quarter of a million workers.

In May 1910, the Chain Trade Board announced a minimum wage for hand-hammered chain-workers of two and a half pence an hour, nearly double the existing rate for many women. At the end of the Trade Board's consultation period on 16 August 1910, many employers refused to pay the increase. In response, the National Federation of Women Workers called a strike of chain-makers at Cradley Heath.[225] It lasted 10 weeks and attracted immense popular support from all sections of society. Nearly £4,000 of donations were received by the end of the dispute from individual workers, trade unions, politicians, members of the aristocracy, business community and the clergy. Mary Macarthur (1880-1921), the founder of the National Federation of Women Workers and National Anti-Sweating League (NFWW) in 1906, used mass meetings and the media, including the new medium of cinema, to highlight the plight of the striking women to a wider audience.[226] Within a month, 60 per cent of employers had signed the 'White List' and agreed to pay the minimum rate, the dispute finally ended on 22 October when the last employer caved in.[227] Further inquiries into home-work by the Factory Department took place in 1925 and 1931, but by then many of the old 'sweated' trades had died away.

Conclusion

Certain attitudes about women's work especially low pay and the sexual division of labour were accepted by employers, trade unionists, experts on employment practices and by many women workers. Why or how this oppressive and exploitative state of affairs had come about was explained by its 'natural' basis, that it was 'historical' and that things had always been that way. 'Natural' explanations were justified by the innate differences between men and women and there is anecdotal evidence that women had definite ideas of what was their work and what was men's.

Women were committed, or assumed to be committed, to marriage, home life and a family and their employment was temporary and linked to their life cycle. It was assumed that most women were unwilling to undertake the training that might have given them access to better-paid, higher-status work. It was also argued that women's productive power was lower than men's in quality and

---

[225] 'Women on Strike', *Nottingham Evening Post*, 31 August 1910, p. 7.

[226] Hamilton, Mary A., *Mary Macarthur: A Biographical Sketch*, (Parsons), 1925, pp. 76-96, examines her contribution to the strike. See also, Hunt, Cathy, *The National Federation of Women Workers, 1906-1921*, (Palgrave Macmillan), 2014, pp. 23-63, considers the period between 1906 and 1914.

[227] Ibid., Blackburn, Sheila C., *A fair day's wage for a fair day's work?: sweated labour and the origins of minimum wage legislation in Britain*, pp. 121-142, examines the Cradley Heath dispute.

quantity. This economic reasoning was used to reinforce innate difference: men deserved better pay than women because men were better workers than women. An ideology of separate spheres and the principles of the free market oppressed working women by seeking to exclude them from the paid workforce. But women were not a homogenous mass with the same attributes and aspirations ignoring regional and occupational differences and the considerable diversity of women's experience of paid work.

Cultural experiences?

In 1780, popular culture was public, robust and gregarious, largely masculine and involved spectacle and gambling with an undercurrent of disorder and physical violence. The distinction between high and popular culture, between opera and drama on the one hand and spectacle, circus and showmanship on the other had broken down: Shakespeare, melodrama and performing animals not merely co-existed but intermingled. The late-eighteenth and first half of the nineteenth century saw two major changes in the cultural experience of English society.[228] There was erosion of the older popular culture because of the withdrawal of patronage by the governing elite and the gradual dismantling of the agrarian social and economic frameworks that gave it justification. By contrast, a more commercial culture developed, entrepreneurial, market-led and largely urban and bourgeois. This led to the modification of both the content and transmission of high culture and, in the nineteenth century, the promotion of popular cultural for profit. Cultural experiences, like economic and social ones, were adaptable.

Attacks on popular culture after 1780 were a response to pressures on existing forms of social control, of demographic and urban growth and the consequent erosion of paternalism and had been gathering pace since the sixteenth century. It had two linked thrusts: a religious belief that popular culture was profane, irreligious and immoral and a secular concern that it was

---

[228] Easton, S., Howkins, A., Laing, S., Merrick L., and Walker, H., *Disorder and Discipline: Popular Culture from 1550 to the Present*, (Temple Smith), 1988, and Borsay, Peter, *A History of Leisure: The British Experience since 1500*, (Palgrave), 2006, are good general surveys. Malcolmson, R.W., *Popular Recreation in English Society 1700-1850*, (Cambridge University Press), 1973, and Cunningham, H., *Leisure in the Industrial Revolution*, (Allen and Unwin), 1980, provide perspectives on the issue of custom and leisure. Bailey, P., *Leisure and Class in Victorian England: rational recreation and the contest for control 1830-1885,* (Routledge), 1978, takes the arguments forward into the late-nineteenth century. Holt, R., *Sport and the British: A Modern History*, (Oxford University Press), 1989, Tranter, N., *Sport, Economy and Society in Britain, 1750-1914*, (Cambridge University Press), 1998, and Kirk, Neville, *Change, Continuity and Class: Labour in British Society, 1850-1920*, (Manchester University Press), 1998, pp. 111-140, 212-230, Colls, Robert, *This Sporting Life: Sport and Liberty in England, 1760-1960*, (Oxford University Press), 2020, are the best introduction to this area of leisure.

detrimental to economic efficiency and public order. Evangelical campaigners succeeded in getting agreement across the governing elite to its central moral tenets through groups such as the Society for the Reformation of Manners and the Society for the Suppression of Vice.[229] Methodism had greater impact on the working population and on artisans and small shopkeepers through its incessant attacks on the worldliness and sensuality of popular culture. Its views were prevalent with mercantile, commercial and professional groups, who looked with distaste at the irrational and sinful nature of much popular culture and were appalled by gratuitous cruelty to animals this involved. This was also evident amongst secular radicals as it offended their emphasis on reason and stress on moral and intellectual self-improvement; books, education and debating rather than bear baiting, races and circuses. The desire to turn people into sober, virtuous and godly citizens motivated by an interest in work and social discipline is generally held to have been resolved by the cultural shift to recreation and sport, 'justifying God to the people' through the 'soft-hearted benevolence' of cricket, cycling and football. Sport was the perfect vehicle for a humanistic, 'unmystical' morality that defines the secularity of the twentieth century.[230]

Leisure to 1850

The staging of contests between animals was still one of the most common and popular forms of recreation in England in the early-nineteenth century.[231] Cock fighting was normal at fairs and race meetings involving the mingling of all social groups, though only men, and accompanied by heavy betting and often local and regional rivalries.[232] Hunting and hawking were widespread. Small children were notorious for amusing themselves in torturing living creatures but they were merely reflecting the standards of the adult world. This was largely what Keith Thomas calls 'the cruelty of indifference' as animals were outside the terms of their moral reference.[233] During the eighteenth century the feelings of animals became a matter of very great concern and led to agitation in the early-nineteenth century culminating in the formation in 1824 of the Society (later

---

[229] Harrison, Brian, 'Religion and recreation in nineteenth-century England', *Past & Present*, Vol. 38, (1967), pp. 98-125.

[230] On this issue see, Erdozain, Dominic, *The Problem of Pleasure: Sport, Recreation and the Crisis of Victorian Religion*, (Boydell Press), 2010.

[231] Ritvo, H., *The Animal Estate: the English and other creatures in the Victorian Age*, (Penguin), 1990, and Harrison, B., 'Animals and the State in Nineteenth Century England', *English Historical Review*, Vol. 88 (1973), pp. 786-820, reprinted in his *Peaceable Kingdoms: Stability and Change in Modern Britain*, (Oxford University Press), 1982, on cruelty to animals.

[232] Jobey, George, 'Cock-fighting in Northumberland and Durham during the eighteenth and nineteenth centuries', *Archaeologia Aeliana*, 5th series, Vol. 20, (1992), pp. 1-25, is a good local study.

[233] Thomas, Keith, *Man and the natural world: changing attitudes in England 1500-1800*, (Allen Lane), 1983, p. 148.

Royal Society) for the Prevention of Cruelty to Animals and the passage of legislation against cruelty to horses and cattle in 1822, to dogs in 1839 and 1854 and against animal baiting and cock-fighting in 1835 and 1849. There are various reasons why this changed occurred. There had long been a tradition that unnecessary cruelty to animals was wrong not because of any moral concern with animals but because of its brutalising effects on human character.[234] It did not go unnoticed that the poisoner William Palmer--hanged in 1856--had conducted cruel experiments on animals as a boy.

British theatre and opera was produced not only for the cultivated and informed but for mass audiences for whom melodrama, lavish stage sets and live animals were essential and whom managers and actors bored at their peril.[235] Growing audiences funded the extensive rebuilding of Covent Garden, Drury Lane and Sadler's Wells as well as theatres outside the West End and entrepreneurs gave melodrama a legitimate place on the stage as well as developing the modern pantomime, an example followed by provincial theatres.[236] Developments in sport showed the same commercialism and capacity to survive in the face of the hostility of authority.[237] Shooting and hunting were the only sports to remain exclusively elitist. Until 1831, shooting was legally restricted to owners of land worth more than £100 and the Games Laws ensured that poaching was severely punished.[238] While shooting showed a horizontal cleavage in rural society, foxhunting had a far greater community interest. Although dominated by the landed aristocracy and country gentlemen, it was open to urban gentry and professionals and the poorer sections of the community followed the spectacle on foot. Some hunts were the property of single great landowners but were expensive to maintain and subscription hunts became more common: there were 69 packs of hounds in Britain in 1812, 91 by 1825.[239]

Horse racing was the sport of both the rich and poor. It could not maintain its exclusiveness though different prices charged for the stands, the paddocks and the ordinary enclosures were as much an expression of social

[234] Li, C. H., 'A union of Christianity, humanity, and philanthropy: the Christian tradition and the prevention of cruelty to animals in nineteenth-century England', *Society & Animals*, Vol. 8, (2000), pp. 265-285.
[235] Jackson, Lee, *Palaces of Pleasure. From Music Hall to the Seaside to Football, How the Victorians Invented Mass Entertainment*, (Yales University Press), 2019.
[236] Borsay, Peter, *The English Urban Renaissance: Culture and Society in the Provincial Town 1660-1770*, (Oxford University Press), 1991, pp. 117-149.
[237] Ibid., Borsay, Peter, *The English Urban Renaissance: Culture and Society in the Provincial Town 1660-1770*, pp. 173-196.
[238] Munsche, P. B., *Gentlemen and poachers: the English game laws 1671-1831*, (Cambridge University Press), 1981.
[239] On this issue see Carr, Raymond, *English Fox Hunting: A History*, (Weidenfeld), 1976, Griffin, Emma, *Blood Sport: Hunting in Britain since 1066*, (Yale University Press), 2007, pp. 124-162, and Itzkowitz, David C., *Peculiar privilege: a social history of English foxhunting, 1753-1885*, (Harvester Press), 1977.

hierarchy as different classes of railway travel. Horse racing combined two obsessions: the love of horses and gambling. Professional bookmakers appeared around 1800; by 1815, the 'classic' races, the Derby, the Oaks, the One Thousand and Two Thousand Guineas, the St. Leger and the Ascot Gold Cup, were all established and by 1837, there were 150 places in Britain where race meetings were held. [240] By 1850, off-course betting had been established, further broadening participation.[241] Pugilism or prize fighting began as a sport of the labouring population but attracted aristocratic patronage by 1800. Like horse racing, it was increasingly commercialised and its champions such as Tom Spring,[242] Tom Crib and Dutch Sam were full-time professionals. Both flourished as industries with their own specialist newspapers yet they were also evocative of an older, perhaps imaginary, culture where sporting squires and labourers rubbed shoulders in a common appreciation of animals and physical prowess. Upper-class support for prize fighting waned after 1830 but it retained its popularity among the working population and its real decline did not occur until after 1860.[243] Other sports like cricket, rowing and pedestrianism proved similar to horse-racing and prize fighting becoming more organised and professional, more dependent on attracting spectators and accompanied by extensive gambling.[244] Cricket originated as an activity of the labouring population in southern England and was then take up by the aristocratic elite and especially by the middle-classes spreading across the British Empire from Australia to the Caribbean, New Zealand to South Africa, India and Pakistan.[245] Pedestrianism and rowing also began as popular sports before becoming more exclusive later in the nineteenth century.[246]

---

[240] Church, Michael, *The Derby Stakes: the complete history 1780-2006*, (Raceform Ltd), 2006, Seth-Smith, Michael, and Mortimer, Roger, *Derby 200: the official story of the blue riband of the turf*, (Guinness Superlatives), 1979, and Huggins, Mike *Flat racing and British society, 1790-1914: a social and economic history*, (Cass), 2000.

[241] See, Clapson, Mark, *A bit of a flutter: popular gambling in England, c.1820-1961*, (Manchester University Press), 1992.

[242] Hurley, Jon, *Tom Spring: bare-knuckle Champion of All England*, (Stadia), 2007.

[243] See, Anderson, Jack, 'The Legal Response to Prize Fighting in Nineteenth Century England and America', *Northern Ireland Legal Quarterly*, Vol. 57, (2006), pp. 265-287, and Sheard, K. G., '"Brutal and degrading": the medical profession and boxing, 1838-1984', *International Journal of the History of Sport*, Vol. 15, (3), (1998), pp. 74-102.

[244] Wigglesworth, Neil, *A Social History of English Rowing*, (Routledge), 1992, pp. 1-91, and Halladay, Eric, *Rowing in England: a social history: the amateur debate*, (Manchester University Press), 1990.

[245] See Underdown, David, 'The History of Cricket', *History Compass*, Vol. 4, (1), (2006), pp. 43-53, Birley, Derek, *A Social History of English Cricket*, (Aurum Press), 1999, and Stone, Duncan, *Different Class: The Untold Story of British Cricket*, (Repeater), 2022.

[246] Lile, Emma, 'Professional Pedestrianism in South Wales during the Nineteenth Century', *The Sports Historian*, Vol. 20, (2000), pp. 94-105, Swain, Peter, 'Pedestrianism, the Public House and Gambling in Nineteenth-century South-east

Many traditional customs continued until after 1850. There is evidence for unchanged New Year mumming festivals in northern England until the 1870s. Guy Fawkes' Night was still celebrated despite attempts by various authorities to suppress bonfires and the burning of effigies.[247] Changes to traditional customs were not easily enforced even in areas, like Lancashire, where factory discipline was most firmly established. The Lancashire Wakes Weeks, traditionally the most important event of the recreational year, were forced on millowners rather than freely given.[248] It was not simply employers who attacked wakes and fairs. Moral reformers, the magistracy and the police recognised that these acted as a focus for criminal activity, could potentially lead to violence and threatened public order. That they continued until the late-nineteenth century was due not to lack of opposition but to disagreement about what action to take.

By 1850, a clear distinction was evident between much popular recreation and rational liberalism and evangelicalism with their argument for a self-conscious and moralistic cultivation of respectability. From the formation of the Proclamation Society in 1787, the campaign for reform gathered momentum. By the 1830s, other societies were established, for instance, the Lord's Day Observance Society founded in 1831 and the British and Foreign Temperance Society. Parliamentary reform in 1832 gave such societies slightly more influence over Parliament and as the police force grew after 1830 they gained the means to enforce legislation. Betting was an early and obvious target for reform but lotteries were not made illegal until 1823 and 1825 and further measures to discourage gambling had to wait until the 1840s and 1850s.[249] Reform was not achieved easily, quickly or completely. Neither was it the prerogative, nor was it dictated by the interests, of any one social group. It traversed class boundaries, dividing all groups, especially among the working-classes.[250]

Drinking

In the early-nineteenth century ale, wine and spirits were cheap and consumed in large quantities.[251] With dangers of disease from untreated water town-

---

Lancashire', *Sport in History*, Vol. 32, (3), (2012), pp. 382-404.

[247] Sharpe, J. A., *Remember, remember the fifth of November: Guy Fawkes and the gunpowder plot*, (Profile), 2005, looks at remembrance.

[248] Poole, Robert, 'Lancashire wakes week', *History Today*, Vol. 34, (8), (1984), pp. 22-29.

[249] Munting, R., 'Social opposition to gambling in Britain: an historical overview', *International Journal of the History of Sport*, Vol. 10, (1993), pp. 295-312, Raven, James, 'The abolition of the English state lotteries', *Historical Journal*, Vol. 34, (1991), 371-389, and Woodhall, Robert, 'The British state lotteries', *History Today*, Vol. 14, (7), (1964), pp. 497-504.

[250] Itzkowitz, David C., 'Victorian bookmakers and their customers', *Victorian Studies*, Vol. 32, (1988), pp. 7-30.

[251] Burnett, John, *Liquid pleasures: a social history of drinks in modern Britain*, (Routledge), 1999, provides an excellent overview.

dwellers relied on alcohol and on water that had been boiled with tea and coffee. As Chadwick's inspectors found from London slum-dwellers in the 1840s people did not believe that local water would ever be safe to drink. There were alternatives to alcohol: milk, though this was considered a dangerous drink even when fresh; soda-water was not made commercially until 1790 and ginger-beer was not sold in London until 1822. Tea[252] had become a necessity for the working-classes by 1780 and per capita coffee consumption increased faster than tea between 1820 and 1850.[253] Alcohol was more than just a thirst-quencher; it was thought to impart physical stamina, extra energy and confidence. Agricultural labourers, for instance, believed that it was impossible to get in the harvest without their 'harvest beer'. Alcohol was a painkiller: it helped dentists and surgeons before anaesthetics, quietened babies and gave protection against infection. It also relieved psychological strain, curbing the sense of social isolation and enhanced festivity.

Drinking places provided a focus for the community.[254] Before 1780, drinking was not rigidly segregated by rank. Squires, for instance, often drank with their social inferiors. However, by 1830 some social segregation had developed and by 1860 no 'respectable' urban Englishman entered an ordinary public house.[255] Private, as opposed to public, drinking was now the mark of respectability. Drinking was a predominantly male preserve and encouraged men to enjoy better living standards than their wives. On paydays, drinking houses were often besieged by wives anxious to get money to feed and clothe their children before it was drunk away. The drinks trade comprised a large complex of different interests.[256] Of particular importance was the powerful landed interest that helps to explain the regional variations in support for the temperance movement. The barley crop was important to farmers and without the distillers' demands for grain, land in Scotland and Ireland might not have been cultivated. Politically the drinks trade drew its prestige from the importance of drink taxes for national revenue. Attitudes to alcohol were deeply ingrained in British society. Abandoning drinking was, for the working-classes, more than

---

[252] Fromer, Julie E., *A necessary luxury: tea in Victorian England*, (Ohio University Press), 2008, and the broader Griffiths, John, *Tea: the drink that changed the world*, (André Deutsch), 2007.

[253] Bramah, Edward, *Tea and coffee: a modern view of three hundred years of tradition*, (Hutchinson), 1972.

[254] Holt, Mack P., (ed.), *Alcohol: a social and cultural history*, (Berg), 2006, provides an overview.

[255] Jennings, Paul, *The local: a history of the English pub*, (Tempus), 2007, Haydon, Peter, *The English pub: a history*, (Hale), 1994, and Kneale, James, ''A problem of supervision': moral geographies of the nineteenth-century British public house', *Journal of Historical Geography*, Vol. 25, (1999), pp. 333-348.

[256] Gourvish, T. R., and Wilson, R. G., *The British brewing industry, 1830-1980*, (Cambridge University Press), 1994.

simply not going to public houses as it isolated workers from much popular culture and a range of recreational activities.

The temperance movement that emerged in the 1830s was one of several attempts to inculcate a middle-class style of life and arose at a time when drunkenness was already becoming unfashionable.[257] The anti-spirits movement that developed was not planned, at least initially and arose independently in different places. Sobriety had the support of influential groups. Since the 1790s, medical opinion attacked the physical and psychological effects of alcohol and evangelicals saw excessive drinking as a sin. Radicals attacked alcohol for its effects on working-class standards of living and coffee trades wished to popularise their product. The movement would not have made such an impact without the techniques of agitation and mass persuasion used by evangelical humanitarians, especially the anti-slavery campaign. Though any clear link between industrialisation and temperance is difficult to establish, the earliest anti-spirits societies originated in textile manufacturing areas in Ulster and Glasgow and spread to England though the textile centres of Preston, Leeds and Bradford.[258] Some employers welcomed the more reliable workforce that temperance encouraged. Money not spent on drink could be spent on home-produced goods and some industrialists welcomed the movement as a means of accelerating economic growth and educating people on where to spend their wages.

During the 1830s and 1840s, a debate within the temperance movement raged between those whose concern was spirits while backing moderation elsewhere and those with a teetotal stance who believed in total abstinence. But while these approaches gained support among those sections of the working population for whom respectability was an objective, the appeal of temperance was of more limited appeal for the poor, for whom alcohol provided temporary escape.[259] Representing the ideals of self-control and self-denial, the temperance movement epitomised middle-class Victorian values. Its values were shaped by the Evangelical movement that was concerned with salvation and the Utilitarian movement that was concerned with efficiency and valued self-control and self-denial. Joseph Kidd, a late-Victorian journalist for the *Contemporary Review* wrote:

---

[257] Greenaway, J. R., *Drink and British politics since 1830: a study in policy-making*, (Palgrave Macmillan), 2003, and Nicholls, James, *The Politics of Alcohol: A History of the Drinks Question in England*, (Manchester University Press), 2009.

[258] Hargreaves, John A., "Arresting the progress of this degrading and brutalising vice': Temperance, Methodism and Chartism in Halifax and its hinterland 1832-48', *Transactions of the Halifax Antiquarian Society*, Vol. 20, (2012), pp. 130-160.

[259] Harrison, B., *Drink and the Victorians: The Temperance Question in England 1815-1872*, (Faber), 1971, 2nd ed., (Keele University Press), 1994, Lambert, W. R., *Drink and Sobriety in Victorian Wales*, (University of Wales Press), 1983, and King, E., *Scotland Sober and Free: The Temperance Movement, 1829-1979*, (Glasgow Museums and Art Galleries), 1979, provide the best analysis on the issue of temperance.

To be able to rule self and transmit to children an organisation (society) accustomed to self-restraint and moderation in all things is one of the chief delights and aspirations to the moral nature of a true man.[260]

The temperance movement was a major cause of social reform in Victorian Britain and was an integral part of the radical ethos.[261] Many contemporaries--working- as well as middle-class--were concerned with the impact of poverty. The evils associated with drunkenness were obvious and this led many reformers to exaggerate its significance as the cause of poverty. Abstaining was an expression of the dignity of class. John Fraser, who spent much of his life campaigning for temperance, went as far as to suggest that 'Drinking radicalism is a contradiction in terms.'[262] Working men were divided over temperance and temperance meetings were often disrupted. For instance, the annual meeting of the Newport Pagnell Temperance Society with visitors from Aylesbury and led by the Dunstable teetotal band was heckled, its flag torn up and several of its members assaulted by drunk working men in October 1840.[263] Some saw drink as an integral part of working-class culture: for instance, a Trowbridge Chartist promised his audience 'plenty of roast beef, plum pudding and strong beer for working three hours a day' and Ernest Jones (1819-1869), the Chartist leader in the 1850s, repeatedly emphasised that 'the Charter was not to be found at the bottom of a glass of water'.[264] For Feargus O'Connor (1796-1855), temperance was only possible when working people were no longer exploited writing in 1846:

Ah! If I were monarch for twenty-four hours, I'd level every gin palace with the dust....and in less than a month I'd produce a wise representation of a sober and thoughtful national mind.[265]

In the early-twentieth century beer, wine and spirits were relatively cheap and consumed in large quantities. At the outbreak of war in 1914, drink became a major political issue with convictions for drunken behaviour regularly exceeded 200,000 per year.[266] There was growing concern in the increased levels

---

[260] Kidd, Joseph, 'Temperance and Its Boundaries,' *Contemporary Review*, Vol. 34, (1879), p. 353.

[261] Yeomans, Henry, 'What did the British Temperance Movement Accomplish? Attitudes to Alcohol, the Law and Moral Regulation', *Sociology*, Vol. 45, (1), (2011), pp. 38-53.

[262] Cit, Wilson, Alexander, *The Chartist Movement in Scotland*, (Manchester University Press), 1970, p. 134.

[263] 'Attack on a Temperance Meeting', *Northern Star*, 31 October 1840, p. 3.

[264] Cit., Jones, David V., *Chartism and the Chartists*, (Allen Lane), 1975, p. 46.

[265] 'The Charter and No Surrender', *Northern Star*, 10 October 1846, p. 13.

[266] *Nottingham Guardian*, 2 May 1914. 'The Flying Inn', *Nottingham Evening Post*, 21 May 1914, p. 4, suggested that a 'general diminution of drunkenness reported

of drinking by women described in contemporary newspapers. This was not a new problem: 'If a woman is out drinking all day long, the home is neglected'.[267] It appears, at least as far as the authorities were concerned, to have been exacerbated by the war. Although women probably accounted for between 25 and 30 per cent of all pub patrons before 1914, most came from the working-classes. During the war, novel drinking habits began to emerge with an unprecedented increase in the number of upper working- and middle-class women who patronised pubs. The *Aberdeen Journal* reported: 'Having more money in their hands than usual, there were only too many ready to help them to spend it in the wrong way.'[268] In November, Carnarvon magistrates restricted the hours during which women could purchase alcohol.[269] The following year, Theophilus Simpson, a member of the county magistracy, expressed his shock in the *Manchester Evening News* at counting:

> ...26 women enter a licensed house in ten minutes, with 16 coming out who he had not seen enter...Some people said women have a right to spend their money as they liked; they might as well say that they had a right to sell themselves if they like.[270]

In 1916, the *Liverpool Echo* reported a debate of the Bootle Licensing Magistrates during which a Captain Oversby said: 'In the opinion of the committee, the great increase in the number of women visiting public-houses during the past year has demanded drastic treatment.' A number of different measures were discussed to reduce this including a refurbishment of all public houses: 'All licensed houses to be provided with clear plate-glass windows; partitions, snugs and other obstacles likely to facilitate secret drinking, be done away.' a member of the Flintshire Police Committee described women as 'The Thirsty Sex' two months before the war ended.[271] The scale of the problem, even if it applied to only a 'small minority of the soldiers' wives', and its impact was made clear in a report produced by the Dundee Society for the Prevention of Cruelty to Children in 1918: the number of women drinking in 1915 was reported to be 275 and 175 soldiers' wives or 55 per cent; in 1916, the respective

---

throughout the country...'

[267] 'Teignmouth Inn', *Western Times*, 12 February 1914, p. 2. 'A Plague Spot: Clarendon Hotel License Opposed', *Nottingham Evening Post*, 9 March 1914, p. 5, 'the landlord was charged with harbouring women of immoral character...The women were behaving in a more unbecoming manner, dancing ragtime and smoking as if they were men.'

[268] 'Drinking among Wives of Soldiers', *Aberdeen Journal*, 25 November 1914, p. 3. See also, 'Drinking amongst Women', *Daily Gazette for Middlesbrough*, 3 November 1914, p. 4, 'Drinking and Women', *Manchester Evening Post*, 7 November 1914, p. 2.

[269] 'Women's Drinking Hours', *Liverpool Echo*, 18 November 1914, p. 8.

[270] 'Soldiers' Wives', *Manchester Evening News*, 5 April 1915, p. 4, see also, 'Manchester Morals', *Manchester Evening News*, 11 December 1915, p. 5.

[271] 'What Becomes of the Beer', *Sheffield Evening Telegraph*, 5 September 1918, p. 2.

numbers were 260 and 172 or 66 per cent; and in 1917 263 and 189 or 71 per cent.

> In many cases the Service allowance to soldiers' wives was larger than the ordinary labouring man's wide was accustomed to receive from her husband...the result [of drinking] was neglect of the children, and abandonment of parental responsibility, and not infrequently unfaithfulness to the husband at the front.[272]

Growing control over licensed premises predated the war at least in part motivated by concerns about women drinking with calls for the government to take action to keep women out of bars, for publicans to stop serving them, and even for changes to the design of pubs, to discourage female drinkers.[273] The 1908 Licensing Bill, with the enthusiastic backing of Lloyd George (1863-1945) a long-time supporter of the temperance movement, sought to limit the number of licensed premises in each local authority area and one of its provisions included the banning of women from working behind the bar. Unlike the suffrage movement that called a truce for the duration of the war, temperance reformers saw it as a call to arms with immediate calls from some for total prohibition. It was believed that military efficiency would be enhanced by abstinence.[274] Many prominent public figure including King George V (1865-1936), Lloyd George and Lord Kitchener (1850-1916) endorsed a pledge to abstain from alcohol for the duration of the war as a means through which the whole population, should they take the pledge, could contribute to the war effort. British teetotalism, therefore, was seen as a crucial weapon to be deployed against beer-drinking Germany.[275]

It was not uncommon for pubs to open between 5.00 am and midnight. At the end of August 1914, the Intoxicating Liquor (Temporary Restriction) Act gave licensing authorities the power to curtail drinking hours allowing pubs to be open for a maximum of six hours a day with a compulsory afternoon break but it was never applied universally. Rising concern that drink impeded the war effort prompted the government to launch a new policy of regulating selective areas through the Liquor Traffic Central Control Board (CCB). Created in May 1915, the CCB addressed insobriety with radical ideas that transformed virtually every aspect of drinking–from hours, liquor strengths and increasing alcohol taxes to

---

[272] 'The Dundee Liquor Problem. The Care of the Soldier's Wife', *Evening Telegraph and Post*, 25 February 1918, p. 3.
[273] Donnachie, I., 'World War I and the Drink Question: State Control of the Drink Trade', *Journal of the Scottish Labour History Society*, Vol. 17, (1982), pp. 19-26, Gutzke, David W., 'Gender, Class and Public Drinking in Britain during the First World War', *Histoire social/Social History*, Vol. 27, (1994), pp. 367-391.
[274] 'Drink and the Cost of War', *Women's Dreadnought*, 8 May 1915, p. 2.
[275] Yeomans, Henry, 'Discussion Paper: Providentialism, The Pledge and Victorian Hangovers: Investigating Moderate Alcohol Policy, 1914-1918', *Law, Crime and History*, Vol. 1, (1), (2011), pp. 95-107.

retailing and social customs, for instance banning the buying of rounds (the 'No Treating Order') in 1915.[276] Shorter, broken licensing hours ranked as one of the key changes.[277] Arrests for drunkenness, already down one-quarter in 1915, decreased by two-thirds over the next two years. Still weaker beer at comparably higher prices in 1918 cut drunkenness by almost a further two-fifths.[278] When the war ended, arrests were less than one-fifth the level of 1914.[279] Between 1914 and 1916, although alcohol consumption had decreased by 17 per cent, actual expenditure had increased by 24 per cent largely because of higher taxation.

The CCB protected women from discriminatory policies that some authorities had introduced in 1914 to banish women from licensed premises after 6 or 7pm. This appealed to a government that dreaded the revival of the pre-war violent strife with the women's suffrage movement especially after the National Union of Women's Suffrage Societies reacted with outrage when the Chief Commissioner of Police in London sought to bar women from buying alcohol before 11.30 am. Concerns about female insobriety took second place to threats to public harmony. Despite the alarm expressed by local newspapers, there appears to have been a waning of the stigma attached to women drinking in public. Their large numbers, coupled with far fewer men drinkers and more women running pubs for husbands away at war, helped to make the pub more respectable. This did not stop affronted local magistrates seeking to divest women of newly-attained drinking rights, a process that accelerated in the final years of the war, as part of a strategy to restore pre-war gender segregation.

Hostility against women drinkers reflected a north-south divide. It was strongest in the ports and industrial centres of northern England, areas most committed to preserving existing drinking habits and was less the case in southern England where respectable women had traditionally found less opposition to drinking in pubs. The issue was female independence—one social, the other sexual—and both threatened patriarchal authority. Drinking alcohol in pubs defied established norms and women were regarded as flagrantly challenging the gender status quo. Female drinkers, whether respectable or not, were seen as feckless, disorderly and unpatriotic and, consequently, not only unfit to use licensed premises but also unfit to have the vote.

---

[276] 'Entertainment Control', *Liverpool Daily Post*, 24 February 1915, p. 9.

[277] Carter, Henry, *The Control of the Drink Trade: A Contribution to National Efficiency, 1915-17*, (Longman, Green and Co.), 1918, pp. 136-148.

[278] 'The Cabinet's Drink Proposals. Heavy Surtax on Spirits and Strong Beer…', *Birmingham Daily Post*, 30 April 1915, p. 12, 'Double Duty to be paid on Spirits and Tax on Heavy Beer', *Daily Mirror*, 30 April 1915, p. 3, 'State Control of Drink in War Munition Areas', *Manchester Courier and Lancashire General Advertiser*, 30 April 1915, p. 1.

[279] Wilson, George B., *Alcohol and the Nation: A Contribution to the Study of the Liquor Problem in the United Kingdom from 1800 to 1935*, (Nicholson & Watson), 1940, pp. 432, 435-436. See also, ibid., Nicholls, James, *The Politics of Alcohol: A History of the Drink Question in England*, pp. 130-160.

Leisure after 1850

Leisure was often associated with idleness so while it was recognised that spare time could bring benefits, its dangers were also acknowledged. In a society where the gospel of work was so deeply ingrained, it was inevitable that leisure time would be regarded with suspicion. Drunkenness, violence and fornication, it was claimed, were on the increase. This belief that moral standards were declining combined with fear that the social stability of the country was being undermined. MP Robert Slaney (1791-1862), argued that it was the duty of those governing the working-classes to provide suitable alternative recreations for those people who otherwise 'will fly to demagogues and dangerous causes.'[280]

Urbanisation and enclosures saw a loss of public spaces restricting the scope of working-class leisure activities. This can be seen in the demise of Brandon Hill near Bristol as a centre for political meetings. In 1819, several mass meetings were held on Brandon Hill and in Queen's Square in the city, the 'people's spaces', following Peterloo.[281] Chartist meetings[282] suddenly stopped on Brandon Hill in August 1839, as a result of the draconian regime of surveillance and harassment but also because local leaders lacked the capacity to draw an audience[283] but were briefly revived in 1848.[284] Populist spaces for working-class activities were significantly restricted by the growing surveillance powers of the Victorian state but it was not until the opening of the Birkenhead and Manchester parks in the 1840s that serious consideration was given to setting up controlled places of amusement within the parks themselves for the playing of games and sports.[285] This was a gradual process but between 1850 and the mid-

---

[280] See, Richards, Paul, 'R. A. Slaney, the industrial town, and early Victorian social policy', *Social History*, Vol. 4, (1979), pp. 85-101. See also, *Hansard*, House of Commons, Debates, 4 February 1840, Vol. 51, cc1222-1247, and *Hansard*, House of Commons, Debates, 22 May 1849, Vol. 104, cc870-874, for Slaney on working-class discontent.

[281] Poole, Steve, 'Till our liberties be secure: popular sovereignty and public space in Bristol, 1780-1850', *Urban History*, Vol. 26, (1), (1999), pp. 40-54.

[282] Chartist meetings on the Hill are reported in *Bristol Journal*, 5, 26 January 1839, 2 February 1839; *Bristol Gazette*, 26 December 1838, 2 May, 12 June, and 17 July 1839.

[283] Latimer, John, *Annals of Bristol in the Nineteenth Century*, (W. & F Morgan), 1887, p. 246.

[284] 'Meeting of Chartists', *Bristol Mercury*, 8 April 1848, p. 6, is the most detailed account of the initial meeting. See also, 'The National Convention', *Northern Star*, 8 April 1848, p. 25; ibid., Latimer, John, *Annals of Bristol in the Nineteenth Century*, pp. 353-354. There was a further meeting of around 2,000 people on 17 April: 'Chartist Meeting on Brandon-Hill', *Bristol Mercury*, 22 April 1848, p. 7.

[285] See, for instance, Elliott, Paul, 'The Derby Arboretum (1840): the first specially designed municipal public park in Britain', *Midland History*, Vol. 26, (2001), pp. 144-176, Taylor, A., ''Commons-stealers, land-grabbers and jerry-builders': space, popular radicalism and the politics of public access in London, 1848-80', *International Review of Social History*, Vol. 40, (1995), pp. 383-407, and MacGill, Lynn, 'The emergence of

1870s municipal parks were established in most provincial towns and cities. Nearly all places of cultural improvement from which the working-classes could benefit–art galleries, botanical gardens, libraries and museums–were denied to them, either because they could not afford the subscriptions or entrance fees or because they were, if not positively excluded, not welcomed.

The Museums Act of 1845 gave boroughs with a population of 10,000 or more the power to raise ½d in local taxes to build museums. In 1849, a Select Committee argued that existing public supply of libraries was inadequate and that their provision would steer people towards temperate and moderate habits. It also suggested that the government should make grants to enable the foundation of libraries and that the Museums Act should be extended to allow for local taxes to fund public libraries. This led to the Public Libraries Act of 1850 for England and Wales—it was extended to Scotland and Ireland in 1853—and to boroughs with populations over 10,000 after two-thirds of ratepayers consented in a local referendum to the creation of a public library.[286] The rate levied could be no more that ½d in the £ and could be used for buildings and staff but not the purchase of books. In 1855, the rate levied was raised to 1d in the £ and boroughs were allowed to buy books. By 1860, only 28 public libraries had been set up but by 1900, this had increased to 295. In 1914, there were over 5,000 libraries authorities established in Britain under the terms of the 1850 and 1853 Acts, collectively circulating between 30 and 40 million volumes a year. However, it was not until 1919, when the rate limit was abolished that a comprehensive and free library service was possible.[287]

Leisure requires 'free' time. After 1800, there was an extension of working hours with factories imposing a twelve or thirteen hour day as opposed to the ten-hour day of pre-industrial society.[288] Coalminers, whose hours in the eighteenth century were relatively short–six to eight hours a day–were by 1842

---

public parks in Keighley, West Yorkshire, 1887-93: leisure, pleasure or reform?', *Garden History*, Vol. 35, (2007), pp. 146-159.

[286] On libraries generally , see, Pettegree, Andrew & der Weduwen, Arthur, *The Library: A Fragile History*, (Profile Books Ltd.), 2021. Hewitt, Martin, 'Extending the public library 1850-1930', in Black, Alistair, and Hoare, Peter, (eds.), *The Cambridge History of Libraries in Britain and Ireland: Vol. 3: 1850-2000*, (Cambridge University Press), 2006, pp. 72-81, Peatling, Gary K., 'Public libraries and national identity in Britain, 1850-1919', *Library History*, Vol. 20, (2004), pp. 33-47, Johnman, W. A. P., and Kendall, H., 'A Commission Appointed to Inquire into the Condition and Workings of Free Libraries of Various Towns in England (1869)', *Library History*, Vol. 17, (2001), pp. 223-238, Fletcher, J., 'Public libraries, legislation and educational provision in nineteenth-century England', *Journal of Educational Administration & History*, Vol. 28, (1996), pp. 97-113, and Sturges, Paul, 'The public library and its readers 1850-1900', *Library History*, Vol. 12, (1996), pp. 183-200.

[287] Black, Alistair, *The Public Library in Britain, 1914-2000*, (British Library), 2000.

[288] Hopkins, E., 'Working hours and the conditions during the Industrial Revolution: a re-appraisal', *Economic History Review*, 2nd series, Vol. 35, (1982), pp. 52-66.

nearly all working a twelve hour day with only short breaks for refreshment. Agricultural workers too suffered an increase in hours by the 1830s. In mining, agriculture, domestic service and the 'dishonourable' sections of the artisan trades and in all domestic work, hours were longer. After 1850, the campaign for the nine-hour day started in the building trade with limited success until the economic boom of the early 1870s when most organised trades achieved a 54 hour week through collective bargaining. Despite pressure in the 1890s, reducing hours nationally was not achieved until 1919 and 1920 when seven million workers achieved an eight-hour day and this remained the norm until 1945. There were, nonetheless, variations between different trades and parts of the country. For instance, in 1924, cement workers had a 49.9 hour week while in tobacco it was 40.3 hours.[289]

There had been a sharp decline in the number of holidays that were recognised and observed since the seventeenth century. They continued to be observed, with some regional variation, around Christmas or New Year, at Easter and Whitsuntide, at the local fair, feast or wake and on national days such as the 5 November and Shrove Tuesday. There were as yet no holidays with pay. The Bank Holidays Acts of 1871 and 1875 were not the first legislative recognition of holidays but they were the first in which the state's intervention was widely applauded.[290] In the late-nineteenth and early-twentieth centuries, employers increasingly conceded holidays to their workforce. Brunner Mond, Lever Bros., the Gas Light and Coke Company, the London and North-Western Railway Company and the Royal Dockyards did so by the 1890s. In 1897, the Amalgamated Society of Railway Servants negotiated one-week's paid holiday after five years' service. Other unionised workers, in coal and iron, for instance, were putting forward similar claims before 1914. It was, however, the war that made the issue national and after 1917 nearly all industries called for holidays with pay and by 1922, district and national agreements included about a million workers. Further trade union pressure saw major advances in the late 1930s with holiday pay agreements covering 3 million manual and 4.75 million non-manual workers. By 1945, pay agreements covered 10 million manual workers. Casual or part-time workers—many of them women—were without holidays, paid or not.[291]

The growth and decline of artisanal leisure culture paralleled their economic status. It flourished until the 1850s but as artisans were absorbed into the structure of capitalist industry, they began to lose the distinctive feature of their culture: independence. Independence in the workplace was paralleled in

---

[289] Johnson, Paul A., and Zaidi, Asghar, 'Work over the life course', in ibid., Crafts, Nicholas F. R., Gazeley, Ian, and Newell, Andrew, (eds.), *Work and pay in twentieth-century Britain*, pp. 98-116.

[290] See, Smart, Eynon, 'Bank holidays...and much else', *History Today*, Vol. 21, (12), (1971), pp. 870-876.

[291] Cunningham, Hugh, *Time, Work and Leisure: Life Changes in England since 1700*, (Manchester University Press), 2016, pp. 92-154.

the leisure culture which rejected patronage from above. Artisans made their own goods and also made their own culture. If the workplace was one factor leading to independence, masculinity and age were others; this was a leisure culture of adult males. Women were rarely admitted and only on sufferance and young apprentices, who had once had a culture of their own, were now firmly subordinated. In Birmingham, artisans formed debating societies and clubs and attended the theatre.[292] Friendly societies and trade unions had their strongest support among artisans and they were instinctively radical in their politics. But it was not an expansive, assertive culture that spread its way of life more widely. By 1850, the heavy drinking artisan culture was restricted to certain trades and regions and a more respectable, even family-based, culture began to replace it. In Edinburgh, the clubs that artisans joined for horticulture, golf and bowling and their participation in the patriotic Volunteer Force suggested a new conformity to the middle-class values . These clubs, however, retained their own independence. Artisan culture may have become more respectable, but it was a respectability generated by artisans rather than one imposed from outside.[293]

Urban popular culture focused on the home and the street offered various kinds of satisfaction to different sections of the population.[294] It was mass culture that leached across communities and was based on participant competition. There were activities that people paid to attend as spectators, audience or readers. This included theatres, circuses and fairs and later in the century, music halls, professional football, horseracing, the popular press, seaside excursions and cinemas.[295] This was commercial leisure in which the size of crowds with resulting financial returns was important to pay the stars and professionals. People also generated leisure activities within their own communities. The pub played a pivotal role and was the location for far more than the consumption of alcohol. Its activities included brass bands, mass choirs, shows and the allotments that provided their flowers and vegetables and fishing and pigeon fancying.[296] Competitiveness was one of the marks of its overriding masculinity: pub against pub, club against club; stars and professionals were absent; there was

---

[292] See Money, J., *Experience and Identity: Birmingham and the West Midlands 1760-1800*, (Manchester University Press), 1977, pp. 80-120, Tholfsen, T. R., 'The artisan and the culture of early Victorian Birmingham', *University of Birmingham Historical Journal*, Vol. 4, (1954), pp. 146-166.
[293] Beaven, Brad, *Leisure, Citizenship and Working-class Men in Britain, 1850-1945*, (Manchester University Press), 2005, pp. 16-124.
[294] Johnes, Martin, 'Pigeon Racing and Working-class Culture in Britain, *c.* 1870-1950', *Cultural and Social History*, Vol. 4, (2007), pp. 361-383, examines one aspect of urban community leisure.
[295] See, Russell, Dave, 'Popular entertainment, 1776-1895', in Ibid., Donohue, Joseph, (ed.), *The Cambridge History of British theatre: Vol. 2, 1660 to 1895*, pp. 369-387.
[296] Willes, Margaret, *The Gardens of the British Working Class*, (Yale University Press), 2014, pp. 113-169, Burchardt, Jeremy, *The Allotment in England 1793-1873*, (Royal Historical Society), 2002.

little formal separation of performers and spectators; and, the participants were mainly adult males. Finally, most working-class women focused not on activities but on space and were confined to the home and the street. They created their own separate culture there and was a key component of the 'traditional working-class culture' from 1870 to 1950. Women's leisure was not seen as leisure but something that accompanied work. This female network of support was based on the separation of male and female world after marriage. In its more social aspects in the street, its most typical form was chatting within a culture heavily based on a sense of neighbourhood. Popular urban leisure was to a considerable degree fractured along lines of gender.[297]

The pub had close ties to this commercialised urban popular culture and was the main location of what was by far the largest single item of leisure expenditure, alcohol. It was itself a commercial undertaking, increasingly under the control of the major brewers. Despite this, the pub also managed to be the main organising centre for the self-generating culture. Publicans often sponsored activities with an eye to profit. In addition, the pub offered a space for socialising and clubs of all kinds met in pubs. The community generated by the pub expressed itself in the annual outing. Above all, within the pub men could take part in a range of competitive activities: darts,[298] draughts, bowls and card playing and gambling of all kinds. The significance of participant competitiveness is underplayed in accounts that focus on music hall, cinema and spectating generally. As communications improved many of these competitions became regional and national. Brass bands, for instance, were competitive from their creation on a significant scale in the 1840s.[299]

After 1780, a print culture developed that complemented and eventually replaced existing oral popular culture. The expanding newspaper press of the eighteenth century reached a largely middle-class audience primarily because of cost, but during the first half of the nineteenth century, a new literate popular culture emerged grounded in the radical and often 'unstamped' press and in the growth of melodramatic 'penny dreadfuls'.[300] It is difficult to establish an

---

[297] Beaven, Brad, *Leisure, citizenship and working class men in Britain 1850-1945*, (Manchester University Press), 2005, pp. 16-43, 128-154, 211-234.
[298] Chaplin, Patrick, *Darts in England, 1900-39: A social history*, (Manchester University Press), 2012.
[299] Herbert, Trevor, (ed.), *The British Brass Band: a musical and social history*, (Oxford University Press), 2000.
[300] On the press Read, D., *Press and People 1790-1850: Opinion in Three English Cities*, (Edward Arnold), 1961, is excellent on the impact of the middle-class press while Hollis, P., *The Pauper Press: A Study in Working-Class Radicalism of the 1830s*, (Oxford University Press), 1970, Wickwar, W. H., *The Struggle for the Freedom of the Press 1819-1832*, (Allen & Unwin), 1928, and Weiner, J., *The War of the Unstamped: the movement to repeal the British newspaper tax, 1830-1836*, (Cornell University Press), 1969, on the popular press. Hewitt, M., *The Dawn of the Cheap Press in Victorian Britain. The campaigns against the taxes on knowledge, 1849-1869*,

accurate profile of the readership by age, gender and class. Men, until after 1870, had higher levels of literacy than women and had easier access to literature. They were the main readers of the popular Sunday newspapers that by 1850 were read by one adult in twenty. Sunday was much more a day of leisure for men than women.[301] Sporting literature, a genre of popular literature with its emphasis on 'manly' sports, also reached a dominantly male audience. By 1900, daily newspapers were read by one adult in five and Sunday newspapers by one in three. By 1920, respective figures were one in two and four in five adults. The number of books published rose from 6,000 in 1901 to 18,000 in 1951 while sale of books grew even more dramatically from 7.2 million in 1928 to 26.8 million in 1939. By the mid-1930s, public libraries were within the reach of the entire population with a dramatic rise in the book borrowing public.[302] Parallel to this mass consumption, there was an expansion in the specialist press that catered for different hobbies and also the growing popular market among the young and women.[303]

Reading was not the only option for those who wanted to stay at home. By the 1930s, radio was an alternative to public leisure for many working men and women, something aided by the dramatic fall in the cost of radio sets.[304] By 1939, 70 per cent of UK households has radio licences but this left a third without radios. Regional differences reflected the lack of programming in some rural areas and the relative affluence of growing areas. In the Midlands, 80 per cent of households had a radio, while 61 per cent of Scottish households had licences. Working-class listeners liked entertainment and variety programmes. One survey found that 82.5 per cent of working-class respondents listed variety as their favourite programmes and two-thirds of the wealthiest respondents also preferred variety. Dance and light music found a ready audience. Radio played a pivotal role in engaging the whole nation in the war effort and, for the first

---

(Bloomsbury Academic), 2013.

[301] See, Kamper, D. S., 'Popular Sunday newspapers, respectability and working-class culture in late Victorian Britain', in Huggins, Mike, and Mangan, James Anthony, (eds.), *Disreputable pleasures: less virtuous Victorians at play*, (Cass), 2004, pp. 83-102, and Kamper, D. S., 'Popular Sunday newspapers, class, and the struggle for respectability in late Victorian Britain', Hewitt, Martin, (ed.), *Unrespectable recreations*, (Leeds Centre for Victorian Studies), 2001, pp. 81-94.

[302] McAleer, J., *Popular Reading and Publishing in Britain 1914-50*, (Oxford University Press), 1992, Rose, Jonathan, *The Intellectual Life of the British Working Classes*, 2nd. ed., (Yale University Press), 2010, pp. 237-255, 365-392. See also, James, Rhodes, *Popular Culture and Working-class Taste in Britain, 1930-39*, (Oxford University Press), 2010, pp. 13-38, 106-123.

[303] Langhamer, C., *Women's Leisure in England 1920-1960*, (Manchester University Press), 2000.

[304] Hendy, David, *The BBC: A People's History*, (Profile Books), 2022, Scannell, P., and Cardiff, D., *A Social History of British Broadcasting, Vol. 1: 1922-1939: Serving the Nation*, (Basil Blackwell), 1991.

time, news of the conflict reached people's homes. For instance, Chamberlain's announcement of war on 3 September was broadcast live as were reports of the Blitz and the D-Day landings. Churchill's speeches in the House of Commons were re-recorded for radio. It was also a major propaganda tool, a means of sending coded messages across Europe as well as 'fake news'.[305] The first regular television broadcasts occurred on 2 November 1936 from Alexandra Palace to the London area. By May 1937 when the coronation of George VI was the first major television outside broadcast, 9,000 TV sets were sold in the London area and by 1 September 1939 it is estimated that there were 20,000 TV sets in Britain. Broadcasts were suspended during the war and did not resume until 7 June 1946.[306]

After 1850, growing numbers of people attended popular entertainments. Music hall was first to make its mark.[307] Charles Morton's (1819-1904) opening of the Canterbury Music Hall in Lambeth in 1851 gained him immediate attention, but there were important precedents in the saloon theatres that had flourished since the 1830s and in the 'music halls' that already existed in the larger provincial towns across the United Kingdom.[308] What is striking about the 1850s and 1860s was the many ways in which people could experience what was eventually to become standardised as 'music hall'. The focus on songs has distracted attention from the range of entertainment on offer in the halls; dance, acrobatics, mime drama and clowning as well as occasional facilities such as a museum, art gallery or zoo, were part of the 'variety' of the halls from the beginning. The emergence of music halls that were architecturally similar to theatres came relatively late during the second great wave of music hall building in the late 1880s and 1890s. It was in the 1890s that there was a partially successful attempt to win middle-class audiences.[309]

---

[305] Stourton, Edward, *Auntie's War: The BBC during the Second World War*, (Doubleday Books), 2017.

[306] Aldridge, Mark, *The Birth of British Television*, (Palgrave Macmillan), 2012.

[307] On music, see, Russell, Dave, *Popular Music in England 1840-1914: A Social History*, (Manchester University Press), 1987, 2nd edition, 1997, and Bowan, Kate, and Pickering, Paul A., *Sounds of Liberty. Music, radicalism and reform in the Anglophone world, 1790-1914*, (Manchester University Press), 2017. Bratton, J. S., (ed.), *Music hall: performance and style*, (Open University Press), 1986, Till, Nicholas, '"First-Class Evening Entertainments": Spectacle and Social Control in a Mid-Victorian Music Hall', *New Theatre Quarterly*, Vol. 20, (2004), pp. 3-18, Scott, Derek B., 'Music and social class in Victorian London ', *Urban History*, Vol. 29, (2002), pp. 60-73, and Kift, Dagmar, *The Victorian music hall: culture, class and conflict*, (Cambridge University Press), 1996.

[308] For instance, Maloney, Paul, *Scotland and the Music Hall, 1850-1914*, (Manchester University Press), 2003, pp. 24-56, 183-212.

[309] Faulk, Barry J., *Music Hall and Modernity: The Late-Victorian Discovery of Popular Culture*, (Ohio University Press), 2004, pp. 23-49.

Cinema can be seen as superseding music hall as the most popular form of mass entertainment but there was a lengthy period of overlap. Music hall was indeed the commercial cinema's first home. From 1906, onwards, however, cinemas acquired their own homes, some 4,000 of them by 1914.[310] There are no accurate figures for admission before 1934 but an average of 7 or 8 million a week is plausible in the years immediately before 1914 or 400 million admissions a year. In 1934, there were 903 million admissions[311] and in 1946 this reached a peak of 1,635 million. From the earliest cinemas, the low cost of seats meant that audiences were largely working-class of both genders and all ages and this had not changed noticeably by 1945. In 1934, 43 per cent of cinema tickets cost less than 6d and another 37 per cent less than 10d. By 1937, 20 million people—40 per cent of the total population—went to the cinema at least once a week.[312] In Britain, the cinema was never more popular—or more important—than during the Second World War. Although promising escape from the hardships and terrors of wartime life, the cinema was so intimately woven into the fabric of British society that it could not itself escape the war.[313]

Spectating at professional sport was already common by 1850 but the next century saw a shift in popularity. Rowing ceased to be a major spectator sport and amateur athletics never achieved the crowds of the professional pedestrianism that it replaced. Football, on the other hand, attracted numbers that grew from the late-nineteenth century.[314] The average football cup tie attendance rose from 6,000 in 1888-1889 to 12,000 in 1895-1896 and to over 20,000 in the first round in 1903. In 1908-1909, in the English First Division 6 million people watched matches with an average crowd size of 16,000. It was dominantly a male pastime and was regionally concentrated in the Lowlands of Scotland, northern and Midland England and to a lesser extent London.

Women's football exploded during the First World War when women were drafted into munitions factories across the country. The Dick, Kerr

---

[310] Much of the research on early cinema is in the form of studies of particular localities or entrepreneurs but see, Hiley, Nicholas, '"Nothing more than a 'craze'": cinema building in Britain from 1909 to 1914', in Higson, Andrew, (ed.), *Young and innocent? The cinema in Britain, 1896-1930*, (University of Exeter Press), 2002, pp. 111-127, and McKernan, Luke, 'A fury for seeing: Cinema, audience and leisure in London in 1913', *Early Popular Visual Culture*, Vol. 6, (2008), pp. 271-280.

[311] Rowson, S., 'A statistical survey of the cinema industry in Great Britain in 1934', *Journal of the Royal Statistical Society*, Vol. 99, (1936), pp. 67-129.

[312] Richards, J., *The Age of the Dream Palace: Cinema and Society in Britain 1930-1939*, (Routledge), 1984, Sedgwick, John, *Popular Filmgoing in 1930s Britain*, (University of Exeter Press), 2000, pp. 39-54.

[313] Farmer, Richard, *Cinemas and Cinemagoing in Wartime Britain, 1939-45: The Utility Dream Palace*, (Oxford University Press), 2016, pp. 92-125, 199-234.

[314] See, Taylor, Matthew, *The Association Game: a history of British football*, (Pearson Longman), 2008, and Gibbons, Philip, *Association Football in Victorian England: a history of the game from 1863 to 1900*, (Minerva), 2001.

locomotive factory in Preston was repurposed for the war effort and its female workforce soon formed the most formidable team in the country playing matches in front of crowds of between 20,000 and 30,000.[315] On Boxing Day 1920, Dick, Kerr Ladies took on St. Helen's Ladies in a charity match at Goodison Park on behalf of unemployed and disabled ex-Service men. They romped home 4-0 before a sell-out crowd of 53,000 with receipts over £3,000 exclusive of tickets and 14,000 turned away at the turnstiles.[316] Almost a year later, on 5 December 1921, the Football Association stated that it felt 'impelled to express their strong opinion that the game of football is not for females and ought not to be encouraged. Women's teams were banned from playing on FA-affiliated ground, somethings not overturned until the 1970s.[317]

Commercialised sport grew in the inter-war period by appealing to men of all ages. First Division matches attracted crowds of 30,000 and men who could not afford the 1s. or 1s.6d. tickets watched local clubs that were often linked with local churches and chapels. For instance, in the North Lancashire and District League in 1920, there were teams called St. Joseph's, Marsh Wesleyans and Marsh Wesleyan Reserves and YMCA Reserves with obvious religious links. In Wales, Rugby Union survived the economic crisis with large crowds throughout the 1930s and Rugby League supported dozens of clubs despite its failure to gain support beyond parts of northern England. The BBC broadcast a wide variety of sporting events with live coverage of rugby, cricket, the FA Cup, the Derby and tennis from Wimbledon in 1927. Professional boxing also proved popular with young working-class spectators between the wars. Two new commercialised sports—dog racing and speedway—developed large working-class support. The first greyhound track was constructed in 1926 and by 1932 over 20 million watched racing at 187 tracks. Seen as the 'poor man's racecourse', tracks offered on-course betting, cheap admission, evening races and arenas in working-class districts. By contrast, most horse-racing took place during working hours and in largely rural locations.[318] Speedway arrived from Australia in 1927 and soon attracted a strong following among women as well as men. Often speedway shared facilities with greyhound racing and may have drawn crowds of 80,000 people.[319]

---

[315] Newsham, Gail J., *In A League of Their Own: The Dick, Kerr Ladies, 1917-1965*, (Paragon Publishing), 2018, pp. 6-113.

[316] 'Christmas Day Football', *Lancashire Evening Post*, 28 December 1920, p. 5.

[317] Williams, Jean, *A Game for Rough Girls? A History of Women's Football in Britain*, (Routledge), 2003, pp. 25-45, Williams, Jean, *The History of Women's Football*, (Pen & Sword History), 2021, Tate, Tim, *Girls with Balls: The secret History of Women's Football*, (John Blake), 2013, pp. 5-98.

[318] Huggins, Mike, *Horseracing and the British 1919-39*, (Manchester University Press), 2003.

[319] Williams, J., "A wild orgy of speed': responses to speedway in Britain before the Second World War', *The Sports Historian*, Vol. 19, (1999), pp. 1-16.

Sports clubs organised a variety of sports and pubs sponsored local football clubs. Matches, especially on Sunday afternoon, drew large crowds of spectators. Working-men's clubs, pubs and employers organised angling clubs particularly for working-class men. Competitions drew thousands of fishermen and, for instance, in 1920 the Annual Angling Competition of the Birmingham and District Anglers' Association saw 1,800 anglers take part in a competition that extended 17 miles along the River Severn.[320] Gambling was central to the appeal of sport in working-class communities and appealed to women as well as men. The football pools began in 1923 and rapidly gained widespread support with 10 million people playing in 1939 with stakes totalling over £40 million. In 1937 there was a special mail train from Liverpool to Birmingham each week carrying 235,000 football coupons for the Birmingham area.

The 1920s was famed for fashions, flappers, jazz and booming stock markets but many were concerned about the baleful effects of new leisure activities. There was considerable moral censoriousness about the spread of working-class gambling whether on horses or more the recent phenomena of greyhound racing and football pools. A Manchester Federation of Evangelical Free Churches reported on the new Belle Vue greyhound tract. It had little interest in the stadium, but spoke in harsh tones about other event at the venue especially on-course betting:

> Betting seems the great and real business...There must have been hundreds of them [bookies] and there is not the least vestige of apology for their presence. I believe if they were not there the crowd would be absent.[321]

The Manchester churches were not alone in their disgust. The National Anti-Gambling League, whose members included Ramsay MacDonald, the Labour prime minister, opposed gambling, as did Winston Churchill. There is a recurring pattern that new recreations provoke moral panics while the reality is less exciting. When moving pictures acquired sound in the 1930s, Sir Alfred Knox (1870-1964), Conservative MP for Wycombe from 1924 to 1945, was appalled that American accents would in the future be spread to impressionable young people warning that 'there can be no doubt that such films are an evil influence on our language'.

Many of the leisure activities that developed in the nineteenth century persisted well into the twentieth century. The street remained an important leisure space for walking and playing and, for women in particular, talking. Fish and chips[322] became a major nutritionally beneficial part of working-classes' diet

---

[320] 'Seventeen Miles of Anglers', *Tewkesbury Register and Agricultural Gazette*, 18 September 1920, p. 5. Trench, C. P. C., *A History of Angling*, (Hart-Davies MacGibbon), 1974.

[321] National Archives, Memo from the Manchester Federation of Evangelical Free Churches, 1926.

[322] Walton, John K., *Fish and Chips, and the British Working Class, 1870-1940*,

while during the inter-war years millions of bananas were imported becoming the fruit of the poor. New leisure opportunities diverted money and attention away from the long-established local pub but drink remained important in working-class lives. For many working-class adults, the cinema or dance hall had little appeal compared to the 'local'. Regulars gathered in the tap-room that was off-limits for women. Women were more welcome in the lounge or 'snug' but attitudes to women's drinking varied with many women accompanying their husbands to the pub while some women went on their own.[323] A vibrant street life, dance halls, cinemas, radio, small-scale betting especially on horses and football and the local corner pub characterised working-class leisure until the mid-1940s.

War to war 1914-1945

By 1914, the working-classes was a very stable and mature structure. Their social horizons were limited and even those who crossed into non-manual occupations seldom travelled beyond the insecure margins of the lower middle-classes.[324] They were rarely far from the abyss of poverty and the shadow of the workhouse. This was summed up by E. M. Forster (1879-1970):

The boy, Leonard Bast, stood at the extreme edge of gentility. He was not in the abyss but he could see it, and at times people he knew had dropped in, and counted no more...[325]

In the First World War, one in 10 men under 45 were killed, and this was particularly marked amongst the 750,000 who had enlisted in the first two months of the conflict.[326] The total of enlisted men reached nearly 2.5 million volunteers by the end of 1915 but despite this, demand for soldiers soon outran supply and in 1916 the government introduced conscription. By the Armistice in November 1918, just under 6 million British men had served in the war. More than 40 per cent were casualties and over 720,000 were killed. 300,000 of those killed were in unknown graves and three million families lost a family member. The working-classes were underrepresented in these figures as they volunteered

---

(Leicester University Press), 1992, pp. 1-22, 137-161.

[323] Gutzke, David W., *Women drinking out in Britain since the early Twentieth Century*, (Manchester University Press), 2016, pp. 14-69.

[324] Bourke, Joanna, *Working-Class Cultures in Britain 1890-1960: Gender, Class and Ethnicity*, (Routledge), 1994, McKibbin, Ross, *Classes and Cultures in England 1918-1951*, (Oxford University Press), 1998, pp. 106-203, 332-384, 419-456, and Todd, Selina, *The People: The Rise and Fall of the Working Class*, (John Murray), 2014, are important on twentieth century developments.

[325] Forster, E. M., *Howards End*, (Edward Arnold), 1910, p. 193.

[326] Meyer, Jessica, *Men of War: Masculinity and the First World War in Britain*, (Palgrave Macmillan), 2009, Silbey, David, *The British Working Class and Enthusiasm for War, 1914-1916*, (Frank Cass), 2005, pp. 15-37.

less often than middle-class men. More manual workers enjoyed reserved status because their jobs qualified as war-work. When conscription was introduced, 28 per cent of those working in industry had signed up compared to 40 per cent in commerce and finance. Although officers–overwhelmingly middle-class–suffered higher casualties than other ranks, 96 per cent of soldiers killed were not officers and most were working men.[327]

Many of those not involved in fighting enjoyed better living standards than before the war. This was the result of higher wages, overtime pay, expanded provision of meals for children and munitions workers and separation allowances of £1 for soldiers' wives. Housing was the exception as construction slowed dramatically as costs rose and workers moved to better paid work in war industries or in military service. Crowded and insanitary housing conditions grew more common though one consolation was the introduction of rent controls that fixed rents at 1914 levels. Loyalty was not guaranteed and the 'awful clutching fear' that sapped morale presented the British government with the formidable task of rallying not only the troops but the entire nation to the war effort. The Independent Labour Party, No Conscription Fellowship, Union of Democratic Control, Fellowship of Reconciliation, and the Women's International League opposed the war. There were anti-war demonstrations in 'Red Clydeside', industrial action in essential industries, rent strikes and even calls for a Marxist revolution.

Between the wars, some industries especially farming, coal-mining, textiles and clothing, which had been in decline before 1914, shrank further. Other industries notably engineering and the metal trades expanded because of technical change while social change led to the growth in professional and financial services and public administration. Building, transport and distribution changed little in relative importance. More generally, the shift in occupational and social structures led to a move away from manual to non-manual labour. The workforce in manual jobs declined from 79.7 per cent in 1911, to 76.5 per cent in 1931 and more rapidly to 69.6 per cent in 1951. The new 'light' manufacturing industries had a higher ratio of supervisory and administrative staff to manual workers than the older staple industries. This was evident in the decline in those employed in manufacturing from 6.27 million in 1911 to 4.84 million by 1931. There was also a decline in the working-classes as a percentage of the total occupied population from 74.6 per cent in 1911 to 72 per cent in 1921 down to 70.3 per cent in 1931 even though the number occupied increased from 13.65 million in 1911 to 14.78 million in 1931. This decline reflected major developments in services and clerical occupations with the numbers employed rising from 6.95 million in 1911 to 9.53 million by 1921 and 11.85 million ten years later. There was an increase in management and administrative workers from 3.4 per cent in 1911 to 8.2 per cent in 1971; clerical

---

[327] Ugolini, Laura, *Civvies: Middle-Class Men on the English Home Front*, (Manchester University Press), 2013.

workers increased from 4.8 per cent in 1911 to 13.9 per cent in 1971; and foremen, inspectors and supervisors from 1.3 per cent in 1911 to 3.9 per cent in 1971.[328]

The First World War saw a change in the distribution of wealth in Britain though less than that of income. In 1913, the wages of skilled workers lay closer to the earnings of foremen than they did to unskilled manual workers and they earned as much as two-thirds of the lower professional income. Skilled workers earned 68 per cent more than the unskilled; but this fell to 40 per cent in 1923 before increasing to 51 per cent in 1931. By 1922, foremen's earnings were half as much again as skilled workers while lower professionals earned almost double. The wages of skilled workers came closer to those of the semi- and unskilled workers than other social groups producing a more homogeneous working-class. During the war, levels of income tax on the well-off rose substantially and did not revert to pre-war levels after 1918. This was offset to some extent by higher indirect taxes that bore most heavily on those with lower incomes. Although lower incomes escaped most direct taxation, a married man with three children earning £200 a year or less in 1937-1938 contributed an average of 8-10 per cent of his income in indirect taxation, double the pre-war proportion. By 1939, the social distribution of income had changed. Much of this was because of higher taxation and public spending that benefited the poorer rather than richer members of society. The gradual upgrading of society also played an important part especially a rise in salaried occupations. In 1911, there were 15.2 million wage-earners and 1.7 million salary earners. By 1939, the number of salary earners had more than doubled to 3.8 million while those earning wages had fallen by 170,000.

Victory might not have been possible but for the sacrifice of millions of men at the front and of women largely on the Home Front in support of the war effort. Yet, most of the changes that occurred during the war proved either short-lived or continued processes already evident by 1914. The decline in working-class fertility predated the war as had the beginnings of local authorities building council houses. Most women who had replaced male industrial workers left their jobs when it ended; they were given little choice by employers. The immediate post-war period was marked by deteriorating class relations, industrial strife and global economic collapse while in the 1930s social tensions in Britain were to a significant extent diffused by the rise in both real incomes and mass consumerism. Britain's economic recovery and painful period of readjustment implies a redefinition of interwar depression as essentially a regional problem arising out of the concentration of heavy industry in particular areas in the North of England, South Wales and Central Scotland. A retreat of trade unionism especially in its old industrial strongholds after the labour militancy in the decade

---

[328] Ibid., Boyer, George R., *The Winding Road to the Welfare State. Economic Insecurity and Social Welfare in Britain*, pp. 217-259, looks at living standards between the wars.

before 1926 and their slow growth in the new industries demonstrated class disunity. But 'mass' unemployment was confined to particular regions and specific industrial communities rather than uniformly experienced by the majority of the workforce nationally, most of whom even at the peak of the depression kept their jobs, nor was the economic slump continuous or comprehensively experienced by all industry.

Revisionist versions sought to counter an crushing picture of industrial decline and unrest, deprivation and unemployment in Northern England, South Wales and Central Scotland in the 1920s and early 1930s with relative prosperity and job security elsewhere in the country for a significant proportion of the working population in regular employment, particularly after 1931.[329] Rather than an era of unremitting social deprivation and disappointment, there was a transformation in some sections of mass manufacturing through innovation in product design and technology as well as advances in communications, distribution and retailing. The failure of staple industries had an intense pauperising effect on working-class communities in the North, Scotland and South Wales. By contrast, on the outskirts of London and in towns such as Oxford and Luton, new industries and new manufacturing plants mushroomed and unemployment was lower. This created new opportunities in an expanding technical and service sector and a consumer boom. Real wages rose by an average of 1.21 per cent per annum over between 1913 and 1938, while wage differentials between unskilled and semi-skilled workers and their skilled counterparts narrowed and consumers benefited from a period of virtually continuous deflation. The benefits of economic change were therefore more widely distributed than traditional accounts of this period imply. The economic insecurity of the inter-war years may have promoted a common sense of class identity among the working-classes but the salient feature of these decades was the disparate experience of workers from different regional economies and various levels of unemployment.

Living standards during the Second World War were determined by the existence of full employment. In July 1939, the number of insured unemployment was 1.27 million and this fell to 645,000 a year later and to 60,000—its lowest point—in July 1943 when the average level of unemployment was 0.6 per cent. William Beveridge (1873-1963) suggested that the lowest rate of post-war full employment would be about 3 per cent.[330] Pressure on labour demand can be seen in the contrast between wage rates and earnings. The index of wage rates had risen by almost 50 per cent between October 1938 and July 1945 while average weekly earnings for all industrial workers rose by 80 per cent from 53s. 3d. to 96s. 1d. The war saw an increase in the relative weekly rate of

---

[329] See in particular, Pugh, M., *We Danced All Night: A Social History of Britain Between the Wars*, (Vintage), 2008.
[330] Beveridge, W. H., *Full Employment in a Free Society*, (Allen & Unwin), 1944, p. 128.

agricultural workers from 34s. 8d in 1939 to 67s. 10d. in 1945. Coal miners and railway workers also recovered some of the wage loss of the 1920s and 1930s. Wartime hours of work were longer than in peacetime where a notional working week was 47 hours before overtime. In practice hours were determined in factories rather than centrally and in industries critical to the war effort such as munitions, aircraft production and shipbuilding rose dramatically to 60 hours a week. Although rising living standards benefited many in the working-classes, inflation fell hard on those with low wages and large families especially in the first year of the war. For the whole war inflation adversely effected the class of 'newly poor', the wives and children of servicemen away from home who struggled on inadequate incomes. Taking all allowances into account, a private soldier's wife with two children received only 32s. a week in 1939 rising to 43s. in 1942 and they were most likely to fall into debt.[331]

Rationing was introduced much faster than during the First World War and lasted considerably longer. Butter, sugar, bacon and ham were rationed from 8 January 1940, meat followed on 11 March and tea and margarine in July. Rationing of jams and other preserves from March 1941 and cheese, eggs and cooking fat from May 1941. All these foods were rationed by weight other than meat that was rationed by value and eggs by number (one fresh egg a week plus allowance for dried eggs). Each person had allowance of 1s. 10d. to be spent on meat and this was reduced to 1s. 2d. in January 1941, the equivalent of about 1 lb a week. Some rations were generous with 8oz of bacon a week, more than pre-war consumption while tea was restricted to 2oz per person per week. The sugar ration, originally 12oz soon fell to 8oz, a sharp reduction on pre-war consumption. Fourteen years of food rationing ended at midnight on 4 July 1954 when restrictions on the sale of meat and bacon stopped.[332]

People were encouraged to provide their own food at home. The 'Dig for Victory' campaign started in October 1939 and called for every man and woman to keep an allotment.[333] Lawns and flower-beds were turned into vegetable gardens and chickens, rabbits, goats and pigs were reared in town parks and gardens. Food rationing system led people to have a balanced diet and as a result the health of the nation improved. Clothes rationing began on 1 June 1941 and ended on 15 March 1949. Each person was given 60 coupons to last them a year that was later reduced to 48 coupons, then 36 and finally 20 coupons per adult. Children were allocated an extra 10 clothing coupons above the standard ration to allow for growing out of clothes during a year. Petrol rationing was introduced in September 1939 and initially tiny amounts were allowed to private motorists.

---

[331] Gardiner, Juliet, *Wartime Britain 1939-1945*, (Headline Review), 2005, Todman, Daniel, *Britain's War*, 2 Vols. (Allen Lane), 2016, 2018.
[332] *How Britain was Fed in War Time: Food Control, 1939-1945*, (Ministry of Food), 1946, Chevalier, Natacha, *Food In Wartime Britain: Testimonies from the Kitchen Front (1939-1945)*, (Routledge), 2020.
[333] Ibid., Willes, Margaret, *The Gardens of the British Working Class*, pp. 264-287.

This ended in the summer of 1942 after the Japanese occupied Malaya and U-Boat attacks in the Atlantic intensified. Some goods such as cigarettes and alcohol were never officially rationed but were often in short supply. Although the public accepted the introduction of rationing, evasion was widespread and a black market flourished. For instance, in March 1941, 2,141 prosecutions were brought under the Food Control Order and there were 1,994 convictions, a success rate of 93.1 per cent. The following month this had increased to 2,300 prosecutions and 2,199 convictions with a higher success rate of 95.6 per cent.[334]

The major threat to the civilian population and to the war economy came from bombing.[335] The government had laid down plans for evacuation[336] that were executed in the early hours of 1 September and before war was declared on 3 September, 1.47 million people were removed from crowded cities across Britain including 826,959 unaccompanied schoolchildren and 523,670 mothers and accompanied children. In addition, 2 million people evacuated themselves largely to small market towns and rural areas in western England or Wales. In June 1940, with the imminent threat of invasion, many parents made desperate efforts to send their children abroad to safety. Thousand left for America, Canada, Australia and other countries.[337] Evacuation was not confined to children and the hospital population was sharply reduced in the expectation of mass bombing casualties. Many patients were discharged prematurely including 7,500 tubercular patients contributing to the rise in TB death rate in 1940 and 1941. The welcome evacuees received varied from warm responses to resentment that welled-up in the reception areas. Many children had head lice, were inadequately toilet-trained and were just dirty and poorly dressed. Many evacuees swiftly returned to their homes when the expected bombing did not materialise and by January 1940 59 per cent had done so. This process was reversed once the blitz began in the autumn of 1940 and by February 1941, the official number of evacuees rose to 1.39 million. The ending of the blitz saw another return until the V1 and V2 campaign in 1944 and 1945 again pushed the number of evacuees to over a million in September 1944.

During the war two houses in every seven were affected by enemy action. Some 222,000 houses were destroyed or damaged beyond repair with 4.70 million houses sustaining varying degrees of damage, sometimes more than

---

[334] Roodhouse, Mark, *Black Market Britain, 1939-1955*, (Oxford University Press), 2013, pp. 77-113, 195-211.

[335] Süss, Dietman, *Death from the Skies: How the British and Germans Survived Bombing in World War II*, (Oxford University Press), 2014, Gardiner, Juliet, *the Blitz: The British under Attack*, (HarperPress), 2010, MacKay, Robert, *Half the Battle: Civilian Morale during the Second World War*, (Manchester University Press), 2002..

[336] Jackson, Carlton, *Who Will Take our Children? The British Evacuation Program of World War II*, revised ed., (Marfarland), 2008, Mawson, Gillian, *Evacuees: Children's Live on the WW2 Home Front*, (Pen and Sword), 2014.

[337] Mann, Jessica, *Out of Harm's Way: The Wartime Evacuation of Children from Britain*, (Hachette), 2004.

once. Half the destruction or damage occurred in London and this was especially the case in the most blitzed areas such as the docks and the East End. In Bermondsey, for instance, only four houses in every hundred came through the war unscathed. Damage was not confined to London with 127 major raids on UK cities between 7 September 1940 and 16 May 1941 of which 71 were in London. South coast ports such as Plymouth, Portsmouth and Southampton were severely damages with, for instance, up to one in four of Plymouth's houses destroyed or rendered uninhabitable. Air raid shelters provided some protection for the civilian population with Anderson shelters semi-buried in gardens and the Morrison shelter for indoor use. There were public shelters and notably, in London, the underground system was taken over by popular action sheltering up to 177,000 people a night by late-September 1940. During the worst raids, many people trekked from the towns into the surrounding countryside in search of shelter. During the raids on Liverpool in May 1941, perhaps 45,000 headed for the countryside while in Plymouth the numbers leaving reached some 50,000. The effects of bombing were not as bad as government and experts, who had thought in terms of massive casualties, had envisaged in the 1930s. It is estimated that civilian deaths due to the war—largely bombing—were between 60,500 and 62,500 with over 82,000 seriously injured and almost 151,000 slightly injured. It was not until 1942 that the number of civilian deaths was exceeded by loss of life in the Armed Forces and for the whole of the war total British war deaths, including civilians, was 450,000.

The Second World War did not blur the gap between social classes as contemporaries believed but heightened class identity.[338] Workers emerged from the war conscious of their role in saving the nation and convinced that in post-war Britain they were owed a better life and greater opportunities. The 1945 General Election campaign was won, not by the Conservatives who emphasised the heroic role of Churchill in winning the war but by Labour with its stress on inter-war failure and on dealing with poverty, unemployment and social division.

Homes for Heroes

Before 1914, private builders had supplied virtually all new housing in towns and cities. A few philanthropic industrialists, like brothers Hesketh Lever, 1st Viscount Leverhulme (1851-1925) and James Lever (1854-1916) at Port Sunlight and George (1839-1922) and Richard Cadbury (1835-1899) at Bournville created 'model villages' or 'garden suburbs' for their workers. Ebenezer Howard (1850-1928) created a 'garden city' at Letchworth (1903) with green public spaces and social amenities normally only experienced by the prosperous middle classes. The architect Raymond Unwin (1863-1940) had designed houses

---

[338] Field, Geoffrey G., *Blood, Sweat and Toil: The Making the British Working Class 1939-1945*, (Oxford University Press), 2011, pp. 299-335, and more generally, Calder, Angus, *The People's War: Britain 1939-1945*, (Jonathan Cape), 1969.

and green spaces for the 'garden suburb' at Hampstead (1906). Why could such houses and estates not be built for the working class?

Although councils had the power to build houses before 1919, most had had little involvement.[339] Some corporation family housing was provided, mainly in London, Liverpool and Glasgow, often to rehouse those displaced as the result of street improvement schemes. London's local councils had begun to build houses in the 1890s and one of its earliest schemes—the Millbank Estate in Westminster—was completed in 1902. The estate provided affordable rented flats for 4,430 people on a site that had previously been Millbank prison. In other areas, efforts to clear slum areas exceeded house construction effectively reducing the number of low cost housing available. Most pre-1919 corporation housing was built cheaply: high density tenement blocks of flats with small rooms and limited facilities including shared kitchen and toilets and no running hot water. Rents were high that was no comfort to those on low and irregular wages and did not provide housing for the extremely poor. One reason for high rents was that before 1919 no corporation dwellings received subsidy from central government. It was not until after the First World War that housing became a real priority and the view that housing policy could no longer be left to the vagaries of the market was increasingly accepted.[340]

During the war, house building came to a virtual standstill and by 1918 it was clear that the country faced an acute housing shortage. Building costs were inflated and this, combined with a scarcity of materials and labour, made it impossible for the private developers to provide houses with rents within reach of the average working-class family. The close of the war also brought a new social attitude that focused the Government's attention on a national responsibility to provide homes, giving rise to Lloyd George's famous promise of 'homes fit for heroes' for many soldiers returning from the war but also as a means of countering growing industrial and political unrest.[341] The initial response, if the statement in the 1921 Census by James Bartley who lived in one rented room in Hove with his wife and three children under five is an indicator was far from positive:

---

[339] Daunton, M. J., *A Property-owning Democracy? Housing In Britain*, (Faber), 1987, Daunton, M. J., (ed.), *Councillors and tenants: local authority housing in English cities, 1919-1939*, (Leicester University Press), 1984.

[340] Bowley, Marion, *Housing and the State 1919-1944*, (Allen & Unwin), 1945, Colquhoun, Ian, *RIBA Book of British Housing 1900 to the present day*, 2nd ed., (Architectural Press), 2008, pp. 2-10, provides a succinct discussion up to 1951, see also, Lowe, Stuart, *The Housing Crisis*, (The Policy Press), 2011, pp. 53-79. Richardson, H. W., and Aldcroft, D. H., *Building in the British Economy between the Wars*, (Allen & Unwin), 1968.

[341] Orbach, Laurence F., *Home for Heroes: A Study of the Evolution of British Public Housing, 1915-1921*, (Seeley), 1977, Swenarton, M., *Homes Fit for Heroes: the politics and architecture of early state housing in Britain*, (Heinemann), 1981.

'Stop talking about your homes for heroes,' wrote Mr Bartley at the bottom of his form. 'Start building some houses and let them at a rent a working man can afford to pay.'

The Housing and Town Planning Act of 1919 was seen as a watershed in the provision of council housing. The Minister for Health, Dr Christopher Addison (1869-1951),[342] pledged substantial government subsidies to build half a million new homes within three years. In fact, as the economy weakened during the early 1920s, subsidies were cut and by July 1921 when the 'homes for heroes' era ended only around 170,000 houses had been built. The Addison Act was passed initially as a temporary measure to meet the housing needs in the country and at a time when private builders could not meet demand. It was generally assumed that the private sector would resume responsibility for working-class housing once the British economy recovered. Councils were thrust to the forefront and began to plan their post-war housing programmes. Addison Act houses with their generous dimensions, provided a blueprint for the inter-war suburban home making them amongst the most spacious council houses ever developed in Britain. Housing Committees were set up, working largely from recommendations produced by the central government's advisory committee--the Tudor Walters (1866-1933) Committee--and encouraged to build through the provision of generous subsidies. The subsidy arrangements shared the costs of this new housing between the tenants, local rate payers and the Treasury. Councils in areas of high housing need could apply for these subsidies. The London County Council (LCC) also raised money by selling housing bonds that promised investors a 6 per cent return and raised £4 million during the 1920s. Neville Chamberlain's Housing Act of 1923 gave a further subsidy to private builders that led to the building of a further 438,000 houses

The most ambitious estate built to reward soldiers and their families after the war was the massive Becontree estate in Dagenham that was the largest council housing estate in the world.[343] Work by the LCC on the estate started in 1921, farms were compulsorily purchased and by 1932 over 25,000 houses had been built and over 100,000 people had moved to the area. The new houses had gas and electricity, inside toilets, fitted baths and front and back gardens.[344] Access to indoor plumbing and a bathroom had become important markers of working-class respectability while a survey of the Wythenshawe estate in Manchester found that 90 per cent of respondents valued their gardens.[345] The

---

[342] Morgan, Kenneth O., and Morgan, Jane, *Portrait of a Progressive: The Political Career of Christopher, Viscount Addison*, (Oxford University Press), 1980.

[343] Olechnowicz, Andrzej, *Working-class Housing in England between the Wars: The Becontree Estate*, (Oxford University Press), 1997.

[344] Scott, Peter, *The Making of the Modern British Home: The Suburban Semi & Family Life between the Wars*, (Oxford University Press), 2013. On the issue of gardens see Willes, Margaret, *The Gardens of the British Working Class*, (Yale University Press), 2014, pp. 264-317.

[345] Hughes, A., and Hunt, K., 'A culture transformed? Women's lives in Wythenshawe

LCC had strict rules for new tenants on housework, house and garden maintenance, children's behaviour and the keeping of pets. The estate expanded over the Essex parishes of Barking, Dagenham and Ilford with nearly 27,000 homes in total creating a virtual new town with dwellings for over 30,000 families. Most of the new council estates provided superior quality housing for the better-off working-classes but since rents were high, did not provide a solution for the poorer people in society. Migration to suburbia offered both access to the hygienic, semi-rural, residential environment promoted by this new model of working-class respectability and escape from the constraining influence of inner-urban communities. Moving from traditional neighbourhoods to the suburbs often incurred social opprobrium, as it was interpreted as a rejection of community values yet by 1939 about a quarter of non-agricultural working-class families are estimated to have been living on new suburban estates.[346]

Suburban estates were initially communities of strangers lacking the support network of extended families and neighbours of the inner city communities. Owning and displaying prestige goods was a feature of status competition in traditional working-class communities but generally focused around one or a few prized possessions. New suburban working-class respectability involved adopting--or at least projecting to the outside world--a broader 'lifestyle' that encompassed all aspects of noted consumption. This created 'consumption communities', tied together not by background, workplace or religion but by shared material values.[347] It was what was visible or accessible to neighbours that was regarded as most important: the garden, hall and the front room received most attention. The new urban respectability involved a more restrained, less intrusive pattern of neighbourliness summed up in the phrase 'keeping ourselves to ourselves', a preference for greater privacy and private space that, at least in part, explains the move to the suburbs. Neighbourliness became regarded as an activity that occurred outside the home--in gardens, whilst cleaning front paths and sills, at local shops and while taking the children to school. Mutual house visiting was a rarity.[348]

---

in the 1930s', in Davies, A., and Fielding, S., *Worker's Worlds: Cultures and Communities in Manchester and Salford 1880-1939*, (Manchester University Press), 1992, pp. 74-101.

[346] Baines, D., and Johnson, P., 'In search of the 'traditional' working class: social mobility and occupational continuity in interwar London*, Economic History Review*, Vol. 52, (1999), pp. 692-713.

[347] Stone, Duncan, 'Suburbanization and cultural change: the case of club cricket in Surrey, 1870-1939', *Urban History*, Vol. 44, (1), (2017), pp. 44-68.

[348] The findings of Swenarton, M., and Taylor, S., 'The Scale and Nature of the Growth of Owner-Occupation in Britain between the Wars', *Economic History Review*, Vol. 38. (1985), pp. 373-392, that the 1930s' owner-occupation boom was essentially a middle-class phenomenon have been questioned in more recent studies. Speight, G., *Building Society Behaviour and the Mortgage Lending Market in the Interwar Period: Risk-taking by Mutual Institutions and the Interwar Housing Boom*, D. Phil., Thesis, Oxford

Planners promoted the construction of new suburban 'garden' estates, situated on the outskirts of cities.[349] Mainly consisting of three bed semi-detached 'Addison-style' houses for families, the design of the estates aimed to create self-contained communities of low density often with no more than 12 houses per acre based on the standards instituted by the Tudor Walters Committee. Facilities, including churches, schools and shops, were provided; public houses were initially excluded from the plans.[350] On most estates, houses had generous sized gardens to encourage tenants to grow their own vegetables. These new conditions were an improvement on slum housing where tenants had experienced overcrowding and often were without basic facilities. The quality of the housing was generally high. Although some slum clearance took place during the 1920s much of the emphasis at this time was to provide new general needs housing on greenfield sites. The initially high building standards were gradually eroded with the need to reduce construction costs. Passed by the Labour government, the principal objective of the Wheatley Act of 1924–that increased council houses by 520,000–was to secure a continuous building programme for 15 years and to erect houses let at lower rents to meet the needs of lower wage earners. This put pressures to reduce the size and standard of houses and called for new higher density council estates to be developed. For instance, by the late 1920s new municipal three-bedroomed semis were often only 620 square feet compared to over 1,000 square feet in 1919 and were more standardised in construction. Councils rapidly developed a preference for a 'neo-Georgian' styles of plainer houses in near-identical rows as a means of economising on cost, emphasising their municipal identity and widening access to lower income families. Developers of owner-occupier estates provided houses of varied design drawing on English vernacular tradition and producing the 'Tudorbethan' semi as a result.[351]

After this initial burst of building activity targeted at reducing the post-war housing shortage, local councils began to tackle the problem of its slum housing.[352] The Housing Act of 1930, known as the Greenwood Act after the MP Arthur Greenwood (1880-1954) who steered it through Parliament, encouraged slum clearance and councils demolished poor quality slum housing replacing it with new housing. Using powers available under the Act to acquire and demolish

University, 2000, and Crisp, A., *The Working class Owner-occupier House of the 1930s*, M. Lit., Thesis, University of Oxford, 1998, revealed a far greater level of working-class owner-occupiers.

[349] Hollow, Matthew, 'Suburban Ideals on England's Interwar Council Estates', *Garden History*, Vol. 39, (2), (2011), pp. 203-217.

[350] Cole, Emily, *The Urban and Suburban Public House in Inter-War England 1918-1939*, (Historic England), 2015.

[351] Sugg Ryan, Deborah, *Ideal Homes, 1918-1939: Domestic Design and Suburban Modernism*, (Manchester University Press), 2018.

[352] Yelling, J. A., *Slums and Redevelopment: Policy and practice in England 1918-45*, (UCL Press), 1992, focusses on London.

privately owned properties, slum clearance schemes were put into action across the country. By 1933, all authorities had to submit a programme of building and demolition aimed at eliminating their slums. Bristol calculated that it had 25,000 people living in houses unfit for human habitation and proposed the replacement of 5,000 unfit dwellings.[353] Unlike the garden estates built directly after the First World War, much of the slum clearance was replaced with flats, mostly three to five storeys high. They were often modelled on schemes in continental Europe such as the Quarry Hill flats in Leeds that were inspired by a tour the Karl Marx building of workers flats in Vienna.

Local councils tried to rehouse people locally in existing communities but this was confined to relatively small schemes and most new houses were built on estates located on the fringes of the cities. This was a combination of central policy and the excessive cost of inner city land. New tenants had to weigh up the disadvantage of longer journeys to work and sense of isolation against the benefits of new well-equipped homes.[354] Rents were generally lower than for earlier schemes built under the 1919 Housing Act. Despite this and a general commitment to house those in most need, in practice the ability to pay the rent played a crucial factor in allocation. Tenancy conditions were strict and regulations were enforced from the start and some tenants were put off by the oppressive housing management. In Liverpool, for instance, women housing managers were employed to inspect properties and instruct tenants on good housekeeping.

The extent to which inter-war building reducing the housing problem that existed in 1914 is uncertain. There is broad agreement that by 1931 the problem was much worse than it had been in 1914. In the 1930s, the shortfall was reduced and by 1938, there were an extra 1.68 million families in the UK since 1931 and an extra 2.59 million houses had been built. Compared to 1914, the absolute shortage had either been reduced or was somewhat worse depending on which estimate of previous shortage is applied. Rent control had been introduced in 1915–following a successful rent strike largely by working-class women in Glasgow against attempts by landlords to raise rents by a quarter- -and restricted rents to their August 1914 levels. The greatest shortage was for cheap rentable housing after 1918 and this was one reason rent controls were retained after the war ended. By 1937, rent controls had been largely withdrawn from more expensive properties but still covered 44.1 per cent of houses in Britain.[355]

The outbreak of war in 1939 again put a stop to house building but by 1945 Britain faced its worst housing shortage of the twentieth century.

---

[353] Jevons, Rosamund, and John, Madge, *Housing Estates: A Study of Bristol Corporation Policy and Practice between the Wars*, (Arrowsmith), 1946.

[354] 'Suburban Neurosis up to Date', *The Lancet*, 18 January 1958, pp. 146-147.

[355] Marshall, J. H., 'The Pattern of Housebuilding in the Inter-war Period in England and Wales', *Scottish Journal of Political Economy*, Vol. 15, (1968), pp. 184-203.

Thousands of houses had been lost by heavy bombing and many more were irreparably damaged. It was estimated that 750,000 new homes were required in England and Wales in 1945 to provide all families with accommodation. Plans were drawn up for a major building programme and housing policy was central to their welfare reforms in the Labour manifesto that underpinned its landslide victory in the 1945 election.[356] Aneurin Bevan (1897-1960), the Minister of Health, was responsible for the housing programme that focused heavily on local authority involvement rather than reliance of the private sector. In 1944, Churchill announced the 'Temporary Housing Programme' that aimed to provide large numbers of houses quickly and economically. Part of the initial response was a programme of short-term repairs to existing properties and the rapid construction of 'prefabs', factory-built single storey bungalows. The first prefabs were completed June 1945 only weeks after the war ended. Although they were intended as a temporary measure to last no more than ten years, they proved popular with residents and some still remain as residential properties. Unlike traditional houses they had fully fitted kitchens and bathrooms. Despite the construction of 156,622 prefabs the country still faced an acute housing shortage and waiting lists soared in urban areas.[357]

A New Towns Committee created government-sponsored corporations in 1945 that were given power to acquire land to establish new towns and the New Towns Act passed the following year provided the government with the power to implement these plans. The result was the creation of 22 new towns between 1946 and 1972, many serving as satellite towns to Greater London. Local authority house building resumed in 1946 and of the 2.5 million new houses and flats built up to 1957, 7 per cent were local authority owned. Council-house building peaked under the Conservative government of the 1950s, when the end of rationing and a growing economy meant that 250,000 new local authority homes a year were being put up. By 1951, local authorities accommodated a quarter of the population in council housing compared to 10 per cent in 1938. The gradual clearance of inner-city slums meant that architects and city planners were able to put into practice modernist theories on urban design. 'Streets in the sky' was the term used to describe the new tower blocks that were built during the 1950s and 1960s that sought to encourage a sense of local community with mixed estates of low and high-rise building with mixed results.[358]

Unemployment between the wars

---

[356] Bullock, Nicholas, *Building the Post-War World: Modern architecture and reconstruction in Britain*, (Routledge), 2002.

[357] Vale, Brenda, *Prefabs: A history of the UK Temporary Housing Programme*, (Routledge), 2003.

[358] Malpass, Paul, *Housing and the Welfare State: The Development of Housing Policy since 1945*, (Macmillan), 2005, Balchin, Paul, 'Housing', in Cullingworth, Barry, (ed.), *British Planning: 50 Years of Urban and Regional Policy*, (Athlone Press), 1999, pp. 14-30, provides a succinct summary.

The inter-war years were dominated by unemployment that affected women as well as men. In many cases, the man was the sole breadwinner so that when he lost his job the whole family suffered. Women were forced to 'make ends meet' either by maintaining the home on a limited budget or, if they were fortunate, by seeking often poorly paid work in domestic service or in retail as shop assistants. Unemployment led to poverty that affected the physical and mental health of those who suffered from its effects. Services continued to be introduced outside the Poor Law including the 'means test', initially intended to offer out-relief without the stigma of pauperism but it became as hated as the Poor Law itself. [359]

During the 1920s, unemployment varied between 10.6 and 12.7 per cent of the insured labour force, averaging 11.3 per cent between 1923 and 1929. Feinstein estimates that the proportion of all unemployed workers in the economy was 8.4 per cent meaning that unemployment was about a third higher than before 1914. From 1918 to 1921, means-tested 'out-of work donations', originally meant for ex-servicemen, were extended to unemployed people. Mindful of the Russian Revolution, the government feared popular violence if nothing was done to cope with unemployment associated with demobilising military forces. It set two important precedents. It offered benefits of 24s for an adult man and 20s for a women, a level higher than that offered by the National Insurance Act 1911. It also, for the first time, offered allowances for dependents: 6s for the first child and 3s for the others. These principles were enshrined in the Unemployment Insurance Act passed in August 1920. It shielded all manual workers and other employees earning less than £250 a year but did not cover the whole workforce as employers and the self-employed were excluded as were farm workers until 1936, private domestic service, the public sector, the railways and military service. The benefit rates were higher than in the 1911 Act rising from 7s to 15s for men and 7s to 12s for women with dependents' allowances.

The problem with the insurance scheme in the 1920s was that, because of the important levels of unemployment, it could not prevent the needy having recourse to the Poor Law. Successive government grappled with this issue. The Labour government introduced 'extended benefits' in 1924 and three years later the Conservatives brought in 'transitional' payments for up to a year for the unemployed. In 1922, 1.9 million people were in receipt of relief though this fell to 1.5 million in 1924. Most of this was 'outdoor' with the workhouse population fluctuating between 200,000 and 300,000. The rise in relief placed pressure on local government finances. Between 1911 and 1914, Poor Law spending averaged £16.4 million a year including £2.7 million from central government but between 1921 and 1925, the figures were £40.6 million and £3.1 million. Poor rates rose significantly as a result. In 1929-1930, a survey in

---

[359] Constantine, Stephen, *Unemployment in Britain between the Wars*, (Routledge), 2013, Garside, W. R., *British Unemployment 1919-1939: A Study in Public Policy*, (Cambridge University Press), 2002.

London found that about 10 per cent of its population were living at subsistence levels.

From 1930, one of the major effects of the global slump in trade and industrial production was the massive rise in unemployment.[360] By 1933, world unemployment topped 30 million people including some 3 million people in Britain. The worst hit areas in Britain were those still dependent on the old heavy industries especially in south Wales and in the north-east of England. In 1938, the unemployment rate in coal, cotton, shipbuilding and steel was twice other forms of work. The government responded to the crisis by trying to cut costs beginning with the benefits paid to the unemployed. A man without work was entitled to benefit or dole under the unemployment insurance scheme for the first six months. However, in order to qualify for dole, a worker had to pass a means test that was introduced in 1931. Public Assistance Committees were created to investigate a family's finances thoroughly before benefits could be given. The intrusiveness of means tests and the insensitive manner adopted by some officials who carried them out offended many people. The usual rate for the dole was 15s per week for man and wife and about 5s for each child. The British Medical Association estimated that a family of two adults and three children needed at least 22s 7d for food for a week.

The Depression caused a major political crisis in 1931. Labour's grip on power, never sure after it won the most seats but no majority in May 1929, began to falter in early 1931 as the economy weakened.[361] By August 1931, its Parliamentary position was becoming increasingly unsure amid calls for spending cuts and the growing cost of rapidly rising unemployment. That put pressure not just on the budget but on the pound, expensively reattached to the Gold Standard by Winston Churchill (1874-1965) in 1925. The day before the summer recess, an 'economy committee' chaired by Sir George May (1871-1946), a city businessman reported Britain faced a £120m deficit: the country, his report implied, might not be able to pay its way. In retrospect, this was an exaggeration, but at the time the May Committee--established in February 1931 under cross-party pressure--was treated as an unquestionable authority. The reaction to it brought down the government.[362] On August 13 Ramsay MacDonald (1866-1937) met the Conservative leaders Stanley Baldwin (1867-1947) and Neville Chamberlain (1869-1940), to discuss the position. A week later leading politicians from all parties met again to hear MacDonald promise that Britain would balance the budget. Spending cuts would help bridge the gap, including salary cuts for teachers and the police. This was not what most Labour

[360] Stevenson, John, and Cook, Chris, The Slump: Britain in the Great Depression, 3rd ed., (Routledge), 2014, pp. 40-109, 183-211, Pugh, Martin, We Danced All Night: A Social History of Britain between the Wars, (Vintage), 2009, pp. 76-101.
[361] Riddell, Neil, Labour in Crisis: The second Labour government, 1929-31, (Manchester University Press), 1999.
[362] Smart, Nick, The National Government, 1931-40, (Macmillan), 1999.

MPs or ministers believed they had been elected to do. On 23 August, the Cabinet met but balked at cutting unemployment benefit and the government collapsed. On 24 August, MacDonald agreed to the creation of a National Government composed of men from all parties with the specific aim of balancing the Budget and restoring confidence. All but 14 Labour MPs refused to stand by MacDonald and went into opposition. On 10 September, the government raised taxes and cut spending and 10 days later took Britain off the Gold Standard. With widespread media and public acclaim for its handling of the crisis, MacDonald asked the King to dissolve Parliament on 6 October. The General Election held on 27 October confirmed the position of the new government with the National government taking 554 seats with the Labour Party reduced to 52.[363]

The vast majority of people in traditional industrial areas could not easily escape the Depression. The government's apparent inability to deal with the Depression convinced many people that there was no alternative but to protest. A mass demonstration with popular support and maximum publicity might force the government into positive action. Thousands of people became involved in resisting the Depression and protesting against its effects and the continuing unemployment and hardship. During the 1930s, as well as local protests, there were also many protest marches from the north-east of England and south Wales.[364] The people living in these areas were becoming more militant because they had been experiencing high levels of unemployment, poverty, malnutrition and disease for some time. The government seemed incapable of dealing with the problems or, at worst, appeared to be indifferent to the plight of the poor. Protesting in the areas where they lived appeared to have insignificant impact on the government, so it was decided to widen the protest. Marches to London were organised to confront the government and, in so doing, gain much needed publicity. It was hoped that the media would be encouraged to report their story and highlight their plight. In October 1932, there was a large-scale march on London by 2,500 workers from all over the country. Trade unionists played a leading role in organising the march and in arranging food and shelter for the marchers. They presented a petition to Parliament demanding the abolition of the means test and protesting about the 10 per cent cut in benefits. Perhaps the most famous protest march was the Jarrow Crusade of 1936, but there were also marches from south Wales.[365] Most demanded government action to create jobs and better benefits for the unemployed.

Historians are divided about the impact of these protest marches. Even

[363] Thorpe, Andrew, *The British General Election of 1931*, (Oxford University Press), 1991.
[364] Ward, Stephanie, *Unemployment and the State in Britain: The means test and protest in 1930s south Wales and north-east England*, (Manchester University Press), 2013, pp. 33-64, 116-159.
[365] Perry, Matt, *The Jarrow Crusade: Protest and Legend*, (University of Sunderland Press), 2005.

contemporaries were mixed in their opinions about the effectiveness of these marches. As the newspaper feared, some ministers in the government were less than impressed with the marches. Historian A. J. P. Taylor (1906-1990) offered a more balanced evaluation of the effectiveness of the hunger marches and the march for jobs:

> Select bands of unemployed from the depressed areas marched on London, where they demonstrated to little purpose. Their progress through the country, however, was a propaganda stroke of great effect. The hunger marchers displayed the failure of capitalism. Middle-class people felt the call of conscience. They set up soup-kitchens for the marchers and accommodated them in local schools.[366]

As unemployment continued to rise, the government was faced with a new problem: what to do about people who had been unemployed for more than six months and had used up their dole. The government passed the Unemployment Act of 1934 that set up two bodies: the Unemployment Insurance Statutory Committee to deal with benefits earned by paying National Insurance when in work; and the Unemployment Assistance Board (UAB) to provide means-tested payments for the long-term unemployed for workers who had exhausted their insurance benefits.

From 1936, the UAB set up training schemes and provided help to workers who wanted to move to another area to find work. It also took over some of the work of the Labour Exchanges and continued to administer the dole and means test. UAB officials were often less severe than officials from the Public Assistance Committees, although reports from the Trades Union Congress show that there was still a great deal of discontent with the low levels of benefit. How those 'desperately in need' were defined varied from area to area with some UABs applying the means test more rigorously than others. To solve this apparent inequality, the government decided that unemployment benefit rates would be set nationally rather than locally. In addition, the 1934 Unemployment Act separated dole and insurance benefits and the 10 per cent cut in dole was reversed. In 1940, the UAB became the Assistance Board responsible for paying a supplement to those on a fixed income that was inadequate to subsistence. According to Richard Titmuss (1907-1973), an average of 150 Britons died every day between 1928 and 1938 as a result of malnutrition and fear of being thrown on the economic scrapheap haunted even the suburban bourgeoisie.

Given that unemployment was *the* problem of the inter-war years, it is remarkable that government made no real attempt to investigate its social consequences and it was not until the late 1930s that the serious government investigations began to appear. The furthest it went was to examine the

---

[366] Taylor, A. J. P., *English History 1914–1945*, (Oxford University Press), 1965, p. 349.

distribution of industrial population in the Barlow Report in 1938 and various reports of the Ministry of Labour on industrial conditions.[367] Almost all the work on social conditions was conducted by voluntary groups or on the initiative of individuals or publishers. In the interim, a literary genre dealing with the problems of unemployment and depression made its appearance. Walter Greenwood's (1903-1974) *Love on the Dole*, a novel set in depression-scarred south Lancashire, Ellen Wilkinson's (1891-1947) *The Town That Was Murdered* about Jarrow and George Orwell's (1903-1950) *The Road to Wigan Pier* are the most famous. These books formed one part of a generally left-wing attack on the performance of the National Government, the other was on appeasement of the European dictators. It is not surprising that the outpouring of 'dole literature' as it was called was not always well received. Arthur Bryant (1899-1985), the historian was extremely critical of Orwell's classic in his preface to an autobiography of G. A. W. Tomlinson, a coal-miner:

> *The Road to Wigan Pier*...was written by a young man of refined tastes who at some apparent inconvenience to himself had 'roughed it' for a few weeks in Wigan and Sheffield...The weakness of the argument lies in the fact that revolutionary change...involves not only a blood-bath...but the loss of individual freedom of choice and the end of democratic government: the experience of Russia and Spain proves this. But there is an even more fatal weakness in his premises, for though Wigan and Sheffield may genuinely seem Hell to a super-sensitive novelist, they do not seem Hell to the vast majority of people who live there.[368]

A comparison of the rhetoric of extremism of both left and right in the 1930s and the actual numerical basis of support for extremism shows the validity of this conclusion. It is interesting that much of the 'dole literature' dates from the mid-to late-1930s–Orwell is no exception here–when the worst of the depression was over. This had also been the case in the 1840s: the 'social industrial' novels of Benjamin Disraeli (1804-1881), Charles Kingsley (1819-1875), Elizabeth Gaskell (1810-1865) and Charles Dickens (1812-1870) were published after 1845. What 'dole literature' did was to add an important dimension to study of social problems. But it reached a much wider audience than the more scientific and more impartial studies of academic investigators and in that sense, did more than any other single source to shape our perceptions of the 'Hungry Thirties' or what Taylor called 'the Devil's Decade'.

This all changed with the publication of *The Road to Wigan Pier* on 8 March 1937. Orwell had an established pedigree in portraying poverty and his vivid autobiographical account of his days among the poor of Paris and London,

---

[367] The question of 'dole literature' is discussed in my 'Orwell, Unemployment and 1984', in Brown, Richard, *People and Places: Britain 1780-1950*, (Authoring History), 2017, pp. 135-152.

[368] Preface to Tomlinson, G. A. W., *Coal Miner*, (Hutchinson and Co. Ltd.), 1937, pp. 10-11.

published as *Down and Out in Paris and London* in 1933 as well as articles in *The Adelphi*, the unofficial voice of the Independent Labour Party. For Victor Gollancz (1893-1967), publisher and noted supporter of left-wing causes, who had decided to commission a writer to spend some time in the north of England, Orwell was an obvious choice. He began the book by letting his audience of mostly southern intellectuals believe that he agrees with them. There is a cult of northernness, he writes, in which: 'you and I and everyone else in the south of England' is written off as snobbish, effete, and lazy. By contrast the northerner sees himself as gritty, warm-hearted, and democratic. Yorkshiremen secretly believe all other peoples to be inferior whereas they belong to a 'rather uncouth tribe.' In the 1930s, the major barrier to people acting on behalf of the unemployed and the deprived was sheer ignorance. Unemployment was geographically concentrated in areas of heavy industry and this disguised the enormity of the problem. Orwell's writings helped to bring this into the open and gave detail lacking in official statements. It is his perception of the debilitating effects of unemployment and his response to government inaction that is most valuable. Orwell was at his most powerful when describing the hated 'means test':

> The most cruel and evil effect of the Means Test is the way in which it breaks upon families...There is no doubt about the deadening, debilitating effect of unemployment upon everybody, married or single and upon men more than women...how the devil is he to fill up his empty days?[369]

Orwell concluded that the thirties opened with unemployment as a social problem and it was not until it was politicised and the alternative Keynesian view that favoured government spending during a recession took root that anything positive could really be done. The classical policy of budgetary control and retrenchment led government to be concerned not with removing the problem of unemployment but only with mitigating its effects through unemployment relief. In response to occupation centres, Orwell said: 'Keep a man busy mending boots and he is less likely to read the *Daily Worker*' and 'Twenty million people are underfed but literally everyone has access to the radio...It is quite likely that fish and chips, art-silk stocking, tinned salmon, cut-price chocolate, the movies, the radio, strong tea and the Football Pools have between them averted revolution.'

The social conditions that Orwell described and the existence of poverty and unemployment became the relevant evidence in the political debate that was to have profound consequences for the post-war world. He contributed but one dimension to this debate that was accentuated by the outbreak of war in 1939. His belief in 'social justice' was echoed in the *Beveridge Report* of 1942, in the Butler Education Act of 1944 and in Archbishop William Temple's (1881-1944)

---

[369] Ibid., Orwell, George, *The Road to Wigan Pier*, pp. 147-148.

126

Christianity and the Social Order with its arguments for minimum social standards acceptable in a Christian community. The Welfare State was a logical consequence of Orwell's writing and the present debate on the role of the state in welfare provision makes his ideas doubly important. Seebohm Rowntree (1871-1954) concluded his *The Human Needs of Labour* with the prophetic statement:

> I submit that the day is past in which we could afford to compromise between the desires of the few and the needs of the many or to perpetuate conditions in which large masses of the people are unable to secure the bare necessities of mental and physical efficiency.[370]

Women and work 1914-1945

The First World War was the nation's first experience of 'total war' impacting on the lives of everybody in society, not simply those directly involved in the fighting.[371] There were changes in diet and habits resulting from food rationing and government propaganda and controls were more extensive than in pre-war society.[372] Many upper- and middle-class women experienced taking up paid employment for the first time. Many more kept things going at home in their traditional role as morale-builders. There was widespread sense of loss with the death of family and friends and the emotional trauma suffered by many men who were forced into uniform because of conscription. The social, cultural and emotional impact of the war was such that it has led some historians to argue that the period after 1918 witnessed a fundamental realignment of moral and social attitudes.

The nature and extent of women's manual work had been a matter of considerable debate before 1914.[373] The 1911 Census recorded that about one-third of all women were doing some paid work though these figures under-record informal work and unemployment. Campaigns on the issue of women's employment were important in informing opinion about women's waged work. Society needed fit mothers and children and was seen as a major consideration in regulating employment or wages emphasising the social determinants of women's work. These arguments are evident in the views of women's trade

---

[370] Rowntree, B. Seebohm, *The Human Needs of Labour*, (Thomas Nelson and Sons), 1918, pp. 81-82.

[371] Wall, Richard, and Winter, Jay, (eds.), *The Upheaval of War: Family, Work and Welfare in Europe, 1914-1918*, (Cambridge University Press), 1988, is a valuable comparative collection of essays.

[372] Dewey, Peter, 'Nutrition and living standards in wartime Britain', in Ibid., Wall, Richard, and Winter, Jay, (eds.), *The Upheaval of War: Family, Work and Welfare in Europe, 1914-1918*, pp. 197-220.

[373] Molinari, Véronique, 'Le droit de vote accordé aux femmes britanniques à l'issue de la Première Guerre mondiale: une récompense pour les services rendus?', *La revue LISA*, Vol. 6, (4), (2008), pp. 71-87.

unions. The image of women's work was based on their concentration in the low skill-low pay 'sweated trades' in which married women were often the main breadwinners especially in areas where male unemployment was high. This was not, as contemporary newspapers reported, about earning 'pin-money'. A Fabian Women's Group survey found one-third of all women workers were supporting dependants, reflecting life in areas of high levels of female work such as in Lancashire, Belfast and Dundee but also demonstrated the connection between women's work and low wages, one of the reasons for male hostility to women in the workplace.[374] This view was strengthened by public discussion of gender buttressing the notion that women were inherently deficient as workers because they were physically weaker, lacked a tradition of work and were inhibited by family responsibilities.[375]

The need to involve women in war work and in auxiliary military services forced society to confront beliefs about the traditional roles of women. Although the government encouraged women to take on previously 'masculine' tasks, it did not seek to undermine the traditional ideal of women's 'true' vocations in homemaking and mothering. Women were both celebrated as heroines for taking on non-traditional 'war work' but also criticised for having loose morals as a result of doing so. The problem was that with male breadwinners away at the front or dead, women were forced by economic conditions to work to support their families but they were also condemned for abandoning their proper roles as mothers and homemakers. Moving women into the work-force was not easy and contemporary debates reflected concerns that women were taking on roles defined as masculine and were often accused of taking men's jobs whilst they were serving their country.[376]

How many women workers who entered new jobs during the war were replacing men? Propaganda gave a misleading impression that women replaced

---

[374] Morley, Edith, (ed.), *Women Workers in Seven Professions: A Survey of their Economic Conditions and Prospects*, (Routledge), 1914, *The War, Women and Unemployment*, Fabian Tract 178, March 1915, printed in ibid., Alexander, Sally, (ed.), *Women's Fabian Tracts*, pp. 283-312, and *Wage-earning women and their dependants by Ellen Smith on behalf of the Executive Committee of the Fabian Women's Group*, November 1915.

[375] See, Reid, Alastair, 'The impact of the First World War on British workers', and Thom, Deborah, 'Women and work in wartime Britain', in ibid., Wall, Richard, and Winter, Jay, (eds.), *The Upheaval of War: Family, Work and Welfare in Europe, 1914-1918*, pp. 221-234, 297-326.

[376] Marwick, Arthur, *Women at war*, (Fontana), 1977, is both well written and well-illustrated. Braybon, Gail, *Women workers in the First World War*, (Routledge), 2nd ed., 1989, looks in greater detail at industrial workers. Twinch, Carol, *Women on the land: their story during two world wars*, (Lutterworth Press), 1990, considers the agrarian dimension. See also, Woollacott, Angela. *On Her Their Lives Depend: Munitions Workers in the First World War*, (University of California Press), 1994, pp. 17-58, 188-216, and ibid., Grayzel, Susan R., *Women in the First World War*, pp. 27-50, 106-111.

men in factories wholesale.[377] Initially women increased their share of the adult workforce in clerical and commercial occupations. By 1915, textile production had begun to recover and more women were taken on as manufacturing diversified into serge and khaki. Between 1914 and 1918, an estimated two million women replaced men in employment and the total number of women employed during the war rose from 3.28 million in 1914 to 4.94 million by 1918: the percentage of women in the British workforce increased from 23.6 to 37.7 per cent between 1914 and 1918.[378] Thom, however, suggests that the figure was 46.7 per cent by the end of the war, a difference explained by whether England and Wales or the whole of Britain is being considered and which categories of employment are included in the calculations.[379] Some changes were particularly striking. By November 1918, 947,000 women were employed in the munitions industry, unpleasant and potentially dangerous work in which more than 300 women lost their lives because of TNT poisoning and explosions.[380] Just 2,000 women had been employed in government dockyards, factories and arsenals in July 1914, but by November 1918, this figure had risen to 247,000. Those employed in metalworking rose from 170,000 to 594,000, in transport from 18,200 to 117,200 and in commerce from 505,200 to 934,000.

The Women's Land Army evolved from a disparate group of training and educational programmes into a national effort to organise women for home food production. Between managing the overstated propaganda expectations for women farm workers and combating public fears about the unwomanly activities of Land Girls, organisers successfully recruited, trained and placed thousands of women on British farms and helped feed the nation during the turbulent years of 1917 to 1919.[381] In national and local government, the number of female employees rose from 262,000 to 460,000. In August 1914, there were 66 women clerks in the Bank of England whose role was confined to typing and counting notes. As a result of the enlistment of many of the Bank's junior male clerks, the number of temporary and permanent women clerks increased to a peak of 2,463 in June 1919 and many had greater responsibility. At the same time as the

---

[377] Ibid., Braybon, Gail, *Women workers in the First World War*, pp. 154-172, on women's public image.

[378] Kirkaldy, A. W., (ed.), *British labour replacement & conciliation 1914-21*, (I. Pitman), 1921, Table XIII.

[379] Thom, Deborah, 'Women and work in wartime Britain', in Ibid., Wall, Richard, and Winter, Jay, (eds.), *The Upheaval of War: Family, Work and Welfare in Europe, 1914-1918*, p. 306.

[380] Ibid., Woollacott, Angela, *On Her Their Lives Depend: Munition Workers in the Great War,* and Thom, Deborah, "A Revolution in the Workplace'? Women's Work in Munitions Factories and Technological Change, 1914-1918', in Groot, Gertjan de, and Schrover, Mariou, (eds.), *Women workers and technological change in Europe in the nineteenth and twentieth centuries,* (Taylor and Francis), 1995, pp. 97-118.

[381] White, Bonnie, *The Women's Land Army in the First World War*, (Palgrave Macmillan), 2014.

number of women in munitions and factories went up, the numbers working in 'traditional' areas of female employment such as domestic service and the clothing trade declined.

After 1918, the sexual division of labour again became a source of friction. The press had already begun to lose its enthusiasm for women workers who were being urged to surrender their jobs to returning soldiers. Employers who had praised female docility, eagerness and dexterity in 1916 were by 1918 deploring their poor time-keeping, lack of commitment to work and low productivity. Legislation was passed including the Sex Disqualification (Removal) Act in 1919 that made it illegal to exclude women from jobs because of their gender. The Act was often ignored and women were excluded from certain professions on marriage. This improved opportunities for middle-class women such as the right to enter the legal profession and to obtain degrees in Cambridge and Oxford on the same terms as men. The Restoration of Pre-War Practices Act 1919 forced most working-class women to leave their wartime roles as men came home and factories switched to peacetime production. 750,000 women were made redundant in 1919. Munition workers were given two weeks' pay in lieu of notice and a train fare home. By the 1920s, it was clear that there had not been a fundamental revision of the role of the sexes and women, especially older married women, were increasingly excluded from employment by the combined actions of employers, government and male-dominated trade unions.[382]

More than 700,000 British men—15 per cent of the male population aged 15-29 in 1911—were killed during the First World War, a tragic loss of life affected the lives of women in the 1920s and 1930s.[383] War deaths resulted in gender imbalance particularly between the male and female populations of people aged 25 to 34 and in the 1921 Census there were 1,158,000 unmarried women and 919,000 unmarried men.[384] Ten years later, half of the women who were 25 to 29 years old in 1921 remained unmarried. Although the results of the 1921 Census were sensationalised in both the national and provincial press by using terms such as 'surplus' and 'superfluous' women, the imbalance of Britain's population was not new.[385] In the 1851 Census, 30 per cent of English

---

[382] Beddoe, Dierdre, *Back to Home and Duty: Women between the wars 1918-1939*, (Pandora), 1989.

[383] Nicholson, Virginia, *Singled Out: How Two Million Women Survived Without Men after the First World War*, (Penguin), 2008, pp. 13-33, Holden, Katherine, *The Shadow of Marriage: Singleness in England, 1914-60*, (Manchester University Press), 2007, pp. 11-29, Todd, Selina, *Young Women, Work and Family in England 1918-1950*, (Oxford University Press), 2005.

[384] 'Britain's Surplus of Women', *Hull Daily Mail*, 23 May 1921, p. 3.

[385] 'Many Old Maids in Birmingham', *Evening Telegraph*, 30 August 1921, p. 3, is symptomatic of the attitude taken in the press in its article headings; the article itself simply reported the conclusions from the Census reports though its conclusion that 'Probably there would have been no ordinary pronounced disparity had the war not

women aged 20 to 40 were unmarried and the imbalance of men and women continued into the early-twentieth century.

The general economic and international situation worked against women's rights between the wars. Successive governments implicitly oppose women's involvement in the working industrial process, maintaining that if married females earned money, they deprived men and unmarried females of the opportunity to earn their living. With unemployment never falling below a million and peaking at three million in 1933, many employers, politicians, trade unionists and married women saw women workers as a threat to men's employment and blamed them for down-grading working conditions and pay. An example of attitudes can be found in a household entry from Leeds in the 1921 Census:

It is disgusting that unemployed ex-servicemen should be deprived of Government work by appointing women enumerators and an insult to send these women to ex-soldiers' houses with Census papers.

The householder Edwin Taber put 'House Duties' as the 'occupation' of his wife. Women were also divided, with single and widowed women claiming a right to employment over married women. For instance, Isobel M. Pazzey of Woolwich reflected a widely-held view when she wrote to the *Daily Herald* in October 1919:

No decent man would allow his wife to work, and no decent woman would do it if she knew the harm she was doing to the widows and single girls who are looking for work...Put the married women out, send them home to clean their houses and look after the man they married and give a mother's care to their children. Give the single women and widows the work.

It was a source of concern for those who felt that middle-class women were not contributing their share to the renewal of the population and should be encouraged to stay at home and have more children. In December 1919, the Glamorgan Education Committee proposed that married women teachers be given three months' notice.[386] The idea quickly caught on and by the mid-1920s, the marriage bar was widespread in teaching, administration and the Civil Service and there were also unofficial marriage bars in some commercial companies where women had to resign upon marriage. In some occupations, single women insisted on excluding their married sisters. In 1921, female civil servants passed a resolution calling for the banning of married women from their jobs. This was enforced in teaching until 1944 and in the civil service until 1946.

Waged women's employment in the inter-war years was shaped by sex-typing and segregation.[387] Women were seen to be fitted to certain types of work,

---

occurred' is questionable.

[386] 'Glamorgan's Married Teachers Must Go', *Llais Lafur*, 6 December 1919, p. 1.

often routine, usually lower paid, and in areas where their feminine and maternal natures could best be utilised. The proportion of single and married women in the workforce rose during the 1930s as new industries provided new opportunities. Increasing numbers of women worked in light assembly-line industries and in clerical and service work. On average, a woman working in industry was likely to be paid less than half what a man would be paid and in some industries, less than a third. During the inter-war years, women made inroads into all public occupations but despite this they were to remain a reproductive rather than a productive force and their employment options were constrained and regulated as part of a process that narrowed their prospects outside motherhood. Between 1931 and 1939, the overall number of employed women dropped by over a million. The working woman was not supported by many in society, politicians or the unions that saw them as a threat to male employment and also not by a significant number of other women.

From 1940 to 1945, Ernest Bevin (1881-1951), Minister of Labour was responsible for Britain's manpower resources. He introduced the Essential Work Order (EWO) that became law in March 1941 tying workers to jobs considered essential for the war effort and prevented employers from sacking workers without permission from the Ministry of Labour. The large rise in the numbers of women in paid employment during the war was not achieved by voluntary means alone. Uniquely, the wartime Coalition Government went further than any other state in the world in enforcing the mobilisation of women, principally for munitions work. From March 1941, it became compulsory for women aged between 19 and 40 to register at Labour Exchanges for war work and by 1943 the upper age limit was 50.[388] Conscription of women began in December following the National Service (Number Two) Act.[389] Unmarried 'mobile' women between the ages of 20 and 30 were called in up and given a choice between joining the services or working in industry. Pregnant women, those who had a child under the age of 14 or women with heavy domestic responsibilities could not be made to do war work, but they could volunteer. 'Immobile' women, who had a husband at home or were married to a serviceman, were directed into local war work. In practice, many women with dependent children were forced to work for financial reasons, as separation

---

[387] Walby, Sylvia, *Patriarchy at Work: Patriarchal and Capitalist Relations in Employment*, (Polity Press), 1986, Lewis, Jane, *Women in England 1870-1950: Sexual Divisions and Social Change*, (Wheatsheaf Books), 1984, Hakim, Catherine, *Key Issues in Women's Work: Female Heterogeneity and the Polarisation of Women's Employment*, (Athlone), 1996, and Bradley, Harriet, *Men's Work, Women's Work: A Sociological History of the Sexual Division of Labour in Employment*, (Polity Press), 1989.

[388] Summerskill, Edith, 'Conscription and Women', *The Fortnightly Review*, Vol. 151, (1942), pp. 209-214.

[389] *Hansard*, House of Commons, Debates, 9 December 1941, Vol. 376, cc1412-1500, 11 December 1941, Vol. 376, cc1718-1792.

allowances paid to service families were inadequate. By 1943, 7.25 million women were in paid work with 8 per cent of married women and 90 per cent of single women contributing to the war effort, a rise of over two million from the pre-war figures.

Despite the wartime message of acceptable participation, post-war magazines encouraged the female labour force back into their traditional domestic roles. They fully supported the pro-natalist policies of the Labour government after 1945, worried by the 1944 Royal Commission on Population and the 1946 *Survey of Childbearing in Great Britain*, but also increased the public discussion about companionate marriage Although magazines made their own editorial decisions, recent work suggests that they promoted a largely monolithic view of the role of women, especially the young wife and mother in the post-1945 period.[390]

Conclusions

How people see themselves and how they are seen by others is an issue of great complexity. It has many dimensions–for instance, cultural, ethnic, historical, geographical, political and religious–and many layers: individual, family, community, civic, as well as regional and national. Identity is personal but usually involves a sense of belonging to a community or a place leading to a geographical identity that is, for most people, very local. People may relate to their street, estate or village more than their district, town or city, but they may include all of these things. Regions and nations are created by states through nationalism. Although political and official boundaries are important, boundaries recognised and understood by people are more significant in personal and community identity. Community and national identities are supported by group myths or national stories that perpetuate their own versions of history.[391] Class determined the life opportunities and choices available to the individual and was constructed through the operation of the market. Language, whether political or not, shaped experiences and helped govern possible actions. It was not just a product of wider social forces; it helped to create them by determining the range of possibilities available at any given time.

Workers identified themselves in terms of a common class but there were other concepts that played a significant, perhaps more important, role. 'Skill' and 'status' were crucial concepts for male workers and the retention of skilled status was an ideal to which all workers aspired. 'Work' was defined narrowly and took little account of unpaid housework. 'Community' increasingly

---

[390] Szreter, Simon, *Fertility, class and gender in Britain 1860-1940*, (Cambridge University Press), 1996, pp. 503-525.

[391] Briggs, Asa, 'The Sense of Place', in *The Fitness of Man's Environment, Smithsonian Annual*, Vol. 2, (Harper and Row), 1968, pp. 78-97, and completely rewritten for *The Collected Essays of Asa Briggs, Volume One: Words, Numbers, Places and People*, (Harvester Press), 1985, pp. 87-105.

supplemented kin as the crucial welfare network for the urban working-classes. Settled and stable, especially after the 1850s, most envisaged a future spent within the narrow confines of the town or city in which they had been brought up, secure in the protection of the customs and mores of a particular district. The idea of community was portable property as much as furniture and clothes and it was transported with emigrants and recreated in and modified by white-settler societies. Contacts with home were nurtured through links between the burgeoning colonial press and British newspapers. There were Caledonian, Hibernian and Welsh societies, churches and eisteddfods and newspapers across the empire through which people voiced their own nationalities. Communities were not simply defined in territorial terms but often by the experience of social interaction among those of similar attitudes, beliefs and interests. The community combined pubs, churches, chapels, co-ops and various special interest groups that were locality-based and served the needs of relatively independent urban villages, delineating districts within which the working-classes moved and married. Men who travelled out of the neighbourhood to work hurried back to their 'local' for a drink, now patronised in preference to the trade pub close to the workplace. Community meant a convivial communality of interests.

Within the workplace or the community, the working-classes were marked by its divisions and sub-divisions on the basis of levels of skill, wages, gender, levels of control and so on. This highlights the unsatisfactory nature of any simple division between aristocrats and plebeians, between skilled and unskilled labour or between men and women. Most workers found themselves on complex wage ladders with many steps up and down along which they generally expected to move at different stages of their working lives.[392] There may have been greater social mobility after the First World War with some in the upper-working-class making their way into the lower middle-class[393] and the percentage of manual workers in the occupied population declined but the working-classes were the largest social grouping in 1780 and remained so in 1945.

[392] Breuilly, John, 'The labour aristocracy in Britain and Germany: a comparison', in Breuilly, John, (ed.), *Labour and Liberalism in 19th-century Europe: essays in comparative history*, (Manchester University Press), 1992, pp. 26-75, provides a valuable perspective.
[393] Hubka, Thomas C., *How the Working-Class Home Became Modern, 1900-1940*, (University of Minnesota Press), 2020, is a valuable study of the working-classes in the USA.

3: The Middle-Classes

In the 1940s, George Orwell suggested that England was 'the most class-ridden country under the sun' and it was moulded in a middle-class image.[1] Who were the 'middle-classes'?[2] They were often seen as a peculiarly British phenomenon; less politically extreme than the Continental bourgeoisie but perhaps less enterprising than their equals in the United States. George Kitson Clark (1900-1975) rightly counselled caution:

Of course, the general expression 'middle-class' remains useful, as a name for a large section of society .... [but] it is necessary to remember that a belief in the importance and significance of the middle-class in the nineteenth century derives from contemporary opinion .... They do not always say clearly whom they have in mind, and since the possible variants are so great a modern writer should follow them with great caution....[3]

The middle-classes can be distinguished from the aristocracy and gentry not so much by their income as their need to earn a living and from the working-classes not by their higher income—there was often little difference between the incomes of the skilled working-class and lower middle-class—but by their property, however small, represented by stock in trade, tools or by their investment in education. Crucially, they did not engage in manual labour either in the workplace or ideally at home. The distinction between their 'mental' labour and the 'manual' labour of the working-classes remains an enduring source of class division across Britain.

---

[1] Orwell George, 'The Lion and the Unicorn', in *Collected Essays, Journalism and Letters, Volume 2: 1940-1945*, (Penguin), 1970, pp. 87-88.
[2] James, Lawrence, *The Middle Class: A History*, (Little, Brown), 2006, is a detailed study. See also, Gunn, Simon, and Bell, Rachel, *Middle Classes: Their Rise and Sprawl*, (Phoenix), 2003, Wahrman, Dror, *Imagining the Middle Class. The Political Representation of Class in Britain c.1780-1840*, (Cambridge University Press), 1995, and Kidd, Alan, and Nicholls, David, (eds.), *The Making of the British Middle Class? Studies of Regional and Cultural Diversity*, (Sutton), 1998, analyse their emergence. Nossiter, T. J., *Influence, Opinion and Political Idioms in Reformed England: Case Studies from the North-East 1832-1874*, (Harvester), 1975, and Crossick, G., and Hauge, H. G., (eds.), *Shopkeepers and Master Artisans in Nineteenth-Century Europe*, (Methuen), 1984 contain some useful comments on the 'shopocracy'. Crossick, G., (ed.), *The Lower Middle Class in Britain 1870-1914*, (Croom Helm), 1977, is the most useful collection of papers and Anderson, G., *Victorian Clerks*, (Manchester University Press), 1976, deals with one occupational group. See also, Searle, G. R., *Entrepreneurial Politics in Mid-Victorian Britain*, (Oxford University Press), 1993, and Searle, G. R., *Morality and the Market in Victorian England*, (Oxford University Press), 1998.
[3] Clark, G. Kitson, *The Making of Victorian England*, (Methuen), 1965, p. 96.

Today the middle-classes exude a sense of faded permanence and solidity but this obscures the fact that they are a recent invention. Their origins can be traced back to the early-eighteenth century though they only became an important feature of society after 1780.[4] Yet, the divide that was emerging was not the Marxist division between those who control capital and ownership—the bourgeoisie—and the majority—the proletariat—who laboured for them for exploitative wages and salaries in which the middle-classes had no relevance but:

> ...a cultural one, between the patrician landowner, banker, lawyer, clergyman or merchant on the one hand and the plebeian tradesman and manufacturer on the other.[5]

The middle-classes were increasingly defined as a 'class' in the late-eighteenth century.[6] As a class, they benefited from the changes in the economy and, though not exclusively urban, were increasingly found in the flourishing towns of the provinces. Their growing sense of identity came from a common social and political ideology that they promoted with missionary zeal. Evangelicalism, whether Anglican or Nonconformist, provided a firm religious foundation grounded in a 'call to seriousness'. This contrasted with the perceived immorality of the aristocracy and the 'baser instincts' of the working-classes. It emphasised the virtues of hard work, plain and moral living, respectable family life and above all conscience. The ideas of Jeremy Bentham (1748-1832) allowed attacks on the inefficiency of the aristocratic conception of society and its corrupt and self-serving institutional framework. Tradition, restriction and 'influence', the values peculiar to landed society, were compared, generally unfavourably, with middle-class virtues of order, discipline, merit and application. Finally, Political Economy provided an economic justification for their growing power with its focus on the freedom of the market and the virtues of individual enterprise.

By the 1830s, the middle-classes embraced city bankers and large industrialists with incomes from investment and profits of over £500 per year and small shopkeepers and clerks with annual earnings of only £50.

---

[4] Earle, Peter, *The Making of the English Middle Class: Business, Society and Family Life in London, 1660-1730*, (Methuen), 1989.

[5] Clark, J. C. D., *English Society 1688-1832*, (Cambridge University Press), 1985, p. 71; see also his *The Language of Liberty 1660-1832*, (Cambridge University Press), 1993.

[6] For the development of the professions see Reader, W. J., *Professional Men: the rise of the professional classes in Victorian England*, (Weidenfeld), 1966. Searle, G. R., *Entrepreneurial Politics in Mid-Victorian Britain*, (Oxford University Press), 1993, is an important statement of the position of the middle-classes in politics.

The provincial elite was a small group of men and families who controlled growing industrial and commercial complexes and in London, there were the merchant bankers. However, this elite, on familiar and sometimes marrying terms with the aristocracy, was not representative of the middle-classes as a whole. The lower middle-classes were composed of smaller manufacturers, shopkeepers, milliners, tailors, local brewers as well as the rapidly growing number of clerks in both business and government, schoolteachers, an emerging managerial class, accountants, pharmacists and engineers.[7] This diversity reflected the 'middling sort' that always referred to a broad band in society between the aristocracy and the working population.

White-collar employment increased accounting for 2.5 per cent of the employed population in 1851 to 5.5 per cent by 1891. Such employment was found in all towns but especially in commercial and financial centres such as Glasgow, Manchester, Liverpool and Bristol. White-collar workers were a diverse group: insurance and bank clerks commanded the highest incomes of over £3 per week and the greatest prestige; in contrast railway clerks often earned little more than skilled manual workers but had greater status and security of employment. White-collar employees certainly perceived themselves, and were seen by others, to be in a secure and privileged position. They could afford not only a decent terraced house, but by 1880 could commute to work using public transport, especially after the suburban railway and tram networks were established. Despite long hours for clerks and shopkeepers, their occupations were less hazardous than most factory work and, with more regular incomes and healthier housing, they were more likely to enjoy better health and living standards than most industrial workers.

Creating middle-classes

The first reference to the middle-classes in the *Oxford English Dictionary* is dated 1766 but references to it before 1800 were uncommon. It was more likely that people would refer to the 'middle ranks' or 'middling sort' to describe the emergent bourgeois group of manufacturers, tradesmen, merchants, lawyers and shopkeepers. The traditional view is that the middle-classes were created by industrialisation, urbanisation and empire between 1780 and 1850. Industrialisation created new types of manufacturer and factory owner, leaders in forming a new class identified with the expanding industrial towns and cities of the Midlands and North of England, South Wales and the industrial Lowlands of Scotland. As well as businessmen linked with the growth of manufacturing, there were

---

[7] Pollard, Sidney, 'The genesis of the managerial profession: the experience of the Industrial Revolution in Great Britain', *Studies in Romanticism*, Vol. 4, (1965), pp. 57-80.

increasing numbers of small entrepreneurs such as shopkeepers and merchants who transported and retailed the fruits of industry and empire. The increased scale of industry and overseas trade, together with the expansion of empire fuelled the spread of commerce and finance such as banks, insurance companies, shipping and railways run by clerks, managers and salaried professionals. The expansion of cities, towns and the economy produced new spaces that needing regulating and running leading to a massive expansion of local government and the centralised state This provided occupations for vast numbers of civil servants, teachers, doctors, lawyers and government officials as well as the clerks and assistants who helped these institutions and services to operate.

While industrialisation, urbanisation and the growth of empire played an important part in the emergence of the middle-classes, they built upon an already existing 'middling ranks'. People who later formed the middle-classes were numerous in the 'middling sort' and industrialisation was a gradual and uneven process whose impact on the creation of middle-classes was limited. Urbanisation also did not create middle-class social and cultural institutions since the public sphere of newspapers, libraries, coffee houses, gentlemen's societies and tradesmen's clubs had existed in provincial centres for at least a century. Such diversity makes a satisfactory definition of the middle-classes impossible. Although there were some individuals that accumulated spectacular wealth through entrepreneurial activity, there were many more businessmen who scraped a living while others worked for wages as public servants, managers or clerks. The economic boundary of the 'middle-class' was unclear.[8]

Such economic and financial divergences were deepened by disparities in religion, background and politics. In the debates over the French Revolution, the 'middle-classes' were seen as the 'middle way' of moderate reform between the two extremes of Paineite radicalism and Burkean traditionalism, a 'political' not a social 'middle'.[9] The right to vote before the 1832 Reform Act lay with the possession of property; this did not change after 1832 severing the pragmatic alliance between middle-class reformers, who were prepared to accept property as a condition of voting and the more moderate working-class radicals who wanted the vote as an individual right.[10] Whigs believed it essential to 'attach' the middle-

---

[8] Iwama, Toshihiko, *The Middle Class in Halifax, 1780-1850*, Ph. D., University of Leeds, 2003, is an excellent local study.

[9] Claeys, Gregory, *The French Revolutionary Debate in Britain: The Origins of Modern Politics*, (Palgrave Macmillan), 2007, provides an excellent summary of the reception of French Revolutionary ideas in Britain.

[10] Brock, Michael, *The Great Reform Act*, (Heinemann), 1973, is the standard work. Pearce, Robert, *The Great Reform Act*, (Cape), 2003, and Fraser, Antonia, *Perilous Question: The Drama of the Great Reform Bill 1832*, (Weidenfeld & Nicolson), 2013, are more recent analyses. Two books by Gash, Norman, *Politics*

classes to the institutions and government of the country but reform in 1832 did not weaken the continued attack of a mobilised middle-class on the landed aristocracy especially over the vexed question of the protection afforded the landed classes through the Corn Laws.[11] Repeal was achieved in 1846 after almost a decade of agitation from the Anti-Corn Law League and was heralded as a middle-class triumph. Richard Cobden, however, was somewhat premature in urging Sir Robert Peel, the Conservative Prime Minister, to embrace the political ascendance of the middle-classes[12] but there is a sense in which the middle-classes had eroded their political exclusion from an unrepresentative and corrupt state.

Religion exacerbated the sense of political grievance felt by the middle-classes especially since many were Nonconformists.[13] This contributed to the construction of a middle-class sense of their historical 'mission' and they fashioned their own history at the same time that they were carving out their distinct political identity. A substantial part of the urban middle-classes did not belong to the Church of England and in Birmingham, Manchester and Leeds, Nonconformists were in the majority. They were denied important civil liberties such as being elected MPs, taking degrees at Oxford and Cambridge and marrying or being buried in their own chapels but still had to pay church rates for the upkeep of Anglican churches. What they sought was 'free trade in religion'. Calls for civil and religious liberty were important throughout the nineteenth century with civil disabilities finally removed with the repeal of the Test and Corporation Acts in 1828, Catholic Emancipation the following year and the Marriages Act 1836 and the abolition of compulsory church rates in 1868.[14]

---

in the Age of Peel, (Harvester Press), 2nd ed., 1978, and his *Reaction and Reconstruction in English Politics 1832-1852*, (Oxford University Press), 1965, provide classic analysis of the operation of the electoral system after 1832.

[11] Prentice, Archibald, *History of the Anti-Corn Law League*, 2 Vols. (W. & R. G. Cash), 1853, is a valuable source by a leading participant. McCord, N., *The Anti-Corn Law League 1838-1846*, (Allen and Unwin). 1958, should in read in conjunction with Pickering, Paul A., and Tyrell, Alex, *The People's Bread: A History of the Anti-Corn Law League*, (Leicester University Press), 2000, pp. 139-164. The political strategies of the League can be approached through Hamer, D. A., *The Politics of Electoral Pressure*, (Harvester), 1977, pp. 58-90.

[12] See, for instance, Cobden's speech during the twelfth night of the adjourned debate on commercial policy and the Corn Laws, *Hansard*, House of Commons, Debates, 27 February 1846, cc275-292.

[13] Yates, Nigel, *Eighteenth Century Britain: Religion and Politics 1714-1815*, (Longman), 2007, Brown, Stewart, *Providence and Empire 1815-1914*, (Longman), 2008, Brown, Callum, *Religion and Society in Twentieth-Century Britain*, (Longman), 2006, provide a summary of developments.

[14] Watts, Michael R., *The Dissenters, Volume 1: From the Reformation to the*

Reform only occurred because of sustained public campaigns involving prominent Dissenting clergymen, pressure groups such as the voluntaryist Liberation Society and the Nonconformist press. For instance, in March 1843, the Home Secretary, Sir James Graham introduced a Factory Bill that included three hours' daily education for children in schools largely controlled by the Church of England. He expected opposition and took care in drafting the proposal for state assistance in the education of factory children. His proposal sought to raise the 'moral feeling' of the people and act as a counter to radical political agitation but Nonconformists and Roman Catholics believed it unfairly favoured the Church of England.[15] Fear and prejudice came together in the massive campaign by Nonconformist pressure groups coordinated by the United Conference, stressing the virtues of 'voluntarism' and professing concerns about the 'Romanising' effects of the Oxford Movement. Within two months, it had organised a petition to Parliament containing over two million signatures. In June 1843, the education clauses were withdrawn but the government remained committed to proceeding with the remainder of the bill that passed in an amended form the following year.[16]

There were urban Anglican merchants and professionals as well as Nonconformists, a cause of frequent local tensions. Both groups had a common evangelicalism especially a mission to reform the morals and manners of the nation. This was evident in their attack on the dissolute behaviour of the aristocracy. The defining event in this campaign was the unsuccessful attempt by the new king, George IV to divorce his estranged wife Caroline of Brunswick.[17] He had long lived apart from his wife whose

French Revolution, (Oxford University Press), 1978, Watts, Michael R., *The Dissenters, Volume 2: The expansion of Evangelical Nonconformity 1791-1859*, (Oxford University Press), 1995, and Watts, Michael R., *The Dissenters, Volume 3: The Crisis and Conscience of Nonconformity*, (Oxford University Press), 2015, are the most valuable surveys.

[15] Ward, J. T., and Treble, James H., 'Religion and education in 1843: reaction to the 'Factory Education Bill'', *Journal of Ecclesiastical History*, Vol. 20, (1969), pp. 79-110.

[16] Graham gave his reasons for withdrawing the educational clauses, *Hansard*, House of Commons, Debates, 15 June 1843, Vol. 69, cc1567-1570.

[17] Clark, Anna, *Scandal: The Sexual Politics of the British Constitution*, (Princeton University Press), 2004, pp. 117-207, includes the most recent discussion of the Queen Caroline affair. See also, Robins, Jane, *Rebel Queen: How the trial of Caroline brought England to the brink of revolution*, (Simon and Schuster), 2006, Smith, E. A., *A queen on trial: the affair of Queen Caroline*, (Alan Sutton), 1993, and Macdonald, C. M. M., 'Abandoned and beastly?: The 'Queen Caroline Affair', in Scotland', in Brown, Y. G., and Ferguson, R., (eds.), *Twisted Sisters: Women, Crime and Deviance in Scotland since 1400*, (Tuckwell Press), 2002, pp. 101-113.

behaviour had been a cause of concern since the mid-1800s. In June 1820, she returned from Italy to claim her rights as queen to which George IV was totally opposed. The government was instructed to dissolve the marriage.[18] Caroline became the unlikely recipient of a wave of outraged public sympathy, seen as a 'wronged woman' who was struggling to uphold her rights against an insensitive and corrupt political establishment.[19] A Whig campaign in favour of Caroline gained support among the middle-classes who held the king, widely regarded as extravagant, selfish and dissolute, in contempt. With widespread economic distress, the king's ministers were also condemned for their alleged corruption and use of repressive legislation, as well as for their servile harassment of the Queen. Faced with widespread opposition, on 9 November 1820 the government was forced to abandon its attempts to deprive Caroline of her title and dissolve the marriage. The affair exposed a system of corruption and injustice damaging the prestige of both Crown and Parliament.[20]

The agitation subsided with surprising suddenness. Early in 1821, there was a loyalist reaction, sustained by the lurid evidence presented during the Lords' trial of Caroline's immoral behaviour.[21] In the following months, Caroline became an increasingly isolated figure and, when she attended the king's coronation in July, she was shut out of Westminster Abbey. A month later she died suddenly. The London crowds forced the military to take her coffin through the City on its way to Harwich and to her family home in Brunswick but her political importance had already diminished.[22] The affair made the government very unpopular but had little lasting impact on either radical or moderate movements for reform. The Whigs failed to topple the government in 1820 but they succeeded in establishing themselves as the leaders of moderate reform that emphasised middle-class respectability. The Caroline affair went to the heart of the evangelical view of private life that sanctified marriage, family and home.

---

[18] Melikan, R. A., 'Pains and Penalties Procedure: How the House of Lords 'Tried' Queen Caroline', *Parliamentary History*, Vol. 20, (2001), pp. 311-332, Hunt, Tamara L., 'Morality and Monarchy in The Queen Caroline Affair', *Albion*, Vol. 24, (4), (1991), pp. 697-722, Carter, Louise, 'British Masculinities on Trial in the Queen Caroline Affair of 1820', *Gender & History*, Vol. 20, (2008), pp. 248-269.

[19] The cultural impact is examined in Gardner, John, *Poetry and Popular Protest: Peterloo, Cato Street and the Queen Caroline Controversy*, (Palgrave Macmillan), 2011, pp. 157-217.

[20] Hone, J. Ann, *For the Cause of Truth: Radicalism in London, 1796-1821*, (Oxford University Press), 1982, pp. 306-319, 346-351.

[21] Fulcher, Jonathan, 'The Loyalist Response to the Queen Caroline Agitations', *Journal of British Studies*, Vol. 34, (1995), pp. 481-502.

[22] Palmer, S. H., 'Before the Bobbies: The Caroline Riots of 1821', *History Today*, Vol. 27, (1977), pp. 637-644.

Evangelicals also believed in an idealised relationship between men and women grounded in distinct roles for men and women.

The Reform Act 1832 and the Municipal Corporations Act[23] three years later are often regarded as the origin of middle-class political power.[24] More important is its institutionalising of division between the working- and middle-classes by marking out the boundary separating them. It is true that the new Parliamentary franchise and municipal franchise increased middle-class representation mainly in municipal politics but also aimed to reduce the power of newly wealthy owners of corrupt boroughs and give fresh legitimacy to the traditional influence of the landed interest. The middle-classes may have dominate municipal elections but as late as the 1860s, almost two-thirds of the country's MPs came from landed backgrounds, over one-third were hereditary aristocrats and around half of the cabinets of both parties were still aristocratic.[25] It was not until after the Reform Act in 1867 that major changes in the nature of the political elite emerged. The Act extended the franchise to certain sections of the urban working-classes leading to a shift from local patterns of influence to professionally organised political machines. This was enhanced by further extensions of the franchise in 1884 but also by the Secret Ballot Act 1872 and the restriction of candidates' spending on elections by the Corrupt Practices Act 1883. After 1885, there was a further dilution in aristocratic power through awards of peerages in recognition of wealth and political service and the introduction of elections for local government in the counties in 1888 and 1894.

Middle-classes 1850-1914

By 1850, the middle-classes represented a distinctive political, religious, moral and cultural force in Britain. These ideas and values included a tradition of opposition to the landed classes and the state, the importance of individual conscience and a claim to represent the moral backbone of the nation. When people spoke of the 'middle-classes', it was their moral

---

[23] Finlayson, Geoffrey, 'The Municipal Corporation Commission and Report, 1833-5', *Bulletin of the Institute of Historical Research*, Vol. 36, (1963), pp. 36-52, and 'The politics of municipal reform, 1835', *English Historical Review*, Vol. 81, (1966), pp. 673-692; Phillips, John A., and Wetherell, Charles, 'Probability and political behaviour: a case study of the Municipal Corporations Act of 1835', *History and Computing*, Vol. 5, (1993), pp. 135-153.

[24] Garrard, John Adrian, 'The middle classes and nineteenth century national and local politics', in Garrard, John Adrian, Jary, David, Goldsmith, Michael, and Oldfield, Adrian, (eds.), *The middle class in politics*, (Saxon House), 1978, pp. 35-66, and Briggs, Asa, 'Middle-class consciousness in English politics, 1780-1846', *Past & Present*, Vol. 9, (1956), pp. 65-74, provide a brief overview.

[25] Ibid., Searle, G. R., *Entrepreneurial Politics in Mid-Victorian Britain*, is the clearest statement of the position of the middle-classes in politics.

and political nature rather than their social character that was being described. There was no clear sense of who the middle-classes were and where they began and ended. They were an extremely heterogeneous body embracing at one end bankers and large industrialists with incomes from investment and profits of over £1,000 per year and at the other end small shopkeepers and clerks with annual earnings of under £50. The middle-classes can be divided into two groupings. The upper middle-class was divided into two distinct groups: the metropolitan financiers and merchants and the manufacturers of the North and Midlands. The former were generally wealthier, of higher social status and closer to the landed elites than the industrialists.[26] London bankers and City merchants were among the wealthiest people in the country and their origins predate the emergence of the northern manufacturers. Most of the largest fortunes, such as those of the Rothschild, Morrison, Baring or Sassoon families, came from commerce or finance rather than manufacturing and industry.[27] The provincial elites, those men and families controlling the growing industrial complex, dominated industry. Factory owners were usually wealthy but in most cases not immensely wealthy.[28] By 1880, and earlier, Britain was as much the 'Clearing House of the World' as the 'Workshop of the World'.

A lower middle-class emerged after 1800 and consisted of three main groups: smaller manufacturers, shopkeepers, dealers, milliners, tailors, local brewers; the rapidly expanding ubiquitous 'clerk' in both business and government; and finally, the growing professionals, schoolteachers, railway officials, an emergent managerial class, accountants, pharmacists and engineers.[29] Middle-class 'occupations' grew from 6.5 per cent of the

---

[26] See, Cassis, Y., 'Merchant bankers and City aristocracy', *British Journal of Sociology,* Vol. 39, (1), (1988), pp. 114-120, Nenadic, S., 'Businessmen, the urban middle classes, and the "dominance" of manufacturers in 19th century Britain', *Economic History Review,* Vol. 44, (1991), pp. 66-85.

[27] On banking and the middle-class, see, Cassis, Y., 'Bankers and English society in the late 19th century' *Economic History Review,* Vol. 38, (1985), pp. 210-229, and *City bankers, 1890-1914,* (Cambridge University Press), 1994, 2009. See also, Camplin, Jamie, *The rise of the plutocrats: wealth and power in Edwardian England,* (Constable), 1978.

[28] Crouzet, François, *The First Industrialists: The Problem of Origins,* (Cambridge University Press), 1985, 2008, pp. 99-115, Howe, A., *The Cotton Masters 1830-1860,* (Oxford University Press), 1984, pp. 50-89.

[29] Crossick, G., 'The Emergence of the Lower Middle Class in Britain: a discussion', in ibid., Crossick, G., (ed.), *The lower middle class in Britain, 1870-1914,* pp. 11-60; Savage, Michael, 'Career mobility and class formation: British banking workers and the lower middle classes', in Miles, Andrew, and Vincent, David, (eds.), *Building European society: occupational change and social mobility in Europe, 1840-1940,* (Manchester University Press), 1993, pp. 196-

working population in 1851 to 7.8 per cent by 1871. Structural changes towards a larger service sector in the late-Victorian economy saw growth in the number of clerical and administrative employees.[30]

Aware of their 'caste', they maintained a distinction between themselves as salaried or fee-earning employees and wage-earning manual workers though they lacked the easily recognisable middle-class badge of having servants. Dorothy Marshall argues:

> Some of these employments were lucrative, some poorly paid, but the men who engaged in them were united in the conviction that they were socially superior to the manual worker, however skilled. The struggling clerk, who earned less than the expert fine cotton spinner, underlined his superiority by his dress, his speech and his manners. These, and not his income, were what distinguished him from the working-class.[31]

Little had changed when E. M. Forster wrote prosaically of Leonard Bast a clerk:

> The boy, Leonard Bast, stood at the extreme verge of gentility. He was not in the abyss, but he could see it and at times people whom he knew had dropped in and counted no more. He knew that he was poor and would admit it: he would have died sooner than confess any inferiority to the rich...[32]

There is an intended irony when the self-improving Leonard is eventually killed, crushed by a bookshelf. There was an unresolved tension between the need to maintain the symbols of middle-class status and the constraints of economic reality.[33] While sharing the ambitions and values of the class above them, the lower middle-class was under pressure to differentiate itself from the working-classes whose ways of life they rejected. They this did by developing the cult of the genteel for fear of losing prestige and status. This façade had many features: thrift, sobriety, disapproval of frivolity, abhorrence of debt, suppression of sexuality and above all an emphasis on keeping up appearances. They could not join

---

216.
[30] Anderson, G. I., 'The Social Economy of Late-Victorian Clerks', in ibid., Crossick, G., (ed.), *The lower middle class in Britain, 1870-1914,* pp. 113-133.
[31] Marshall, D., *Industrial England 1776-1851*, (Routledge), 1973, p. 96.
[32] Ibid, Forster, E. M., *Howards End*, p. 42.
[33] Hammerton, A. James, 'The English weakness? Gender, satire and "moral manliness" in the lower middle class, 1870-1920', in Kidd, Alan J., and Nicholls, David, (eds.), *Gender, civic culture, and consumerism: middle-class identity in Britain, 1800-1940*, (Manchester University Press), 1999, pp. 164-182, and Hammerton, A. James, 'Pooterism or partnership?: marriage and masculine identity in the lower middle class, 1870-1920', *Journal of British Studies*, Vol. 38, (1999), pp. 291-321.

the secure world of literary and philosophical societies or afford subscription libraries but could not join the pub world of the upper working-class. The lower middle-class was the more amorphous, least neighbourly and gregarious and assertive class in society and made little impact on cultural or intellectual issues—theirs was a cultural desert. George Grossmith's (1847-1912) *The Diary of a Nobody*, published in 1892 and illustrated by his brother Weedon (1854-1919), that made Mr Pooter into the stock comic figure of Victorian petty gentility did nothing to raise the status of the class and the lower middle-class was held in universal contempt by the literati.

For the late-Victorian middle-classes drawing lines to distinguish oneself from those below and above was especially important, a reflection of the uncertainty many had about their own status. Religious attendance was a marker of respectability, if not of middle-class status itself. Religious denominations had their social tones. Congregationalists and Unitarians attracted the wealthy urban elite while Methodism had a more popular appeal. By 1900, half the church-going population were Nonconformists and in industrial and mining areas, they formed a majority. This dominance did not go unchallenged and after 1850 Anglicanism was able to regain a foothold in the North. For the urban middle-classes, regular attendance was a social event as well as a religious rite. In the suburbs, churches and chapels functioned as centres for a range of activities such as missionary, philanthropic and community pursuits as well as recreations.

Emphasis on the future—practical as well as spiritual—formed a fundamental part of middle-class culture until after 1945. Education, especially secondary and tertiary, was central to this process reflecting the growing importance of 'mental culture' as the middle-classes became dependent on knowledge and expertise to define their livelihoods. For middle-class boys—and from the 1860s girls—attendance at public school either as a day or boarding pupil followed by university became established as a foundation of middle-class identity. The expense of educating their sons was seen as providing the entrée into a professional career or failing that work as a clerk in government offices or in commercial houses. Both conferred respectability that working with your hands—even though many commentators urged parents to get their sons to learn a trade—did not. A skilled engineer might earn more than a clerk but he worked with his hands and was irredeemably a member of the lower classes.

After 1867, helped by the growing numbers of white-collar workers, small shopkeepers, tradesmen and businessmen took political control of the cities. This was achieved by a three-pronged infiltration into urban affairs as ratepayers and councillors and as the core of the new local government bureaucracy. With the withdrawal of the more substantial middle-classes from local politics and expansion of local responsibilities that, as ratepayers they generally disapproved of because of cost and ideology, the lower middle-classes achieved dominance in municipal politics be default rather than design. Their rates may not have been high compared to the 'villadom' of the upper middle-classes, but collectively they were a considerable electoral force within communities. Small traders and businessmen felt especially aggrieved having to pay rates on their businesses as well as their own houses and if they happened to be landlords, rates on the properties they owned. Ratepayers associations, largely consisting of the lower middle-class, were a recurrent feature of Victorian towns in organising resistance to proposed municipal spending.[34] For instance, in early 1841, anti-Poor Law feelings focused on the construction of a new workhouse 'of extreme size'[35] in Nottingham and, for the increasingly depressed working-classes in Nottingham it seemed large enough to house them all.[36] The alarm of the poor was matched by the dismay of the ratepayers at the cost of constructing this 'pauper palace' and an opponent of the new workhouse succinctly summed this up when he declared in favour of the Old Poor Law that it:

...was far more satisfactory than the present sweeping system of centralisation, with all its cumbrous machinery—a system which abridged the comforts of the poor and increased the taxes of the ratepayers. [37]

The hours of work for the working-classes are easy to establish compared to the middle-classes as there are no national statistics and only scattered and unreliable data. Within the professions and the civil service hours were relatively short until the late-nineteenth century, perhaps six hours a day. In the private sector, clerks worked rather longer hours, generally 40 hours per week in five days. Businessmen worked long hours in the first half of the nineteenth century but by 1900 followed the 9 to 5 norm. Finally, at the lower end of the middle-classes, amongst shop-workers, hours were notoriously long and remained so. After fifty years of effort to curtail hours, a House of Lords Select Committee in 1901 could only confirm that many shops were working 80 or 90 hours a week. The 1911 Shops Act did, however, enact a half-day holiday. As far as annual holidays were concerned middle-class workers undoubtedly had the

[34] Prest, John M., *Liberty and Locality: Parliament, Permissive Legislation and Ratepayers' Democracies in the Nineteenth Century*, (Oxford University Press), 1990.
[35] It was 364 feet long with a roof reservoir providing hot and cold water and there was also a water closet on each floor. However, these amenities did little to allay the fears of working people.
[36] 'An Address to the Inhabitants of Nottingham...', *Nottingham Review*, 2 April 1841, p. 3.
[37] 'Nottingham Board of Guardians, June 15', *Nottingham Journal*, 18 June 1841, p. 4.

advantage over the working-classes. In 1875 the Civil Service Inquiry Commission stated that clerks working for insurance companies, solicitors, banks, railway companies and the civil service were at getting at least two week's holiday a year. They had achieved this some seventy-five years before the bulk of manual workers.

The growing importance of its entrepreneurial values has often been used to imply that the middle-classes were the dominant group after 1850.[38] In fact, what characterised the middle-classes was its aspiration for economic, political and cultural power rather than the achievement of that aspiration. The relative aristocratic power and the emergent bourgeoisie illustrates this. Rubinstein[39] used probate calendars and assessments of incomes in different Inland Revenue districts to analyse the relative wealth of different groups of property owners.[40] Each of these sources is subject to technical qualifications but it is nonetheless clear that the wealth of landowners was dominant for longer than has been assumed. Among the increasingly important non-landed wealth-holder, industrial employers came third behind bankers and merchants with only 30-40 per cent of non-landed fortunes at their peak in 1850.[41] Until the 1880s, over half of the very wealthiest still had the bulk of their property in land.[42] Even when income from rents began to fall from the 1870s, large landowners were able to increase their incomes from coal and mineral royalties and from urban rents, while landowners of all sizes were able to supplement their

---

[38] Read, D., *The English Provinces c.1760-1960: a study in influence*, (Edward Arnold), 1964, is a tentative attempt to explore provincial society where the middle-classes were at their strongest. See also, Trainor, Richard H., 'The middle class', in Daunton, Martin J., (ed.), *The Cambridge urban history of Britain, Vol. 3: 1840-1950*, (Cambridge University Press), 2000, pp. 673-713.

[39] Rubinstein, W. D., *Men of Property: The Very Wealth in Britain since the Industrial Revolution*, (Croom Helm), 1981, *Elites and the Wealthy in Modern British History*, (Methuen), 1987, and *Wealth and Inequality in Britain*, (Faber), 1986, provide valuable analyses of wealth-holding, point to the relatively low standing of manufacturers and argue that few businessmen brought landed estates and that the aristocracy was a closed elite. See also, Rubinstein, William D., 'Wealth making in the late-nineteenth and early twentieth centuries: a response', *Business History*, Vol. 42, (2000), pp. 141-154, and Nicholas, Tom, 'Wealth making in the nineteenth and early twentieth century: the Rubinstein hypothesis revisited', *Business History*, Vol. 42, (2000), pp. 155-168.

[40] Ibid., Rubinstein, W. D., *Men of Property: The Very Wealth in Britain since the Industrial Revolution*, pp. 9-26, considers the methodological problems in studying the wealthy.

[41] Nicholas, Tom, 'Wealth making in nineteenth- and early twentieth-century Britain: industry v. commerce and finance', *Business History*, Vol. 41, (1999), pp. 16-36.

[42] Berghoff, Hartmut, 'British businessmen as wealth-holders, 1870-1914: a closer look', *Business History*, Vol. 33, (1991), pp. 222-240.

incomes by diversifying into commercial and financial activities in the City of London, then experiencing rapid growth as it emerged as the major service centre for the world economy. As a result, there was a marked concentration of non-landed wealth in London, particularly the City and this was to be found among the middle-classes as well as the very rich.[43] Within the industrial regions the same pattern is repeated: centres of commerce like Liverpool contained the highest general levels of wealth and in cities like Manchester only one out of six recorded millionaires was a cotton manufacturer, the others were bankers and merchants.[44]

The growth of manufacturing employment and the wealth of employers in the northern industries was important but their fortunes were only impressive at small town level.[45] Joseph Gillott, a Birmingham pen manufacturer, for instance, had an extensive and impressive art collection that included works by Gainsborough, Constable, Etty and Landseer but especially by Turner.[46] Patronage of the Arts drew positive comments, as, for instance, in 1857:

The taste of the middle classes, then, for modern pictures is a wholesome fact – good for painters, good for art, good for honesty and truth, which is the cause of all true art.[47]

This was partly the result of the limited extent of the ambitions of

---

[43] Green, David R., 'To do the right thing: gender, wealth, inheritance and the London middle class', in Laurence, Anne, Maltby, Josephine, and Rutterford, Janette, (eds.), *Women and their money, 1700-1950: essays on women and finance*, (Routledge), 2009, pp. 133-150, Rubinstein, W. D., 'The role of London in Britain's wealth structure, 1809-99: further evidence', in Stobart, Jon, and Owens, Alastair, (eds.), *Urban fortunes: property and inheritance in the town, 1700-1900*, (Ashgate), 2000, pp. 131-152.
[44] Stobart, Jon, and Owens, Alastair, (eds.), *Urban fortunes: property and inheritance in the town, 1700-1900*, (Routledge), 2000, highlights the importance of property and inheritance in shaping social, cultural, economic and political structures and interactions within and between towns and cities.
[45] Morris, R. J., 'The middle class and the property cycle during the industrial revolution', in Smout, Christopher, (ed.), *The search for wealth and stability: essays in economic and social history presented to M. W. Flinn*, (Macmillan), 1979, pp. 91-113, Morris, R. J., *Class, sect and party: the making of the British middle class, Leeds, 1820-1850*, (Manchester University Press), 1990, and Morris, R. J., *Men, women and property in England 1780-1870*, (Cambridge University Press), 2005, consider Leeds as an example.
[46] Roberts, Stephen, *Joseph Gillott and Four Other Birmingham Manufacturers 1784-1892*, (Birmingham Biographies), 2016, pp. 16-20.
[47] *A handbook to the gallery of British paintings in the Art treasures exhibition, a repr. of notices orig. publ. in 'The Manchester Guardian': Being a Reprint of Critical Notices Originally Published in The Manchester Guardian*, (Manchester Art Treasures Exhibition), 1857, p. 14.

prosperous family-based firms, as well as of the greater uncertainty and lower rate of return from productive activity compared with landownership and finance and it was closely connected with manufacturers' general avoidance of heavy fixed investment in plant and equipment.[48]

Suburbanisation was not simply a matter of numbers but was also an expression of middle-class values. The cult of privacy rejected street and house arrangements where overcrowding, communality, noise and public access damaged self-discipline and diminished parental responsibility. It was not simply the physical structures that undermined decency and the family unit–there were many examples of generously proportioned and well-maintained terraced housing and tenement flats–it was the congestion with which they were associated. Suburbs were a middle-class response to the death, disease and depravity seen as products of the uncontrolled urban environment and for which middle-class economic power was largely responsible. The filth and stench of the courts, yards and streets were offensive and hazardous to all and with no administrative apparatus to control it or engineering expertise to remove it until the 1870s, fleeing made practical sense. The preference for hillside suburbs exposed to prevailing westerly winds uncontaminated by industrial and domestic pollution was understandable since statistical and medical reasons stressed air-borne contamination. For middle-class women—and this is one of the ironies of suburbanisation—the household lay at the cusp of class relations evident in their relationship and authority over domestic servants. This is apparent in *Mrs Beeton's Book of Household Management,* first published in 1861 that by 1868 had sold nearly two million copies.[49] Now famous for her recipes, the early editions of *Household Management* focused on questions of manners and on how to manage your servants. The critical concern was maintaining the proper boundary between oneself and one's servants since so much of middle-class identity rested on not being working-class.[50]

Many contemporaries believed the development of suburbia to have spoiled village life and the rural social order. E. M. Forster wrote of the

---

[48] Moore, James, *High Culture and Tall Chimneys: Art Institutions and Urban Society in Lancashire 1780-1914*, (Manchester University Press), 2018, considers the role played by the commercial and professional middle-classes in establishing industrial Lancashire as a leading national and international art centre.

[49] Isabella Beeton (1836-1865) wrote for her husband's publications and in 1859 launched a series of 48 page monthly supplements to *The Englishwomen's Domestic Magazine* that were published in one volume in 1861. She died after childbirth in 1865. Hughes, Kathryn, *The Short Life and Long Times of Mrs Beeton*, (Harper-Collins), 2006.

[50] This can, for instance, be seen in 'Literary Article: Household Management', *Dorset County Chronicle*, 20 June 1867, and 'Reviews', *Sheffield Daily Telegraph*, 19 February 1880, p. 8.

'red rust' spreading out of London into the countryside of Surrey and Hampshire.[51] The suburban dream equalled selfishness, a rejection of the obligation and commitment to the city where the suburbanites earned their living.

But it is still more Arcadian to sit under our own pears and apples, which in the summer by their blossom, in the autumn by their fruit, might possibly make, say, Hammersmith look almost like Herefordshire.[52]

Suburbs highlighted class distinctions residentially and the core of the cities became depopulated. Suburban development was prompted by a series of factors. There was the demographic upsurge; of particular importance was the expansion of the lower middle-class. Clerks increased from 2.5 per cent of all occupied males in 1851 to over 7 per cent in 1911: a rise from fewer than 150,000 to over 900,000 individuals.[53]

Clapham, once amongst the most affluent Georgian suburb, remained in the 1860s a citadel of stockbrokers and merchants with easy access to open countryside. By 1900, it was enclosed and had faded socially into a clerkly capital, the location of the man on the eponymous omnibus. Around provincial cities the same process is evident. Acock's Green, a village four miles from the centre of Birmingham, became unbearable for the upper middle-classes as it was engulfed by the expanding city. By 1903, it had become, as the *Birmingham Daily Mail* commented:

...abandoned to the smaller house -- the house adapted to the means of the family man of limited income who like to live just outside the artisan belt encircling the city.[54]

The expansion of suburban railways gave people the ability to extend their journey to work. The combination of rising real wages and reduced hours of work that allowed more travelling time were central to the growth of mass suburbs. The presence of a responsive building industry, ready capital and compliant landowners was essential to organise and effect the transfer. There was also the matter of taste and visions of family privacy and class exclusiveness. Certain negative conditions existed in, for instance,

---

[51] Ibid., Forster, E. M., *Howard's End*, p. 270.
[52] Even in 1888, suburbs were a matter of satire: 'The Leafy Suburb', *Globe*, 9 September 1888, p. 1.
[53] Studies of suburbia have often focussed on London; see, for instance, Dyos, H. J., *Victorian Suburb: A Study of the Growth of Camberwell*, (Leicester University Press), 1966, and Pullen, D.E., *Sydenham: from hamlet to suburban town*, (D. E. Pullen), 1974.
[54] Ibid., Waller, P. J., *Town, City and Nation, England 1850-1914*, p. 148.

the prejudice against apartment building in English cities, if not in Scotland resulted in outward rather than upward building. Purpose-built flats for the poor only emerged after it was clear that they could not take advantage of decentralised housing. The need for cheap, central housing was undeniable for the poor who needed to be close to possible work. The exception was in the industrial north-east where two-storey flats were commonplace. Relatively low-density housing spilling out of open towns was the norm. City centres were vacated for residential purposes and left to bankers by day and prostitutes by night gave a special tone to these constructions.

Entrepreneurs

During the economic revolutions after 1780, entrepreneurs[55] were viewed as the main instruments of change because of their enterprise, organisational innovation skill and their ability to exploit commercial opportunities.[56] Many industrial pioneers operated in a uniquely favourable economic environment; an expanding domestic market buttressed, especially in cotton, by a flourishing overseas demand. This allowed entrepreneurs such as Robert Owen (1771-1858), Benjamin Gott (1762-1840)[57] and his partners, George Newton and Thomas Chambers to exploit profit potentials. In such conditions, substantial profits could be achieved without effective use of power supplies or optimal factory layouts. However, successful entrepreneurs such as Richard Arkwright (1732-1792), Jedediah Strutt (1726-1797) and Sir Robert Peel senior (1750-1830) were not typical of contemporary businessmen. More representative were individuals such as the Wilsons of Wilsontown Ironworks[58] or the Needhams of Litton[59] whose businesses suffered from entrepreneurial

---

[55] Casson, Mark, and Casson, Catherine, *The Entrepreneur in History: From Medieval Merchant to Modern Business Leader*, (Palgrave Macmillan), 2013, provides valuable breadth.

[56] See this issue from a literary perspective, McKinstry, Sam, 'The positive depiction of entrepreneurs and entrepreneurship in the novels of Sir Walter Scott', *Journal of Scottish Historical Studies*, Vol. 26, (2006), pp. 83-99.

[57] See, Heaton, Herbert, 'Benjamin Gott and the industrial revolution in Yorkshire', *Economic History Review*, Vol. 3, (1931-2), pp. 45-66.

[58] Donnachie, Ian L., and Butt, John, 'The Wilsons of Wilsontown ironworks, 1779-1813: a study in entrepreneurial failure', *Explorations in Entrepreneurial History*, second series, Vol. 4, (1967), pp. 150-168.

[59] MacKenzie, M. H., 'Cressbrook and Litton mills, 1779-1835', *Derbyshire Archaeological Journal*, Vol. 88, (1969 for 1968), pp. 1-25, Chapman, Stanley D., 'Cressbrook and Litton mills: an alternative view', *Derbyshire Archaeological Journal*, Vol. 89, (1970 for 1969), pp. 86-90, and MacKenzie, M. H., 'Cressbrook and Litton Mills: a reply', *Derbyshire Archaeological Journal*, Vol. 90, (1972 for 1970), pp. 56-59.

shortcomings coupled with gross mismanagement. Such was the strength of the home and overseas markets, the former benefiting from railways and gradually rising living standards that entrepreneurs had no great inducement to alter the basic economic structure that had evolved before 1830.

Without change in the scale of operations, the relatively slow enlargement of the labour forces of individual enterprises and the close coincidence of firm and plant, meant that the nature of entrepreneurship and the structure of the firm changed little in the middle decades of the century.[60] However, some firms that traced their origins to the Industrial Revolution were already declining and some had already disappeared. Marshalls of Leeds[61] declined from the 1840s lingering on for another forty years by which time many of its leading competitors in flax spinning had already gone: Benyons of Shrewsbury in 1861, John Morfitt and John Wilkinson a few years later. The Ashworth cotton enterprises, built up between 1818 and 1834 by Henry and Edward Ashworth, began their relative decline in the 1840s.[62] In iron, Joshua Walker & Co. did not long survive the end of the French Wars, its steel trade being formally wound up in 1829 and its iron trade finally wasted away in the 1830s. Other ironmasters fared little better: John Darwin, one of Sheffield's leading industrialists, had gone bankrupt by 1828.[63] The Coalbrookdale Company lacked managerial direction after Abraham and Alfred Darby retired in 1849 and Francis Darby died in 1850, faltered and was sustained only by continuing demand for its products.[64]

Entrepreneurship was never confined to the industrial economy and there were also business opportunities for women in leisure industries and several managed theatres either themselves or with their husbands.[65] A young widow Mrs Honey, for instance, managed the City of London

---

[60] Aston, Jennifer, *Female Entrepreneurship in Nineteenth-Century England: Engagement in the Urban Economy*, (Palgrave Macmillan), 2016, pp. 53-138.

[61] Rimmer, W. G., *Marshalls of Leeds Flax-Spinners,1788-1886*, (Cambridge University Press), 1960, 2012.

[62] Boyson, Rhodes, *The Ashworth Cotton Enterprise: The Rise and Fall of a Factory Firm, 1818-1880*, (Oxford University Press), 1970.

[63] 'Samuel Darwin and Sons' Partnership Dissolved, The Partnership between Samuel Darwin and his sons John and Thomas...', *Sheffield Independent*, 6 March 1824, p. 1, 'Bankruptcy', *Sheffield Independent*, 12 January 1828, p. 2.

[64] Thomas, Emyr, *Coalbrookdale and the Darby family: the story of the world's first industrial dynasty*, (Sessions), 1999.

[65] Brooks, Helen, 'Women and Theatre Management in the Eighteenth Century', in Engel, Laura, (ed.), *The Public's Open to Us: Essays on Women and Performance in Eighteenth-Century England*, (Cambridge Scholars), 2009, pp. 73-97, Powell, Kerry, *Women and the Victorian Theatre*, (Cambridge University Press), 1997, pp. 13-75.

Theatre from 1837 until her death six years later. Sara Lane was not born into the business, but like many other working-class girls found the stage an attractive alternative to other occupations. She started aged sixteen as the music hall singer Sara Wilton but went on to become the second wife of Sam Lane, the proprietor of the Britannia Saloon who employed her in 1843.[66] After his death in 1871, she was successfully managed the Britannia Theatre for the next twenty-eight years.[67]

Mrs Honey and Sara Lane achieved their greatest success as widows, but marrying within the profession had its advantages for women wanting to work after marriage. Clarissa Conquest danced at the Garrick Theatre when her husband Benjamin Conquest (1803-1872) was lessee in the 1830s.[68] Mrs Honner, the Irish-born actress Ann-Maria Macarthy (1812-1870) and star of the Pavilion in 1831, appeared with her husband and they managed the City of London Theatre after 1847 while Emma Yarnold appeared with her husband when he was lessee of the Pavilion Theatre in 1848 and managed it after his death. In the 1840s and 1850s the prolific Mrs Henry Denvil (1809-1889), the playwright wife of the manager of the Pavilion Theatre, regularly kept London's East End theatres supplied with melodramas, a necessity when her husband went bankrupt in the 1840s.[69] Emma Cons (1838-1912) was committed to using the arts to improve the quality of life for the poor.[70] In 1880, she took over the management of the Royal Victoria Coffee Music Hall providing a programme of entertainment, concerts, educational and temperance lectures. The committee running the theatre was mainly made up of philanthropists and social reformers. From 1912 her niece, Lilian Baylis (1874-1937), took over the management of the Old Vic. Baylis was to become the most influential woman manager in the twentieth century, turning the Old Vic into a quasi-national theatre.[71]

How competent were entrepreneurs in late-Victorian and Edwardian Britain?[72] Seeing entrepreneurs in the late-nineteenth century as having

---

[66] 'Testimonial to Mrs Sara Lane', *The Era*, 9 October 1886, p. 13.

[67] 'Mrs Sara Lane's Funeral', *Huddersfield Chronicle*, 23 August 1899, p. 4: 'The funeral brought together a very large crowd consisting mainly of the inhabitants of the district [Hoxton, London], Mrs Lane having endeared herself to them by her benevolence and philanthropy…'

[68] 'Death of Mr Benjamin Conquest', *East London Observer*, 13 July 1872, p. 5.

[69] Davis, Tracy C., and Donkin, Ellen, (eds.), *Women and Playwriting in Nineteenth-Century Britain*, (Cambridge University Press), 1999.

[70] Poole, Andrea Geddes, *Philanthropy and the Construction of Victorian Women's Citizenship: Lady Frederick Cavendish and Miss Emma Cons*, (University of Toronto Press), 2014, pp. 96-134.

[71] Schafer, Elizabeth, *Lilian Baylis: A biography*, (University of Hertfordshire Press), 2006, pp. 49-74 on Emma Cons and Lilian Baylis.

[72] Payne, Peter, 'Entrepreneurship and British economic decline', in Collins,

declining initiative and drive rests on the dynamism of their predecessors of the classical industrial revolution.[73] From the 1870s, growth in industrial production declined, there was a relative deterioration in Britain's international economic status and a sluggish rise in productivity that have, to some degree, been blamed on declining entrepreneurial spirit.[74] Landes, for instance, supported this position suggesting that British enterprise reflected a:

...combination of complacency. Her merchants, who had once seized the markets of the world, took them for granted; the consular reports are full of the incompetence of British exporters, their refusal to suit their goods to the taste and pockets of the client, their unwillingness to try new products in new areas, their insistence that everyone in the world ought to read in English and count in pounds, shillings and pence. Similarly, the British manufacturer was notorious for his indifference to style, his conservatism in the face of new techniques, his reluctance to abandon the individuality of tradition for the conformity implicit in mass production.[75]

Entrepreneurial failure was compared adversely with performance elsewhere, usually in Germany and America. However, McCloskey[76] found that the British iron and steel masters exploited technology before 1914 as well as their competitors but was less convinced by the potential of the British coal industry in which productivity was boosted by increasing the labour force rather than by technological means.[77] Similar studies of the cotton industry found that failure to introduce newer technology and

---

Bruce, and Robbins, Keith, (eds.), *British culture and economic decline*, (St. Martin's Press), 1990, pp. 25-58.

[73] Payne, P. L., *British Entrepreneurship in the Nineteenth Century*, (Macmillan), second edition, 1988, is a brief bibliographical study. Dintenfass, Michael, *The Decline of Industrial Britain 1870-1980*, (Routledge), 1992, and Dormois, Jean-Pierre, and Dintenfass, Michael, (eds.), *The British industrial decline*, (Routledge), 1999, supply a challenging account of Britain's long-term decline since the 1870s.

[74] Westall, O. M., 'The competitive environment of British business 1850-1914', in Kirby, M. W., and Rose, Mary B., (eds.), *Business enterprise in modern Britain: from the eighteenth to the twentieth century*, (Routledge), 1994, pp. 207-235, and Kirby, M. W., *The Decline of British Economic Power Since 1870*, (Taylor & Francis), 1981, pp. 1-24, provides a valuable context.

[75] Landes, D., *The Unbound Prometheus*, (Cambridge University Press), 1969, p. 564.

[76] McCloskey, D. N., *Economic maturity and entrepreneurial decline: British iron and steel, 1870-1913*, (Harvard University Press), 1973, pp. 1-21, 56-72, 125-130.

[77] McCloskey, D. N., *Enterprise and Trade in Victorian Britain*, (Allen & Unwin), 1981, pp. 74-93.

reliance on mule-spinning did not lead to a decline in productivity.[78] On the basis of these and other studies, McCloskey argued that there was 'little left of the dismal picture of British failure painted by historians'.[79] Nevertheless doubts remain. British entrepreneurs failed to confront organisational weakness or vigorously embrace new industries. However, they did move into the service sector, whose relatively rapid rate of growth and high productivity between 1870 and 1914 was superior to the old staples and provided buoyancy in Britain's aggregate economic growth. Entrepreneurial hesitations were always present, even during the Industrial Revolution and this became more apparent after 1870.[80]

There is a deep-seated conviction that British culture was the root cause of Britain's industrial decline. British people, especially the middle-classes, have long been averse to industry. Those businessmen who could abandon industry and trade for a life of gentility eagerly did so. This 'gentrification' of the English middle-classes caused a dulling of industrial energies and led to a decline in Britain's economic expertise.[81] Politicians and civil servants whose actions shaped policies within which private enterprise operated were drawn from the gentry or educated in the ideals of service in public schools or the ancient universities. The financiers and traders of London to whom they looked for economic expertise were also imbued with the same anti-industrial spirit. In reality, however, the middle-classes were far less hostile to manufacturing. The upper middle-classes sent a significant number of their sons into business and their flow into manufacturing and commerce was not limited to genteel pursuits like merchant banking. Sons of landowners and professionals accounted for a

[78] Chapman, S. D., 'The Textile Industries', in Roderick, G. W., and Stephens, M. D., (eds.), *Where did we go wrong? Industrial performance, education and the economy in Victorian Britain*, (Taylor & Francis), 1981, pp.125-138.
[79] Ibid., McCloskey, D. N., *Enterprise and Trade in Victorian Britain*, p. 106.
[80] See, for instance, Brown, K. D., 'Entrepreneurial Failure and Retailing: a case-study', *Journal of Industrial History*, Vol. 5, (2002), pp. 71-88, Toms, Steven, 'Windows of opportunity in the textile industry: the business strategies of Lancashire entrepreneurs, 1880-1914', *Business History*, Vol. 40, (1998), pp. 1-25.
[81] The classic modern exposition of this view can be found in Wiener, Martin, *English Culture and the Decline of the Industrial Spirit 1850-1980*, (Cambridge University Press), 1981. See also, Trainor, Richard, 'The gentrification of Victorian and Edwardian industrialists', in Stone, Lawrence, Beier, A. L., Cannadine, David, and Rosenheim, James M., (eds.), *The First modern society: essays in English history in honour of Lawrence Stone*, (Cambridge University Press), 1989, pp. 167-197, and Thomson, F. M. L., *Gentrification and the Enterprise Culture: Britain 1780-1980*, (Oxford University Press), 2003, pp. 19-142, and Robbins, Keith, *Politicians, diplomacy, and war in modern British history*, (Hambledon), 1994, pp. 67-84, on British culture versus British industry.

quarter of British steel manufacturers active between 1865 and 1914 and both groups were markedly over-represented in this heavy industry in comparison with their incidence in the population as a whole.

Mechanisation spread rapidly but it was not until 1924 that factories, distinguished by their use of a power source, were more numerous than workshops. While the numbers employed in the chemical and allied trades grew rapidly between 1881 and 1911, in 1907 they only accounted for 3 per cent of the net output of industry. In new science-based industries, producers clung to outdated methods and failed to develop new ones sufficiently fast.[82] The decline of industrial Britain after 1870 was a matter of the decisions about tools and techniques, education and training and advertising and sales that the men who remained in the offices and on the shop-floors made. There is little direct evidence linking the choices entrepreneurs and managers made about production and marketing with the anti-industrial values to which they supposedly succumbed. If there was a 'gentry cast' to their minds, that strongly influenced business decision-making, there are few traces of it in the records of British enterprises.

The professions

Britain had an increasing, and increasingly prosperous, population. It grew by a third in the last three decades of the century, a higher growth rate than for 1841-1871. There was also diversification of the industrial structure with an increased emphasis on the service sectors whose share of the national income rose from 44 per cent in 1841 to 54 per cent by 1901. It was in the urban centres that the middle-classes mushroomed. Those with incomes over £150 per year increased by about 170 per cent: from 307,000 in 1860-1861 to 833,000 in 1894-1895. The development of a substantial and powerful professional group within the middle-classes gathered considerable pace from the 1840s.[83] This growth came not only those who sought entry into the traditional professional occupations in religion, law, medicine and education but also those who helped to 'professionalise' other occupations connected with the demands of the post-industrial world such accounting, surveying, civil and mechanical engineering and the emergence of the 'service class'. For Perkin, the

---

[82] Reed, Peter, *Entrepreneurial Ventures in Chemistry: The Muspratts of Liverpool, 1793-1934*, (Routledge), 2016.
[83] Corfield, P., *Power and the professions in Britain, 1700-1850*, (Routledge), 1995, provides context. Reader, W. J., *Professional Men: The Rise of the Professional Classes in Nineteenth-Century England*, (Basic Books), 1966, is still the best short introduction to the subject but see also Gourvish, T. R., 'The Rise of the Professions' in Gourvish, T. R., and O'Day, Alan, (eds.), *Later Victorian Britain 1867-1900*, (Macmillan), 1988, pp. 13-36.

professions constituted the 'forgotten middle-class', temporarily ignored in the early stages of the industrial revolution as the aristocratic, entrepreneurial and working-class ideals vied for supremacy.[84] This neglected group benefited from the expanded opportunities provided by industrialisation and by the expansion of education.[85]

In 1800, there were three great liberal professions—divinity, physic and the law—identified in the person of the clergyman, the physician and the barrister or judge. Advancement in these professions came through family connection, patronage and a liberal education based on the classics not a specific body of expert knowledge and not through success in competitive examinations. The nineteenth century saw the creation of institutions that helped the middle-classes define who were members of the professions. In many respects, the idea of professionalism with its self-governing rules and regulations, its codes of ethics, its elaborate hierarchies based on qualifications and seniority was largely a nineteenth century invention even though it adopted some of the forms of older institutions. Apothecaries were the first to establish a system of registration and qualification in the Apothecaries Act 1815 ensuring that those who called themselves shared a common body of knowledge properly not cursorily examined and standards of behaviour. By 1834, the apothecaries' system had changed not only how apothecaries worked but also their social status.

In 1851, certain occupations had acquired social status through their control of a particular area of knowledge and expertise combined with a license to use this knowledge and expertise. The activities of a 'profession' were controlled and regulated by the profession itself through monopolistic restrictive practices.[86] The 'professional class' embraced not only those in the 'learned professions' plus 'literature, art and science' but also those engaged in government and defence. This classification excluded accountants, architects and surveyors who were included on the list of industrial occupations. However, it was the notion of service to the community that was held to justify a privileged position of trust:

This great class includes those persons who are rendering direct service to mankind and satisfying their intellectual, moral and devotional wants.[87]

The late-nineteenth century saw considerable competition for

---

[84] Ibid., Perkin, Harold, *The Rise of Professional Society*, p. xxii.

[85] See, Schwarz, Leonard D., 'Professions, elites, and universities in England, 1870-1970', *Historical Journal*, Vol. 47, (2004), pp. 941-962.

[86] On this issue, see Witz, A., 'Patriarchy and professions: the gendered politics of occupational closure', Sociology, Vol. 24, (1990), pp. 675-690.

[87] 'Remarks on the Industrial Statistics of 1861', *Return on Poor Rates and Pauperism*, July 1864.

professional status as emerging occupations tried to join their more established colleagues. Their numbers rose from about 345,000 in 1861 to 515,000 in 1881 and 735,000 in 1901, an increase of 113 per cent across the period. The professional elements in society increased from about 2.5 per cent in 1861 to 4.0 per cent in 1901 as a percentage of the occupied population.

Between 1861 and 1901, the growth in the established professions was slight. Numbers in religion, law and medicine rose by 30-60 per cent, compared to an overall increase in population of 61 per cent and an increase of 170 per cent in those with incomes over £150. However, some occupations exhibited much higher growth rates. Dentistry established itself as a recognised activity after the Medical Act 1858[88] and the Dentists Act 1878.[89] Writing and journalism and music and entertainment expanded reflecting the growth of leisure activities and their commercial exploitation in the late-nineteenth century. Teaching was stimulated by the expansion of both public and state schools and the 'industrial professions' of architecture, engineering and surveying also expanded. After 1881, the growth of most professional occupations was more modest but two occupations experienced considerable growth. Most of the increase in the numbers of physicians and surgeons were concentrated after 1881 while acting continued to exhibit above-average growth, its 174 per cent increase between 1881 and 1901 receiving special attention in the 1901 Census Report. Employment opportunities for women remained limited in the major professions especially in the more prestigious posts but dominated three occupations, teaching, midwifery and nursing, where status was usually low: of the 230,000 teachers listed in 1901, 172,000 or three-quarters were women.

Between 1860 and 1900, new protective organisations were established in the predominantly male professionalising occupations and there was a considerable increase in educational and training activities but this built on critical earlier decisions. For instance, the British Medical Association was founded in 1856.[90] After 1860, earlier advances were strengthened and local and provincial bodies combined to form national

[88] Roberts, M. J. D., 'The Politics of Professionalization: MPs, Medical Men, and the 1858 Medical Act', *Medical History*, Vol. 53, (2009), pp. 37-56. See also, Lawrence, Christopher, *Medicine in the Making of Modern Britain 1700-1920*, (Routledge), 1994.
[89] Campbell, J. M., 'A brief survey of British dentistry: Charles Allen - Dentists' Act, 1878', *British Dental Journal*, Vol. 52, (1950), pp. 175-181.
[90] Little, E. M., *History of the British Medical Association 1832-1932*, (BMA), 1932, republished, 1984, Pyke-Lees, Walter, *Centenary of the General Medical Council, 1858-1958: the history and present work of the Council*, (General Medical Council), 1958, and Oswald, Arthur, *The Royal College of Surgeons of England*, (Country Life), 1962.

associations. Royal Charters were conferred on existing institutions and other elements of enhanced status were evident in statutory recognition, regulation and privilege. In the law, separation of barristers from the subordinate branch of solicitors and attorneys remained. Barristers took steps to defend restrictive practices through a Bar Committee of 1883, reorganised in 1894 as the Bar Council. Solicitors, who had obtained a monopoly of conveyancing in 1804, obtained more work with the creation of country courts in 1846.[91] Their association, the 'Incorporated Law Society' was entrusted with registration in 1843, given a new charter in 1845, the right to conduct its own examinations in 1877 and established its own Law School in London in 1903. The membership of the Law Society increased fourfold to reach 77,000 by 1901 and the number of practising solicitors rose by 60 per cent over the same period to 16,300.[92] The creation of the 'industrial professions' was, by contrast, emphatically a creation of the nineteenth century. Railways functioned as a major stimulus encouraging change in engineering, accounting, surveying and architecture as well as in specialist branches of the law. Two organisations were established before 1860: the Institution of Civil Engineers in 1818 and a similar body for Mechanical Engineers in 1847.[93] Between 1860 and 1900, a dozen further bodies were established, six in 1860-1873 and six more in 1889-1897. Membership of engineering institutions rose from about 1,700 in 1860 to 23,000 in 1900.

Professional organisations sought to raise status, increase financial rewards and provide occupational security by differentiation, regulation and an emphasis on the gentlemanly virtues of education and middle-class morality. The transformation of the older professions and the emergence of newer branches were part of the general process of socio-political change. Professional activities, whether stimulated by internal factors such as new knowledge or by external changes like industrial growth, urbanisation and the railways were a major element in the process by

---

[91] Christian, E. B. V., *A short history of solicitors*, (Reeves & Turner), 1896, and Garrard, J. A., and Parrott, Vivienne, 'Craft, professional and middle-class identity: solicitors and gas engineers, c.1850-1914', in Kidd, Alan J., and Nicholls, David, (eds.), *The making of the British middle class? Studies of regional and cultural diversity since the eighteenth century*, (Sutton), 1996, pp. 148-168.

[92] Sugarman, David, *A brief history of the Law Society*, (Law Society), 1995.

[93] Pullin, John, *Progress through mechanical engineering: the first 150 years of the Institution of Mechanical Engineers*, (Quiller), 1997. See also, Reader, W. J., *History of the Institution of Electrical Engineers, 1871-1971*, based on research by Rachel Lawrence, Sheila Nemet, and Geoffrey Tweedale, (Peregrinus on behalf of the Institution of Electrical Engineers), 1987, and Buchanan, R. A., 'Institutional proliferation in the British engineering profession, 1847-1914', *Economic History Review*, second series, Vol. 38, (1985), pp. 42-60.

which middle-class elites established and protected their position in an industrial society. This involved a separation from the working-classes and a power-sharing and partial empathy with the old aristocratic order. The rise of the professions pointed both backward and forward: backward since the professions failed to shake off the trappings of aristocratic values; forward in encouraging a greater degree of government intervention in the economy, the hallmark of the modern century state.

The suburban movement represented the beginnings of the gradual move from a society in which most people rented accommodation to one in which many envisaged owning their homes. About 250 building societies existed in 1825 but by 1910 this had risen to 1,723 societies with 626,000 members and total assets of over £76m and had been placed on a statutory basis in 1874 and 1894.[94] In 1914, tenancies remained the norm for 90 per cent of the population. The beginnings of a property-owning democracy was a product of the post-war period.[95]

The suburbs were much criticised by contemporaries. Walter Besant (1836-1901) said they were:

...without any society; no social gatherings or institutions as dull a life as mankind ever tolerated...[96]

Yet their benefits were plain. Thousands gained privacy in a home of their own in quiet and healthy surroundings, within reach of the countryside. Shopping facilities, initially poor, improved dramatically with the displacement of the stall-holder and local craftsmen by the lock-up shop in the 1850s and the emergence of shopping centres in the 1880s containing branches of national retail chains like Boots, Liptons and Freeman, Hardy and Willis.[97] The infrastructure of suburbs was

---

[94] See, for instance, Brabrook, Edward, *Building Societies*, (P. S. King), 1906, Samy, Luke, and Samy, Antoninus, *The Building Society Promise: Access, Risk and Efficiency 1880-1939*, (Oxford University Press), 2016, pp. 1-53, Pooley, Colin G., and Harmer, Michael J., *Property ownership in Britain c. 1850-1950: the role of the Bradford Equitable Building Society and the Bingley Building Society in the development of homeownership*, (Granta Editions), 1999, and more generally Johnson, Paul A., *Saving and spending: The working-class economy in Britain, 1870-1939*, (Oxford University Press), 1985.
[95] See, Daunton, Martin J., *A property-owning democracy?: Housing in Britain*, (Faber) 1987, for the period after 1900.
[96] Besant, Walter, *London in the Nineteenth Century*, (A. & C. Black), 1909, p. 262.
[97] See, Lancaster, Bill, *The department store: a social history*, (Leicester University Press), 1995, Benson, John, and Shaw, Gareth, (eds.), *The evolution of retail systems, c.1800-1914*, (Leicester University Press), 1991, and Chapman, S. D., *Jesse Boot of Boots the Chemists: a study in business history*, (Hodder &

reinforced in other ways with the building of churches, schools, pubs and theatres.

There was also some decentralisation of industrial and business activity, some of which catered entirely for suburban needs: building and repair trades, bakeries and breweries, laundries, gas and electricity works. But lack of space and high rents and rates in city centres were driving other businesses to suburban sites. This development was generally part of the process of evolution of suburban sites. Camberwell, for instance, began as a detached village outside London, became a satellite community and was fully absorbed as a suburb.[98] By 1900, most of its population of 259,000 lived and worked in Camberwell. The extension in railway mileage between 1870 and 1912, from 13,562 to 20,038 miles, was the consequence of rural branch lines or suburban services. Many railways followed rather than anticipated suburban expansion. The growth in third-class suburban travel was of major importance in London but outside the capital railways were underused by commuters. The Nottingham Suburban Railway opened in 1889 could not withstand the competition of trams and closed in 1916.

Domesticity

The emergence of the middle-classes has been treated as 'male' and accounts of middle-class consciousness structured round public events in which women have generally been seen as playing little part.[99] The place of women in conventional historiography lay at the heart of middle-class notions of family and home. Their role was essentially domestic, dependent and private while the male role was one of having dependants and public. Was 'the separation of spheres' and the division between the public and private a given or was it constructed as an integral part of middle-class culture and self-identity? Catherine Hall maintains:

> But one of the ways in which the middle-class was held together, despite many divisive factors, was their ideas about masculinity and femininity. Men came to share a sense of what constituted masculinity and women a sense of what constituted femininity....masculinity meant having dependants, femininity meant being dependent...the idea of a universal womanhood is weak in comparison with the idea of certain types of sexual differentiation being a necessary part of class identity.[100]

Stoughton), 1974.

[98] Boast, Mary, *The story of Camberwell,* rev. ed., (Southwark Local Studies Library), 2000.

[99] On the emergence of the middle-classes Davidoff, L., and Hall, C., *Family Fortunes: Men and Women of the English middle-class 1780-1850,* (Hutchinson), 1987, 2nd ed., (Routledge), 2002, is a major contribution to women's history.

There was no middle-class equivalent to the working-class idea of the 'family wages' that established a notion of economic dependence. The middle-classes took on the aristocratic notion of patrilineal rights to property even though they broke with them at many other points. The Birmingham *Trade Directories* demonstrate the growing dependence of women after 1780 and their increasingly marginal economic role. By the 1840s, however, women were seen as lacking the knowledge and expertise to enter into business: jobs were being redefined as managerial and skilled and therefore masculine. Women could manage the home and the family but not the workshop or the factory.

How were middle-class women represented? The concept of 'respectability' was a complex combination of moral, religious, economic and cultural systems that helped defined the individual's proper relationship with their worlds. The notion of respectability was defined for women in terms of dependency, delicacy and fragility. Independence was unnatural; it signified boldness and sexual deviancy. Female dependency was secured through economic, legal, medical and cultural discourses. Dependency should not be seen in terms of a repressive exercise of power but as a natural and gratifying part of respectable femininity. Male veneration upheld the delicacy and purity of women and, far from oppressing them elevated them to a superior position. Baptist Wriothesley Noel (1799-1873), an evangelical writer stated:

> Women deserve all tenderness; and, made of a more delicate organisation, and of less strength, they need respect and courtesy, protection in danger, the supply of their wants, and above all affection to repay affection.[101]

The characteristics of ideal femininity were a part of a woman's normal biological development. The supposed fragility of middle-class femininity was contrasted with the image of working-class women as inherently healthy, hardy and robust. This myth served the interests of the medical profession and of many middle-class men. The definition of female respectability was part of the wider formation of the domestic ideology and the development of home and family values, the notion of the 'Angel in the House'.[102]

---

[100] Hall, C., 'Gender Divisions and Class Formation in the Birmingham Middle-class 1780-1850', in Samuel, R., (ed.), *People's History and Socialist Theory*, (Routledge), 1981, p. 165

[101] Noel, Baptist, *The Fallen and their Associates*, (James Nisbet and Co.), 1860, pp. 7-8.

[102] Patmore, Coventry, *The Angel in the House: The Betrothal*, (J. W. Parker & Son), 1854.

A cult of domesticity developed with the separation of the home and the workplace during the late-eighteenth and early-nineteenth century and a reconstruction of gender identities.[103] Women were defined 'naturally' as domestic beings, suited to the duties of the home and children. Men were associated with a public sphere, the world of work and politics. The home, for the middle-classes, was emptied of its association with work and was seen in terms of privacy. The home became a haven from the speculation, competition and conflicts of business and public life. It was 'domesticated'. It was, however, much more than:

> The Home is the crystal of society – the very nucleus of national character; and from that source, be it pure or tainted, issue the habits, principles and maxims, which govern public as well as private life. The nation comes from the nursery; public opinion itself is for the most part the outgrowth of the home.[104]

Regulation, control and peace in the home ensured national security and prosperity. The breakdown of domestic order was seen in terms of a total social disintegration. The ideologies of the home and separate spheres were fundamental elements in the formation of an ideal for the middle-class 'Perfect Lady'. This presupposed a plentiful supply of money, provided by working husbands, to create the cosy sanctuary, the home. However, for women in the working-classes the ideal corresponded little to the reality of their lives. The economic realities for the great majority of the middle-classes meant that they had insufficient income to employ a legion of cooks, maids, nannies and governesses. The lot of most middle-class women was often one of hard work and making ends meet, whilst helped in the house often by a single young maid-of-all work.

Most middle-class women could not afford the idleness or other trappings of this stereotype. In reality, there are doubts whether many women indulged in the hypersensitivity with which the Perfect Lady is usually accredited. Ill-health among lower middle-class women was far more likely to arise from overwork and from non-stop childbearing than from inertia. Yet, this sickly facet of the Perfect Woman stereotype is important.[105] The view of women as consumptive weaklings could not have been projected without active support from the medical profession that

---

[103] Hall, Catherine, 'The Early Formation of Victorian Domestic Ideology', in ibid., Hall, Catherine, *White, Male and Middle-class,* (Basil Blackwell), 1994, pp. 75-93, provides a valuable discussion of the development of this central concept between the 1790s and 1840s. It provides a fundamental context for later developments.

[104] Smiles, Samuel, *Self-Help,* (John Murray), 1859, p. 274

[105] See in particular Duffin, Lorna, 'The conspicuous consumptive: woman as invalid', in Delamont, Sara, and Duffin, Lorna, (eds.), *The Nineteenth Century Woman,* (Croom Helm), 1978, pp. 26-56.

attempted to exert social control over their lives by producing medical arguments in favour of the 'traditional female role'. Their views on the health of women actually differed hugely by class. Middle-class women were regarded as inherently sick if they tried to step outside their prescribed role; working women, on the other hand, were seen as health hazards, who harboured the germs of cholera, typhoid and venereal disease and who bore numerous sickly working-class babies. Social and economic conditions made it impossible for working-class women to attain the ideal of the Perfect Lady and there was rarely a separation between work and home. Yet many in the working-classes admired the ideal.

Middle-class writers who were popular among the working-classes wrote about the moral purity of the reputable working-class and the deserving poor. Dickens, Mrs Gaskell and George Eliot (1819-1880) portrayed the sanctity of the working-class home in the face of the moral carelessness of upper-class men who thought they could freely dally with women beneath them. In most respects the Perfect Lady represented only a small minority but there is no doubt of the influence of the ideal. The notion of the wife at home looking after the house and family became gradually more desirable and even if she could not afford servants or idleness, she could be respectable, chaste and virtuous.

This message was widely projected from the pulpit, in religious tracts, in poems, in magazines, in painting and in manuals on the behaviour of women. The Perfect Lady had to acknowledge and inwardly assimilate the fact that she was inferior to men. Mrs Sarah Stickney Ellis (1799-1872), author and mid-century commentator, put the message succinctly:

> As women, then, the first thing of importance is to be content to be inferior to men – inferior in mental power, in the same proportion that you are in bodily strength.[106]

The young girl would be educated in her role of service to the male and in childhood she could practise this submissive and servile role upon her demanding brothers. As for the Victorian woman who really could not dupe herself into believing that she was inferior to man, there was the persuasive and pervasive doctrine of the 'separate spheres'. John Ruskin (1819-1900), in a series of lectures given to women in Manchester in 1864 and later published under the precious and obscure title *Sesames and Lilies*, shied away from the reality that man ruled and women were his subjects. He could not countenance:

---

[106] Ellis, Sarah Stickney, *The Daughters of England: Their Position in Society, Character and Responsibilities*, (Appleton), 1843, p. 6.

...the idea that woman is only the shadow and attendant image of her lord owing him thoughtless servile obedience.[107]

She was, according to Ruskin, man's complement and helpmate. Man was the doer of deeds and the great function of women was to praise. So much for 'separate but equal', an insidious doctrine designed to subvert women from seeking change.

The proper sphere of the Perfect Lady was the home and it was she who converted mere bricks and mortar into that bastion of Victorian cosiness. The outside world was a wicked place, full of terrors and it was small wonder that Victorian businessman sought refuge close to his own warm hearth. Within the home the male willingly submitted to the devoted ministrations of his dear wife–the angel in the house. She was totally untainted by the grimy realities of industrial capitalism. If the outside world was dark, discordant and evil, the angel in the home brought light and harmony to the secure domestic world. Victorian magazines, many with the word 'Home' in the title, glorified the domestic role and reinforced the dominant female image.

The Perfect Lady stereotype was gradually rejected. Middle-class women launched the attack on the inactivity and economic dependence that was expected of them. They claimed control over property, economic independence and admission to education and to the professions, wider employment opportunities and the franchise. There were several economic and social reasons why feminism emerged and why it often focused on the Sex Question. Some argue that feminism was the result of the break-up of the old productive family unit that left single women redundant. Others pursue the sex ratio theory, showing that a 'surplus' female population existed by the 1840s and that these surplus, unsupported spinsters broke down the barriers to entry into the professions. The emergence of a distinct middle-class closed many of what would previously have been middle-class female occupations. It was this group of middle-class women, dissatisfied with their assigned place that sought to redefine women's social position. They provided the majority of 'New Women'. It was these bourgeois women whom John Stuart Mill (1806-1873) had in mind when he pleaded for equality of the sexes in *The Subjection of Women* in 1869 and it was they who assumed the challenge.

The 'New Women' were in part the product of changed socio-economic conditions and in part the result of the efforts of individual women who suffered social ostracism for their beliefs. The suffrage movement, educational reform, the campaign against the Contagious Diseases Acts and the fight to distribute birth control information all contributed to the decline of hypocrisy and rigidity. Women increasingly

---

[107] Ruskin John, *Sesames and Lilies*, (John Wiley & Sons), 1867, p. 77.

demanded and gained constructive and useful roles in society. Job opportunities were opening to every class and the typewriter and telephone had a profound impact of work for women. Social attitudes were beginning to change: in the 1880s and 1890s, W. S. Gilbert (1836-1911) was far softer in his satire of middle aged spinsters than his predecessors in the music halls and in popular literature independent women became heroines for the first time. But this was a slow process.

The New Woman was lampooned and shown in a variety of 'unladylike' postures such as playing golf and riding bicycles. The pages of *Punch*, a journal renowned for its anti-feminism, peddled the popular caricature of the 'New Woman'. Her aspirations to education were derided in its pages throughout the 1890s. The entry of women to the professions was similarly a great joke. On the women's campaign for the vote, *Punch* was equally biting: Suffragettes were uniformly old, ugly, butch and bespectacled. In Thomas Hardy's (1840-1928) novel *Jude the Obscure* (1896) there can be no happiness for Sue Bridehead: she recoiled from marriage to a good man, Jude; her children die horribly and she finally breaks down. George Gissing's (1857-1903) portrayal of spinsters in *The Odd Women* (1892) showed the unhappiness to which their course had led them. The images that are most frequently presented of the New Woman were cruel, mocking and hostile. However, others took a more understanding attitude towards 'new women'.[108]

It is difficult to know how satisfied middle-class women were with their lot. A woman who was discontented would seek an individual rather than a group solution to her predicament. Clearly limited choice of employment, especially before the 1890s, and low pay for all classes of women meant that marriage was the most attractive option. But the fluidity of society meant that women could not remain within a static role of domesticity. Even the most contented could not help but be affected by the intense debate on the position of women that swirled about them. By the 1860s, middle-class women were taking on a growing number of tasks that required public agitation while a few hoped to broaden the definition of women's 'proper sphere'. Respectability remained the goal of outsiders, from actresses to shopkeepers and its possession the prize of even the most militant feminist. In 1914, women were still largely excluded from circles of power, authority and prestige; marriage was still held out as the goal of every young woman. It was the First World War and its immediate

---

[108] Ledger, Sally, 'The New Woman and feminist fictions', in Marshall, Gail, (ed.), *The Cambridge Companion to the Fin de siècle*, (Cambridge University Press), 2007, pp. 153-168, Bickle, Sharon, '"Kick(ing) Against the Pricks": Michael Field's *Brutus Ultor* as Manifesto for the "New Woman"', *Nineteenth Century Theatre and Film*, Vol. 33, (2006), pp. 12-29.

aftermath that, for a time, provided women with a significant degree of emancipation but by the mid-1920s feminism was again in retreat.

Symptomatic of changing sexual attitudes and heightened anxieties over women's sexual behaviour were 'flappers'.[109] They were free-spirited in their behaviour, modern in dress rejecting the corseted restrictions of the pre-war fashion for freer, revealing, shorter dresses or trouser suits, silk stockings, cosmetics and cropped hair and progressive in their love of dancing, jazz and frivolity. Seen as irresponsible and undisciplined, many were appalled by the precocity of their sexuality portraying them as man-hungry vamps or boyish lesbians who preyed on either sex, an ever-available temptation for men and women whether married or not. Images in the media from magazines to films portrayed women firmly placed within marriage and family; the flapper, a differing model of femininity, was often derided. The war with its opportunities for war-work and financial independence had opened up new vistas for women, but after 1918, the re-entry of men into civilian jobs saw women's opportunities for a life, other than traditional domesticity slowly narrowing.

A cult of domesticity was being promoted at the expense of all other models of womanhood. Fulfilment for a woman was to be found at home with a husband and children and few women would have disagreed. Electrolux's 1924 tagline for its vacuum cleaners—'Give her pleasure. Give her Leisure. Give her an ELECTROLUX for Christmas'—could not have been more explicit in identifying leisure as the ultimate goal of the housewife:

There should be no drudgery in the house. There must be time to think, to read, to enjoy life, to be young with the growing generation, to have time for their pleasures, to have leisure for one's own - to hold one's youth as long as possible, to have beauty around us - line and colour in dress, form and colour in our surroundings; to have good food without monotony, and good service without jangled tempers.[110]

---

[109] Ibid., Dyhouse, Carol, *Girl Trouble: Panic and Progress in the History of Young Women*, pp. 70-104.

[110] Braithwaite, Brian, Walsh, Noelle, and Davies, Glyn, (eds.), *Ragtime to Wartime: The Best of Good Housekeeping, 1922-1939*, (Ebury Press), 1986, p. 11.

Middle-class women and employment

The distinction between public and private was never absolute. Among business owners listed in commercial directories between 1780 and 1860, about 10 per cent were female. Women were active businesswomen in towns, many of whom had served an apprenticeship and had earned the 'freedom' of the trade from the appropriate guild. Women were apprenticed to a wide variety of trades, including butchery, bookbinding, brush making, carpentry and ropemaking and as silversmiths. Single women, married women and widows are included in these numbers. Sometimes widows carried on the businesses of their deceased husbands, not simply as figureheads but because they had been active in management of the business while their husband was alive.[111] Most firms were small family partnerships and wives and daughters played an important role, especially behind the scenes, in retailing, book keeping, correspondence and dealing with clients.

By the 1830s, although many middle-class women had successfully entered trades, they faced growing obstacles. Female apprentices declined but this may not have been a major barrier to employment. Women received less education than men though the extent to which this restricted their access to trade is questionable given the limited practical use of education. Women found it harder than men to raise capital because English law did not consider a married woman to have any legal existence; she could not sue or be sued. A married woman was a *feme covert* and technically could not make any legally binding contracts and this may have discouraged others from loaning money to or making other contracts with married women. However, this law was not as limiting in practice in theory because a married woman engaged in trade on her own account was seen by the courts as a *feme sole* and was responsible for her own debts.[112]

---

[111] Tradesmen considered themselves lucky to find a wife who was good at business. In his autobiography James Hopkinson, a cabinetmaker, said of his wife, 'I found I had got a good and suitable companion one with whom I could take sweet council and whose love and affections was only equall'd by her ability as a business woman': Goodman, J. B., (ed.), *Victorian Cabinet Maker: The Memoirs of James Hopkinson, 1819-1894*, (Routledge), 1968, p. 96.

[112] In 1764, James Cox and his wife Jane were operating separate businesses, and both went bankrupt within the space of two months. Jane's creditors sued James' creditors for the recovery of five fans, goods from her shop that had been taken for James' debts. The court ruled that, since Jane was trading as a *femme sole*, her husband did not own the goods in her shop, and thus James' creditors had no right to seize them. See, Blackstone, William, *Reports of Cases determined in the several Courts of Westminster-Hall, from 1746 to 1779*, London, 1781, pp. 570-575.

Women's economic agency was entangled within local relations and family networks. In practice, women found legal ways of getting around *coverture* using other legal instruments—settlements, trusts and bonds, pre-marital and other private contracts—to circumvent its restrictive features. This often gave married women greater economic flexibility and power than the Common Law allowed and provided a platform in which to engage in business and enterprise. For instance, customary law gave women in certain urban boroughs, including London, Cambridge, Chester, Lincoln and Worcester, the possibility of being granted *feme sole* status allowing them to trade independently from their husbands. Women could also exercise their equitable right to establish a marriage contract that gave them control over their own 'separate estate', the money or property they owned before marriage. Where a woman brought business interests into marriage, the principle of 'separate estate' protected her assets from her husband's creditors who, at Common Law, might have a claim on the wife's property. The Courts of Equity and especially the Court of Chancery provided women with a valuable means of avoiding some of the rigidities of the Common Law and had been successfully used by enterprising women since the beginning of the eighteenth century to protect their interests.[113] The law was increasing seen by women as a flexible rather than constraining force on economic activity. The ability of women to function as independent traders depended less upon their marital status than upon the degree to which their local communities felt they could be regarded as trustworthy economic agents.

Women's association with a culture of domesticity is seen as a constraint on their economic agency. Davidoff and Hall argued this gendered separation of roles to be at the heart of middle-class identity and central to the formation of bourgeois social groups within industrialising England.[114] The difficulty with their position is that the articulation of such gender roles in popular discourse did not necessarily accord with the realities of men's and women's lives. The ideology might have been a cultural aspiration, but it was not an impenetrable barrier to female enterprise and, like the law, it was something that women could and did work around. The same applied to the view that business activity was incompatible with bourgeoisie femininity and domestic gentility. There is also a danger in reading the nineteenth century domestic ideology back into the eighteenth century. Contemporary ideologies that sought to marginalise and oppress middle-class women and to deny women

---

[113] Stebbings, C., *The Private Trust in Victorian England*, (Cambridge University Press), 2002, pp. 128-162.

[114] Davidoff, L, 'Gender and the 'great divide': public and private in British gender history', *Journal of Women's History*, Vol. 15, (2003), pp. 11-27, provides a useful summary of their position.

economic power and agency—and ideology is not necessarily a good guide to everyday experience—were a product of the mid-nineteenth rather than the eighteenth century.

Unlike working-class women, employment for middle-class women was also linked to their claims for independence, for a share of the public domain, and with demands for an identity defined by self-respect rather than dependence to middle-class men. Working-class and some poorer middle-class women could not afford the luxury of employment as an expression of their identity. For them, it was a matter of subsistence.[115] The issue was not whether middle-class women worked, which they clearly did, or whether working was compatible with the emerging 'domestic ideology', which for many middle-class men it was not, but how middle-class women, who lacked the financial resources necessary not to work battled against the voice of propriety that sought to define them within an exclusively domestic environment.[116]

Finding suitable employment

By the 1850s, there was a rapid growth in the ranks of middle-class women for whom marriage was to prove unattainable and the increasing failure of middle-class families to maintain large retinues of unproductive and unmarried daughters. The number of single women between the ages of 15 and 45 rose by 72 per cent, from 2.76 million to 3.29 million in the twenty years between 1851 and 1871.[117] This situation was exacerbated by the rising age of marriage that also left more single women waiting for, and often not achieving, marriage. In 1851, a question about marital status on the British census sparked concern about the decline of the family as the moral and reproductive basis of British society triggering the debate about

---

[115] Holcombe, Lee, *Victorian Ladies at Work: Middle-Class Working women in England and Wales, 1850-1914*, (David & Charles), 1973. See also, Davidoff, Leonore, and Hall, Catherine, *Family fortunes: men and women of the English middle class 1780-1850*, (Hutchinson), 1987, 2nd ed., (Routledge), 2002, 3rd ed., (Routledge), 2019, Morris, R. J., *Men, women, and property in England, 1780-1870: a social and economic history of family strategies amongst the Leeds middle classes*, (Cambridge University Press), 2005, and Gordon, Eleanor, and Nair, Gwyneth, 'The economic role of middle-class women in Victorian Glasgow', *Women's History Review*, Vol. 9, (4), (2000), pp. 791-814, Young, Arlene, *From Spinster to Career Woman: Middle-Class Women and Work in Victorian England*, (McGill-Queen's University Press), 2019

[116] Shiman, Lilian Lewis, *Women and Leadership in Nineteenth Century England*, (St. Martin's Press), 1992, pp. 72-90, considers the issue of economic disabilities in relation to employment.

[117] Vicinus, Martha, *Independent Women: Work and Community for Single Women 1850-1920*, (Virago), 1985, examines the lives and ambitions, work and communities of single middle-class women.

the 'surplus woman' problem. The debate can be viewed in the context of larger nineteenth-century discourses about population, surplus, nation, and empire. Levitan uses the background of the census in order to place the surplus woman problem in a larger context. The census viewed single women who were not reproducing as one among many unproductive groups within the nation.[118] For such women who would be regarded as 'ladies', the spectre of a double failure loomed large: the inability to attract a husband and not fulfil their proper role in life as wives and mothers marked them out in the circles of Victorian gentility, while their upbringing and education did not prepare them for the world of work.[119]

The feminist campaigns of the late-1850s and 1860s were concerned with the problem of finding suitable employment for single women. Theodosia, Lady Monson (1803-1891) hired and furnished at her town expense new offices for the *English Woman's Journal* at 19 Langham Place, an extensive property in which she also created a committee room, reading room and coffee shop that was open from 11 am to 10pm.[120] In 1860, it was advertised as 'The Ladies Institute' and it soon became the meeting place for a group of liberal, politically-minded women who became known as the Langham Place group or circle and included Helen Blackburn (1842-1903), novelist, journalist and part-time actress Matilda Hays (1820-1897), women's rights activist and publisher Emily Faithfull (1835-1895),[121] Jessie Boucherett (1825-1905), women's educator Emily Davies (1830-1921) and Lady Manson. It offered a central metropolitan conduit from which a variety of radical and feminist experiments flowed and was the earliest feminist group to be involved in the area of women's employment.

Central to activities of the Langham Place group was in developing journals in which feminist issues were discussed.[122] The *English Women's*

---

[118] See Levitan, Kathrin, 'Redundancy, the 'Surplus Woman' Problem, and the British Census, 1851-1861', *Women's History Review*, Vol. 17, (3), (2008), pp. 359-376. See, for instance, Boucherett, Jessie, 'How to Provide for Superfluous Women', in Butler, Josephine, (ed.), *Women's Work and Women's Culture*, (Cambridge University Press), 1869, pp. 27-39. See also, Holloway, Gerry, *Women and Work in Britain Since 1840*, (Routledge), 2005, pp. 36-51, on surplus women.

[119] Dollard, Catherine L., *The Surplus Woman: Unmarried in Imperial Germany, 1871-1918*, (Berghahn Books), 2012, a valuable comparative study.

[120] Alexander, Sally, 'Why feminism? The women of Langham Place' in Alexander, Sally, (ed.), *Becoming a woman*, (Virago), 1994, pp. 135-148, and Lacey, C. A., (ed.), *Barbara Leigh Smith Bodichon and the Langham Place Group*, (Routledge), 1987.

[121] Stone, James S., *Emily Faithfull: Victorian Champion of Women's Rights*, (P. D. Meany), 1994.

[122] Herstein, Sheila, 'The Langham Place circle and feminist periodicals of the

Review was established two years before the Langham Place Group and marked the beginning of a prolific decade of feminist periodicals. In 1857, it changed its name to the *English Women's Review* and after four issues, Bessie Rayner Parkes and writer Matilda Hays (1820-1897), who had been trying to found a feminist publication for ten years took over as editors. They moved it from Edinburgh to London and one of the essays it published was a hard-hitting article by Barbara Leigh Smith Bodichon[123] entitled 'Women and Work'. The cost of purchasing the magazine proved too high and in March 1858 Bessie Rayner Parkes (1829-1925)[124] and Barbara Leigh Smith Bodichon (1827-1891) founded the *English Woman's Journal* in its place.[125] Published monthly, it ran for six years initially under the editorship of Parkes and Isa Craig, from 1862 to 1864 by Emily Davies and finally Elizabeth Eiloart (1827-1898), from the 1860s a prolific novelist. It had an impressive circulation: from 1860, it was printing 1,000 copies a month to sell and 250 to store to cover demand for back copies. It ceased publication in August 1864 and Parkes then founded the short-lived *Alexandra Magazine and Woman's Social and Industrial Advocate* but when it failed, she withdrew from feminist activity. It was refounded as the *Alexandra Magazine and Englishwoman's Journal* in 1864 and 1865. Jessie Boucherett took over the magazine in 1866 and it was renamed the *Englishwoman's Review.*[126]

The aim of the mid-century feminists through their organisations, letter-exchange and journals was to extend women's capabilities and qualifications through effective networking, education and training and to combat the prejudice that barred women from many avenues of

---

1860s', *Victorian Periodicals Review*, Vol. 26, (1993), pp. 24-27, and relevant articles in *Dictionary of Nineteenth-Century Journalism in Great Britain and Ireland*, (Academia Press and The British Library), 2009. Schroeder, Janice, ''Better Arguments': The *English Woman's Journal*, and the Game of Public Opinion', *Victorian Periodicals Review*, Vol. 35, (3), (2002), pp. 243-271.

[123] Herstein, Sheila R., *A mid-Victorian feminist, Barbara Leigh Smith Bodichon*, (Yale University Press), 1985, Hirsch, Pamela, *Barbara Leigh Smith Bodichon: Feminist, Artist and Rebel*, (Chatto & Windus), 1998.

[124] Parkes, Bessie Rayner, *Essays on Woman's Work*, (Alexander Strahan Publisher), 1865, Lowndes, Emma, *Turning Victorian Ladies into Women: The Life of Bessie Rayner Parkes, 1829-1925*, (Academica Press), 2012.

[125] Schroeder, Janice, ''Better Arguments': The *English Woman's Journal*, and the Game of Public Opinion', *Victorian Periodicals Review*, Vol. 35, (3), (2002), pp. 243-271.

[126] Jordan, Ellen, and Bridger, Anne, ''An Unexpected Recruit to Feminism': Jessie Boucherett's 'Feminist Life' and the importance of being wealthy', *Women's History Review*, Vol. 15, (2006), pp. 385-412, examines how she used her wealth to fund the initial women's suffrage campaign and to direct the strategies of the activist groups to which she belonged.

172

employment.[127] Conscious of women's need for autonomy, the major focus of *English Women's Review* was employment and the associated need to improve the education of women of all classes. The reading room set up at Langham Place became the first of the women's employment societies.[128] Founded in 1859 by Jessie Boucherett, Barbara Bodichon and Adelaide Proctor (1825-1864), the Society for Promoting the Employment of Women (SPEW) had two stated aims: to train women and to find employment for them.[129]

Creating a register of women seeking employment and it also launched classes in arithmetic and bookkeeping, skills of increasing social value.[130] Maria Rye (1829-1903) set up an office copying legal documents in Lincoln's Inn Fields and in 1862, with Bodichon's help, founded the Female Middle-Class Emigration Society.[131] Under Emily Faithfull, it also established the Victoria Press, where she trained working-class girls to be compositors and it rapidly became the leading feminist printing house of the period.[132] SPEW proved highly effective in maintaining a high profile in the press and by lobbying leading MPs as well as using its extensive social networks to persuade influential figures to employ women. Lord Shaftesbury was the President of SPEW from its launch until his death in 1885. It had women accepted successfully into the clerical branches of the Civil Service and many girls were apprenticed in occupations previously available for men such as hair-dressing, china-painting, gilding, watch-making photography, and telegraphy.[133] Later feminist involvement in

[127] Simon-Martin, Meritxell, *Barbara Bodichon's Epistolary Education: Unfolding Feminism*, (Palgrave Macmillan), 2020.

[128] Bridger, Anne, and Jordan, Ellen, *Timely Assistance: The Work of the Society for Promoting the Training of Women, 1859-2009*, (Society for Promoting the Training of Women), 2009.

[129] See, for instance, Boucherett, Jessie, 'How to Provide for Superfluous Women', in Butler, Josephine, (ed.), *Women's Work and Women's Culture*, (Cambridge University Press), 1869, pp. 27-39.

[130] *The Times*, 8 June 1860, *Morning Post*, 30 June 1860, p. 7.

[131] 'Social Science Association', *Morning Post*, 15 October 1863, p. 2.

[132] See, Stone, James S., *Emily Faithfull: Victorian Champion of Women's Rights*, (P. D. Meany), 1994, Faithfull, Emily, 'The Victoria Press', reprinted in ibid., Lacey, C. A., (ed.), *Barbara Leigh Smith Bodichon and the Langham Place Group*, pp. 281-286, Fredeman, William E., 'Emily Faithfull and the Victoria Press', *The Library*, 5th ser., Vol. 29, (1974), pp. 139-164, Stone, James, 'More Light on Emily Faithfull and the Victoria Press', *The Library*, 5th series, Vol. 33, (1978), pp. 63-67. See also, Frawley, Maria, 'The Editor as Advocate: Emily Faithfull and The Victoria Magazine', *Victorian Periodicals Review*, Vol. 31, (1), (1998), pp. 87-103, and 'Feminism, Format and Emily Faithfull's Victoria Press Publications', *Nineteenth-Century Feminisms*, Vol. 1, (1999), pp. 39-63. See also, Ratcliffe, Eric, *The Caxton of her age: the career and family background of Emily Faithfull (1835-95)*, (Images Pub.), 1993, pp. 60-81.

employment campaigns lay in publishing feminist periodicals devoted principally either to this issue or at least offering coverage of new trades for women, as well as carrying job applications. Emily Faithfull, for instance, published a weekly, eight page *Women and Work* from 1874 to 1876 as 'a complete and reliable organ for women seeking employment and employers seeking workers.'[134] They were cheap with *Women and Work* selling for 1d and introduced women to a whole range of related feminist issues.[135] As there were limited ways in which women could find available work, these ventures played an important role.

SPEW succeeded in placing women in jobs but initially the number was small. The organisation created a fresh set of attitudes based not on the threat of poverty but on the dignity and fulfilment that waged-work could offer. The campaign for employment raised two question about the appropriate sexual division of labour: to what extent should the Langham Place feminists support the employment of married women and how far should women who sought employment be constrained by notions of gentility and the appropriateness of employment for a 'lady'? Its concern was that work could be a worthy and indeed morally beneficial alternative to the domestic role and though paid employment was quite clearly an urgent necessity for many middle-class women, the feminists were also concerned with aspects of choice. Payment was a central issue. The prevalent presence of women in philanthropic endeavour was acceptable only because of their volunteer status, a declaration of respectability and of moral sanctity. When their labours were a source of gain rather than personal sacrifice, the issue became one of respectability.[136]

The tightrope of respectability was only one of a host of problems faced by feminist campaigners. Parkes, as editor of the *English Women's Review*, and SPEW tried to broaden the range of occupations that women of different classes might do beyond the saturated markets for governesses and needlewomen. Increasingly, however, Parkes condemned the work of married women outside the home, though Boucherett and Faithfull argued that 'every woman should be free to support herself by the use of whatever faculties God has given her', without obstruction by prejudice or legislation.[137] Middle- and working-class women shared the problem of

---

[133] SPEW was renamed the Society for Promoting the Training of Women (SPTW) in 1926 and is still in existence.

[134] *Women and Work*, 6 June 1874.

[135] This was, for instance, also evident in the publication of guides for women searching for work such as Grogan, Mercy, *How women may earn a living*, (Cassell & Co.), 1883, and Davidson, J. E., *What our daughters can do for themselves: a handbook of women's employments*, (Smith, Elder, & Co.), 1894.

[136] On this issue, see, Jordan, Ellen, *The women's movement and women's employment in nineteenth century Britain*, (Routledge), 1999, pp. 3-21.

[137] Faithfull, E., 'Open council', *English Woman's Journal*, Vol. 10, (1862), pp.

limited fields of opportunity. To become a governess, Jane Austen (1775-1817) observed, was to 'retire from all the pleasures of life, of rational intercourse, equal society, peace and hope, to penance and mortification for ever.'[138]

The 'governess problem' summarised the difficulties imposed since there was a dearth of employment available for middle-class women, governesses became overstocked and hugely exploited field of labour.[139] *English Women's Review* argued that alternative professions were more respectable because, if too many women become governesses, there was a real risk that they would become destitute and ultimately resort to prostitution. Feminists pointed to the absurdity of delivering educational responsibilities into the hands of women unprepared and untrained for the task. The campaign on employing middle-class women centred on the opportunities and choices open to single women, and implied their choice of whether or not to marry.[140] There was also a potential conflict with orthodox political economy, which argued that women's work depressed the wages of men when they were in free competition. Some, like Boucherett were prepared to face the consequences of a free market in labour. Parkes and others adopted a more cautious position suggesting ways in which association and co-operation among women might moderate the harshness of the free market. There were differences over whether their work should continue, as Parkes believed, to be primarily concerned with women or play its part in mixed campaigns and voluntary associations, as Davies argued.

70-71, at p. 70.

[138] Austen, Jane, *Emma: A Novel*, (John Murray), 3 Vols. 1816, Vol. 2, p. 25.

[139] On the issue of governesses see Hughes, Kathryn, *The Victorian Governess*, (Hambledon), 1993, Renton, Alice, *Tyrant or victim? A history of the British governess*, 1991, Raftery, Deirdre, 'The nineteenth-century governess: image and reality', in Whelan, Bernadette, (ed.), *Women and paid work in Ireland, 1500-1930* (Four Courts), 2000, pp. 57-68, and Horn, Pamela, 'The Victorian governess', *History of Education*, Vol. 18, (1989), pp. 333-344.

[140] Faithfull, Emily, *Choice of a Business for Girls*, (Victoria Press), 1864, and Faithfull, Emily, 'On some of the Drawbacks connected to the present Employment of Women: paper read before the National Association for the Promotion of Social Science, in London, June 11th, 1862', *Transactions of the National Association for the Promotion of Social Science*, (John W. Parker), 1863, pp. 809-810.

Professionalising women's work

The development of substantial and powerful professional groups within the middle-classes gathered momentum from the 1840s.[141] This growth came not only those who sought entry into the traditional professional occupations in religion, law, medicine and education[142] but also those who helped to 'professionalise' other occupations such as civil and mechanical engineering, accounting, surveying and the emergence of the 'service class'. The activities of a 'profession' were regulated by the profession itself through powerful, male-controlled protective organisations that sought monopoly power through restrictive practices. However, it was the notion of service to the community that was held to justify a privileged position of trust.

Activist women could extend the cause of women's employment was by moving into new areas of opportunity.[143] Many prominent feminists did this by taking up employment in government jobs as factory and sanitary inspectors, in the new female professions of nursing and teaching or by fighting for entry to hitherto closed professions such as medicine and the Law though the advance into the professions should not be exaggerated. Problems became more acute for women entering nursing or teaching, precisely because they were the areas that rapidly became associated with and almost defined, women's professionalism. Nursing was an exclusively female profession by the 1850s unlike teaching where women employees were concentrated in the lower ranks of the profession and were paid less than their male counterparts. By 1891, among the 'Professional Class' in the census categories, almost 10,000 women worked for the national government with a further 5,000 as local officials. There were 166 women law clerks, 101 doctors, 2 veterinarians, more than 50,000 sick nurses and midwives and almost 145,000 women teachers, professors or lecturers. Altogether more than 400,000 women were in the 'professional class'. This is in addition to the explosion of women's work as typists, telephone operators, telegraphers and commercial clerks. By 1901, women were also nearly 11 per cent of the newly certified occupation of 'dispensing chemist'.

The 'white-blouse' revolution

The 1851 Census listed only fourteen women as commercial clerks in England and Wales but by 1921, 46 per cent of Britain's clerks were

---

[141] See above pp. 157-162.

[142] The civil service and armed forces may also be seen as part of this group but, equally, they may be seen as part of 'government'.

[143] On this issue, see Witz, A., 'Patriarchy and professions: the gendered politics of occupational closure', *Sociology*, Vol. 24, (1990), pp. 675-690.

women. This represented a massive shift in gender. In the mid-nineteenth century, clerks were men generally employed in the counting-houses of merchants and manufacturers as well as in the growing bureaucracies of central and local government. Although in some instances their income of £50 a year in the 1850s was often less than skilled workers, most clerks saw themselves as socially superior with higher levels of literacy and educational achievement. Before the 1880s, male clerks pursued their careers largely untroubled by serious competition in the labour market increasing from 2.5 per cent of all occupied males in 1851 to over 7 per cent in 1911. However, women began to be recruited in increasing numbers especially in the two decades before the First World War but though they made major inroads into the commercial office, they were largely absent in the male reserves of banking, railways and the law. This was the 'white-blouse revolution'.[144]

Why this feminisation occurred was the result of changes in office organisation, technological developments and better education for girls. Changes in business especially the growth of joint-stock companies and amalgamation of companies created larger and more complex structures from the smaller counting-houses. The increased volume of office work saw an increase in the size of the office workforce. Employing more male clerks was an option but this would have led to a rising wages bill when Boards of Directors were trying to curtail costs. Employing women as office workers was cheaper but even so in 1911, male clerks outnumbered female workers by four to one.

Technological change was a major cause of feminisation. Telegraphy and the telephone speeded up communications but it was the typewriter that from the 1880s revolutionised the production of documents in offices.[145] The first Remington model was sold in Britain in 1878; 304 Remington Model IIs were sold in 1880, 27,000 in 1887 and 65,000 in 1890. Although typewriting is gender-free, few male clerks learned typing skills especially when it became clear that typists were unlikely to be promoted.[146]

---

[144] Anderson, Gregory, (ed.), *The White-Blouse Revolution: Female Office Workers since 1870*, (Manchester University Press), 1988, especially pp. 1-66.

[145] Zimmeck, Meta, "The Mysteries of the Typewriter': Technology and Gender in the British Civil Service, 1870-1914', in Groot, Gertjan de, and Schrover, Mariou, (eds.), *Women workers and technological change in Europe in the nineteenth and twentieth century*, (Taylor and Francis), 1995, pp. 67-96, and Shiach, Morag, 'Modernity, labour and the typewriter', in Stevens, Hugh, and Howlett, Caroline, (eds.), *Modernist Sexualities*, (Manchester University Press), 2000, pp. 114-129.

[146] Davy, Teresa, "A cissy job for men: a nice job for girls': women shorthand typists in London, 1900-30', in Davidoff, L., and Westover, B., (eds.), *Our Work, Our Lives, Our Words: Women's History and Women's Work*, (Macmillan), 1986, pp. 124-144.

However, once shorthand was linked with typewriting, it was quickly feminised and explains why girls, initially largely from the better educated middle-classes, became the backbone of office work. By the 1890s, working-class boys and girls and those from less secure middle-class backgrounds were taking evening continuation classes in commercial subjects provided by local School Boards and by voluntary organisations increasing numbers of suitably qualified young women who could become clerks.[147]

What motivated large numbers of young women to invest in classes in shorthand and typing was the economic benefits that came from office work. In 1910, female clerks earned on average a £1 a week in commerce and more in insurance compared to the 12 and 18 shillings a week paid to female cotton workers. In other female white-collar occupations, nurses earned between £24 and £40 a year and only in school teaching did women earn substantially more than clerks. A small number of female clerks earned higher wages than almost all women and most men with the elite private secretaries in top London offices by 1911 earning between £150 and £220 a year.

Office work fulfilled the middle-class requirement of genteel and economically secure employment and apart from nursing and teaching and the higher reaches of shop work was the only occupation that allowed women to be 'ladylike' in and outside work. It is also clear that female clerks generally left the labour market when they married. The process of feminisation of office work was slow and women only made up a fifth of clerks in 1911 largely because they were not hired to replace men. Women clerks were largely confined in their own clerical grades and departments and had little prospect of promotion. It was not until 1951 Census that women clerks outnumbered men.

Nursing

There were three options open to people in need of hospital care. They could go to the local Poor Law workhouse where they would be inexpertly treated by other inmates or be admitted to a voluntary hospital where conditions were often poor and where contagious diseases were endemic or they could also be treated at home.[148] In the early-nineteenth century,

---

[147] Carnaffon, Gladys, 'Commercial education and the female office worker', in ibid., Anderson, Gregory, (ed.), *The White-Blouse Revolution: Female Office Workers since 1870*, pp. 67-87.

[148] Hawkins, Sue, *Nursing and Women's Labour in the Nineteenth Century*, (Routledge), 2010, places nursing in the context of women's wider role in British society. See also, Hallett, C. E., 'Nursing, 1830-1920', in Borsay, Anne, and Hunter, Billie, (eds.), *Nursing and Midwifery in Britain since 1700*, (Palgrave

nursing in hospitals was almost exclusively working-class in character.[149] By 1900, it had evolved into a profession composed largely of middle-class women. Professionalisation of nursing drew on established social norms of female behaviour and nurses were increasingly seen as paragons of female virtue: dedication to duty, reliability and efficiency. These idealised female qualities existed in the context of total obedience to male doctors, their asexual character reinforced by nurses living in segregated lodgings and a dedication to a vocation that was almost religious in intensity. Although it provided important opportunities for middle- and working-class employment, the professionalisation of nursing provided little liberation from male-domination. In fact, Florence Nightingale (1820-1910) was anxious not to rouse male opposition in the medical profession by equating nursing with feminism. Yet, by 1918, nurses had created a strong professional identity and a clear role within the cultural constructs of femininity.[150]

The Nightingale nurse did not emerge as the standard model for nursing until the 1890s. It took time for new ideas on nurse training and discipline to gain support. Contemporaries and later historians have considered Florence Nightingale, with her training school established at St. Thomas' Hospital in 1860, as the founder of modern nursing. The role played by Jamaican businesswoman Mary Seacole (1805-1881) in the Crimea and after was downplayed largely because of her colour.[151] The Nightingale school has not been judged a great success but its achievement was to associate her name in the public mind with a particularly disciplined form of nurse training.[152] Rather than the beginning of nursing reform, Nightingale nursing built on two earlier reforms: doctor-driven reform that came to be called the 'ward system' and the reforms of the Anglican Sisters, known as the 'central system' of nursing.[153] There were two main

---

Macmillan), 2012.

[149] Borsay, Anne, 'Nursing 1700-1830', in ibid., Borsay, Anne, and Hunter, Billie, (eds.), *Nursing and Midwifery in Britain since 1700*, pp. 23-45.

[150] Abel-Smith, Brian, *A History of the Nursing Profession*, (Heinemann), 1960, and Maggs, C. J., *The Origins of General Nursing*, (Croom Helm), 1983, provide valuable studies of the development of nursing in the nineteenth century.

[151] Robinson, Jane, *Mary Seacole: The Charismatic Black Nurse who became a Heroine in the Crimea*, 2005, (Robinson), 2019.

[152] Baly, Monica, 'The Nightingale nurses: the myth and the reality', in Maggs, C., (ed.), *Nursing History, the state of the art* (Croom Helm), 1987, pp. 33-59, and her more extensive *Florence Nightingale and the nursing legacy*, (Croom Helm), 1986. See also, McDonald, Lynn, 'Florence Nightingale a Hundred Years on: why she was and what she was not', *Women's History Review*, Vol. 19, (2010), pp. 721-740.

[153] Helmstadter, Carol, and Godden, Judith, *Nursing before Nightingale, 1815-1899*, (Ashgate), 2011. See also, Helmstadter, Carol, 'Building a New Nursing

reasons for these reforms. Hospital doctors found the old independent nurse practitioners a threat to the development of new medical practices and welcomed the spread of middle-class values by philanthropists. By contrast, Helmstadter and Godden argue that the real cause of reform was the development of new scientific medicine that emphasised supportive therapies and became heavily dependent on skilled nursing for successful execution of these treatments. The old hospital nurses could not meet the requirements of the new medicine. Recruitment and retention of working-class persons was also extremely difficult because nursing in the early-nineteenth century formed the lowest rung of the occupation of domestic service and was a job of last resort. It was still more difficult to recruit educated women or 'ladies' and there were intricate interactions between the requirements of clinical nursing under hospital medicine's new regime and the contemporary ideal of a lady.

The importance of Florence Nightingale, forever fixed in the public imagination as the 'Lady with the Lamp' in the Crimea, lies in her role in establishing a set of rules and expectations of what a nurse should be.[154] Her view of nursing, expressed in *Notes on Nursing* in 1860, was based on moral rather than scientific principles. Candidates for her training schemes had to demonstrate that they had the stamina and character to fulfil her highest moral requirements. They had to be dedicated to the role, to suppress their own personal interests and to be disciplined and self-controlled. Before a nurse was considered fit to control and care for patients, she had to be in total control of herself. There was little emphasis here on scientific progress. Cleanliness was next to godliness so nurses had to have the highest standards of hygiene but apart from that, the major objective was complete dedication to patient care. Even nurses' uniforms were modelled on those of nursing sisters in religious orders. Nursing was less a profession than a calling.[155]

Before 1861, there were under a thousand women acting as hospital nurses but by 1901, this had risen to 12,500 nurses in general hospitals. The reasons for this are clear. The nursing profession was based on a

Service: Respectability and Efficiency in Victorian England', *Albion*, Vol. 35, (4), (2004), pp. 590-621.

[154] Bostridge, Mark, *Florence Nightingale: The Woman and the Legend*, (Viking), 2008, 200th Anniversary Edition, (Penguin), 2020, Nightingale, Florence, *Florence Nightingale to Her Nurses: A Selection of Miss Nightingale's Addresses to Probationers and Nurses of the Nightingale School at St Thomas' Hospital*, (Jungle), 2007, McDonald, Lynn, (ed.), *Collected Works of Florence Nightingale: The Nightingale School*, (Wilfred Laurier University Press), 2009, pp. 557-712, for *Notes on Nursing*, originally published in 1860.

[155] Hallett, Christine E., 'Nursing, 1830-1920: Forging a Profession', in ibid., Borsay, Anne, and Hunter, Billie, (eds.), *Nursing and Midwifery in Britain since 1700*, pp. 46-73.

hierarchical system based on the domestic sphere of women's accepted world and middle-class women were attracted to a role without any loss of social status and this was reflected in their pay and conditions. Matrons were given low salaries because it was assumed that they were from affluent families and had a private income. Nursing attracted working-class girls because, though it resembled domestic service, it was not limited by the confines of a household and had a degree of freedom and independence. They too were poorly paid but this was balanced by a roof over their heads, regular meals and by professional status especially after the establishment of formal training and certification for nurses after 1881. Without working-class nurses the problem of recruiting sufficient nurses would have proved impossible but this was not without difficulties. Most working-class nurses had little education and most training courses did little to address this issue. There were also opportunities for working-class girls as untrained domestics who performed menial and cleaning tasks on low pay. Although they called themselves nurses, they had no formal training and outnumbered trained nurses well into the 1930s. There were also important openings in nursing beyond hospitals with the emergence of district nurses from the 1860s and especially after 1880.[156]

State registration of the medical profession began in 1858 but, although many observers argued for a similar system for nursing, it was not until the 1890s that pressure for state registration grew.[157] Both the Hospitals Association, an organisation representing the interests of hospital administrators and the Matrons' Committee were committed to registration by the early 1880s but they disagreed about the length of training: the Hospitals Association supported a one year period while the Matrons' Committee argued for three years. In 1887, the Hospitals Association overruled matrons and established a non-statutory voluntary register leading to a split in the Matrons' Committee between those who supported the Association and those who followed Ethel Gordon Fenwick (1857-1947), former matron of St. Bartholomew's Hospital opposing the new register and aligning themselves more closely with the medical profession. In 1887, Fenwick formed the British Nurses' Association with its own register and claimed over two thousand members within two years.[158]

---

[156] Howse, Carrie, ''The Ultimate Destination of All Nursing': The Development of District Nursing in England, 1880-1925', *Nursing History Review*, Vol. 15, (2007), pp. 65-94.

[157] McGann, Susan, *The Battle of the Nurses: A study of eight women who influenced the development of professional nursing, 1880-1930,* (Scutari Press), 1992, is a valuable biographical approach to the registration struggle.

[158] Griffon, D. P., ''Crowning the Edifice': Ethel Fenwick and State Registration', *Nursing History Review*, Vol. 3, (1995), pp. 201-212. See also, ibid., McGann, Susan, *The Battle of the Nurses*, pp. 35-57.

This was a small proportion of the 50,000 nurses listed in the 1891 Census.

The pressure for state registration was undermined by unresolved disagreements over the desired form and purpose of the regulatory system: was it to ensure clinical competence and expertise or to improve the social status of nurses? Florence Nightingale, for instance, objected to state registration since its proponents within the British Nurses' Association wanted to exclude working-class nurses, whom she believed included many of the most competent, and make nursing a profession only for ladies. Fenwick argued that without working-class nurses, the profession would be more attractive to ladies but, as Nightingale pointed out, other spheres of work for educated women were opening and attracting many middle-class women who might formerly have gone into nursing. In 1902, the Midwives Registration Act established the state regulation of midwives and two years later, a House of Commons Select Committee set out a detailed and persuasive case for nursing registration, but the government took no action because of the unresolved disagreements over the desired form and purpose of the regulatory system.[159]

Over the next decade, several private member's bills to establish regulation were introduced but all failed to achieve sufficient support in Parliament. The First World War provided the final impetus to the establishment of nursing regulation, partly because of the specific contribution made by nurses to the war effort and also as a reflection of the increased contribution of women more generally in society. The College of Nursing, later the Royal College of Nursing was established in 1916 and three years, a private member's bill to establish a regulatory system was finally passed in December 1919.[160] The separate Nurses Registration Acts for England and Wales, Scotland and Ireland established the General Nursing Council for England and Wales that controlled registration until legislative changes in 1979.[161]

The fight for female doctors

Florence Nightingale transformed the image and practice of nursing in the

---

[159] Dale, Pamela, and Fisher, Kate, 'Implementing the 1902 Midwives Act: assessing problems, developing services and creating a new role for a variety of female practitioners', *Women's History Review*, Vol. 18, (2009), pp. 427-452, and Nuttall, 'Midwifery, 1800-1920: The Journey to Registration', in ibid., Borsay, Anne, and Hunter, Billie, (eds.), *Nursing and Midwifery in Britain since 1700*.

[160] McGann, Susan, Crowther, Anne, & Dougall, Rona, *A History of the Royal College of Nursing, 1916-1990: A Voice for Nursing*, (Manchester University Press), 2009, pp. 1-24, considers the foundations of the institution.

[161] Bendall, Eve, and Raybould, Elizabeth, *A History of the General Nursing Council for England & Wales, 1919-1969*, (H. K. Lewis), 1969.

1860s but it was still assumed that doctors would be men. It is ironic that the campaign fought by women to become doctors, one of the great epics of the women's movement, is far less well-known than the professionalising of nursing.[162] Women would feel more comfortable and confident if, at times of illness, they could be attended by women doctors. Although Florence Nightingale was a Victorian icon and popularly endured in poem and story book, Sophia Jex-Blake (1840-1912) who pioneered female doctors is a less familiar figure.[163] Yet, both women had a number of features in common. They were of superior social status and financial security, refused to be intimidated, were both able publicists and had the devoted admiration of individuals of both sexes. But while images of the Lady with the Lamp were widespread and popular, no female doctor achieved the same level of instant recognition.

Florence Nightingale was keen to show that nursing was suitable employment for ladies and Jex-Blake was making same point for the women doctors. Nursing did not reach down to the uneducated daughters of the very poor since nurses were trained on the job and most were supported financially while doing so but attracted women from the lower middle-classes and also the daughters of skilled workers.[164] This range of social background was not found amongst women medical students who had to pass entrance examinations for the medical schools, pay high levels of fees and had the lengthy training period and, unlike nurses, women doctors were trying to break into a highly competitive, masculine profession. Most came from middle-class backgrounds but Alice Vickery (1844-1929)[165] was upper working-class. She was born in Devon in 1844 but moved to London by 1861 where she began her medical career in 1869 at the Ladies' Medical College training as a midwife qualifying in 1873. She also met Charles Drysdale, her partner and co-worker, at the College. Both objected to the institution of marriage and, though they had two children, never married remaining together until his death in 1907. Vickery went to France in 1873 to study medicine at the University of Paris completing her training at the London Medical School for Women

[162] Blake, Catriona, *The Charge of the Parasols: Women's Entry to the Medical Profession in Britain,* (Women's Press), 1990, examines how women fought for and obtained entry into the medical profession. Campbell, Olivia, *Women in White Coats: How the First Women Doctors Changed the World of Medicine,* (Harlequin Enterprises), 2002.

[163] Roberts, Shirley, *Sophia Jex-Blake: A Woman Pioneer in Nineteenth Century Medical Reform*, (Routledge), 1993, 2014.

[164] Workhouses provided training schemes for nurses that went further down the social hierarchy.

[165] Hall, Lesley A., 'Vickery, Alice (1844-1929)', *Oxford Dictionary of National Biography*, (Oxford University Press), 2004; [http://www.oxforddnb.com/view/article/39448, accessed 26 January 2022]

in 1877 and finally obtained her medical qualification three years later.

Elizabeth Blackwell (1821-1910), a Nonconformist who had gained her training in America, was able to practise in England after the 1858 Act recognised foreign degrees, though the following year this was rescinded, and spoke of the loneliness of being the only woman doctor.[166] It was a decade later when the first female medical students, led by Sophia Jex-Blake entered the University of Edinburgh but the University refused to award them degrees. Jex-Blake and the other female students took the University to court but lost their case in 1873.[167] Several then went abroad to qualify.[168] In 1864, the University of Zurich had admitted female students while the universities of Paris, Berne and Geneva followed suit in 1867. Jex-Blake went to Switzerland to study medicine at the University of Berne. Elizabeth Garrett Anderson (1836-1917) had her name entered on the medical register in 1865 by gaining the diploma of the Apothecaries Society and obtained a degree from the University of Paris in 1870.[169] Elizabeth Garrett and Sophia Jex-Blake established the London School of Medicine for Women in 1874 and gradually there were enough courses and lecturers for women to gain a good medical education.[170]

In 1876, Russell Gurney's Bill was accepted by Parliament and British examining bodies were permitted to include women if they wished: by slow stages, first licenses and then university degrees were open to medical women. The following year, the Royal Free Hospital admitted women medical students for clinical training and the University of London adopted a new charter in 1878 that allowed women to graduate

---

[166] See, Baker, Rachel, *The First Woman Doctor: The Story of Elizabeth Bakewell, M. D.*, (George C. Harrap and Co. Ltd.), 1946, and Chambers, P., *A Doctor Alone: A Biography of Elizabeth Blackwell: The First Woman Doctor*, (Bodley Head), 1956.

[167] Ibid., Roberts, Shirley, *Sophia Jex-Blake: A woman pioneer in nineteenth century medical reform*, pp. 71-124, considers this issue.

[168] On Jex-Blake's women, their education and careers, see Crowther, M. Anne, and Dupree, Marguerite W., *Medical Lives in the Age of Surgical Revolution*, (Cambridge University Press), 2007, pp. 152-175.

[169] Anderson, Louisa, *Elizabeth Garrett Anderson, 1836-1917; by her daughter*, (Faber & Faber), 1939, and Manton, Joan, and Manton, Grenville, *Elizabeth Garrett Anderson*, (Methuen), 1965. See also, Cherry, Deborah, and Walker, Lynne, 'Elizabeth Garrett Anderson: image, identity and space in the modernization of 19th-century medicine', *Visual Culture in Britain*, Vol. 3, (2), (2002), pp. 33-56, and Brock, Claire, 'Elizabeth Garrett Anderson and the professionalism of medical publicity', *International Journal of Cultural Studies*, Vol. 11, (3), (2008), pp. 321-342.

[170] Molinari, Véronique, "Schools of their own': the Ladies Medical College and the London School of Medicine for Women', in Andréolle, D., and Molinari, V., (eds.), *Women and Science, 17th century to present: Pioneers, Activists and Protagonists*, (Cambridge Scholars), 2011, pp. 99-124.

from their courses. Individual institutions were slowly forced to permit women to hold their degrees, though some, like Oxford and Cambridge, resisted until 1920 and 1948, respectively. One by one, often with great personal difficulty and dedication, a handful of women were able to qualify through this indirect route. By 1880, there were five, a modest achievement after so much effort. The numbers were small but rising. In the 1881 Census, there were 25 women doctors in England and Wales or 0.17 per cent of all doctors. By 1891, 101 women doctors practised in the British Isles and the following year, the British Medical Association was finally forced to admit women doctors. In the 1911 Census, there were 495 women practitioners or 1.98 per cent of all doctors.[171]

In the drive towards the professionalisation of medicine in the mid-nineteenth century, the power of the male doctor and the range of remedies he was ready to use for all kinds of ailments had increased. In the prevailing social and cultural context, women were at the mercy of the professional man. In intimate matters, especially those related to female problems, women could feel intimidated by male doctors. The women trained to be doctors were missionaries with a cause: the well-being of their own sex. To compound this moral stance, men fought doggedly to stop them. Women had considerable difficulty attending classes in anatomy and surgery, 'indelicate' subjects not suitable for mixed classes and some doctors refused to instruct women at all. Fear of competition from female doctors for female patients, the most lucrative part of most general practices was enough to sustain solidarity amongst the ranks of the medical schools and universities that awarded medical degrees and thus controlled entry into the profession.[172] This should not, however, be over-emphasised since women doctors who worked in mixed hospitals were restricted to junior posts and if they wanted to work exclusively with women and children needed the capital to establish their own hospitals. However, the specialist societies of obstetrics and gynaecology were notoriously hostile to the women; for it was in these areas that they offered the greatest threat.[173]

The problem faced by women doctors, unlike nurses, was that they

---

[171] Little, E. M., *History of the British Medical Association 1832-1932*, (BMA), 1932, republished, 1984, Pyke-Lees, Walter, *Centenary of the General Medical Council, 1858-1958: the history and present work of the Council*, (General Medical Council), 1958, and Oswald, Arthur, *The Royal College of Surgeons of England*, (Country Life), 1962.

[172] Brock, Claire, '*The Lancet* and the Campaign against Women Doctors, 1860-1880', in Caleb, Amanda Mordavsky, (ed.), *(Re)creating science in nineteenth-century Britain*, (Cambridge Scholars), 2007, pp. 130-145.

[173] Brock, Claire, *British Women Surgeons and their Patients, 1860-1918*, (Cambridge University Press), 2019, pp. 1-25, examines the 'obstinate hostility' to women and surgery.

could not be accommodated into existing female stereotypes. They demonstrated that, contrary to existing medical wisdom, they had the necessary intellectual abilities to qualify even if as contemporaries believed they would develop their brains at the expense of their reproductive organs. In fact, medicine was one of the few professions in which women could combine motherhood and a career. Jex-Blake remained single but Elizabeth Garrett Anderson combined marriage and motherhood with her private practice and later running the London School of Medicine for Women. Married women could combine their profession with domesticity in general practice. The first female doctors married men who were either practitioners themselves or had substantial middle-class incomes: in either case, they were well supported with domestic help for child-care. All practised in towns, with surgeries usually attached to their residences and they did not undertake the arduous rounds of the country practitioner.

Women doctors often had independent incomes and, once past the hospital residence stage, lived independent lives. They were associated with feminism and several of Jex-Blake's more radical followers later became active suffragettes. Dr Alice Ker (1853-1943) from Liverpool was imprisoned for breaking Harrods' windows during a demonstration while her daughter, a medical student, was also jailed for burning mail in a post-box. By contrast, many women doctors saw their role as one in helping women to undertake their natural roles especially that of mother. Alice Vickery used her knowledge to alleviate women's sufferings on a wider scale than her medical practice, becoming President of the Malthusian League and was an articulate advocate of family limitation and birth control. In the 1890s, she became involved with the Legitimation League that was established to protest against the legal penalties borne by the illegitimate children. She also joined the National Society for Women's Suffrage, later moving on to the more militant Women's Social and Political Union, and then the Women's Freedom League though she was never a leading figure in the political struggle. She also became an early member of the Eugenics Education Society and was also involved in divorce law reform and the international birth control movement. But they did not see this as part of a larger possibility of changing the medical profession from within and making it more conscious of gender prejudices. This position at least earned them the support of most of their male colleagues.

Women in uniform

Women also served as volunteers supporting the armed forces.[174] The Women's Emergency Corps that evolved into the Women's Volunteer

---

[174] Gould, J., 'Women's Military Services in First World War Britain' in

Reserve, (WVR) was formed by wealthy suffragette Evelina Haverfield (1869-1920) and Decima Moore (1871-1964) after the German naval attack on the East Coast in December 1914[175] and was the major voluntary military organisation for women. Its declared aims were two-fold: to 'free more men for the firing line' and to 'organise more succour for the helpless ones in the community'. It was soon joined by many women from the upper- and upper-middle classes and was an unlikely mix of feminists and conservative women. The WVR was an exclusive organisation as members had to pay for their own uniforms costing more than £2, beyond the means of lower-middle- and working-classes. Its role included running canteens for soldiers, transporting the wounded, camp cooking, first aid and motoring but its role was primarily domestic fund-raising.

Its members wore a khaki uniform, a colour associated with the 'sacrifice' of the armed forces, learned to parade and drill, named their local groups battalions and their members privates and officers and were sometimes offered the opportunity of training to bear arms. This proved controversial and the organisation faced criticism about the pertinence of its military symbolism, something that many people felt should be reserved for male combatants. In 1915, the less militaristic volunteer Women's Legion was formed by Edith Chaplin, Marchioness of Londonderry (1878-1959).[176] It did not practise drill and the work undertaken by its members, such as cookery and waitressing in military canteens, remained more clearly within an established female sphere and because of this the Women's Legion was more socially acceptable than the WVR. The work of these women represented the first official recognition by the British Army of its need for female labour in total war, but also helped to reinforce established, gendered patterns of work and status.

The Women's Army Auxiliary Corps (WAAC) was formed in March 1917 in response to the review of women's role in wartime and the introduction of male conscription the previous year.[177] Despite the influx

Higonnet, M., Jenson, J., Michel, S., and Weitz, M. Collins, (eds.), *Behind the Lines: Gender and the Two World Wars*, (Yale University Press), 1987, pp. 114-125, Watson, J., 'Khaki Girls, VADs and Tommy's Sisters: Gender and Class in First World War Britain' *International History Review*, Vol. 19, (1), (1997), pp. 32-51, Noakes, L., 'Eve in Khaki: Women Working With the British Military 1915-1918', in Cowman, K., and Jackson, L., (eds.) *Women and Work Culture: Britain c1850-1950*, (Ashgate), 2004, pp. 213-228, and Noakes, Lucy, *Women in the British Army: War and the Gentle Sex, 1907-1948*, (Routledge), 2006, pp. 39-81.

[175] 'Bombardment of Hartlepool', *Illustrated London News*, 26 December 1914, pp. 4, 5.

[176] Urquhart, Diane, 'Ora et Labora: The Women's Legion, 1915-1918', in McIntosh, Gillian and Urquhart, Diane, (eds.), *Irish Women at War: The Twentieth Century*, (Irish Academic Press), 2010, pp. 1-16.

of conscripts in 1916, the catastrophic causalities on the Somme meant that the need for more manpower remained critical. If the army made use of female labour, it was argued, men would be released for front line duties.

Because the WAAC was closely regulated by the War Office and Army Council, despite wearing khaki uniforms, it avoided the criticisms made in 1916 about the WVR. Women worked in five main areas: domestic, cookery, mechanical, clerical and tending war graves. However, it took the death of nine members of the WAAC in a bombing raid at Abbeville and their funeral with full military honours before the organisation was accepted and derogatory rumours about its members as both 'mannish' and unfeminine and as sexual predators, preying on the male soldiers of the British army, were quashed. The WAAC were renamed the Queen Mary's Army Auxiliary Corps (QMAAC) in April 1918 and officially ceased to exist on active service in September 1921, when the last thirty-one active members, who had been working with the Directorate of Graves Registration and Enquiries in France, were sent home.[178] By the Armistice on 11 November 1918, between 80,000 and 90,000 women had served in the British auxiliary forces. In addition to the WAAC, women had also served in the Women's Royal Naval Reserve and the Women's Royal Air Force formed respectively in November 1917 and April 1918. Although they had fewer members than the WAAC and QMAAC, women in these auxiliary organisations worked in similar roles.

Three organisations were formed to exploit Britain's agricultural resources. The Women's Land Army was formed in February 1917 in spite of male resistance in farming communities, in an attempt to provide a full-time, properly regulated workforce for agricultural industries. It was not part of the army or even under the control of the War Office and was funded and controlled by the Board of Agriculture and Fisheries. As an organised body supporting the war effort, it deserves its place in any reflection of the fighting forces. It eventually employed 113,000 women; female labour made up some one-third of all labour on the land, the remainder being a mix of enemy prisoners, Army Service Corps, infantry labour units and agricultural workers outside military age. The Women's Forage Corps was formed by the government in 1915 under the control of

---

[177] Robert, Krisztina, 'Discipline with Home-Like Conditions': The Living Quarters and Daily Life of the Women 's Army Auxiliary Corps in First-World-War Britain and France', in Hamlett, Jane, Hoskins, Lesley, and Preston, Rebecca, (eds.), *Residential Institutions in Britain, 1725-1970: Inmates and Environments*, (Pickering & Chatto), 2013, pp. 141-154.

[178] Shaw, Diana, 'The forgotten army of women: Queen Mary's Army Auxiliary Corps', in Cecil, Hugh P., and Liddle, Peter H., (eds.), *Facing Armageddon: The First World War experienced*, (Leo Cooper), 1996, pp. 365-379.

the Army Service Corps to deal with the demand of the British army, which largely ran on horses, for reliable sources of forage. The Women's Forestry Corps, controlled by the Timber Supply Department of the Board of Trade, was responsible for maintaining a reliable supply of wood for industrial and paper production at home and for construction in theatres of war.

Nursing

Women also made a major contribution to the war effort as nurses[179] and to a lesser extent, as doctors.[180] The Army Nursing Service had provided nurses for military hospitals from 1881 until the general reorganisation of the Army Medical Services in 1902. As a result, the Queen Alexandra's Imperial Military Nursing Service (QAIMNS) was formed in March 1902 and by 1914 consisted of 297 well-trained and educated matrons, sisters and staff nurses. During the war, the establishment remained unchanged, as it was considered unwise to employ more women permanently than would be needed after the war ended.[181] Any women who left the service were replaced, but the many thousands of nurses recruited during the war joined on short-term contracts with clauses that enabled the War Office to end their employment at its convenience. There were 40,850 in Queen Mary's Auxiliary Army Corps by 1918. The Territorial Force Nursing Service (TFNS) was established by R. B. Haldane as part of the new Territorial Force in the army reforms of 1908 and was the equivalent to the regular army's QAIMNS. It provided nursing staff for the twenty-three territorial force general hospitals planned for the United Kingdom in the event of war with a total establishment of 2,760 women, who in peacetime went about their normal duties in civil hospitals and private homes, but with a commitment to the War Office in the event of conflict. Over the course of the war, 8,140 women served at some time as mobilised members of the Territorial Force Nursing Service and of these 2,280 served overseas.

Following Haldane's Territorial scheme of 1907, new possibilities arose of co-operation between voluntary agencies and the Army, and on the 16 August 1909 the War Office issued its *Scheme for the Organisation of Voluntary Aid in England and Wales* with a similar scheme for Scotland

---

[179] Hallett, Christine, *Veiled Warriors: Allied Nurses of the First World War*, (Oxford University Press), 2014, Lee, Janet, *War Girls: The First Aid Nursing Yeomanry in the First World War*, (Manchester University Press), 2005.
[180] Ibid., Brock, Claire, *British Women Surgeons and their Patients, 1860-1918*, pp. 181-33, examines women surgeons in the theatre of war.
[181] McEwen, Yvonne, *In the Company of Nurses: The History of the British Army Nursing Service in the Great War*, (Edinburgh University Press), 2014, an authorised history.

in December. Detachments were organised for their local Territorial Force Association by the Red Cross, and received preliminary training in first aid and nursing from the St. John's Ambulance Association. After October 1914, this responsibility was transferred to the Joint War Committee of the British Red Cross Society and St. John of Jerusalem, a wartime amalgamation of the two organisations. The scheme proved popular and immediately before the outbreak of war, there were 1,823 female detachments and 551 male detachments registered with the War Office. The First Aid Nursing Yeomanry (FANY), a select upper-class organisation established in 1907, collaborated with the Red Cross principally as ambulance drivers. It only had 120 members in France in August 1918.

The women who joined Voluntary Aid Detachments (VADs) had a wide range of ages and different sorts of life skills. As a group, they were defined as middle- or upper middle-class, most were young women who had never had any paid employment, and of those who eventually went on to wartime service, more than three-quarters had either never worked outside the home or had done paid work. From August 1914, members of female detachments staffed VAD hospitals and auxiliary units and individual members quickly came to be referred to by the initials of their organisation. As the number of medical units both at home and abroad grew, the difficulties of keeping so many hospitals fully-staffed became increasingly difficult. In the spring of 1915, the War Office agreed that VADs could be employed in the large military hospitals at home to augment trained staff and also by early summer in general hospitals overseas. During the course of the war more than 90,000 women served as VADs in some capacity; 10,000 worked in hospitals under the direction of the War Office, and of those, 8,000 served overseas, in France, Malta, Serbia, Salonika, Egypt and Mesopotamia.[182]

Doctors

Those women trained in the medical professions made a significant, if subsequently under-valued, contribution to the war effort. The work and responsibilities of female doctors increased dramatically during the war as their male colleagues left for service in the Royal Army Medical Corps.[183] As a result, hospitals were increasingly prepared to offer women a wider range of jobs, albeit at longer hours. By 1918, 40 per cent of medical

---

[182] Donner, Henriette, 'Under the cross: why VADs performed the filthiest tasks in the dirtiest war: Red Cross women volunteers, 1914-1918', *Journal of Social History*, Vol. 30, (1997), pp. 687-704.
[183] Ibid., Brock, Claire, *British Women Surgeons and their Patients, 1860-1918*, pp. 234-284, examines women surgeons on the Home Front.

students were women. The war had many positive aspects for women physicians, but none of these advances persisted after the Armistice. Even when there was an excess of patients, female doctors and nurses, as well as untrained yet keen female volunteers, sometimes found themselves pushed aside by the military authorities. For instance, when Dr Elsie Inglis (1864-1917) offered the services of the Scottish Women's Hospitals that she founded in 1914 to the British army she was told to 'go home and sit still'. [184] She was, however, welcomed by the French and Serbian armies establishing field hospitals, dressing stations and other medical units in 1914. By the end of the war, 14 SWH had been established in six different countries, with over 1,000 women serving.[185] Under the leadership of the former militant suffragists Flora Murray[186] and Louisa Garrett Anderson, a group of women doctors calling themselves the Women's Hospital Corps (WHC) successfully ran two military hospitals in France from September 1914 to January 1915.[187] In 1915 the War Office invited them to run a military hospital. The 573-bed Endell Street Military Hospital, the first British hospital established for men but staffed and administered entirely by medical women, operated from May 1915 to December 1919 and during those years its doctors saw 26,000 patients and performed over 7,000 major operations. A key feminist organisation of the First War, the WHC has largely been forgotten, Geddes suggests partly because of its relatively small size and partly because of its anomalous status as a female-run hospital under the direct patronage of the War Office.

Towards the end of the war, women in uniform became a more widely accepted feature of society and women not wearing uniforms were increasingly criticised for their perceived lack of patriotism. No scheme for the demobilisation of militarised women existed at the end of the war. As they had enrolled rather than enlisted, they officially remained civilians

---

[184] Leneman, Leah, *In the service of life: The story of Elsie Inglis and the Scottish Women's Hospitals*, (Mercat), 1994.

[185] McDermid, Jane, 'What's in a Name? The Scottish Women's Hospitals in the First World War', *Minerva Journal of Women and War*, Vol. 1, (2007), pp. 102-114, Smith, Andrea, 'Suffragists at war: the Scottish Women's Hospitals and the vote', in Le Jeune, Françoise, (ed.), *Paroles de femmes, histoires de femmes: actes du colloque, Université de Nantes, Janvier 2000*, (Centre de recherches sur les identités nationales et l'interculturalité), 2003, pp. 105-112.

[186] Murray, Flora, *Women as army surgeons: being the history of the Women's Hospital Corps in Paris, Wimereux and Endell Street, September 1914-October 1919*, (Hodder and Stoughton), 1920, Moore, Wendy, *Endell Street: The Trailblazing Women who ran World War One's Most Remarkable Military Hospital*, (Atlantic), 2020.

[187] Geddes, J. F., 'The Women's Hospital Corps: forgotten surgeons on the First World War', *Journal of Medical Biography*, Vol. 14, (2), (2006), pp. 109-117.

and were released from service according to demand for their skills in the workplace or their role in the home. Married women and women with children were released first. Although the expansion of women's work and, in particular, their uniformed work with the military threatened to undermine the division between male and female war experience, the control and regulation of every aspect of women's work meant that these boundaries were largely maintained.

The leisure industries

Boundaries of class, gender, age and of geography were reproduced in leisure and may have reinforced those boundaries and not merely passively reflected them. The issue is not one of leisure but of different leisure cultures that were not hermetically sealed against each other but overlapped and influenced each other. Urban popular culture in the nineteenth and early-twentieth centuries developed three important dimensions. It was a mass culture that permeated across communities. There were activities that people paid to attend as spectators or as the audience. This included theatres, circuses and fairs and later in the century, music halls, professional football, horseracing, the popular press, seaside excursions and cinemas.[188]

Despite contemporary attitudes towards working in the leisure industries—being an actress was the last career any middle-class mother would have chosen for her respectable daughters—they provided important and growing employment opportunities for women but at a cost.[189] For many in the middle-classes, 'actress' was a euphemism for 'prostitute'. As late as 1898 Clement Scott (1841-1904), a theatre critic, believed that the temptations faced by actresses meant that it was nearly impossible:

> ...for a woman to remain pure who adopts the stage as a profession...Her prospects frequently depend on the nature and extent of her compliance, and, after all, human nature is very weak.[190]

---

[188] See, Russell, Dave, 'Popular entertainment, 1776-1895', in Donohue, Joseph, (ed.), *The Cambridge history of British theatre: Vol. 2, 1660 to 1895*, (Cambridge University Press), 2004, pp. 369-387. Jackson, Lee, *Palaces of Pleasure. From Music Halls to the Seaside to Football, How the Victorians invented Mass Entertainment*, (Yale University Press), 201, pp. 32-94.

[189] Eltis, Sos, 'Private lives and public space: Reputation, celebrity and the late Victorian actress', in Luckhurst, Mary, and Moody, Jane, (eds.), *Theatre and Celebrity in Britain, 1660-2000*, (Palgrave Macmillan), 2005, pp. 169-188, and Eltis, Sos, 'The fallen woman on stage: maidens, magdelans and the emancipated female', in Powell, Kerry, (ed.), *The Cambridge Companion to Victorian and Edwardian Theatre*, (Cambridge University Press), 2004, pp. 222-236.

[190] Jones, Stanley, *The Actor and His Art: Some Considerations of the Present*

Despite the debased reputation of the theatre, there was never a shortage of actresses, or women to work backstage. Girls who worked in a factory or sweat shop would have found more interest in a theatre job such as a dresser or seamstress, with the chance of an occasional walk-on part. Many of them followed relatives into the theatre, also a common way of becoming an actress. With only the benefits of training on the job, many actresses remained relatively obscure as extras or chorus girls, needing additional work, which included prostitution, as well to make a living wage.

Between 1871 and 1911, the population of England and Wales rose on average by 0.8 per cent per year and the number employed in the arts and entertainment by 4.7 per cent per year. The number of actors and actresses peaked in 1911 at over 19,000, having quadrupled in the previous thirty years.[191] In nearly every section of the leisure industries there were attempts to raise the status of entertainers. The outcome was the achievement of stardom for the select few while the rank and file had to be content with wages at roughly semi-skilled level. The best actors and actresses were already getting £150 per week in the 1830s. Between 1906 and 1914, the wages of performing musicians doubled reaching £200 per year but only a minority got that amount. On the whole, however, complaints about wages and conditions of service within the entertainment world were muted. The lure of acceptance as a profession, the hope of stardom for the individual and the sense that to be in entertainment was unlike any other job, for the most part curtailed any open conflict.

Controlling entry

With the growth of the numbers of women in professional and white-blouse work, employers tended to play a more direct and central role in maintaining sexual segregation and women, particularly those in the professions, faced rather more direct discrimination by employers in respect to recruitment and promotion than manual workers. In the higher professions, employers were also the men who controlled entry to the profession. For instance, until 1914 very few teaching hospitals admitted women wishing to train as doctors despite opening the Medical

---

Condition of the Stage, (Downey & Co.), 1899, p. 151. Clement Scott had made the comment in an interview for an evangelical periodical *Great Thoughts*, 1 January 1898. His intemperate attack on the morals of theatricals, and particularly actresses, led to an uproar in the press and to his dismissal as a columnist for the *Daily Telegraph* the following year when theatre managers united in barring him from their premises.
[191] Pécastaing-Boissière, Muriel, *Les actrices victoriennes: Entre marginalité et conformisme*, (L'Harmattan), 2003.

Register to women several decades earlier. The medical profession at least proved malleable in this period but the law remained unassailable before 1914. As the number of qualified women increased, and it became usual for middle-class girls to work on leaving school, the lines of sexual segregation were increasingly closely defended. Ideas regarding the proper role of married women in particular lay behind the introduction of the marriage bar, particularly after 1918. The assumption was that all married women could be treated as a reserve army of labour because of their primary responsibility to home, family and husband.[192]

Women were first employed as clerks in the Post Office and the Playfair Commission 1874-1875 maintained that, because this had been successful, women's employment could be extended to other departments if they 'could be place in separate rooms, under proper female supervision'.[193] This view was reiterated by the Ridley Commission in 1890. At first women were recruited by nomination to the clerical level, or they joined the service by open competition to posts in the lower grades and rose to the clerical level by promotion. The MacDonnell Royal Commission suggested that women should be eligible for administrative posts but it was not until 1925 that the first woman was recruited to the administrative class in the Civil Service.[194] The few women who were appointed to senior posts, such as Mrs Jane Nassau Senior (1828-1877), who was hired to inspect girls' education in workhouses in 1874[195] or Adelaide Anderson (1863-1936), who became the Chief Woman Inspector of Factories were the social equals of the

---

[192] Ibid., Holcombe, Lee, *Victorian Ladies at Work: Middle-class working women in England and Wales 1850-1914*, and Vicinus, Martha, *Independent Women: Work and community for single women 1850-1920*, (Virago), 1985, provide a much needed focus on the problems facing middle-class women who either did not wish to enter into marriage or for whom work was necessary within marriage. Ibid., Hughes, Kathryn, *The Victorian Governess*, and Gathorne-Hardy, Jonathan, *The Rise and Fall of the British Nanny*, (Weidenfeld), 1993, provide valuable insights into two areas where middle-class women found a niche (albeit an insecure one). Prochaska, F. K., *Women and Philanthropy in Nineteenth Century England*, (Oxford University Press), 1980, is a subtle study of the lives and motivations of middle-class women as well as about their 'causes'.

[193] *First Report of the Civil Service Inquiry Commission* [Chairman: Lyon Playfair]. ([C. 1113] H.C. (1875). XXIII, 1; Appendix. ([C. 1113-I] H.C. (1875). XXIII, 31.; *Second Report*. ([C. 1226] H.C. (1875). XXIII, 451.); *Third Report*. ([C. 1317] H.C. (1875). XXIII, 569; *Index*. ([C. 1444] H.C. (1876). XXII, 561.

[194] Martindale, Hilda, *Women Servants of the State, 1870-1938: A History of Women in the Civil Service,* (George Allen & Unwin), 1938, pp. 15-86, considers women's involvement to 1918.

[195] Oldfield, Sybil, *Jeanie, an 'Army of One': Mrs Nassau Senior, 1828-1877, the First Woman in Whitehall*, (Sussex Academic Press), 2008.

men they worked with. In 1892, May Tennant née Abraham (1869-1946), Clara Collet (1860-1948), Eliza Orme (1848-1937), in 1888 the first woman to gain a law degree in England and Margaret Irwin (1858-1940), a Scottish trade unionist were appointed to the Royal Commission on Labour as assistant commissioners. The following year, the Kensington Vestry appointed two women sanitary officers, Rose Squire and Lucy Deane. By 1896, five women were employed by the Factory Department of the Home Office, whilst Clara Collet had taken up an appointed with the Board of Trade in 1893. These early appointees were women with a strong academic or vocational training. Clara Collet, for instance, was not only the first female fellow at University College London, but was the first women to receive an MA.[196]

Since the eighteenth century, hundreds of British women defied social convention to seek adventure and influence on the global stage. Some became travellers and explorers; others were business-owners or buyers while some devoted their lives to international causes, from anti-slavery and women's suffrage to the League of Nations and world peace. What influence they had was informal and played little part in the formulation of foreign policy. This position was reinforced in a White Paper issued on 28 April 1936 by the Foreign Office—that denizen of reactionary resistance to modernity in government—making clear that women should not represent their country abroad in the Diplomatic Service.[197] This decision, some eight years after women over 21 had finally achieved the vote, was arcane and *Punch*—hardly a supporter of women's rights—mocked the Foreign Office for its prejudice. It was not until 1946 that women officially represented Britain abroad and 1976 before Anne Warburton (1927-2015) was appointed the first female ambassador to Denmark.

Male teachers were also incensed by the growing number of women teachers.[198] Between 1875 and 1914, the number of women elementary teachers increased by 862 per cent compared to a 292 per cent increase in men leading to the proportion of female teachers rising from 54 per cent in 1875 to 75 per cent by 1914. Unlike doctors and top civil servants, male teachers were not in a position to control recruitment that was in the hands of school boards and then local authorities after 1902. The nineteenth century pupil-teacher system had encouraged the entry of

---

[196] McDonald, Deborah, *Clara Collet, 1860-1948: An educated working woman*, (Woburn Press), 2004.

[197] McCarthy, Helen, *Women of the World: The Rise of the Female Diplomat*, (Bloomsbury), 2014, pp. 136-151.

[198] Oram, Alison, *Women Teachers and Feminist Politics, 1900-39*, (Manchester University Press), 1996, and Phipps, Emily, *History of the National Union of Women Teachers*, (National Union of Women Teachers), 1928.

working-class girls into teaching.[199] Like nurses, they learned on the job.[200] Pupil teaching did not enjoy a high status and it was not unusual for such girls to be considered in the same bracket as shop assistants or clerks. Many female teachers remained uncertificated: in 1913 the ratio for women was 1 in 9 compared to 1 in 3 for men. After 1907, the bursary system of teacher training replaced the pupil-teacher scheme. Boys or girls intending to become teachers had to stay on longer at school and become student teachers at seventeen. As a result, more middle-class women entered the profession and its status rose.[201]

In 1911, of the 117,057 female commercial clerks, 114,429 were single and 95 per cent under thirty-five. Most of these girls only expected to work until they married and employment practices in both private and public sectors were based on this prospect. Discrimination was not solely the prerogative of employers and male-dominated trade unions; in some occupations, single women in the public sector insisted on excluding married women. For instance, in 1921, female civil servants passed a resolution asking for the banning of married women from their jobs and the resulting ban was enforced until 1946. In Ireland, the ban on primary school married women lasted until 1958.[202] There were other setbacks. During the First World War, hospitals had accepted female medical students but in the 1920s, women were again rejected by hospitals on the grounds of modesty. The National Association of Schoolmasters campaigned against the employment of female teachers. In 1924, the

---

[199] See, *Report of the departmental committee on the pupil teacher system*, 2 Vols. (HMSO), 1898.

[200] Before the Education Act 1902, the training of teachers was largely carried out under a pupil-teacher system, first established in 1846. It had received various modifications throughout its existence, but by the turn of the century elementary school children were selected as pupil-teachers and received three years concurrent training and education taking the Queen's/King's Scholarship Examination at 18. Originally, both their training and education took place at their elementary schools under the supervision of the headmaster, but after the Elementary Education Act 1870 their instruction was undertaken at separate establishments called pupil-teacher centres, run by local school boards, with teaching practice at their elementary schools.

[201] See, Trouvé-Finding, Susan, 'Unionized Women Teachers and Women's Suffrage', Boussahba-Bravard, Myriam, (ed.), *Suffrage outside suffragism: women's vote in Britain, 1880-1914*, (Palgrave), 2007, pp. 205-230, Oram, Alison, ''Men must be educated and women must do it': the National Federation (later Union) of Women Teachers and contemporary feminism 1910-30', *Gender & Education*, Vol. 19, (6), (2007), pp. 663-667, and Kean, Hilda, *Deeds not words: the lives of suffragette teachers*, (Pluto), 1990.

[202] Redmond, J., and Harford, J., ''One man one job': the marriage ban and the employment of women teachers in Irish primary schools', *Paedogoq Hist*, Vol. 40, (5), (2010), pp. 639-654.

London County Council make its policy explicit when it changed the phrase 'shall resign on marriage' to 'the contract shall end on marriage'. In the private sector, the same exclusionary policy tended to be informal but nonetheless universal.

Reforming women's lives

The symbolic importance of the vote has meant that women's broader political culture and history has been obscured. The possession of the vote qualified women finally to enter the purely masculine and public world of national politics from which they had so long been excluded. Women's interest in securing access to political rights was not limited to the campaign for Parliamentary suffrage. Feminists agitated on a range of issues that affected public policy from education through official attitudes to prostitution.[203] Nineteenth century Britain was a society in which class boundaries were increasingly complex and gender was one of the influences determining women's loyalties and interests.[204] There were other loyalties, most obviously to class and community. Nineteenth and twentieth century women employed the language of their own experience, of motherhood, of domestic labour, of religious commitment, whether their links were primarily with other women or when they were operating in male-dominated social institutions or political movements. While challenging injustice, many drew their considerable strength from what they regarded with pride as their most fulfilling tasks, as wives and mothers.

Rights

Before 1830, political and individual rights were allowed only to men from the wealthier sections of society.[205] The basis for these rights was male

---

[203] Women's participation in public life is explored in Hollis, Patricia, *Ladies Elect: Women in English Local Government 1865-1914*, (Oxford University Press), 1987, and in the collection of documents Hollis, Patricia, (ed.), *Women in Public: The Women's Movement 1850-1900*, (Allen & Unwin), 1979, and in Jalland, Pat, *Women, Marriage and Politics 1860-1914*, (Oxford University Press), 1986. Rendall, Jane, (ed.), *Equal or Different: Women's Politics 1800-1914*, (Basil Blackwell), 1987, contains a variety of papers on the politicisation of women in the nineteenth and early-twentieth centuries.

[204] On this issue see Pedersen, Joyce S., 'The historiography of the women's movement in Victorian and Edwardian England: varieties of contemporary liberal feminist interpretation', *The European Legacy*, Vol. 1, (1996), pp. 1052-1057.

[205] Cornish, William, Anderson, Stuart, Cocks, Raymond, Lobban, Michael, Polden, Patrick, and Smith, Keith, (eds.), *The Oxford History of the Laws of England*, Vol. XIII, (Oxford University Press), 2010, pp. 723-747, on the legal relationship between men and women. Cornish, William, Banks, Steve, Mitchell,

claims to have 'reason' while women were thought as incapable of rational thought. Before 1850 women, especially if married, had few legal rights. Under the Common Law, married women had no legal identity apart from that of their husbands. Their position was defined by the doctrine of *coverture* under which a woman lost all rights to economic independence and ownership of property during marriage.[206] William Blackstone (1723-1780), the eighteenth century jurist laid down the legal relationship:

> By marriage, the husband and wife are one person in law; that is, the very being or legal existence of the women is suspended during the marriage, or at least is incorporated and consolidated into that of the husband: under whose wing, protection and cover, she performs everything.[207]

Under the law, men gained considerable control over their wives' lives. A husband assumed legal possession or control of all property that belonged to his wife on marriage and of any property that might come to her during marriage. The law distinguished between real property, mainly freehold land that the husband could not dispose of without his wife's permission though he could control it and its income and personal property that passed into his absolute possession and which he could use in any way he chose. The husband's rights also extended to any children of the marriage; they were his children and if a marriage was dissolved custody was always ceded to the man. Married women could neither sue nor be sued, nor enter into contracts and her debts were her husband's responsibility. He could even set aside her will on her death. Husbands had the right to decide where and how to live. They were legally entitled to beat their wives and could, and sometimes did, lock them up.

In practice, married women used the law as a means of evading the control of their husbands and were able to avoid the constraints imposed by the Common Law. Women played a dominant role in actions in ecclesiastical consistory courts in actions for sexual slander and initiated 97 per cent of breach of promises cases in the early-nineteenth century.[208]

Charles, Mitchell, Paul, and Probert, Rebecca, *Law and Society in England 1750-1950*, 2nd ed., (Hart Publishing), 2019, chapter 5, and Steedman, Carolyn, *History and the Law: A Love Story*, (Cambridge University Press), 2020.

[206] Cornish, William, Anderson, Stuart, Cocks, Raymond, Lobban, Michael, Polden, Patrick, and Smith, Keith, (eds.), *The Oxford History of the Laws of England*, Vol. XIII, (Oxford University Press), 2010, pp. 723-747, provides a succinct discussion of the legal relationship between men and women. See also, Phillips, Nicola, *Women in Business, 1700-1850*, (Boydell), 2006, pp. 23-47.

[207] Blackstone, William, *Commentaries on the Laws of England in Four Books*, 1765-1769, Vol. 1, chapter 15

[208] Meldrum, Tim, 'A Woman's Court in London: Defamation at the Bishop of London's Consistory Court, 1700-1745', *London Journal*, Vol. 19, (1994), pp. 1-

There were several ways in which women could evade *coverture*. The law of necessaries recognised that although married women could not make economic contracts in their own right, they were empowered to make contracts on their husbands' behalf. Finally, women took actions in the Court of Requests and the County Courts that functioned as small claims courts.[209] Women enjoyed more favourable property rights under the laws of Equity than under Common Law through the trust settlement of property. The Court of Chancery allowed the creation of separate property or separate estate of a married woman.[210] Married women had unrestricted rights over their separate property, enjoyed contractual capacity and could make binding contracts, lend money and incur debts, conduct a business and dispose of it freely. It was impractical to tie up small sums of money in trust settlements and consequently trusts only accounted for 10 per cent of all marriage in England and Wales in the early-nineteenth century. However, one in ten non-elite women appear to have protected their property using informal settlements.[211]

Women had no responsibility or competence within marriage and were tied to a moral standard to which their partners were not expected to adhere. Before 1857, responsibility for divorce lay in the hands of the church.[212] Since ecclesiastical law recognised very few grounds for divorce, the only other recourse was the obscure and costly–a private petition to Parliament. Consequently, it remained a rare and restricted option with only about 200 such petitions ever being granted. In cases heard in Parliament before the marriage reforms of the 1850s, few women came forward as petitioners. Where they did present cases involving adultery by their husbands, their bid for divorce was rejected, while adultery on the part of the wife was always sufficient grounds for a husband's petition. Feminists campaigning centred on inequalities and problems relating to the institution of marriage and on efforts to wipe out the double standard of morality based on gender that licensed male freedom but suppressed women, a double standard enshrined in matrimonial legislation.[213]

20, and Frost, Ginger S., *Promises Broken: Courtship, Class and Gender in Victorian England*, (University Press of Virginia), 1995, pp. 13-40, 80-97.

[209] Finn, Margot C., *The Character of Credit: Personal Debt in English Culture, 1740-1914*, (Cambridge University Press), 2003, pp. 266-272.

[210] Ibid., Phillips, Nicola, *Women in Business, 1700-1850*, pp. 69-93.

[211] Erickson, Amy, *Women and Property in Early Modern England*, (Routledge), 1993, pp. 145-146.

[212] Stone, Lawrence, *Road to divorce: England, 1530-1987*, (Oxford University Press), 1990.

[213] Gibson, Colin, *Dissolving Wedlock*, (Routledge), 1994, provides insight into this area of women's experience looking at divorce over a long period. Horstman, Allen, *Victorian Divorce*, (St Martin's Press), 1985, is more specific. Holcombe, Lee, *Wives and Property: Reform of the Married Women's Property*

Marriage, Divorce and Property

The prominence of marriage and its centrality in women's lives determined their status whether they were married or not and made it an obvious and important feminist concern. Although its religious character remained, Parliament intervened creating provision for civil marriage in 1836 and divorce in 1857. Married women achieved greater legal status especially in relation to their property and fathers lost their exclusive right to the custody of their children. There were also attempts to ease the plight of working-class women by allowing local magistrates' courts to issue judicial separations. Feminists campaigning centred on inequalities and problems relating to the institution of marriage and on efforts to wipe out the double standard of morality based on gender that licensed male freedom and female suppression embracing the property of married women, their access to divorce, custody of children, violence within marriage and the controversy over marriage to a deceased wife's sister finally resolved in the Deceased Wife's Sister's Marriage Act of 1907.[214]

The centrality of marriage in most women's lives made it an obvious feminist concern. In 1854, Barbara Leigh Smith published a tract on women's legal disabilities entitled *A Brief Summary, in plain language, of the most important laws of England concerning Women, together with a few observations thereon.* It began the campaign that was to become one of the more prominent and indeed successful of all feminist agitation. In 1856, a petition with 3,000 signatures was presented to both Houses of Parliament demanding change in laws affecting married women's property. The Divorce and Matrimonial Causes Act was hurriedly passed in 1857 to head off the more alarming prospect of a proposed married women's property bill. Legislation on divorce arose largely from the government initiated Royal Commission on Divorce set up in 1850 whilst the less successful attempts to change the law on married women's property arose directly from feminist lobbying.[215]

Law in nineteenth-century England, (Toronto University Press), 1983, and Shanley, Mary Lyndon, *Feminism, Marriage and the Law in Victorian England 1850-1895*, (Princeton University Press), 1989, provide an entree into how the law was changed. Doggett, Maeve, *Marriage, Wife-Beating and the Law in Victorian England*, (University of South Carolina), 1993, looks at a neglected subject.

[214] Anderson, Nancy F., 'The 'Marriage with a Deceased Wife's Sister Bill' Controversy: Incest Anxiety and the Defence of Family Purity in Victorian England', *Journal of British Studies*, Vol. 21, (1982), pp. 67-86.

[215] Ibid., *The Oxford History of the Laws of England*, Vol. XI, pp. 742-756, and ibid., *The Oxford History of the Laws of England*, Vol. XIII, pp. 781-796, consider the operation of the Divorce Court. Shanley, M. L., ''One must ride behind': married women's rights and the divorce act of 1857'. *Victorian Studies*,

The 1857 Act was unsatisfactory in three respects. Its provision for deserted wives was inadequate and it enshrined a double standard in the grounds in established for securing a divorce. It was also an alternative to more controversial legislation and set back the cause of married women's property by more than a decade. Women's access to divorce was limited to cases where the husband's adultery was compounded by further sexual misdemeanours (bigamy, cruelty, desertion or incest) while for the man his wife's adultery alone was sufficient cause. Major deficiencies in the 1857 Act only surfaced again when organisations like the Women's Emancipation Union made divorce reform a plank of their policies in the early 1890s.[216] The Clitheroe case of 1891 was also instrumental in re-opening the wider question of women's status within marriage. Mr and Mrs Jackson had lived apart throughout their brief marriage and when Jackson returned from New Zealand, his wife refused to live with him. He abducted her and held her captive in his sister's house in Blackburn while a legal suit was set in train. The judges initially upheld Jackson's claim but this was overturned by the Court of Appeal that set Mrs Jackson free. A husband could no longer physically compel his wife to live with him.[217]

It was not until 1891 that the High Court ruled that the husband did not have the right to imprison his wife in pursuit of his conjugal rights and not until 1991 that a similar ruling denied him the right to rape her.[218] The Court could order a return to cohabitation when either the man or woman had separated from the other party without lawful excuse, and, if the Court's order were disobeyed, this might result in an action for desertion and contempt of court, the injured party petitioning for an

---

Vol. 25, (1982), pp. 355-376; Anderson, Olive, 'Hansard's hazards: an illustration from recent interpretations of married women's property law and the 1857 Divorce Act', *English Historical Review*, Vol. 112, (1997), pp. 1202-1215; Shanley, Mary Lyndon, *Feminism, Marriage, and the Law in Victorian England*, (Princeton University Press), 1993, pp. 22-48.

[216] See, for instance, *Women's Emancipation Union: women and the law courts: paper read at the Birmingham Conference, 25th October 1892*, 1892, and *The Women's Emancipation Union: its origin and its work*, (Guardian Printing Works), 1892

[217] Elmy, E. C. Wolstenholme, *The decision in the Clitheroe case and its consequences: a series of five letters by Mrs Wolstenholme Elmy*, (Guardian Print), 1891, ibid., Shanley, Mary Lyndon, *Feminism, Marriage, and the Law in Victorian England*, pp. 156-188, and Frost, Ginger, 'A shock to marriage? The Clitheroe Case and the Victorians', Robb, George, and Erber, Nancy, (eds.), *Disorder in the court: trials and sexual conflict at the turn of the century*, (Macmillan), 1999, pp. 100-118.

[218] Savage, Gail, '...the instrument of an animal function': Marital Rape and Sexual Cruelty in the Divorce Court, 1858-1908', in Delap, Lucy, Griffin, Ben and Wills, Abigail, (eds.), *The Politics of Domestic Authority in Britain since 1800*, (Palgrave Macmillan), 2009, pp. 43-57.

accelerated hearing. By 1914, however, it had been shown that such a decree was almost worthless if the wife chose to ignore it, and since 1886 the court had been able to order periodic payments to the petitioner by the respondent as seemed just. The remedy of restitution of conjugal rights was abolished in 1970.

In the decade after 1857, there were 1,279 dissolutions of marriage and 213 judicial separations. The cost of an action remained high, and the legal procedures took about eighteen months to complete. There were some 150 divorces per year in the 1860s, a surprisingly high proportion of them (perhaps approaching half) among the working- and lower-middle-classes. One repercussion of the Married Women's Property Acts in 1882 was an increase in the divorce rate. In England before 1880, the number of divorces rarely rose above 300 annually but after 1882 it only once fell below that number. Divorces continued to rise each year reaching over 1,000 in 1914. After women received the vote in 1918, the number of divorces rose again, tripling within two years. In Scotland, this trend was even more marked. In 1879, there were 55 divorces. The highest number of divorces in a single year had been 66 in 1878, the year after Scotland got its first Married Women's Property Act. In 1880, there were 80 divorces and numbers never again fell below 65 divorces in a single year. By the end of the decade, there were usually over 100 divorces a year, almost doubling the pre-Act numbers and by 1900 had reached 200 divorces a year. Scotland also saw a rise in post-war divorces, with 297 divorces in 1917, 485 in 1918 and 829 in 1919, a figure not reached again until the late 1930s.

After the failure of many marriages during the First World War[219] and a 90 per cent increase in the divorce rate between 1913 and 1922, the Matrimonial Causes Act 1923 allowed divorce on the petition of the wife solely because of her husband's adultery. The administration of divorce also became less centralised in London when, in 1922, several of the towns in which Assizes were held had been named as suitable for hearing some kinds of uncontested divorce. In 1927, twenty-three district registries were made available for the filing of petitions where, within ten years, a quarter of all petitions were being filed with decrees issued by the Supreme Court.

The concoction of bogus cases in which men provided their wives with suitable pre-arranged evidence of 'adultery', by sitting up all night in a hotel that catered for the trade with a lady provided by an agency, became common and was ridiculed by A. P. Herbert (1890-1971) in his series of

---

[219] Thane, Pat, 'The Impact of World War 1 on Marriage, Divorce and Gender Relations in Britain', in Brée, Sandra and Hin, Saskia, (eds.), *The Impact of World War 1 on Marriages, Divorces, and Gender Relations in Europe*, (Routledge), 2020, pp. 50-68.

Misleading Cases and his novel *Holy Deadlock* in 1935. Both parties to a marriage might admit that they had been unfaithful, but that was not grounds for divorce. This also applied to desertion, though there might be grounds for judicial separation. So, if there was mutual agreement to end the marriage, the man usually took it upon himself to be 'the guilty party' in this way. Incompatibility was irrelevant, there had to be 'the outward visible sign of physical misconduct'. Herbert promoted the Matrimonial Causes Act in 1937 that greatly extended the grounds for divorce and came into force on 1 January 1938. A marriage could now be made void because of desertion for three years or for cruelty and insanity. The Act also gave the courts power to pronounce a decree of presumption of death and consequent dissolution of marriage. The Second World War caused the collapse of many marriages and by 1950, there were about 20,000 divorces a year. Assisted by the introduction of legal aid after 1949, the number of divorce cases increased rapidly. Legal aid was not normally available in undefended divorce and judicial separation cases, but in disputed cases it was available to those whose disposable income was under £420 a year and whose disposable capital, not including the house or household effects, was under £500.

From the 1850s, the marriage debate had also focussed on the property issue.[220] The first Married Women's Property Committee was set up in 1855 but it failed in its legislative attempts in 1856-1857. It was an issue that raised interest across class barriers, more particularly in relation to a husband's rights over his wife's earnings. Property campaigns combined Parliamentary manoeuvre with bills and amendments through the late 1860s and 1870s and hard propaganda and lobbying. When the first and inadequate Married Women's Property Act passed in 1870, campaigners maintained their attacks.[221] Women could now keep up to £200 of the money they earned. Bills and amendments came before Parliament in 1873, 1874, 1877, 1878, 1880 and 1881 before finally

---

[220] Ibid., Holcombe, Lee, *Wives and property: reform of the married women's property law in nineteenth-century England.*

[221] The 1870 Act allowed all wives to retain any property or earnings acquired after marriage rather than, as before, losing them to their husbands. For contemporary details of the legislation see, *The Married Women's Property Act, 1870: its relations to the doctrine of separate use, with notes*, (Stevens and Haynes), 1873. See, ibid., Shanley, Mary Lyndon, *Feminism, Marriage, and the Law in Victorian England*, pp. 49-78, Combs, Mary Beth, 'A Measure of Legal Independence": The 1870 Married Women's Property Act and the Portfolio Allocations of British Wives', *Journal of Economic History*, Vol. 65, (4), (2005), pp. 1028-1057, and Morris, R. J., 'Men, women and property: the reform of the Married Women's Property Act, 1870', in Thompson, F. M. L., (ed.), *Landowners, capitalists and entrepreneurs: essays for Sir John Habakkuk* (Oxford University Press), 1994, pp. 171-191.

becoming law in August 1882. The 1882 Act was widely regarded as a victory equalising the rights and responsibilities of women irrespective of marital status.[222] Legislation two years later finally allowed women to keep all their personal property that they brought to the marriage or acquired during it but it was not until 1893 that the rights of married women to property became the same as for unmarried women. A woman was no longer a 'chattel' but an independent and separate person. Even after 1884, relatively few women had sufficient income or property to live conformably alone or with children after divorce.

Domestic violence

Of growing concern in the 1870s were anxieties over domestic violence.[223] Legal opinion did little to prohibit male violence. It was Frances Power Cobbe's (1822-1904) denunciation of wife-abuse, an act she saw as resulting in large part from the degrading pressure of poverty that re-opened the marriage debate in the late 1870s.[224] She argued that the new divorce courts remained an option beyond the reach of poor women, whom she felt to be more at risk. The passage of the Matrimonial Causes Act in 1878 established a class distinction: wealthier women could still obtain full divorces under the 1857 Act, while working women were offered the cheaper but more restricted alternative of a separation order granted through a magistrate's court that prohibited the option of re-marriage. Women could now secure a separation on the grounds of cruelty and claim custody of their children. Magistrates even authorised

---

[222] The 1882 Act allowed women to retain any property possessed at the time of their marriage, thus extending to all women with property a right which the better-off had previously been able to acquire through establishing a trust in equity. See, Thicknesse, Ralph, *The Married Women's Property Act, 1882*, (W. Maxwell & Son), 1884, and ibid., Shanley, Mary Lyndon, *Feminism, Marriage, and the Law in Victorian England*, pp. 103-130.

[223] On domestic violence, see, Hammerton, A. James, *Cruelty and companionship: conflict in nineteenth-century married life*, (Routledge), 1992, and 'Victorian marriage and the law of matrimonial cruelty', *Victorian Studies*, Vol. 33, (1990), pp. 269-292; D'Cruze, Shani, *Crimes of outrage: sex, violence and Victorian working women*, (UCL Press), 1998, Savage, Gail, "A State of Personal Danger': Domestic Violence in England, 1903-1922', in Watson, K. D., (ed.), *Assaulting the past: violence and civilization in historical context*, (Cambridge Scholars), 2007, pp. 269-285.

[224] *Life of Frances Power Cobbe: By herself*, (S. Sonnenschein & Co.), 1904, pp. 556-634, considers 'the claims of brutes' and gives a clear statement of her views. Mitchell, Sally, *Frances Power Cobbe: Victorian feminist, journalist, reformer*, (University of Virginia Press), 2004, pp. 267-304, Williamson, Lori, *Power and protest: Frances Power Cobbe and Victorian society*, (Rivers Oram), 2005, and Hamilton, Susan, *Frances Power Cobbe and Victorian feminism*, (Palgrave Macmillan), 2006, pp. 125-144.

protection orders to wives whose husbands have been convicted of aggravated assault.

The 1878 Act was seen by Cobbe as a means of empowering women. Yet her suggestions were more far-reaching than those actually implemented in the legislation. She argued that the right of separation should be amplified by automatic maternal custody of children and by maintenance orders for a wife and children against the offending husband. From 1883, about 8,000 separation orders per year were being granted. The subsequent history of these changes shows that women largely used the option of separation while divorce remained primarily a vehicle used by men. The social stigma attaching even to an 'innocent' divorced woman in respectable circles, though not to a separated wife in the working-class, figures suggest may have remained a considerable deterrent to ending a marriage.

Children

The medieval distinction between legitimate and illegitimate children was central to the fundamental premise of the strict notion of primogeniture to the succession to titles and to property. A father could not even legitimate his child by subsequently marrying the mother. The only obligation that could be imposed on the father of an illegitimate child arose from the Poor Laws. The law imposed little by way of substantial responsibility on fathers in relation to legitimate children. There was a social expectation that fathers were under a duty to maintain, protect and education their children but it was a moral rather than a legal obligation. Private law was largely concerned with rights of custody and access and the basic premise in both law and equity in custody disputes was one of strict patriarchy. In the case of disputes between parents, neither Common Law courts nor courts of Equity would exercise their authority to remove a child from a father.

The perceived harshness of these rules, together with a number of high profile cases, led to a campaign for reform.[225] Caroline Sheridan Norton (1808-1877) is credited for bringing the issue of divorce and custody of children to public and Parliamentary scrutiny and was instrumental in achieving passage of the Infant Custody Act of 1839 and the Divorce and Matrimonial Causes Act of 1857.[226] She married George

---

[225] Ibid., *The Oxford History of the Laws of England*, Vol. XIII, pp. 802-822, considers family law and children after 1820.

[226] See Chedzoy, Alan, *A Scandalous Woman: The Story of Caroline Norton*, (Allison & Bushby), 1992, Atkinson, Diane, *The Criminal Conversation of Mrs Norton*, (Preface Publishing), 2012, and Fraser, Antonia, *The Case of the Married Woman: Caroline Norton: A 19th Century Heroine who wanted Justice for Women*, (Weidenfeld & Nicolson), 2021.

Norton (1800-1875) in 1827 and had three sons but in 1836, he sued Prime Minister Lord Melbourne (1779-1848) for damages for 'criminal conversation' (adultery) with his wife as a first step to obtaining divorce by Act of Parliament. Although the jury acquitted Melbourne, Caroline Norton's reputation was damaged but her legal exoneration made divorce impossible. Norton took their three sons out of England forbidding Caroline to see them. She then began a series of campaigns to reform the laws asking for legal protection for women similar to that recently provided for paupers, the insane, prisoners and other helpless groups. In 1839, the Custody of Infants' Act said that if the parents separated, the wife should legally be able to claim custody if the children were under seven. Furthermore, if older children were taken by the husband, the mother could claim access. This was extended to 16 and also a wife's adultery ceased to be an automatic bar to custody but remained an influential factor in the Infant Custody Act 1873 and from the Infant Custody Act 1886 the welfare of the child rather than the 'guilt' or otherwise of the parents determined custody arrangements.[227] Even then the father remained the sole legal guardian during his lifetime. It was still difficult for a woman to prove the unfitness of a comfortably off father to bring up his heirs in court and, if she succeeded, to support them on her own.

The financial problem was most acute in case of illegitimate offspring. Many feminists believed that the bastardy clauses in the Poor Law Amendment Act 1834 and effective until the 1870s were another means of sanctioning and protecting male vice.[228] This catalysed feminist action. One of the most controversial parts of the Act were its 'bastardy clauses' that made obtaining affiliation orders for maintenance more difficult and expensive to obtain.[229] Before 1834, unwed mothers had been legally entitled to receive support from the fathers of their children and affiliation orders were obtained through the local Petty Sessions courts. After 1834, they were heard at the county Quarter Sessions and could only be initiated by Overseers or Guardians. Paternity claims now had to be 'corroborated in some material particular', evidence often difficult to find. The Act made illegitimate children the sole responsibility

---

[227] On the 1886 legislation, see, ibid., Shanley, M. L., *Feminism, Marriage, and the Law in Victorian England*, pp. 131-155.

[228] Henriques, Ursula, 'Bastardy and the New Poor Law', *Past & Present*, Vol. 37, (1967), pp. 103-129. See also, Zlotnick, Susan, "The Law's a Bachelor': *Oliver Twist*, Bastardy and the New Poor Law', *Victorian Literature and Culture*, Vol. 34, (1), (2006), pp. 131-146.

[229] This proved highly contentious in the House of Commons on 18 June 1834 and in the House of Lords on 28 July with, for instance, debate over whether freeing the father from all consequences of his actions would increase illegitimacy.

of their mothers until they were 16 years and if mothers were unable to support their families, they and their children would have to enter the workhouse. It was hoped that this would discourage women from risking extra-marital pregnancy.

The new laws did not lead to a reduction in bastardy and in some parts of the country, it increased. There was also concern that the new law had stimulated an increase in cases of infanticide and abandonment. This proved a highly unpopular and contentious measure and petitions flooded into Parliament and were diluted in 1839 when, following a Select Committee report on the issue, local magistrates could hear affiliation orders at Petty Sessions and overturned in 1844 when legislation enabled an unmarried mother to seek an affiliation order against the father for maintenance whether she was in receipt of poor relief or not.[230] The Bastardy Act in 1845 simply clarified the procedures established the previous year. The real turning point came in 1872 when the Bastardy Laws Amendment Act allowed Guardians as well as women to initiate proceedings and also increased the amount that could be paid to the mother. The seducer had to pay and this was, it was argued, more likely to reduce immorality than and severe laws on the seduced.[231] The arguments of 1834 had been inverted and the Bill passed the House of Commons without a division.

Many women cut their feminist teeth within this area of protest and through addressing the problems of property within marriage came a clearer understanding of other aspects of female subjugation. The feminist critique was not on marriage and they did not seek to undermine the practice or prevalence of marriage but to realign the rights of partners within that institution. As the movement grew in numbers and in confidence, and as analysis of the position of women grew more sophisticated, so it widened its net to other areas of civil disability. However, changes in the law did not always expand women's rights at the expense of men's. As late as 1889, a Court for Crown Cases Reserved decision in the case of *Regina v. Clarence*[232] overturned the standard opinion of judges and legal textbooks by asserting a husband's right to have intercourse with his wife, even when, as in this case, the husband was suffering from advanced syphilis and his wife, had she known, would not have submitted to his advances.

---

[230] Henriques, U. R. Q., 'Bastardy and the New Poor Law', *Past & Present*, Vol. 37, (1967), pp. 103-129, Davison, Diane M., *The bastardy controversy of nineteenth century Britain*, MA, Thesis, Lehigh University, 1982.

[231] Ibid., Henriques, U. R. Q., 'Bastardy and the New Poor Law', p. 120.

[232] See, Bibbings, Lois S., *Binding Men; Studies about violence and law in Late Victorian England*, (Routledge), 2014, pp. 112-148, for discussion of Regina v. Clarence.

Prostitution and the Contagious Diseases Acts

There was one kind of equality, one sort of liberation about which nineteenth century feminists found it difficult to speak. Higher education for women, better employment opportunities for women, protection at law for women were all 'respectable' issues. Few were afraid to voice opinions upon them, nobody ashamed to sign their name on a petition. But the attack on the infamous 'double-standard' that bedevilled relationships between the sexes did not attract such eager support. Nowhere was the Victorian tendency for melodrama or its view of society as locked in a perpetual battle between good and evil, order and anarchy more clearly expressed than in the debates over prostitution, 'the Great Social Evil'. Contemporary social, medical and moral structures meant that the prostitute's place in the community, her role in the spread and reduction of venereal disease and the threat she posed to the nation's moral well-being were central to the attitudes of a broad spectrum of Victorian society.[233]

Growth in population and in the corresponding preference for urban living mobilised an increasing level of state intervention in the private lives of its citizens.[234] Sanitation and housing, water supplies and the control of disease, all became subject to government regulation, and this was paralleled by an extension of intervention from the definitely public to the obviously private. Government's role was increasingly prescriptive laying down acceptable sexual behaviour and policing sexual relations through laws governing such areas as prostitution, homosexuality and contraception. In many respects, the state assumed the role previously played by the church. This can be seen in its sanctioning marriages and the grounds on which divorce was valid, in its defining the forms of licit and illicit sexual behaviour and in its treatment of prostitution.[235] The interest in prostitution in late-Victorian Britain

---

[233] Kent, Susan Kingsley, *Sex and suffrage in Britain 1860-1914*, (Routledge), 1990, pp. 60-79.

[234] Harling, Philip, 'The powers of the Victorian state', in Mandler, Peter, (ed.), *Liberty and authority in Victorian Britain*, (Oxford University Press), 2006, pp. 25-50, and 'The State', in Williams, Chris, (ed.), *A companion to nineteenth-century Britain*, (Blackwell Publishers), 2004, pp. 110-124, provide a succinct overview.

[235] Walkowitz, Judith, *Prostitution and Victorian Society: Women, Class and the State*, (Cambridge University Press), 1980, and MacHugh, Paul, *Prostitution and Victorian Social Reform*, (Croom Helm), 1980, deal specifically with the debate on the Contagious Diseases Acts. Bartley, Paula, *Prostitution: prevention and reform in England, 1860-1914*, (Routledge), 2000, Mahood, Linda, *The Magdalenes: Prostitution in the nineteenth century*, (Routledge), 1990, Trudgill, Eric, *Madonnas and Magdalens: The origin and development of Victorian sexual attitudes*, (Heinemann), 1976, and ibid., Mort, Frank, *Dangerous Sexualities:*

stemmed from the need to extirpate immoral behaviour through tougher policing.[236]

'The Great Social Evil'

Under the name of the Great Social Evil our newspapers for years have alluded to an awful vice, too evidently of wide prevalence,' wrote Francis Newman in 1869.[237] As middle-class conventions dictated that men could not marry until they could support a family, high levels of urban unemployment caused an increase in unmarried people of both sexes and unfulfilled male sexual desire encouraged prostitution. Victorian writers did not often see the socio-economic factors, preferring moral arguments; the urban environment became a place of vice, depravity and sexual danger. An Anglican clergyman wrote of the dangers in the crowded city:

> The concentrations of vice and their rotaries... the sanction lent by example; the concealment offered by numbers to every sort of sin; the facilities provided by commerce for multiplying the means of enjoyment; the inducements held up by the love of gain to sacrifice integrity to advancement; the very refinement which attaches itself to vice when it has so many elegant appliances.[238]

These factors were said to encourage prostitution and illustrated how cities were transformed from places of opportunity to ones of danger. In the mid-1880s, W. T. Stead (1849-1912) in the first of his articles on 'Maiden Tribute to Modern Babylon' compared London to the Minotaur's labyrinth, awash with women sacrificed to the monster of modern society.[239] Though the bulk of contemporary comment and later analysis focused on London, problems of prostitution existed in urban centres across the country.

Medico-moral politics in England since 1830, pp. 54-73, provide valuable background. Levine, Philippa, 'Rough usage: prostitution, law and the social history', in Wilson, A., (ed.), *Rethinking social history: English society 1570-1920 and its interpretation*, (Manchester University Press), 1993, pp. 266-292, provides a synthesis. Fisher, Trevor, *Prostitution and the Victorians*, (Alan Sutton), 1997, is a useful collection of sources.

[236] Lee, Catherine, *Policing prostitution, 1856-1886: deviance, surveillance and morality*, (Pickering & Chatto), 2013, focuses on the experience in Kent.

[237] Newman, F. W., *The Cure of the Great Social Evil, With Special Reference to Recent Laws Delusively Called the Contagious Diseases' Acts*, (Trübner & Co.), 1869, p. 3.

[238] Walsh, W. P., *The Temptations and Trials Peculiar to Young Men: A Lecture Delivered to the Young Men's Christian Association*, (George Herbert), 1858, p. 3.

[239] *Pall Mall Gazette*, 6 July 1885, p. 5.

For the middle-classes, sexual morals or the lack of them emphasised the divide between them and the working-classes. Josephine Butler argued that men created this divide, that both respectable women and prostitutes were exploited and that the male exploitation of the working-classes upheld the morals of equally repressed but more respectable women:

> The protected and refined ladies who are not only to *be good*, but who are, if possible, to *know* nothing except what is good; and those poor outcast daughters of the people whom they purchase with money, with whom they think they may consort in evil whenever it pleases them to do so, before returning to their own separated and protected homes.[240]

In practice, poor working wages for women formed by far the strongest link between poverty and prostitution. Harriet Martineau (1802-1876) wrote that 'there is the strongest temptation to prefer luxury with infamy to hardship with unrecognised honour' in the face of unemployment.[241] Petty theft was more profitable than petty manufacturing and in turn prostitution could be more profitable than either. The working prostitute did not fit her gender role as a mother or 'angel of the house', instead choosing to work in public. The prostitute was also far from the ideal mother figure: Acton saw the two major sins of motherhood, infanticide and bastardy and from the 1860s, baby-farming to be associated with prostitution.[242] For one anonymous Christian Lady, the assault on prostitution was 'a holy war'.[243] The prostitute did not conform to the role prescribed to her by patriarchal society and branding prostitution as the 'Great Social Evil' helped to reinforce this patriarchal social structure. Given the constraints under which working-class women lived, many young women chose prostitution when seasonal and unskilled work was unavailable but also remained within a network of family and friends.

Legislating to control

---

[240] Butler, Josephine, *Social Purity: An Address*, (Morgan and Scott), 1879, pp. 9-10.

[241] Rubenhold, Hattie, *The Five: The Untold Lives of the Women Killed by Jack and Ripper*, (Doubleday), 2019, is an important revisionist study of prostitution through the medium of the quintet of women killed by 'Jack and Ripper'. A collective biography of Victorian womanhood, blighted by poverty and powerless against casual and constant abuse.

[242] Acton, W., *Prostitution Considered in its Moral, Social and Sanitary Aspects in London and Other Large Cities and Garrison Towns with Proposals for the Control and Prevention of its Attendant Evils*, 2nd ed. (John Churchill and Sons), 1870, p. x.

[243] *Pall Mall Gazette*, 9 July 1885.

In the urban context, increasing anxiety was expressed over the perceived increase in prostitution and of venereal disease. The prostitute's body itself became a pollutant of the city that needed to be regulated or removed to preserve the public's health. Bracebridge Heming (1841-1901) wrote that her disease:

...contaminates the very air, like a deadly upas tree, and poisoning the blood of the nation, with most audacious recklessness... The woman was nothing better than a paid murderess, committing crime with impunity.[244]

Eradication of a social evil energised attempts to regulate conduct in Victorian Britain in many areas. The prostitute was the symbol of degradation and sin in urban society. Prostitution, as a significant vice in the nineteenth century, was associated with the problematic poorer elements of society; their immorality was strongly associated with the criminal nature of the lower social orders.

Let the 'Social Evil' be a punishable offence, whether it be in its rather less sinful, or its more aggravated, form of 'Adultery': the latter being forbidden by God's Holy Commandments as much as murder, theft, or any other offence which our laws admit to the criminal, and the former by God's Holy Word.[245]

Prostitution was associated with venereal disease, and occasionally likened to a disease to be cursed on the body politic:

[Is prostitution] the sore to be neatly and comfortably dressed as it may be, from day to day, with mollifying and deodorising appliances, and suffered to run on? or are the means to be taken to heal and dry it up?[246]

The prostitute's body itself was seen as a pollutant of the city that needed to be regulated or removed to preserve the health of the populace. She became caught up in the Public Health movement and the extended Contagious Diseases Acts of 1866 and 1869 were pushed through by those concerned with this movement. This was an attempt at public health on a social level by combating a disease that stemmed from an individual's actions. Military reports showed a steady increase in venereal infections among troops since the 1820s. A series of government inquiries in the 1850s and 1860s, triggered by the Crimean War, testified

[244] Hemyng, B., 'Prostitution in London' in ibid., Mayhew, H., *London Labour and the London Poor*, Vol. 4, p. 235.
[245] Publicus Mentor, *The 'Social Evil!' Is There No Remedy?* (William Ridgeway), 1875, p. 4.
[246] Miller, J., *Prostitution Considered in Relation to its Cause and Cure*, (Sutherland and Knox), 1859, p. 11.

to the seriousness with which the dual problems of venereal diseases and sexual immorality among the lower ranks was regarded in official circles. In 1862, 29 per cent of all army men admitted to hospital and 12.5 per cent of all naval admissions were for sexually transmitted diseases.[247] From the 1840s, public anxiety had also been focused on prostitution by studies from evangelical clerics and doctors and by rescue and reform societies campaigning for a police crackdown on the London streets.[248] Concerns for the physical and moral health of the military and its readiness to shoulder imperial burdens led to legislation that sought to resolve the problem by dealing with the prostitutes, not their customers. Attempts to subject the enlisted rank-and-file to periodic genital examination met with considerable resistance and government turned instead to the regulation of the women with whom soldiers and sailors consorted in the Contagious Diseases Acts of 1864, 1866 and 1869.

The 1864 Contagious Diseases Act applied in several naval ports and army garrison towns in England and Wales. Under its provisions, police and medical practitioners, acting under the direct supervision of the War Office and the Admiralty, rather than the local constabulary were permitted to notify a magistrate if they suspected a woman of being a 'common prostitute'. The woman would then be detained and taken to a certified hospital for medical examination, where she could be detained for up to three months for treatment if this proved positive. A woman's refusal to co-operate with what was effectively a suspension of habeas corpus could lead to a prison sentence of one month, doubling for any subsequent offence. Infringing hospital rules, or quitting without medical consent, also carried penalties of up to two months imprisonment. In detaining a 'common prostitute', the police relied on certain signs of guilt: residence in a brothel; soliciting in the street; frequenting places where prostitutes resort; being informed against by soldiers or sailors; and lastly,

---

[247] See, *Report of the Committee appointed to enquire into the Pathology and Treatment of the Venereal Disease with the view to Diminish its Injurious Effects on the men of the Army and Navy*, (Harrison and Sons), 1868, pp. xli-xlii, for statistical information for 1864. Hall, Lesley A., 'Venereal diseases and society in Britain, from the Contagious Diseases Acts to the National Health Service', in Davidson, Roger, and Hall, Lesley A., (eds.), *Sex, sin and suffering: venereal disease and European society since 1870*, (Routledge), 2001, pp. 120-136; Blanco, Richard L., 'The attempted control of venereal disease in the army of mid-Victorian England', *Journal of the Society for Army Historical Research*, Vol. 45, (1967), pp. 234-241.

[248] See, for instance, Anon, *Social versus political reform: the sin of great cities: or The great social evil a national sin: illustrated by a brief enquiry into its extent, causes, effects, and existing remedies*, (A. W. Bennett), 1859, and Spurgeon, Charles, *The Great Social Evil. A sermon*, [on *John*, viii, 10, 11], (John Chapter-House Court), 1860.

the admission of the woman herself. There were also penalties for brothel keepers. The Contagious Diseases Acts 1866 and 1869 extended the geographical locations covered by the regulations, while the Admiralty and War Office were now mandated to provide hospital facilities for inspection and treatment. Provision was also made within hospitals for adequate moral and religious instruction of the women and for regular fortnightly inspections of former detainees, while the period of compulsory detention was extended to six months. [249]

Supporters of the legislation did not see the principles of state hygiene as contradicting the moral emphases of the public health movement. Far from the state sanctioning male vice by providing men of the forces with a clean supply of women, it claimed that the Acts were essentially moral in aim and intention. In reality, the Acts were concerned with the regulation of the sexual and moral habits of two particular groups within the urban poor: female prostitutes and the lower ranks of the armed forces. But the tactics used to discipline these two groups were markedly different.[250]

Opposing the Acts

The legislation understandably angered women, and many men, the more so because of the opportunities it afforded the police to harass women. The Acts assumed that prostitution was a permanent and necessary evil. They condoned male sexual access to fallen women and were specifically directed at women in order to protect the health of men. If the priority had been to fight venereal infections, then inspecting the prostitutes' clients would also have been required by the Acts. However, the

---

[249] Ogborn, Miles, 'Law and discipline in nineteenth century English state formation: the Contagious Diseases Acts of 1864, 1866 and 1869', *Journal of Historical Sociology*, Vol. 6, (1), (1993), pp. 28-55, Smith, Francis Barrymore, 'The Contagious Diseases Acts reconsidered', *Social History of Medicine*, Vol. 3, (1990), pp. 197-215, and 'Ethics and disease in the later 19th century: the Contagious Diseases Acts', *Historical Studies: Australia & New Zealand*, Vol. 15, (1971), pp. 118-135.

[250] See, Parliamentary Papers, *Report from the Select Committee on Contagious Diseases Act (1866)*, 1868-1869, *Report of Royal Commission upon the administration and operation of the Contagious Diseases Acts plus Minutes of evidence*, 1871, and *Report from the Select Committee on the Contagious Diseases Acts plus Further reports*, 1880-1881, for the changing nature of the debate on the legislation. Hill, Berkeley, 'Statistical results of the Contagious Diseases Acts', *Journal of the Statistical Society of London*, Vol. 33, (1870), pp. 463-485, and Stansfeld, James, 'On the validity of the annual government statistics of the operation of the Contagious Diseases Acts', *Journal of the Statistical Society*, Vol. 39, (1876), pp. 540-561, give contemporary views on the ways the Acts operated.

assumption was that, while men would be offended at the intrusion, the women were already so degraded that further humiliations were of no consequence. These Acts became a feminist cause because they permitted the police to detain and inspect any woman suspected of venereal infection, and, it was claimed, innocent women found themselves forced to undergo degrading inspections.[251] One obvious problem lay in the fact that the law did not distinguish between prostitutes and other women of the lower classes and another was that, contrary to common Victorian belief that any extramarital sexual experience inevitably doomed women to a life of prostitution and dismal, lonely death, many women only worked intermittently as prostitutes.[252]

Social Science Congresses were an important forum for reformers who wished to bring a social problem to national attention and public scrutiny.[253] Some of those who wished to campaign for the repeal of the Contagious Diseases Acts chose the Congress that was to meet at Bristol in the early autumn of 1869 as the platform from which to launch their campaign. At first the Congress Committee were loath to have the subject debated but changed their mind just before the Congress met.[254] Some leaders of the movement arranged a preliminary meeting at the Royal Hotel, Bristol on 30 September 1869 attended by some seventy persons that passed a resolution strongly condemning the Regulation system with six dissentients. On Monday, 4 October 1869, Dr C. Bell Taylor (1829-1909) of Nottingham read his paper advocating the repeal of the Contagious Diseases Acts, while Dr W. P. Swain, Surgeon, Royal Albert Hospital, Devonport and Mr Berkeley Hill of the Extension Association read papers in favour of the Acts and of their extension.[255] The meeting

---

[251] Lee, Catherine, *Policing Prostitution, 1856-1886: Deviance, Surveillance and Morality*, (Pickering and Chatto), 2013, focuses on how the legislation operated in Kent.

[252] Ibid., Shiman, Lilian Lewis, *Women and Leadership in Nineteenth Century England*, pp. 138-150, examines 'this Revolt of the Women'.

[253] For the Social Science Association, see Yeo, Eileen, *The Contest for Social Science: Relations and Representations of Gender and Class*, (Oram Press), 1996, pp. 148-180, Goldman, Lawrence, 'The Social Science Association, 1857-1886: a Context for mid-Victorian Liberalism', *English Historical Review*, Vol. 101, (*1986*), pp. 95-134, and Goldman, Lawrence, *Science, reform, and politics in Victorian Britain: the Social Science Association, 1857-1886*, (Cambridge University Press), 2002, pp. 113-142, consider the role of women and the Social Science Association.

[254] 'The Social Science Congress', *Pall Mall Gazette*, 18 August 1869, p. 7.

[255] Taylor, Charles Bell, *Observations on the Contagious Diseases Act, (women, not animals): showing how the new law debases women, debauches men, destroys the liberty of the subject, and tends to increase disease: being a reply to Mr. W. Paul Swain's paper on the working of the Act at Devonport*, (Frederick

resolved by an overwhelming majority that the National Association for the Promotion of Social Science should protest against the Acts and take steps to resist their extension and the following day, The National Association for the Repeal of the Contagious Diseases Acts was established.[256]

Initially women were excluded from the Association though it was quick to change this policy. Despite this, women led by Josephine Butler broke away to form the Ladies' National Association for the Repeal of the Contagious Diseases Act.[257] The LNA was well organised and vocal. As soon as it was established, it issued a strongly worded memorial in *The Daily News* on 31 December 1869 signed by prominent figures including Florence Nightingale and Harriet Martineau, claiming the Acts were not only an attack on the civil liberties of all women but also implicated the state in sanctioning male vice. It was widely, if briefly, reported in the provincial press in the first week of January 1870. *The Shield*, a weekly circular giving news of the acts and of protests against them, began publication in March 1870.

The women's protest was received with expressions of outrage and puzzlement by men within the established political culture. Despite this, moral campaigns were unusual in that men allowed women to 'find it in their power to contribute' to a larger extent than anywhere else in Victorian life.[258] Divorce, prostitution and women's emancipation were designated as outside the parameters of political discourse and MPs customarily prefaced speeches on these topics by apologising for intruding on Parliamentary time. Repealers soon grasped this and drew on the only vocabulary able to bear the moral and intellectual weight of their challenge, the militant language of radical dissenting religion. The LNA leadership included veterans of the Anti-Corn Law League and the abolitionist campaigns in which women had forged an important role that stopped short of feminism. LNA women and male supporters, many of whom were Unitarians and Quakers, came from a background of similar, if less explicitly sexual, moral reform campaigns, anti-slavery and temperance in particular. The recognition that class was an important consideration won them support from working-class men fearing the effects of the acts on their own wives and children.[259] The Contagious Diseases Act agitation

Banks), 1869.

[256] Hamilton, M., 'Opposition to the Contagious Diseases Acts, 1864-1886', *Albion*, Vol. 10, (1978), pp. 14-27.

[257] L'Esperance, Jean, 'The Work of the Ladies' National Association for the Repeal of the Contagious Diseases Acts', *Bulletin for the Society for the Study of Labour History* (Spring, 1973), pp.14-16.

[258] M. R., '*The Contagious Diseases' Act: A Letter to The Editor of* The Times', *The Times*, 6 February 1868, p. 15.

[259] Blackwell, Elizabeth, *Wrong and right methods of dealing with social evil: as shown by English Parliamentary evidence*, (A. Brentano), 1883.

proved important in its emphasis on the power given to men over women's bodies adding a feminist dimension to the critique of the Acts. In 1870, a prostitute complained bitterly to Josephine Butler:

> It is *men*, only *men*, from the first to the last, that we have to do with! To please a man I did wrong at first, then I was flung about from man to man. Men police lay hand on us. By men we are examined, handled, doctored, and messed on with. In the hospital it is a man again who makes prayers and reads the Bible for us. We are up before magistrates who are men, and we never get out of the hands of men.[260]

In the wake of the suspension of 1883 and the final repeal of the acts in 1886, many women choose to concentrate not on older-style feminist campaigns such as in education, but on obtaining a single moral standard for men and women alike. The LNA continued as a much smaller group until 1914, focusing attention on the state regulation of prostitution in the colonies and other European countries.[261] This was most clearly evident in India where Butler emphasised the powerlessness of Indian women, in the face of the oppression of British military and imperial strength, yet also the 'mission' of those in a position to redress such oppression.[262]

The timing of the Contagious Diseases Acts was important for British feminism and the campaign against the legislation absorbed women who might otherwise have been attracted to the temperance movement with its comparable stress of women victimised by male vice and power.[263] The LNA's critique of male-dominated society was far

---

[260] Cit., ibid., Walkowitz, Judith, *Prostitution and Victorian Society: Women, Class and the State*, p. 128.

[261] Heath, Deana, *Purifying Empire: Obscenity and the Politics of Moral Regulation in Britain, India and Australia*, (Cambridge University Press), 2010.

[262] There was also an imperial dimension that paralleled the situation in Britain. Virtually every British colonial possession was subject in the latter half of the nineteenth century to Contagious Diseases ordinances and regulations that identified female prostitutes as the principal source of infection. Though most agree that this legislation was put in place primarily to protect the health of British soldiers, a closer examination reveals that the laws were not just about the control of venereal infections but also a conscious instrument of colonial dominance. See, Levine, P., *Prostitution, race and politics: policing venereal disease in the British Empire*, (Routledge), 2003, and Howell, Philip, *Geographies of Regulation: Policing Prostitution in Nineteenth-Century Britain and the Empire*, (Cambridge University Press), 2009.

[263] In the United States, the rise of abolitionism in relation to alcohol arose at the same time as the CDAs and LNA in Britain. Its critique of male attitudes was far less radical. Had the Contagious Diseases legislation not been passed, it is possible that British feminism would have also taken this route. Fletcher, Holly Berkley, *Gender and the American Temperance Movement of the Nineteenth*

more radical. In contrast to the feminist organisations of the 1850s and 1860s, the LNA was national in scope rather than London-based with 92 local associations in 1882 and 500 branches when its protest ended in 1886. It was strong in big cities where prostitution was widespread and in middle-class, Nonconformist families.[264] However, there was a tension between married and single women within the repeal campaign and within feminist agitation generally. Married women received priority in the agitation for property law reform, single women in the push for employment and educational gains. The divisive emphasis on a limited suffrage that would disproportionately benefit single women may have strengthened the determination of married women in the LNA to take the lead on matters where their sexually inexperienced sisters were at a disadvantage.

Josephine Butler (1828-1906) was the daughter of John Grey, a Northumberland agricultural reformer and abolitionist who acted as the chief political agent for his cousin the reformist Prime Minister Lord Grey and was married to George Butler (1819-1890), an Anglican clergyman and educator established in Liverpool.[265] She could speak for the middle-class provincial activist independent of the London elite. Like many women who undertook moral reform, she was driven by religious conviction and faith. She had not herself been an abolitionist but shared with anti-slavery activists an empathy with powerless fellow-women debased by circumstances. The LNA attracted some working-class women to its meetings and Butler, together with its other middle-class leaders,

Century, (Routledge), 2007, Mattingly, Carol, Well-Tempered Women: Nineteenth-Century Temperance Rhetoric, new edition, (Southern Illinois University Press), 2000, Parsons, Elaine Frantz, Manhood Lost: Fallen Drunkards and Redeeming Women in the Nineteenth Century United States, (John Hopkins University Press), 2003.

[264] Wallace, Ryland, 'Organise! Organise! Organise!': A Study of Reform Agitations in Wales, 1840-1886, (University of Wales Press), 1991, pp. 170-183, provides a valuable study of regional development demonstrating that the experiences of the LNA in England were paralleled in Wales.

[265] Butler, Josephine, Personal Reminiscences of a Great Crusader, (H. Marshall), 1896. Jordan, Jane, Josephine Butler, (John Murray), 2001, Petrie, Glen, A Singular Iniquity: The Campaigns of Josephine Butler, (Macmillan), 1971, and Bell, E. Moberly, Josephine Butler: Flame of Fire, (Constable, 1962). See also, Mathers, Helen, 'Evangelicalism and feminism: Josephine Butler, 1828-1906', in Morgan, Sue, (ed.), Women, religion and feminism in Britain, 1750-1900, (Palgrave Macmillan), 2002, pp. 123-137, Mathers, Helen, 'The evangelical spirituality of a Victorian feminist: Josephine Butler, 1828-1906', Journal of Ecclesiastical History, Vol. 52, (2001), pp. 282-312, and her Patron Saint of Prostitutes: Josephine Butler and a Victorian Scandal, (History Press), 2014, and Regard, Frédéric, Josephine Butler (1828-1906): Récit d'une croisade féministe, (Les Edition de Paris), 2021.

stressed that repeal was essentially a women's cause and a cause of all women. She stressed medical, moral and constitutional arguments against the Contagious Diseases Acts. The campaign focused on the underhand ways in which they were passed; their failure to detect or check venereal disease, the unfair way in which they penalised women but ignored their better-off clients and infringed women's civil liberties. It focussed on attempts to condone, sanitise and regulate sin and the physical results that might be visited on innocent married and unmarried women. The Acts were, she argued, a mockery of Victorian veneration of womanhood.

Ultimately, the campaign for repeal was successful, drawing on considerable support from working-class men, from evangelical churches and Nonconformists and from Liberal politicians. Middle-class evangelists had worked with the poor since the early part of the century, attempting to stamp out their alleged immorality. Repealers took far more direct and, on occasions, dangerous action. They sought out registered prostitutes, gave them practical help and moral support in opposing the legislation. Feminists of the LNA supported the contemporary campaign for female doctors and challenged male doctors, politicians and the military establishment with a number of telling points.[266] They rejected the commonly held view, directed at middle-class women, that prostitutes in the public sphere protected virtuous females in the private sphere against unreasonable sexual demands and argued that all women were vulnerable to sexual exploitation within their profession of marriage and that men should raise themselves to women's levels of sexual self-control. The support for the Contagious Diseases Acts by Elizabeth Garrett, who, like male doctors, put checking disease before defending liberty, was an embarrassment to the LNA that was not concerned with the control of venereal disease.[267] Finally, feminists argued that a Parliament of rich men was unfit to legislate for poor women on such matters, contrary to the politicians' assertions that they looked after the interests of disenfranchised females. Feminists resented the way in which women were defined only in relation to men and motherhood.

The campaign against the CDAs did not destroy the double standard of morality for the sexes any more than it materially improved the position of prostitutes.[268] Politicians may have become disenchanted with the

---

[266] Holton, Sandra Stanley, 'State Pandering, Medical Policing and Prostitution. The Controversy within the Medical Profession over the Contagious Diseases Legislation, 1864-86', *Research in Law, Deviance and Social Control*, Vol. 9, (1989), pp. 149-170, explores the debate in the medical profession.

[267] See, Garrett, Elizabeth, *An enquiry into the character of the Contagious Diseases Acts of 1866-69*, (Harrison and Sons), 1870, and 'Justina', *Justina's Letters in Reply to Miss Garrett's Defence of the Contagious Diseases Acts*, (W. Tweedie), 1870, initially published in the *Pall Mall Gazette* on 3 March 1870 and 18 March 1870.

Contagious Diseases legislation and tired of the struggle it provoked, but they had not been persuaded that Parliament should abandon other attempts to regulate vice. For instance, the Vagrancy Act 1898 outlawed sexual soliciting, prescribed fines of 40 shillings for female offenders compared with six months' imprisonment and hard labour for men. In practice, it was massively enforced against women while prosecutions of men were virtually unknown. Women were divided on the issue. Rescue work attracted both feminists and non-feminist members of the LNA and women outside the Association. It reinforced notions of feminine mission and moral superiority that had encouraged female community and justified women's involvement in reform earlier in the century. During the 1880s and 1890s, it led some of them, mobilised in a host of social purity groups like the National Vigilance Association, to believe that legislation could be used to 'force people to be moral'.[269]

Campaigns for social purity

Much of the moral focus of late-Victorian feminists stemmed from fear. Feminists saw themselves as victims of a male ideology, as victims of a lust denied to them, of a right to speak denied to them, of a society shaped by male requirements and from the 1880s demands for a single standard became central to the women's movement. Their position was limited by Victorian ideology, but they inverted its precepts, turning the duties of moral guardianship into a campaign that criticised laxity and degradation of men who ascribed them that role. The element of philanthropy that surfaced in almost all the campaigns is also apparent here: some of the activity centred round the CDA controversy and laid emphasis on the rescue of 'fallen women' and their moral re-education.[270] Campaigns on marital violence pre-dated the 'Jack the Ripper' murders of 1888 and one of the most powerful arguments that campaigners against 'wife-torture' had was the inadequacy of the law in protecting women from reprisal.[271] Frances Power Cobbe and others were convinced that levels of male

---

[268] Laite, Julia, *Common Prostitutes and Ordinary Citizens. Commercial Sex in London, 1885-1960*, (Palgrave Macmillan), 2011.

[269] Cox, Pamela, 'Compulsion, Voluntarism and Venereal Disease: Governing Sexual Health in England after the Contagious Diseases Acts', *Journal of British Studies*, Vol. 46, (2007), pp. 91-115, considers developments between 1885 and 1940.

[270] Roberts, M. J. D., *Making English morals: voluntary association and moral reform in England, 1787-1886*, (Cambridge University Press), 2004, provides a valuable overview. See also, Hall, Lesley A., 'Hauling Down the Double Standard: Feminism, Social Purity and Sexual Science in Late Nineteenth-Century Britain', *Gender & History*, Vol. 16, (2004), pp. 36-56.

[271] This can be seen in Walkowitz, Judith, *City of Dreadful Delights*, (Virago), 1993, that uses the Ripper murders of the autumn of 1888.

violence were made worse by the consumption of alcohol, an analysis not exclusive to feminists as long-standing temperance societies show.

From the early-nineteenth century, until absorbed by the new social purity movements of the 1880s, the Society for the Suppression of Vice, founded in 1802, was the leading organisation campaigning against the obscene. Its work demonstrated the close relationship between private vigilance and public authorities and it was the influence of the Vice Society that led to the Obscene Publications Act 1857.[272] Throughout the 1870s and 1880s, the 'abolitionists' were a major social force and the stimulus for the emergence of vigorous social-purity organisations such as the Social Purity Alliance, the National Vigilance Association, the Association for the Improvement of Public Morals and the Moral Reform Union.

Why was there a major attempt at moral restructuring in the last decades of the nineteenth and first decade of the twentieth centuries? From the 1870s, following what was seen as a decline in standards in the 1850s and 1860s, a new confidence in a moralistic ethic can be detected.[273] In 1885, one Christian lady described it as a 'holy war'. In the early years of the nineteenth century, moral reformers had been sustained by the threat of revolution. No such fears limited them in the 1880s and 1890s but there were a series of causes and scandals that maintained their momentum. Tensions created by economic depression, political upheaval, social reorganisation and demographic imbalance found voice in the seemingly endless debate over private morality. Social purity campaigns became increasingly opposed to 'deviant' sexual practices, including homosexuality, resulting in a 'veil of silence' over sexual topics. The iniquities of the CDA, the scandalous leniency meted out to high class 'madams'—until 1885 prosecuted generally if irregularly by local vestries for keeping a 'bawdy house' under the Disorderly Houses Act of 1751--the exploitation and abduction of young girls in the 'white slave trade' and the divorce cases of Sir Charles Dilke (1843-1911) in 1886 and the Irish leader Charles Stewart Parnell (1846-1891) in 1890 suggested declining moral standards.[274] Also, there was the scandal at Cleveland Street homosexual brothel 1889-1890 said to involve the duke of Clarence, eldest son of the heir to the throne[275] and the Tranby Croft gambling scandal of 1891 that

---

[272] Hunt, Alan, *Governing morals: a social history of moral regulation*, (Cambridge University Press), 1999, pp. 57-76.

[273] Fisher, Trevor, *Scandal: The Sexual Politics of Late Victorian Britain*, (Alan Sutton), 1995, is a useful and readable examination of this issue.

[274] Nicholls, David, *The lost prime minister: a life of Sir Charles Dilke*, (Continuum), 1995, pp. 177-194, ibid., Horstman, Allen, *Victorian Divorce*, pp. 140-141.

[275] On this see Chester, Lewis, Leitch, David and Simpson, Colin, *The Cleveland Street Affair*, (Weidenfeld), 1976, and Hindmarsh-Watson, Katie, 'Male Prostitution and the London GPO: Telegraph Boys 'Immorality' from

did involve Edward, Prince of Wales.[276] Above all in 1895, there was the conviction and imprisonment of Oscar Wilde (1854-1900), the Irish dramatist. Wilde was prosecuted three times for his homosexual behaviour, a sentence of two years hard labour was passed after the third trial and Wilde was imprisoned in Reading Jail. It was here that he wrote *De Profundis* and *The Ballad of Reading Gaol.* On his release from prison Wilde was bankrupt, divorced, his children had been taken from him and many of his friends had deserted him. He left the country dying in exile in Paris in 1900.[277]

There was a constituency ready to be stirred by such scandals in the lower middle-class and the respectable working-class whose values were being attacked by radicals and libertarians.[278] Respectability, with its stress on values such as self-help and self-reliance, the value of work and the need for social discipline and the centrality of the family, was threatened by public immorality. Here was a strong basis for social purity. Behind this, giving the campaigns a tremendous dynamism was an evangelical revival, bringing large sections of the feminist movement into alliance with Nonconformity, an alliance sealed in their common outrage against double standards and the call for a common moral standard that applied equally to men and women. Many of the leaders of the campaigns in the 1880s were products of this Christian revival and W. T. Stead, described himself as 'a child of the revival of 1859-60' that had swept across the Atlantic and won hundreds of thousands of converts. Social purity was also able to mine very deep fears of a more secular kind. 1885 saw the expansion of the electorate in the Third Reform Act, but there were fears of national decline following the defeat and death of General George Gordon (1833-1885) at the hands of the Mahdi in the Sudan, anxieties about Ireland and all this in the context of a socialist revival and feminist agitation. Social purity became a metaphor for a stable society and in 1885 was able to tap an anxiety that found a symbolic focus in the 'twin evils' of enforced prostitution and especially the sexual dangers this posed for children.[279]

Nationalization to the Cleveland Street Scandal', *Journal of British Studies*, Vol. 51, (3), (2012), pp. 594-617. Coleman, Jonathan, *Rent: Same-Sex Prostitution in Modern Britain 1885-1957*, Ph.D., Thesis, University of Kentucky, 2014, takes a broader approach but see pp. 28-67, on Cleveland Street and Oscar Wilde.

[276] Havers, Michel, Grayson, Edward, and Shankland, Peter, *The Royal Baccarat Scandal*, (Souvenir Press), 1988.

[277] Foldy, Michael, *The Trials of Oscar Wilde: Deviance, Morality and Late-Victorian Society*, (Yale University Press), 1997.

[278] Ibid., Hunt, Alan, *Governing morals: a social history of moral regulation*, pp. 140-191, and ibid., Roberts, M. J. D., *Making English morals: voluntary association and moral reform in England, 1787-1886*, pp. 245-289.

[279] Liggins, Emma, 'Prostitution and Social Purity in the 1880s and 1890s',

By the early 1880s, Repealers were also becoming concerned about juvenile prostitution and 'white slavery', the traffic in women abducted through deception or force for the purposes of prostitution.[280] The white slavery metaphor—also used more frequently in the London and provincial press[281] to describe the more general economic exploitation of women in the sweated trades—helped to recast the image of the prostitute, enabling the public to see her sympathetically as the victim of social and economic forces beyond her control. This allowed reformers to shift attention away from the prostitute and toward those who profited by her trade, redirecting censure from victim to exploiter, from individual to society and, most importantly, from women to men. Largely as a result of the efforts of feminists and other social reformers, the Criminal Law Amendment Bill, was introduced into Parliament in the early-1880s with the intent of protecting young women by raising the age of female consent from thirteen to sixteen and making brothels more susceptible to legal controls.

For several years, the Bill languished in Parliament. At a crucial moment, support for it was energised by a sensational report, 'The Maiden Tribute of Modern Babylon' serialised in the Pall Mall Gazette in 1885, documenting the complexity and reach of organised prostitution as an industry and its reliance on both crude and sophisticated techniques for the entrapment of young girls.[282] A House of Lords Select Committee identified the trade in English girls for prostitution in 1859 and from 1874 the Home Office monitored the transportation of English minors to foreign brothels but the articles caused uproar among the working-classes but also raised anxieties among the middle-classes regarding their own daughters. Stead was prosecuted for buying Eliza Armstrong, a thirteen year old girl from her mother and taking her to the continent in order to prove how easy it was to procure child prostitutes and was convicted of kidnapping and abetting indecent assault serving three months in prison.

Critical Survey, Vol. 15, (3), (2003), pp. 39-55.

[280] 'Foreign Trade in English Girls', Liverpool Echo, 8 January 1880, p. 4.

[281] For instance, 'On Things in General', Sheffield Daily Telegraph, 6 March 1880, p. 2, 'House of Lords', Morning Post, 29 February 1888, p. 4, 'The Queen's Reign', Gloucester Citizen, 4 June 1897, p. 1.

[282] Four articles that appeared in the Pall Mall Gazette, Monday, 6 July 1885, pp. 1-6, Tuesday, 7 July 1885, pp. 1-6, Wednesday, pp. 1-5, 8 July 1885, and Friday, 10 July 1885, pp. 1-6, though unsigned, were acknowledged to be the work of W. T. Stead, its editor. 'The Press on the Crimes of Modern Babylon', Pall Mall Gazette, 14 July 1885, pp. 11-12, 16 July 1885, p. 6, prints extracts showing the provincial press' supportive response to the articles. See, Schults, Raymond L., Crusader in Babylon: W. T. Stead and the Pall Mall Gazette, (University of Nebraska Press), 1972, and Eckley, Grace, Maiden Tribute: A Life of W. T. Stead, (Xlibris Corporation), 2007.

His sensational exposé generated a sense of outrage with which a wide range of public opinion found itself in sympathy and, in the ensuing moral panic, the Criminal Law Amendment Act—its Second Reading was being debated at the same time that Stead's articles were published—was passed five weeks after the articles were published.

The Act raised the age of consent for girls from 13 to 16, criminalised 'indecent acts' between men in private as well as in public and outlawed brothel keeping and the procurement of women for prostitution. Brothel keepers and their agents could be fined or sent to prison with hard labour. As a result, landlords became wary of letting rooms to suspected prostitutes meaning that many women became homeless. As a consequence of an amendment introduced by Henry Labouchere (1831-1912), an ambitious Liberal politician, the legislation also provided for up to two years' hard labour in prison for acts of gross indecency between men. Here ideals of masculinity played a crucial role. Medical literature increasingly portrayed homosexuals as effeminate and degenerate, a threat to Victorian manliness. Labouchere amendment also reflected a general belief among social purity campaigners that male homosexuality was a product of the same unrestrained male lust they were trying to curb in their campaign against the double standard and the evils of the CDAs.

In both cases, too, public decency was invoked, along with the need to protect young people. Further changes, in the Vagrancy Act 1898 and, following renewed anxiety about 'white slavery' and the upsurge of interest in the issue after W. T. Stead's death on the *Titanic*, the Criminal Law Amendment Act 1912 for which there was widespread suffragist and suffragette support in a pass-the-bill campaign, underlined new legislative involvement with regulating and criminalising prostitution and homosexuality.[283] Reformers in 1885 had no doubt that their cause was right: a crusade against 'a dark and cruel wrong'. Yet they were directing their energies at many of the wrong targets, illustrating the nineteenth century preference for moral campaigns rather than structural social reforms.[284]

While feminists broadly welcomed the 1885 Act especially the clauses raising the age of consent, they were divided over whether moral attitudes could be changed by state regulation. Some feminists were hostile towards the medical profession and to the use of discourses of

---

[283] Fletcher, Ian Christopher, 'Opposition by Journalism? The Socialist and Suffragist Press and the Passage of the Criminal Law Amendment Act of 1912', *Parliamentary History*, Vol. 25, (1), (2006), pp. 88-114.

[284] Gorham, Deborah, ''The Modern tribute of Modern Babylon Re-Examined': Child Prostitution and the Idea of Childhood in Late-Victorian England', *Victorian Studies*, Vol. 21, (1978), pp. 353-379.

purity and sanitary reform. Widespread female anxiety regarding male violence, both physical and sexual towards women led anti-medical feminists to claim that some pieces of 'sanitary' legislation represented a state-sanctioned violation of the bodies of women and children.[285] Others, Josephine Butler for instance, were concerned that further state regulation threatened civil liberties and regarded a repressive approach with concern:

> Beware of 'Purity Societies'...ready to accept and endorse any amount of inequality in the laws, any amount of coercive and degrading treatment of their fellow creatures in the fatuous belief that you can oblige human beings to be moral by force.[286]

Other feminists saw the legislation as a means of providing protection for women from sexual abuse, joined organisations such as the National Vigilance Association and Moral Reform Union to seek further legislation to regulate sexual behaviour. Some feminists took a more repressive stance and confronted prostitution through the closing of brothels and the expulsion of prostitutes from places of entertainment. Why these women took this approach and why they thought of it as feminist reflected their vision of a 'purified' public and private world that was informed by religious beliefs and adherence to temperance. Churchwomen who were major campaigners for social purity exerted enormous pressure upon the hierarchies of church and chapel, actively reworking Christian readings of the body to bring the moral influence of the churches to bear upon public opinion.[287] Concern with the morality of public spaces also related to women's desire for safety in public places and justified state intervention to achieve this.[288]

Illegitimacy was always regarded as the mother's fault, and it was seen as vitally important to separate these 'bad apples' from the rest of society.[289] Unmarried mothers were considered immoral, single fathers feckless and illegitimate children inherently defective. One tool used by the state was the Mental Deficiency Act 1913, a pernicious piece of legislation that

---

[285] Scott, Anne L., 'Physical purity feminism and state medicine in late nineteenth-century England', *Women's History Review*, Vol. 8, (1999), pp. 625-653.

[286] Josephine Butler writing in 1897 quoted in Higson, J., *The Story of a Beginning: An Account of Pioneer Work for Moral Welfare*, (SPCK), 1955.

[287] Morgan, Sue, "'Wild Oats or Acorns?' Social Purity, Sexual Politics and the Response of the Late-Victorian Church', *Journal of Religious History*, Vol. 31, (2007), pp. 151-168.

[288] Bland, Lucy, "'Purifying' the public world: feminist vigilantes in late Victorian England', *Women's History Review*, Vol. 1, (1992), pp. 397-412.

[289] Robinson, Jane, *In the Family War: Illegitimacy between the Great War and the Swinging Sixties*, (Viking), 2015.

allowed women to be classed as moral imbeciles as well as mental ones. This included unmarried mothers who could not support themselves and those unwed mothers who were pregnant for a second time. Some of these women, who were not medically diagnosed as being an 'imbecile' and who could be committed, if under 21, merely on the word of a parent or guardian—never emerged from the institutions in which they were incarcerated. The Act was not repealed until 1959.

At the heart of the Social Purity movement in Britain and its Empire was the conviction that sexuality had to be controlled.[290] Many reformers believed that because it was basically associated with men, it was woman's mission to re-educate them. By accepting the idea of feminine moral superiority and by implication, the traditional 'separate sphere' for women, the movement was not fully feminist. Nonetheless, in urging women to resist sexual domination and exploitation, it aided the advancement of female autonomy. Its birth control ideas were feminist to the extent that advocates urged voluntary motherhood and women's control over their own bodies yet they were opposed to contraception and abortion. Furthermore, their eugenic arguments that initially aimed to increase woman's power, foundered in a 'cult of motherhood' that was ambivalent in its attitude to woman's professional improvement.

Cultures

The image of the nineteenth century as a period of great opportunity for men of energy and skill has been long established. Historians have argued that an industrious middle-class made great fortunes during the industrial revolution and converted economic success into political power in the 1832 Reform Act. This political power was then used to ensure policy reflected the middle-class interests. Such arguments present the middle-class as a coherent body mobilising their economic and political power to forge society in their image. Challenging landed privilege, the industrial and urban middle-classes are seen as striving to establish a society based on merit rather than on one's birth. Through education reform, schemes of civic improvement and the growth of the market. the middle-classes saw themselves as enabling equality of opportunity by enabling the working-classes to realise their abilities.[291]

---

[290] Butler, Josephine, *Social Purity*, (Morgan and Scott), 1879, an address given in Cambridge in May 1879 and published at the request of the Committee of the Social Purity Alliance, summarised social purity thinking.

[291] Gunn, Simon, *The Public Culture of the Victorian Middle Class. Ritual and Authority in the English Industrial City, 1840-1914*, (Manchester University Press), 2000, Kidd, Alan, and Nicholls, David, (eds.), *Gender, Civic Culture and Consumerism: Middle-Class Identity in Britain, 1800-1940*, (Manchester University Press), 1999.

Political culture

There was a major restructuring of the British Establishment from the 1870s but the extent to which the middle-classes as a whole benefitted from this was limited. It did not give provincial manufacturers an enhanced position nationally.[292] Membership of the ruling elite was extended to include larger numbers of bankers and merchants but contained few manufacturers. The great country houses remained important and the network of power and influence was firmly based in the south of the country and the aristocracy was still the leading part of the ruling classes. The industrial middle-classes was able to exert pressure on the nation's political elite to get the kind of government it wanted. However, restructuring the Establishment owed less to industrialists than occupationally-based pressure groups among both the professional middle-classes and the working-classes that had won major reforms in the 1860s and 1870s and made further advances in the 1890s and 1900s.

Lancashire factory owners became a substantial group in the House of Commons after 1832 but their effectiveness was limited by internal political divisions and by their failure to create alliances with other Parliamentary groupings.[293] In the longer term, factory owners became less active in politics and more conservative in their social behaviour and their attachment to the Tory Party echoed the traditional allegiance of the Lancashire aristocracy. The debate over the Corn Laws and their repeal in 1846 was apparently an assertion of industrial against the landed interest. Repeal was beneficial to manufacturers who had a direct interest in reducing food prices and tariffs on their products but it was by no means disadvantageous to the aristocracy much of whose land was devoted to pastoral farming and whose rents from arable land were largely maintained during the long mid-century boom. It was tenant farmers, caught between the need to pay rents and fear of falling grain prices, who stood to suffer most from repeal and were its most vocal opponents. Repeal was a result of aristocratic concession to popular opinion during a short-term crisis rather than an expression of the long-term growth of middle-class political power.[294] The middle-class 'victory' of 1846 was

---

[292] The economic strength of this group, measured in terms of their share of the national wealth, began to decline from the 1870s under pressure from foreign competition.

[293] Kadish, A.', Free trade and high wages: the economics of the Anti-Corn Law League', and Lloyd-Jones, Roger, 'Merchant city: the Manchester business community, the trade cycle, and commercial policy, c.1820-1846', in Marrison, Andrew (ed.), *Freedom and trade, Vol. 1: Free trade and its reception, 1815-1960*, (Routledge), 1998, pp. 14-27, 86-104.

[294] McCord, N., *The Anti-Corn Law League 1838-1846*, (Allen and Unwin), 1958, and Pickering, Paul A., and Tyrrell, Alex, *The People's Bread: A History*

atypical of their success and did not mark the beginnings of middle-class control of the political system.

So if the position of manufacturers within the British ruling elite was limited, what power did they have within their own industrial regions? Given their wealth, they exercised considerable local power but there were limitations on this. Aristocratic influences persisted in many industrial towns until at least the 1870s offsetting the economic and political impact of the factory elite. There was also competition from non-landed groups, especially mercantile, retailing and professional middle-classes, who were more active in local urban politics than manufacturers. In Bolton and Salford, for instance, in the 1840s over half the councillors were manufacturers but this fell to under 40 per cent by the 1870s. The political dominance of manufacturers was confined to the smaller industrial towns but even there it was not unlimited. The growing mandatory powers of local government led to the creation of regulatory and democratic local procedures.

Urban society soon escaped from the aristocratic and patrician cocoon and by the 1870s the upper middle-class, though it retained substantial economic urban interests and may not have withdrawn entirely to the country, was gentrified in manners, education, values and residential style. It no longer identified with the fortunes and aspirations of any particular town. The most purely urban elements in urban society were the lower middle-class and working-classes but neither was a 'class' with cohesion, consciousness or culture. The working-class was a bundle of classes defined by wages, skills, occupations, unionisation, gender or religion while the lower middle-class was neither a social reality nor cohesive in attitude even amongst those who situated themselves within this cadre.

The dynamic of urbanisation had shoved the lower middle-classes into a prominent position for which its members were unprepared. It had far exceeded their expectations and it lacked the capacity to develop constructive ideas on how to use this position. The working-classes stepped into this vacuum seeking unity through political and industrial organisation that developed in the 1880s and 1890s as it gradually moved away from the 'Lib-Labism' of the 1870s and towards mass unskilled unionism. Political mobilisation saw a growth of working-class involvement in urban local government and after 1906 increasingly as a force in

---

of the Anti-Corn Law League, (Leicester University Press), 2000, provide different perspectives but Prentice, Archibald, *History of the Anti-Corn Law League*, 2 Vols. (W. & F. G. Cash), 1853, new edition with an introduction by W. H. Chaloner, (Cass), 1968, is still a valuable source. The political strategies of the League can be approached through Hamer, D. A., *The Politics of Electoral Pressure*, (Harvester), 1977, pp. 58-90.

Parliament. After 1918 their power in the towns and national politics saw the destruction of the social texture and culture of Victorian towns with the deliberate demolition of its physical fabric. The lower middle-class eventually found its voice in the Thatcher revolution after 1979.[295]

Economic norms

The middle-classes had a relatively low status in terms of wealth-holding and political power, but how far did they mould society in their own image and indirectly influence the behaviour of the more prominent actors? Perkin contrasted the 'entrepreneurial ideal' of the emergent middle-classes with the 'aristocratic' ideal but it is difficult to define 'bourgeois' as opposed to 'aristocratic' values.[296] It is perhaps better to focus on whether the specific interests of manufacturers were represented in the attitudes and values of the ruling classes.[297] Literary culture suggests that manufacturers, far from reshaping dominant attitudes, were consistently rejected unless they conformed to existing social values.

Economic success beyond the exploitation of land was viewed with suspicion and the belief that money was without the reciprocal obligations and duties of landowning retained its influence. Until the 1780s, attitudes were ambiguous, but subsequently the trend was towards literary condemnation of new wealth that reached its peak in the rejection of provincial manufacturers between the 1840s and the 1930s.[298] The only route to acceptance and 'respectability' was to adopt the values of civilised culture and public service associated with the 'gentleman', and later the professional man and to abandon the money-making and sectional interest associated with new wealth.[299] The acquisition of a landed estate was one

---

[295] Roberts, Matthew, *Political Movements in Urban Britain, 1832-1914*, (Macmillan Palgrave), 2008.

[296] Ibid., Perkin, H., *The Origins of Modern English Society 1780-1880*, pp. 218-270.

[297] Gunn, Simon, *The public culture of the Victorian middle class: ritual and authority in the English industrial city, 1840-1914*, (Manchester University Press), 2000, and Kidd, Alan J., and Nicholls, David, (eds.), *Gender, civic culture, and consumerism: middle-class identity in Britain, 1800-1940*, (Manchester University Press), 1999, Green, S., 'In search of bourgeois civilisation: institutions & ideals in 19th century', *Northern History*, Vol. 28, (1992), pp. 228-245, and Morgan, S., "A sort of land debatable': Female influence, civic virtue and middle-class identity, c.1830-c.1860', *Women's History Review*, Vol. 13, (2004), pp. 183-210.

[298] Raven, James, *Judging New Wealth: Popular Publishing and Responses to Commerce in England, 1750-1800*, (Oxford University Press), 1992.

[299] See one dimension in Jeremy, David J., (ed.), *Religion, business, and wealth in modern Britain*, (Routledge), 1998, and Rubinstein, W. D., 'New Men of Wealth and the Purchase of Land in Nineteenth-Century Britain', *Past & Present*,

of the normal 'scales of hierarchy' in the upward rise of a mercantile family.[300] These elite values had an effect on the industrial middle-classes many of whom lived in town houses or holidayed at coastal resorts located on large landed estates. Most sought acceptance by the Establishment and the wealthier sent their sons to public schools and bought their own landed estates. Those who were active in political life did so in the Conservative and Liberal parties led by the aristocracy.[301] There was, however, a significant space for the cultural influence of non-landed groups within the industrial regions. Merchants, retailers and professionals were more active than manufacturers and there were important political and religious differences within local middle-classes with Nonconformists beyond Wesleyan Methodists largely supporting a liberal or radical stance while Anglicans were more conservative in their politics.

The economic and political power of the landed elite came from their ownership and control of land while for industrial entrepreneurs it came from their ownership and control of manufacturing. For both elites the nineteenth century saw important changes. The emergence of managers as a segment of the economic elite reflected changing rates of social mobility.[302] Education became more important for recruitment into managerial occupations and the chances of those from working- or especially middle-class backgrounds of moving into this economic elite improved. The emergence of a managerial sector introduced an important source of potential conflict within the economic elite as a whole. The moral solidarity of the old property-owning elite was undermined. The separation of ownership and control in industry saw the advent of two types of individuals who moved apart in their outlook on and attitudes towards society in general and towards enterprise in particular. The 'individualistic', profit-seeking entrepreneur contrasted with managerial executives whose values stressed efficiency and productivity rather than profits. These differences in ideals and values reinforced divergence in styles of life and social contacts. This in turn produced conflict of interests, sometimes leading to open struggles, since seeking maximum

---

Vol. 92, (1981), pp. 125-147.

[300] See, for instance, Jones, E. L. 'Industrial Capital and Landed Investment: The Arkwrights in Herefordshire, 1800-43', in Jones, E. L., and Mingay, G. E., (eds.), *Land, Labour and Population in the Industrial Revolution*, (Edward Arnold), 1967, pp. 48-71, and Rapp, Dean, 'Social Mobility in the Eighteenth Century: The Whitbread's of Bedfordshire 1720-1815', *Economic History Review*, Vol. 27, (1974), pp. 380-394.

[301] MacLeod, Dianne Sachko, *Art and the Victorian middle class: money and the making of cultural identity*, (Cambridge University Press), 1996.

[302] Pollard, Sidney, 'The genesis of the managerial profession: the experience of the Industrial Revolution in Great Britain', *Studies in Romanticism*, Vol. 4, (1965), pp. 57-80.

returns on capital was not always compatible with safeguarding the productivity and security of the enterprise.[303] Finally, the separation of ownership and control introduced important shifts in the structure of economic power. Within the large joint-stock companies that emerged in the 1850s and 1860s, effective power increasingly devolved into the hands of managers and the sanctions held by the 'owners' of the enterprise were largely nominal.[304]

This separation of ownership and control is not the only factor that led to the disintegration of the old ruling class. There was a general rise in rates of mobility, particularly inter-generational mobility, into elite positions in many institutional spheres during the last thirty years of the nineteenth century. There was some redistribution of wealth and income after 1850 as levels of 'real' wages rose that benefitted some in the working-classes. Parliamentary reform in 1832, 1867 and 1884-1885 initially gave the middle-classes and latterly some in the working-classes a stake in the existing political structure. This needs to be seen in relation in the industrial and political sphere to the mobilisation of the mass of the population. The growth of trade unions, especially after 1851, the expansion in the range of political pressure groups and the emergence of the Labour Party in the early years of the twentieth century potentially placed limitations on the power of elite groups.

Cultural norms

There was an obsession across the middle-classes with religious certainty, moral zeal and purity and respectability but above all keeping up appearances at all costs and this led later generations to accuse them of hypocrisy.[305] But this was not the only or perhaps the most abiding character trait of the middle-classes:

---

[303] This was evident in agriculture after 1870: Hunt, E. H., and Pam, S. J., 'Managerial failure in late Victorian Britain?: land use and English agriculture', *Economic History Review*, second series, Vol. 54, (2001), pp. 240-266, and Hunt, E. H., and Pam, S. J., 'Responding to agricultural depression, 1873-96: managerial success, entrepreneurial failure?', *Agricultural History Review*, Vol. 50, (2002), pp. 225-252.
[304] Alborn, Timothy L., *Conceiving companies: joint-stock politics in Victorian England*, (Routledge), 1998, Taylor, James, *Creating capitalism: joint-stock enterprise in British politics and culture, 1800-1870*, (Boydell), 2006, Johnson, Paul, *Making the Market: Victorian Origins of Corporate Capitalism*, (Cambridge University Press), 2010, and Freeman, Mark, Pearson, Robin and Taylor, James, *Shareholder Democracies? Corporate Governance in Britain and Ireland before 1850*, (University of Chicago Press), 2012.
[305] Bailey, Peter, 'White collars, gray lives?: the lower middle class revisited', *Journal of British Studies*, Vol. 38, (1999), pp. 273-290.

A person of the middle class appreciates the value of the position he occupies; and he will not marry if marriage will so impoverish him as to render it necessary to resign his social position.[306]

Their search was for security, comfort and peace of mind and above all for that social acceptance and approval denoted by respectability.[307] Being respectable meant maintaining a reputable facade and encouraged all the hypocrisies highlighted by contemporary social commentators and novelists. There is now a more subtle appreciation of middle-class values and the extent of 'hypocrisy' now depends on examining particular values rather than the middle-class ideology as a whole.

The eighteenth century urban pursuit of pleasure turned into an anxious scrutiny of the legitimacy of particular pursuits and to a corresponding emphasis on domesticity rather than sociability in the nineteenth and twentieth centuries. There was a relaxation after 1918–though it had been evident since the 1880s–within the safe boundaries of school and suburb. The most obvious and continuing thrust of the culture was towards social exclusivity. Within the wide middle-class boundary, lines to demarcate status were carefully drawn and upper and lower middle-classes would rarely meet in leisure activities. What they had in common was an attitude to leisure and a view of its social function: in leisure people could meet others of similar social status in environments, whether public or private, that conformed to the canons of contemporary respectability.

Urban middle-class culture was distinctively provincial. Until 1800, it was a culture that was more obviously urban than middle-class, expressing many of the values of the urban gentry who were part of the leisure class and its aristocratic way of life. It was inherently social rather than intellectual and its existence can be seen in figures of theatre building. Only ten purpose-built theatres were erected in the larger provincial towns between 1736 and 1760 but more than a hundred were built in the following 80 years.[308] Music festivals were another indicator that the provinces can be said to have led the way.[309] It was not until the 1830s that

[306] Fawcett, Henry, *The Economic Position of the British Labourer*, (Macmillan & Co.), 1865, p. 44.

[307] The briefest discussion of respectability can be found in Best, G., *Mid-Victorian Britain 1851-1875*, (Fontana), 1979, pp. 279-286.

[308] See, Garlick, Görel, 'Theatre outside London', and Schoch, Richard W., 'Theatre and mid-Victorian society', in Donohue, Joseph, (ed.), *The Cambridge history of British theatre: Vol. 2, 1660 to 1895*, (Cambridge University Press), 2004, pp. 165-182, 331-351.

[309] Dale, Catherine, 'The Provincial Musical Festival in Nineteenth-century England: A Case Study of Bridlington', in Cowgill, Rachel, and Holman, Peter, (eds.), *Music in the British provinces, 1690-1914*, (Ashgate), 2007, pp. 325-348,

the patronage and market for classical music in London passed from the aristocracy to the upper middle-classes. The new culture was visible too in the classical style of its architecture and in the design of squares and boulevards that were emphatically the territory of the aristocracy. For this culture was unashamedly exclusive.

After 1780, the intellectual character of this urban culture became more pronounced as did its masculinity.[310] Like-minded men turned to voluntary organisations--the association or club or society--as a forum within which they pursued their interests.[311] After 1660, inns, taverns, coffee-houses and alehouses lodged an array of clubs and societies that grew in number during the urban cultural renaissance in the eighteenth century.[312] They served as a medium through which new ideas, values and forms of regional and local identity were developed and disseminated and interacted with a range of wider developments including the growth of urbanity, the rise of public sociability and paradoxically the evolution of public and private space and growing gender differentiation. They established a network of connections that ranged across the country and were exported to the growing centres of British trade and empire. How many clubs existed in the eighteenth and early-nineteenth century is difficult to determine but Clark suggests that there were over 130 different types of society operating in the British Isles in the eighteenth century and that there may have been up to 25,000 different clubs and societies meeting in the English-speaking world.[313] In the second quarter of the nineteenth century, their leaders took a more direct interest in the social and political problems of their own towns: they formed statistical societies and disseminated 'useful' knowledge. Anxious to influence the ways of life of the working-classes from their narrow but powerful middle-class bridgehead, they were increasingly concerned with the supply of leisure to others than with enjoyment of it themselves.

The emergence of this male, intellectual, socially concerned and distinctly middle-class urban culture marked part of the wider challenge to the lack of seriousness and the frivolity of the urban gentry. Leisure activities such as theatre-going or novel reading or cards or even cricket now had to be scrutinised to see if they served any purpose that God,

---

and Sprittles, Joseph, 'Leeds musical festivals', *The Thoresby Miscellany*, Vol. 13, (1959-63), pp. 200-270, provide good case studies.

[310] Danahay, Martin A., *Gender at work in Victorian culture: literature, art and masculinity*, (Ashgate), 2005.

[311] Clark, Peter, *British Clubs and Societies 1580-1800: The Origin of an Associational World*, (Oxford University Press), 2002, pp. 94-140, 274-308.

[312] Borsay, Peter, *The English Urban Renaissance: Culture and Society in the Provincial Town, 1770-1770*, (Oxford University Press), 1991, 257-306, 321-368.

[313] Ibid., Clark, Peter, *British Clubs and Societies 1580-1800*, p. 2.

rather than Society, would approve. Many such activities ceased to be 'respectable'. The public sociability that had been so highly prized in the eighteenth century ceased to be a virtue. The attraction of a life lived in public within a defined and exclusive society gave way to an emphasis on domesticity and away from frank enjoyment of leisure towards a more calculating performance of duty, towards a 'rational' view of recreation. This 'call to seriousness' began to be relaxed from the mid-nineteenth century. In the 1860s and 1870s the press and pulpit endlessly discussed the legitimacy of this or that activity and of leisure in general. The official view was that leisure was justified not for its own sake but for its ulterior purpose of re-creating men for work. Under this umbrella, however, more and more activities became legitimate and were doubtless enjoyed for their own sake. It was in physical activity, however, that the change was greatest.

Middle-class urban culture, especially in public schools, was able from 1850 to transform the nature and image of sport. Sport encouraged qualities of leadership; it took boys' minds off sex and was the best training for war.[314] As rules were written and enforced, sport became increasingly an analogy for middle-class male life: a competitive struggle within agreed parameters. The middle-classes not only imposed a new ideology on sport; they were also the chief beneficiaries of the expansion of facilities. Up to 1914:

> ...the sporting revolution belonged, in the main, to the middle-classes in their leafy suburbs.[315]

From the 1880s and in parallel with the emerging movement for women's political emancipation, new sporting women—female cricketers, female footballers and female athletes—became a feature of largely middle-class sport. Some saw this as part of their support for women's rights but it was also supported by those who believed in the domestic role of women but who thought women should also be healthy and fit. There was strident opposition with often repeated concerns about the loss of femininity, blurring of sex differences, immodest exposure of female bodies and the female incursion into the male sphere. As women defied opposition and continued to compete, opponents drew on their strongest

---

[314] Lowerson, John, *Sport and the English middle classes, 1870-1914*, (Manchester University Press), 1993, Huggins, Mike, 'Second-class citizens? English middle-class culture and sport, 1850-1910: a reconsideration', *International Journal of the History of Sport*, Vol. 17, (2000), pp. 1-35, and Lowerson, John, 'Sport and British Middle-Class Culture: Some Issues of Representation and Identity before 1940', *International Journal of the History of Sport*, Vol. 21, (2004), pp. 34-49.

[315] Meller, H. E., *Leisure and the Changing City 1870-1914*, (Routledge), 1976, p. 236.

staple argument—sport would ruin women's reproductive capacity.

The New Woman was lampooned and shown in a variety of unladylike postures such as playing golf and riding bicycles. Its absurdity was well illustrated in the great 'bicycle debate' in the early 1890s when the threatened physiological perils of cycling for women were exposed as nonsensical.[316]   Specious medical arguments that excessive riding of bicycles could lead to overstrain of the heart and lead to spinal deformities and was a danger to women's reproductive systems were deployed to restrict the physical mobility and personal freedom of women.   'Bicycle women' were denounced from the pulpit as 'children of Satan' and that 'If something is not done to stop this Satanic contagion the world will soon not be worth saving!'[317]

...Her bicycle, for example, may a good, useful thing, but she will not induce the public to approve of bicycles for women by appearing on it as an offensive caricature of a man. She will not win the world her cause, however just, disgusting it with herself.[318]

This was not the universal view:

Let it at once be said, an organically sound woman can cycle with as much impunity as a man. Thank Heaven, we know now that this is not one more of the sexual problems of the day. Sex has nothing to do with it, beyond the adaptation of machine to dress and dress to machines. With cycles as now perfected, there is nothing in the anatomy or the physiology of a woman to prevent their fully and freely enjoyed within the limits of common sense.... It was expected that women specially might be exposed to injury from internal strains and from the effects and shaking and jarring when riding on the roads. In practice, this has been found to be nothing but a bogey.... Already thousands of women qualifying for general invalidism have been rescued by cycling...[319]

When the motorcar became a more common mode of transport in

---

[316] See Strange, L. S., and Brown, R. S., 'The bicycle, women's rights, and Elizabeth Cady Stanton', *Women's Studies*, Vol. 31, (2002), pp. 609-626, and Vertinsky, Patricia, *The Eternally Wounded Woman: Women, Doctors and Exercise in the late Nineteenth Century*, (Manchester University Press), 1989, pp. 76-81.

[317] 'Denouncing Bicycle Women from the Pulpit', *Hampshire Advertiser*, 24 August 1895, p. 2.

[318] 'The Charm of a Womanly Woman', *South London Chronicle*, 10 October 1896, p. 11.

[319] Fenton, W. H., 'A Medical View of Cycling for Ladies', *The Nineteenth Century*, no. 39, (May 1896), pp. 797, 800. See also 'Women and the Bicycle', *Evening Telegraph*, 26 May 1893, p. 4: 'It is, indeed, of great use to healthy women for them to cycle.'

the 1920s and women took to the wheel, similar warnings were made about its unsuitability for women.[320]

After 1900, middle-class culture became more suburban than urban. Work was urban; leisure suburban. Women were able in the seclusion of the suburbs to develop some autonomy playing tennis or golf while men were at work; at weekends men took precedence. The building of suburban Odeons in the 1930s, styled to appeal to middle-class women, opened up new opportunities for leisure activities. Families increasingly avoided city centres and the home environment became the locus for recreations. Improvements in communications that led to the growth of suburbia also provided the means to escape it. During the summer, middle-class families rented seaside villas in resorts or areas of resorts where there was an appropriate degree of exclusivity. Escaping abroad to Europe became increasingly fashionable with over a million people taking their holidays in Europe in the 1930s.

Supplying leisure

The state, whether at local or national level, created a legal framework and acted as a direct supplier of leisure activities. In the first half of the nineteenth century, its main concern was to control supply through licensing, but later it became a direct supplier of such facilities as parks, libraries and playing fields. One reason why the state intervened was prestige that came from supporting both the production of high culture in the present and the preservation of the high culture of the past. By the 1830s, state aid was necessary to subsidise museums and the public could not be denied right of access. In 1810, admission to the British Museum was made free leading to an increase in visitors from 128,000 in 1824, to 230,000 in 1835 and 826,000 by 1846. It is easy to exaggerate the level of state supply. Central government provided a legal framework within which facilities could be built and run out of the rates but it was also concerned to protect ratepayers from excessive spending. Until 1914, libraries were still largely the result of philanthropy and were only available to 60 per cent of the population. The same was true of museums and parks. Local authorities played an increasingly important role and had the same motives as central government: a concern for prestige in relation to other local authorities and concerns about social order.[321] A more compelling motive was to stimulate prosperity. Seaside resorts led the way after 1875,

---

[320] 'Women as Motor Drivers', *Evening Telegraph*, 18 August 1924, p. 2. 'Why Women Motor Drivers', *Evening Telegraph*, 19 August 1924, p. 2.
[321] See, for instance, Morrison, John, 'Victorian municipal patronage: the foundation and management of Glasgow Corporation Galleries 1854-1888', *Journal of the History of Collections*, Vol. 8, (1996), pp. 93-102.

investing in sea defences, promenades, piers, golf courses and concert halls in an attempt to improve their attractiveness to potential visitors.

A major element in the state's supply of leisure was its concern to regulate the use of space. The home, as a private space, was beyond its physical reach. Licensing the sale of alcohol was the state's major intervention and was intended to preserve public order and provide some means of monitoring the leisure of the poorer sections of society.[322] Public parks, museums and libraries were supported precisely because they were public, open to scrutiny and controlled by bye-laws. The space provided by theatre, music hall and cinema was potentially more dangerous, but the need to license both building and activity made them relatively acceptable.[323] The censorship of both plays and films ensured that public entertainment adhered to acceptable moral and political values. Fire regulations, for instance those imposed on music halls in 1878, not only reduced the dangers of fire but drove many of the smaller, less salubrious halls out of business. The cinema industry established its own form of censorship in 1912 with the British Board of Film Censors.[324] In horse-racing, by contrast, the government banned off-course betting in the Street Betting Act of 1906.[325]

There was much self-made leisure, whether personal or communal or associational. In its communal or associational forms, it was a major means of supply of leisure for the middle-class urban culture, typically in the form of subscription concerts and libraries and of clubs. Founded in 1824, the Ipswich Choral Society is one of the oldest choral society in Britain; the oldest were Coventry Union Choral Society founded in 1813 and the Halifax Choral Society established four years later.[326] By 1885, there were 264 members of Ipswich Choral Society made up of 94

---

[322] Mutch, Alistair, 'Shaping the Public House, 1850-1950: Business Strategies, State Regulation and Social History', *Cultural and Social History*, Vol. 1, (2004), pp. 179-200.

[323] See, Ley, A. J., *A history of building control in England and Wales, 1840-1990*, (RICS Books), 2000, and Gaskell, S. Martin., *Building control: national legislation and the introduction of local bye-laws in Victorian England, (*British Association for Local History), 1983. Harper, R. H., *Victorian building regulations: summary tables of the principal English building acts and model by-laws, 1840-1914, (*Mansell), 1985, shows the extent of regulation.

[324] Robertson, J. C., *The British Board of Film Censors: film censorship in Britain, 1896-1950*, (Croom Helm), 1985, pp. 1-18.

[325] Dixon, David, *From Prohibition to Regulation: Bookmaking, Anti-gambling, and the Law*, (Oxford University Press), 1991.

[326] Lajosi, Krisztina, and Stynen, Andreas, (eds.), *Choral Societies and Nationalism in Europe*, (Brill), 2015, pp. 83-110, Johnston, Roy, and Plummer, Declan, *The Musical Life of Nineteenth-Century Belfast*, (Ashgate), 2015, pp. 21-54, 181-205.

sopranos, 65 altos, 40 tenors and 65 basses. In Bradford in 1900, there were 30 choral societies, 20 brass bands, an amateur orchestra, six concertina bands and a team of hand-bell ringers. Churches and chapels were crucial suppliers of leisure with their young men's and ladies' classes, their debating societies and numerous other activities.[327] Much leisure within the family relied on commercial sources of supply, of games, pianos, books and a wide array of hobbies. By 1910 there was one piano for every fifteen people, far more than the middle-classes alone could have bought.[328]

Voluntary organisations were key agents in both the control and the supply of leisure. The Vice Society (1802), the Royal Society for the Prevention of Cruelty to Animals (1824), the Lord's Day Observance Society (1831), numerous temperance and teetotal societies and the National Council for Public Morals (1911) were constraints on leisure. Middle-class philanthropists and employers who funded parks, libraries, brass bands and football clubs, Mechanics' Institutes, the Pleasant Sunday Afternoon Association, the Girls' Friendly Society (1874) and the Boys' Brigade (1883) supplied different types of leisure. What united these two approaches was a concern to direct people's leisure by control over its supply to wean people away from bad habits by providing respectable 'rational recreation'. As a result, not only would the bad habits disappear or at least diminish but in the process people, largely men of good will from different classes would meet fraternally and come to understand each other's point of view.

The amount of leisure provided was enormous. In Glasgow where ratepayers on three occasions in the second half of the century refused to fund a public library, Stephen Mitchell (1789-1874), a tobacco magnate, left £70,000 for a library that opened in 1877. In Manchester, T. C. Horsfall (1841-1932) raised the funds for an Art Museum opened in 1884. Bristol acquired a municipally owned museum, library and art gallery between 1895 and 1905, all through private funding. Much church and chapel activity was organised from above for people deemed to be in need especially the young. The real problem arose when they left Sunday Schools and it was partly to keep a hold on these children that William Smith (1854-1914) established the Boys' Brigade in Glasgow in 1883 and uniformed youth movements, particularly for boys, attracted a high proportion of the youth population.[329] The Boys' Brigade had its

---

[327] See, for instance, Cusack, Janet, 'Bible classes and boats: church and chapel rowing clubs at Plymouth and Devonport in the early twentieth century', *Mariner's Mirror*, Vol. 87, (2001), pp. 63-75.

[328] McKibbin, R., 'Work and hobbies in Britain 1880-1950', in Winter, J. M., (ed.), *The working class in modern British history: essays in honour of Henry Pelling*, (Cambridge University Press), 1983, pp. 127-146.

denominational rivals and from 1908 faced serious competition from the Boy Scouts. By 1914, between a quarter and a third of the available youth population was enrolled in a youth movement. There were fewer provisions of leisure for girls because they were thought to pose less of a problem. The Girls' Friendly Society, formed in 1874, was predominantly rural and Anglican in outlook and many of its members were young domestic servants. Two further organisations met their needs as they grew older: the Mothers' Union founded in 1885 expanded to 7,000 branches by 1911[330] and Women's Institutes, initially developed in Canada, begun in 1915.[331] Between the wars, Women's Institutes were opened at the rate of five a week and their combined membership was 238,000 by 1939 rising to 349,000 by 1947. Classes, examinations and competitions acknowledged the craft and homemaking skills of women but they also encouraged involvement in local campaigns and discussed social and political issues at their meetings.

Finally, commercial leisure played an increasingly significant role in the supply of leisure between 1780 and 1945. In 1830, it was provided largely for the middle-classes but spread into the working-classes by the 1870s.[332] There was a shift in the nineteenth century from the patron-client relationship that characterised the employment of professionals in cricket and music in 1800 to an employment relationship more akin to that of the industrial world. This was in part because of the seasonal nature of much of such employment, but also because of the lack of control over entry to leisure jobs. The numbers employed were growing, certainly after 1870. Between 1871 and 1911, the population of England and Wales rose on average by 0.8 per cent per year and the number employed in the arts and entertainment by 4.7 per cent per year.

In nearly every section of the leisure industries there were attempts to raise the status of entertainers. The outcome was the achievement of stardom for the select few while the rank and file had to be content with

[329] See, Springhall, John, *Youth, empire and society: British youth movements, 1883-1940*, (Croom Helm), 1977, for an excellent summary of developments with a detailed bibliography.
[330] Beaumont, Caitriona, *Housewives and Citizens: Domesticity and the Women's Movement in England, 1928-1964*, (Manchester University Press), 2013, focuses on the Mothers' Union of the Church of England, the Catholic Women's League, the National Council of Women, the National Federation of Women's Institutes and the National Union of Townswomen's Guilds.
[331] Andrews, Maggie, *The Acceptable Face of Feminism: The Women's Institute as a Social Movement*, (Lawrence & Wishart), 1997, pp. 17-99, and Robinson, Jane, *A Force to be Reckoned With: A History of the Women's Institute*, (Virago), 2011, pp. 29-146, examine the inter-war years.
[332] Malcolm, Dominic, *Globalizing Cricket: Englishness, Empire and Identity*, (A. & C. Black), 2012, pp. 30-62.

wages at roughly semi-skilled level. The best actors and actresses were already getting £150 per week in the 1830s. In 1890, at least ten jockeys were earning £5,000 per season and the better professional cricketers were earning £275 per year. Between 1906 and 1914, the wages of performing musicians doubled reaching £200 per year. The best professional footballers could not earn high wages: the Football Association set the maximum wages at £208 per year but only a minority got that amount.[333] On the whole, however, complaints about wages and conditions of service within the entertainment and sports world were muted.[334] The lure of acceptance as a profession, the hope of stardom for the individual and the sense that to be in entertainment was unlike any other job, for the most part curtailed any open conflict.

The importance of leisure in giving people a sense of national and social identity is matched by the significance placed on leisure in individual life-choices. Between 1780 and 1945, as hours of leisure grew longer, leisure activities took on a more central role in people's lives. 'Rational recreationalists' wanted to 'control' what people, and especially the working-classes, did with that time and they were successful, to a degree, in mitigating the worst excesses of pre-industrial leisure with its potential violence and cruelty. The persistence of large-scale spectating, especially football and horse-racing showed the limits of that success. Alcohol and gambling remained key working-class leisure activities and, despite increased controls by the state, continued to play a major part in defining working-class consciousness throughout this period. Leisure was in 1945, as it had been in 1780, largely male-dominated and escapist but there was a shift towards greater female involvement from the 1880s.

An embourgeoisement of society

In the first half of the twentieth century the social composition and public perception of the middle-classes underwent radical change. Before 1900, the middle-classes were associated with industrialists, bankers and 'ladies'; by 1945, they were more likely to be office workers and housewives. The typical middle-class man was no longer an employer but a salaried employee with the typical middle-class woman no longer the manager of household and servants but a domestic worker herself. George Orwell observed that one of the most important developments in the first half of the twentieth century had been the upward and downward extension of the

---

[333] Polley, Martin, (ed.), *The History of Sport in Britain, 1880-1914, Vol. 1: The Varieties of Sport*, (Routledge), 2004, pp. 1-11.
[334] Vamplew, Wray, *Pay Up and Play the Games: Professional Sport in Britain, 1875-1914*, (Cambridge University Press), 1988, pp. 104-126, on earnings, Anderson, Nancy Fix, *The Sporting Life: Victorian Sports and Games*, (ABC-CLIO), 2010, pp. 137-154, on professionalism.

middle-classes through shifts in employment and the posts created by 'modern industry'.[335]

A broad white-collar stratum had emerged in the late-nineteenth century--a transformed traditional industrial and entrepreneurial artisan class--and a new technical sector that had grown up as a result of the technical innovation generated by modern industrial capitalism and warfare. The number of clerical workers grew from 887,000 in 1911 to 2.404 million by 1951, from 5 to 11 per cent of the workforce. Growth was most marked among engineers and technicians reflecting the shift from industries like textiles and coal to newer, science-based industries such as light engineering and pharmaceuticals. There was a shift from traditional skilled work as a result of new production lines but there was also an increase in supervisory staff such as the foreman and management and administration posts. London saw a massive surge in manufacturing in munitions, transport and communications, electrical and rubber goods and chemicals during the First World War and engineers and other skilled workers were in great demand.

The dramatic collapse of Britain's heavy industries after 1918 was offset in parts of the country by greater opportunities for work in new types of factories and industrial complexes. The manufacture of chemicals, electrical goods and consumer durables all offered opportunities for skilled and semi-skilled employment and inter-generational occupational 'advance' through the increased need for managers, supervisors, technicians, draughtsman, chemists, and industrial engineers. The 1920s saw some mergers and consolidations that created giant new business corporations such as the 'Big Four' railways and ICI, and an unprecedented growth in new industries such as car and motor cycle production. The creation of the National Grid, for instance, helped the relocation of new industrial operations away from traditional manufacturing areas and light industrial plants and factories were built in the Midlands, and in London and the South-East. The Factory Inspectorate registered 20,000 new factories between 1921 and 1931, most built on new trading estates on the outskirts of towns and cities. This was especially evident in West London with 60 per cent of electrical factories employing over 1,000 workers with 53 factories employing 11,000 workers in a two mile stretch along the Great West Road in the 1930s. Firms producing vacuum cleaners, gramophone records and players, cosmetics, cleaning products, tyres, convenience foods, sweets and confectionary, cameras and film stock, whose products became household names. Heinz, Hoover, Kodak, Birds, Plessey, Coty and Lyons all had factories on or around the major roads out of London.

---

[335] Orwell, George, *The Lion and the Unicorn: Socialism and the English Genius*, (Harmondsworth), 1941, p. 66.

After 1918, large sections of the middle-classes saw themselves as the 'new poor'; they had suffered more than other classes both in the war and now in the peace. Ex-officers were unable to find work or were forced into menial jobs and many of their widows and orphans faced extreme financial hardship struggling to survive on dwindling savings and pensions. For the middle-classes, the real problems that many faced during the war and immediately after were, they believed, directly proportional to the supposed gains made by the working classes. Those who could work saw themselves unfairly burdened with increased taxation imposed by the government to meet the needs of an increasingly militant working-class whose interests were now also served by trade unionism at home and the inflamed culture of Bolshevism abroad. The British press targeted its language of populist resentment at a middle- and lower middle-class audience conjuring up a vision of a powerless and apathetic middle-class at the mercy of rampant trade unionism and a profligate and corrupt plutocracy. Many from the wide constituency of the salaried population supported the anti-socialist attitudes of emerging fascism in Italy and Germany in the 1920s and especially the 1930s.[336]

The lower middle-class was affected by the depression of the 1920s but for those in work salary levels were at least maintained if not increased. Some cuts were imposed in 1931 and 1932 but these had been reinstated by 1935 and were to a considerable extent offset by falling prices. The Staff Associations for civil servants, teachers and railway clerks and white collar unions negotiated better pay scales and conditions that resulted in relatively stable conditions for their workers in the 1920s and 1930s. About 5 per cent of the lower middle-class were unemployed in 1931 compared to 14 per cent of skilled and semi-skilled working classes and 30 per cent of the unskilled. In the 1930s, the number of salaried workers increased by 50 per cent and by 1939, 15 per cent of workers were in this category. Most of them earned in excess of £250 a year, a figure that represented the threshold of middle-class status. Rather than an era of disappointment and resentment, for many in the middle-classes and especially the lower middle-class the 1920s and 1930s were years of survival, then consolidation and finally improvement. Arguably there were less embattled victims than enthusiastic protagonists of an emerging modern Britain.

Suburbia

Inter-war Britain saw intense waves of suburbanisation, the result of the sustained housing boom dominated by municipal housing in the 1920s

---

[336] Pugh, Martin, *'Hurrah for the Blackshirts!' Fascists and Fascism in Britain Between the Wars*, (Jonathan Cape), 2005, and Copley, Nigel, *Anti-Fascism in Britain*, 2nd ed., (Routledge), 2017, pp. 1-75.

and owner-occupied housing during the 1930s. Council housing expanded from less than one per cent of Britain's 1914 housing stock to around 10 per cent in 1938, with over 90 per cent of the 1.1 million new inter-war council houses located on suburban estates. Meanwhile owner-occupation is estimated to have increased from around 10 per cent of Britain's 1914 housing stock to around 32 per cent in 1938, mainly due to new developments (an estimated 1.8 million new houses were built for owner-occupiers, compared to 1.1 million existing houses transferred from the privately-rented to owner-occupied sector). The 1914 owner-occupation rate is subject to a substantial margin of error, as it is based on an assumption regarding the volume of pre-1914 housing transferred from the privately-rented to owner-occupied stock by 1938, for which there are no direct estimates. The low level of owner-occupation in 1914 is strongly corroborated by contemporary sources. As with council houses, the vast majority of new owner-occupied housing was located on suburban estates. Around 900,000 houses were also developed for private renting, again concentrated in the suburbs.

The growth of privately owned suburban houses was encouraged by rent controls that had been introduced during the war and extended into the inter-war years that made building for rent unprofitable. For the first time, most houses built in Britain were for private sale and ownership not rent and there was also a large rise in the number of people who owned their own houses. There was working-class ownership in certain industrial towns such as the cotton towns of Lancashire, mining areas of South Wales, some Yorkshire woollen centres and in south-east London, suburbs. Middle-class ownership was found more often in large towns with suburban areas developed by speculative builders who advertised to sell their wares. For instance, Cardiff had an average level of ownership of 7.2 per cent but it was 25 per cent in the new middle-class districts to the east and west of the city. These privately developed houses used ornamentation and other variants such as garage space to distinguish them from council houses. Nationally, by 1938, the level of ownership is estimated to have risen to about 31 per cent.

House prices in the outer suburbs fell rather than increased during the 1920s and 1930s. Cheap mortgages were available encouraged by government in the Housing Acts of 1923 and 1925 that enabled local councils to lend to home buyers. By the 1930s, this role had been taken over by building societies such as the Halifax and the Woolwich whose capital had been boosted after the Wall Street Crash. Financial investors saw building societies as safer than the more volitive stock market. This was helped, especially during the 1930s by the fall in the capital cost of a house and lower mortgage interest rates—they fell from 6.5 per cent in 1924 to 4.5 per cent a decade later. Deposits were normally small often as low as 10 per cent of the purchase price, while the monthly repayment of

£5 10s. on an £800 house in 1928 was less than a quarter of a bank clerk's average monthly wage. Most 'middle earners'—what George Orwell called the 'five-to-ten-pound-a-week' and included teachers, senior clerks and technicians and superior shop assistants—could afford to buy a place in the suburbs. The average cost of a three-bedroomed suburban terraced house fell from £510 in 1925 to £361 ten years later with a 35 per cent reduction in weekly payments on a typical twenty-year mortgage. By 1935, houses worth £500 could be bought for a down-payment of £25-£50 and the fall in the weekly mortgage to 9s. 6d. had brought them within the ambit of the upper working-class though suburbia was not the product of widespread upward social mobility.[337] The number of families paying mortgages reached about 0.5 million in 1920 but reached 1.4 million by 1937 with building societies loaning £32 million in 1923 rising to £140 million by 1936. House ownership became a defining facet of the middle-classes distinguishing them from the working-classes who lived in rented properties.

Migration to the suburbs could have a strong psychological impact on both working- and middle-class housewives; men do not appear to have been similarly affected as they retained their established workplaces. Many would have been new to living in a suburb but also to the region: over a million people migrated to the London area in search of work between 1921 and 1937. For most, it was the newness of the housing that made a lasting impression with electric lights and running hot water and the greenery and space compared to inner-city living. In 1938 in the *Lancet*, Stephen Taylor coined the term 'suburban neurosis' to describe the anxiety states—often with hysterical features and depression—that he found among his patients on new estates.[338] These he attributed to boredom arising from lack of friends and not enough to do or occupy the mind. This combined with anxieties linked to financial pressures arising from the new house and a 'false' set of values leading to failure to achieve unrealistic expectations of suburban married life culminating in a general disillusionment with life. Psychological problems were limited to a small minority of migrants but they nonetheless illustrate the disorienting effect of the new residential environment.

Modernity and domesticity

---

[337] Swenarton, Mark, and Taylor, Sandra, 'The Scale and Nature of the Growth of Owner-Occupation in Britain between the Wars', *Economic History Review*, Vol. 38, (1985), pp. 373-392, Humphries, Jane, 'Inter-War House Building, Cheap Money and Building Societies: The Housing Boom Revisited', *Business History*, Vol. 29, (1987), pp. 325-345.

[338] Taylor, Stephen, 'The suburban neurosis', *The Lancet*, 26 March 1938, pp. 759-761.

The suburbs in the inter-war years like the new industries stood on the frontier between town and country and linked to the urban centres by trains and arterial roads. Both were seen as expressions of modernity with its novels, its femininity and consumerism and its Americanisation. The suburbs was made up of new houses and new social relationships; a new life where people were able to carve their own niche. One of the important differences between middle-class life before 1914 and after 1918 lay in the presence of living-in servants or lack of. In 1914, any family with a serious claim to be middle-class had at least one servant and ideally more. By 1900, there were increasing complaints about the shortage of servants from members of the middle- and upper-classes. It was not simply a matter of wages since these increased steadily throughout the second half of the nineteenth century. The wages still appeared to be low: average annual wages for 1907 were £19 10s for general servants and £26 8s for parlour maids. What is more difficult to compute is monetary value of board and lodgings and uniform provided by the employer. In households where everything was provided, domestic servants had a distinct wage advantage over other female workers since they had a reasonable disposable income out of which it was possible to save. Various reasons have been provided for the 'servant shortage'. An increasing number of women regarded the wages as insufficient compensation for what were regarded as long hours, the hard physical effort and lack of independence. Ellen Darwin (1856-1903), daughter-in-law of Charles Darwin (1809-1882), wrote in an article on the 'servant problem' in 1890 of the 'stale odour of feudalism' round domestic service that had not kept pace with the 'modern spirit of human relations'.[339] There was an increase in alternative employment. While town girls preferred different employment to domestic service, for country girls it represented an easily available and acceptable occupation. However, the difficulty in finding servants by 1914 should be seen in relation to the declining rural population.

The First World War hastened the collapse of traditional women's work especially domestic service. By 1921, government grants given to the Central Committee on Women's Training and Unemployment were tied exclusively to domestic service training.[340] In 1922, the new Insurance Act stipulated that applicants were to accept any job which they were capable of doing and had no right to work with pay and conditions comparable to their previous employment. Consequently, women were forced back into domestic service through legislation and economic expediency. Although domestic service declined in the inter-war years, it

---

[339] Darwin, Mrs Francis (Ellen), 'Domestic Service', *The Nineteenth Century*, August 1890, p. 287.
[340] Lewis, J., *Women in England, 1870-1950: Sexual Divisions and Social Change*, (Wheatsheaf Books), 1984, pp. 190-191.

still represented the largest occupation for women. In 1911, there were 2,127,000 women in domestic service; ten years later the number had fallen to 1,845,000, but this figure still represented almost a third of the female workforce.[341] By 1931, there was a momentary increase of 15 per cent in the number of female indoor servants, caused by high unemployment and the economic recession. But from the mid-1930s, domestic service went into an irreversible decline. By 1951, the numbers had fallen by more than three-quarters of a million to 343,000.[342] However, these figures, as Bowden and Offer point out, may mask the employment of women on a more casual and *ad hoc* basis.[343] J. B. Priestley's (1894-1984) comment in 1927 that domestic service was 'as obsolete as the horse' was premature.[344]

In the 1920s, increasingly only the upper middle-classes could afford to employ live-in servants and there was a shift away from residential servants to dailies amongst the lower middle-classes.[345] For the middle-classes, the decline of domestic servants was facilitated by the rise of domestic appliances, such as cookers, electric irons and vacuum cleaners but the popularity of 'labour-saving devices', usually so expensive that only the more affluent households could afford them, is insufficient to explain the dramatic drop in the servant population.[346] Furthermore, with post-war inflation in the 1920s, many middle-class families, dubbed the 'new poor' by the popular press, struggled to maintain the standards and appearances of their pre-war standards of living. By the 1930s, residents in the new estates of the extraordinary inter-war house building boom bemoaned the lack of servants. They used the discourse of the 'servant problem' to mask the fact that their incomes could not stretch to domestic service, as least not beyond casual help.

---

[341] Lewis, J., 'In Search of a Real Equality: Women Between the Wars' in Gloversmith, F., (ed.), *Class, Culture and Social Change: A New View of the 1930s*, (Harvester), 1980, p. 211.

[342] Glucksmann, M., *Women Assemble: Women Workers and the New Industries in Inter-War Britain*, (Routledge), 1990, p. 246.

[343] Bowden, S., and Offer, A., 'The technological revolution that never was: Gender, class, and the diffusion of household appliances in interwar England', in Grazia, V. de, & Furlough, E., (eds.), *The Sex of Things: Gender and Consumption in Historical Perspective,* (University of California Press), 1996, pp. 244-274.

[344] Priestley, J. B., 'Servants', *Saturday Review*, 19 March 1927, p. 430.

[345] Giles, J., *The Parlour and the Suburb: Domestic Identities, Class, Femininity and Modernity*, (Berg), 2004, Delap, Lucy, *Knowing Their Place: Domestic Service in Twentieth Century Britain*, (Oxford University Press), 2011, pp. 26-62.

[346] Delap, Lucy, *Knowing Their Place: Domestic Service in Twentieth Century Britain*, (Oxford University Press), 2011, pp. 98-139, examines the development of the 'servantless' home.

The modernity of the suburban home was strongly associated with the 'housewife', a new social type in the 1920s. Like married women in Victorian Britain, the suburban housewife was not expected to engage in paid work outside the home. In 1931, over six million women worked outside their homes, about 34 per cent of the total labour force but only 1 in 8 married women worked outside the home.[347] Images in the media from magazines to films portrayed women firmly placed within marriage and family; the flapper, a differing model of femininity, was often derided. A cult of domesticity was being promoted at the expense of all other models of womanhood. Fulfilment for a woman was found at home with a husband and children and few middle-class women disagreed. Of particular importance in this process were widely read women's weekly magazines that, at the zenith of their popularity during the late 1930s, had over 50 titles in circulation. The use of colour printing and glamorous content in titles such as *Woman's Own* established in 1932, *Women's Illustrated* 1936 and *Woman* 1937 appealed to a younger working- and middle-class readership and took advantage of increased standards of living and the expansion in consumer goods. All disseminated an ideology of domesticity, something reflected in regular features on beauty, fashion, baby care, cookery, furnishing and housekeeping, and raised the profile of women's domestic role within the cultural arena.[348]

Central to the development of the 'modern housewife' was the dissemination of ideas on household management especially by the prolific Mrs Constance Peel (1868-1934), who worked for *The Queen Magazine* as well as for the *Daily Mail* and published her *The Labour-Saving House* in 1917 and Clementina Black of the Women's Industrial Council who published *A New Way of Housekeeping* the following year. Modernist household design was led by organisations such as the Design and Industries Association that, during the 1920s, organised a consumer education programme through exhibitions and publications and its contributions to the annual Ideal Home Exhibition. Good design was regarded as a practical and aesthetic solution that saved labour and was part of a moral design for living to liberate housewives from the drudgery of housework but also as one way of reviving the economy.[349] For many

---

[347] Strachey, Ray, *Careers and Openings for Women: A Survey of Women's Employment and a Guide for Those Seeking Work*, (Faber and Faber), 1935, p. 85; Beddoe, Deirdre, *Back to Home and Duty: Women between the Wars 1918-1939*, (Pandora Press), 1989, p. 82. In 1931: 14,790,000 men and 6,265,000 women were employed.

[348] For the context of *Good Housekeeping*, see Cox, Howard, and Mowatt, Simon, Revolutions *from Grub Street: A History of Magazine Publishing in Britain*, (Oxford University Press), 2014, pp. 67-69. See also, Braithwaite, Brian, Walsh, Noelle, and Davies, Glyn, (eds.), *Ragtime to Wartime: The Best of Good Housekeeping, 1922-1939*, (Ebury Press), 1986.

women the application of scientific management techniques and new technologies was an implicit recognition that the home was a site of production. Although there was widespread coverage of labour-saving appliances in magazines and advertisements, they were not as widespread as previously thought.[349] Cost meant that their purchase was aspirational for many women in the 1920s, though mass production meant that costs fell and their use expanded during the 1930s. Modern housewives needed to keep up appearances and were careful not to let the possession of a vacuum cleaner give the impression that they no longer hired domestic help. The term 'labour saving' came to signify a suburban modernity in the inter-war years that was functional rather than aesthetic in character.

The steady fall in prices meant that the 1920s and 1930s were ones of increasing consumer demand. High Streets and Parades boasted 80,000 grocers, 40,000 butchers, 30,000 bakers and 30,000 greengrocers. Most families did not have refrigerators and still shopped locally or had local tradesmen often deliver every day. Sales of ice cream boomed in the 1930s and new kinds of sweets were introduced including Milky Way in 1935, Crunchie in 1929, Snickers and Freddo in 1930, Mars Bar in 1932, Aero and Kit Kat in 1935 and Smarties, Rolo and Milky Bar in 1937. Small traditional and modern shops existed alongside larger, independent family-run department stores and suburban 'multiples' such as Timothy Whites, Woolworths with 600 branches by 1934, Boots, Marks & Spencers and David Greig. The number of multiple grocery shops doubled between 1920 and 1939 and several large firms merged; Co-operative societies expanded again especially in the Midlands and South East and some 24,000 shops served 8.5 million members. There was also a growth of new types of retailing with the emergence of wireless shops, usually linked with music shops, camping shops and shops dealing with motor accessories.[351] For instance, Halfords began as a wholesale ironmongery store in Birmingham in 1892, started selling cycling goods ten years later and opened its two hundredth store in 1931. The 'modern

---

[349] Cieraad, I., "Out of my kitchen!' Architecture, gender and domestic efficiency', *Journal of Architecture*, Vol. 7, (3), (2002), pp. 263-279. Ryan, Deborah S., *Ideal Homes, 1918-39: Domestic Design and Suburban Modernism*, (Manchester University Press), 2018.

[350] Davidson, C., *A Women's Work is Never Done: A History of Housework in the British Isles, 1650-1950*, (Chatto & Windus), 1982; Hardyment, C., *From Mangle to Microwave: The Mechanisation of Household Work*, (Polity), 1988. Bowden, S., and Offer, A., 'The technological revolution that never was: Gender, class, and the diffusion of household appliances in interwar England', in de Grazia, V., & Furlough, E., (eds.), *The Sex of Things: Gender and Consumption in Historical Perspective*, (University of California Press), 1996, pp. 244-274.

[351] Llewellyn-Smith, Sir H., (ed.), *The New Survey of London Life and Labour*, (P. S. King & Son Ltd.), 1933, Vol. 5, pp. 192-193.

woman' was targeted as part of a new commercial culture of feminine consumption and consumer desire for a whole range of toiletries and cosmetics that were not just integral to the small town over-the-counter trade, but many were manufactured or processed in the new suburban factories.

The boom in popular leisure also benefitted light manufacturing, transport and communication industries with the British film industry experiencing considerable growth and investment with the number of studios rising to more than 640 by 1936. Small drapers' shops began to stock cycling and hiking 'kit' to meet the growing demand created by new cycling clubs and other recreational activities like rambling. The Youth Hostel Association (YHA) established in 1929 offered basic accommodation at 1/- a night and by 1939 there were some 150 YHA hostels catering for over 20,000 hikers, ramblers and walkers.[352] Tom Stephenson (1893-1987), a leading writer on outdoor leisure wrote an extensive article in 1934 outlining the prosperity rambling and hiking brought to different industries from entrepreneurs and industrialists to railways and coaches, camping and camera shops as well as inns, hostels and cafes.[353]

Conclusions

Whether in the economy, society, politics or culture, the nineteenth century is often portrayed as one of growing middle-class hegemony in which the entrepreneurial ideal became the dominant social ideology. The problem is that the middle-classes were curiously diverse ranging from financiers and businessmen who were wealthier than many landowners to clerks whose income differed little from skilled workers. The notion of respectability that distinguished them from the excesses of the aristocracy and the working-classes is no longer regarded as the exclusive characteristic of the middle-classes as it dispersed across society. Defining masculinity and femininity in terms of separate spheres played an important part in marking off the middle-classes from other social groups and different sections of the bourgeoisie could agree on the subordinate position of women if nothing else creating a homogeneous ideology between the disparate groups within the middle-classes. The view that all groups of property owners, landed and non-landed were increasingly integrated into a new ruling class after 1850 is questionable. Given the diverse economic functions, different geographical locations and access to wealth and power, it is difficult to establish a viable case for middle-class political hegemony. It is true that the middle-classes were given the vote in 1832, municipal government was reformed in 1835, they managed to get the Corn Laws

---

[352] Coburn, O., *Youth Hostel Story*, (Hunt, Barnard and Company Ltd.), 1950.
[353] Stephenson, T., 'Walking to Prosperity', in *The Passing Show*, 19 May 1934.

repealed in 1846 and their ideological stance, characterised by 'respectability', was of growing significance. But this occurred within a framework of aristocratic economic and political power. The 'power' of the middle-classes, however it is construed, did increase and they became more influential in determining policy directions and agendas. However, this does not mean that they acquired political power in any meaningful sense.

4 The Upper-Classes

In the 1830s, power, economic and political, still lay in the possession and exploitation of land. The great houses and the large landowners still set the aristocratic tone of British society.

Landed England did not survive unchanged. Had there not been flexibility in coming to terms with the economic realities of the industry state, and a willingness to retreat gradually and quietly from untenable positions of political privilege, landed society might not have outlived the end of the century. In fact, it displayed remarkable powers of tenacity and adaptation: it sought to engulf and change some of the new elements in society, though in the process it was itself changed.[1]

Landowners did not simply farm their own land or rent it out to tenant farmers.[2] They exploited their mineral deposits providing stone, slate, sand, brick-clay, timber and coal for growing industries. They rented their urban properties in response to a growing housing shortage. They invested in government stocks, the Bank of England, in industry and transport and benefited from the profits of politics through their monopoly of the offices of state, their patronage and revenues. They were adaptable, if conservative, in outlook. A peerage of three hundred wealthy families dominated the landed classes. The estate and country house were at the heart of their power providing authority and status. They controlled patronage repaying loyalty of friends, family and clients openly and without moral scruple to maintain political power. Below the great landowners were the gentry who dominated the counties as squires, Justices of the Peace, Poor Law officials, churchwardens and backbench MPs. Below the gentry, landed society forked. There was a hierarchy of owner-occupiers or freeholders with incomes ranging from £700 down to as little as £30 per year and tenant farmers who found their profits threatened by falling food prices and were the most vocal proponents of the Corn Laws.

The basis of landed society was mutual obligations within a hierarchical framework of paternalism.[3] This was grudgingly accepted by most people in rural England and Scotland where the landlord was normally of the same nationality and culture. This was less the case in Wales and Ireland where landlords were often both from an alien culture and religion. Yet, the 'bond of dependency' between landlord, tenant

---

[1] Harrison, J. F. C., *The Early Victorians 1832-1851*, (Panther), 1973, p. 123.
[2] Thompson, F. M. L., *English landed society in the 19th century*, (Routledge), 1963; Mingay, G. E., *Land and Society in England, 1750-1980*, (Longman), 1994.
[3] Horn, Pamela, *The Rural World 1780-1850*, (Hutchinson), 1980, Reay, Barry, *Rural Englands*, (Palgrave), 2004.

farmer and labourer were beginning to break down. Food riots in the 1790s, the rural slump after 1815, riots in the Fens in 1816, in Norfolk and Suffolk in 1822, and particularly the 'Captain Swing' riots across southern England in 1830 challenged established values.[4] The traditions of agrarian secret societies in Ireland such as Whiteboys[5] and Captain Rock also had a formidable reputation in the 1820s.[6] Each was largely unsuccessful and harshly repressed but Griffin suggests:

> ...many labourers were willing to dispute their wages, openly question the nature of authority, and even join forbidden political unions, is testimony to a collective will that refused to be beaten into submission by the combined might of capitalist 'logic' and state terror.[7]

The market rather than appeals to custom and established practice, increasingly determined the social behaviour of the landed classes. Agriculture declined relative to other sectors of the economy after 1850 but the aristocratic tone of British society was still set by the great houses and the large landowners.

From the 1780s, manufacturing industry grew steadily in importance

---

[4] Charlesworth, A., *An Atlas of Rural Protest in Britain 1548-1900*, (Croom Helm), 1983, and Griffin, Carl J., *Protest, Politics and Work in Rural England, 1700-1850*, (Palgrave Macmillan), 2013, provide synoptic analysis. For the 1816 East Anglia riots, see Peacock, A. J., *Bread or Blood: a study of the agrarian riots in East Anglia in 1816*, (Gollancz), 1965, and for 1830 Hobsbawm, E. J., and Rudé, George, *Captain Swing*, (Penguin), 1973, and the revisionist study, Griffin, Carl J., *The Rural War: Captain Swing and the Politics and Protest*, (Manchester University Press), 2012; Dunbabin, J. P. D., *Rural Discontent in Nineteenth Century Britain*, (Faber), 1975, and Archer, John E., *"By a flash and a scare": incendiarism, animal maiming and poaching in East Anglia, 1815-1870*, (Oxford University Press), 1990, on arson as a form of protest.

[5] Ó Tuairisg, Lochlainn, 'Whiteboys and faction fighters in pre-famine Ireland', in O'Neill, Michael S., Cullen, Clara and Dennehy, Coleman, (eds.), *History matters*, (University College Dublin Press), 2004, pp. 97-106, Wall, Maureen, 'The Whiteboys', in Williams, T. D., (ed.), *Secret Societies in Ireland*, (Gill and Macmillan), 1973, pp. 13-25, and Powell, Martyn J., Popular disturbances in late eighteenth century Ireland: the origins of the Peep of Day Boys', *Irish Historical Studies*, Vol. 35, (2005), pp. 249-265.

[6] Clark, Samuel, and Donnelly, James S., *Irish Peasants Violence and Political Unrest 1780-1914*, (Manchester University Press), 1983, Donnelly, James S. Jr., *Captain Rock: The First Agrarian Rebellion of 1821-1824*, (University of Wisconsin Press), 2009, Kelly, James, *Food Rioting in Ireland in the Eighteenth and Nineteenth Centuries. The 'Moral Economy' and the Irish Crowd*, (Four Courts Press), 2017.

[7] Ibid., Griffin, Carl J., *The Rural War: Captain Swing and the Politics and Protest*, p. 314.

to dominance within the economy and this was reflected in the structure of class relations. The relationship between agriculture and industry changed tilting the economic balance of power in favour of manufacturing classes while Britain's central position in the international flow of commodities and capital ensured the continuing importance of the financiers and merchants of the City of London.[8] The landed interest was forced to come to terms with changed circumstances. The nineteenth century saw the development of a closer relationship between property owners whether in agriculture or industry. The distinction between the two was never complete, even in the eighteenth century successful industrialists bought landed estates and landowners exploited the mineral reserves beneath their land. Although by 1900, the landed, manufacturing and commercial classes had moved closer together in economic, cultural and political terms, they had not yet coalesced into a unified propertied class.[9]

Changes in the banking system in the second half of the nineteenth century stimulated a closer relationship between the two groups. In 1780, three different types of bank formed the British banking system.[10] At the heart of the London financial system were the private banks such as Hoares, Childs, Coutts and Martins that had often developed out of older goldsmith businesses.[11] The private banks of the West End had many landed clients and were heavily involved in long-term mortgage business. By contrast, the private banks of the City itself were more concerned with the provision of short-term credit for merchant firms and, to a much lesser extent, manufacturing business. The Bank of England and, perhaps less

---

[8] On this issue see Chapman, S. D., *Merchant Enterprise in Britain*, (Cambridge University Press), 1992.

[9] See, for instance, Rothery, Mark, 'The shooting party: the associational cultures of rural and urban elites in the late-nineteenth and early twentieth centuries', in Hoyle, Richard W., (ed.), *Our hunting fathers: field sports in England after 1850*, (Carnegie), 2007, pp. 96-118.

[10] On the development of banking in the nineteenth century see Collins, Michael, *Banks and Industrial Finance in Britain 1800-1939*, (Macmillan), 1995, and Quinn, Stephen, 'Money, finance and capital markets', in ibid., Floud, Roderick, and Johnson, Paul A., (eds.), *The Cambridge economic history of modern Britain, Volume 1: industrialisation, 1700-1860*, pp. 147-174, and Cottrell, P. L., 'Domestic finance, 1860-1914', in Floud, Roderick, and Johnson, Paul A., (eds.), *The Cambridge economic history of modern Britain, Volume 2: Economic Maturity, 1860-1939*, (Cambridge University Press), 2011, pp. 253-279.

[11] Hutchings, Victoria, *Messrs Hoare bankers: a history of the Hoare banking dynasty*, (Constable), 2005, and Temin, Peter, and Voth, Hans-Joachim, 'Credit rationing and crowding out during the industrial revolution: evidence from Hoare's Bank, 1702-1862', *Explorations in Economic History*, Vol. 42, (2005), pp. 325-348, and Temin, Peter, and Voth, Hans-Joachim, *Prometheus Shackled: Goldsmith Banks and England's financial revolution after 1700*, (Oxford University Press), 2013, pp. 39-72.

importantly, Scottish chartered banks were involved in the management of government finances but carried out private banking transactions for the merchant houses that comprised its major shareholders.[12] The Bank was by no means a central bank regulating the rest of the banking system; its main role was to facilitate the formation of the financial syndicates that purchased government stock. The third type of bank was the country bank, private banks located outside London.[13] These often arose as adjuncts of mercantile concerns and had strong banking links with both local landowners and industrialists. Their businesses were localised but the country banks were tied into the national system of capital mobilisation through their use of London agents and correspondent offices, generally . one of the London private bankers.

Major changes in the financial system began with the repeal of the 'Bubble Act' in 1825 and the two Companies Acts of 1856 and 1862.[14] These changes made limited liability and transferable shares more easily available to businesses and did much to stimulate the establishment of joint-stock banks in London and the provinces. The country banks were often involved in the formation of joint-stock banks, a number of them in London. Agency arrangements between London and country banks were, in many cases, formalised in mergers to form large joint-stock banks. The tightening up of the banking system, especially in the 1844 Bank Charter Act, enabled it to become more closely involved in capital mobilisation.[15] Agricultural wealth filtered through the country banks to London from where the money went to finance the industries of the north and midlands and to finance landowners' mortgages.[16]

---

[12] Checkland, S. G., *Scottish Banking: A History, 1695-1973*, (Collins), 1975, Gaskin, Maxwell, *The Scottish Banks: A modern survey*, (Routledge), 2013.

[13] Dawes, M. and Ward-Perkins, C. N., *Country banks of England and Wales: private provincial banks and bankers, 1688-1953*, (Chartered Institute of Bankers), 2000, Brunt, Liam, 'Rediscovering Risk: Country Banks as Venture Capital Firms in the First Industrial Revolution', *Journal of Economic History*, Vol. 66, (2006), pp. 74-102, Caunce, Stephen, 'Banks, communities and manufacturing in West Yorkshire textiles, c.1800–1830', in Wilson, John Francis, and Popp, Andrew, (eds.), *Industrial clusters and regional business networks in England, 1750-1970*, (Ashgate), 2003, pp. 112-129, Cottrell, P. L., 'Britannia's sovereign: Banks in the finance of British shipbuilding and shipping, c. 1830-1894', in Akveld, L. M., Loomeijer, Frits R., and Hahn-Pedersen, Morten, (eds.), *Financing the maritime sector: proceedings from the fifth North Sea history conference*, (Fiskeri- og Søfartsmuseet), 2002, pp. 191-254.

[14] Alborn, Timothy L., *Conceiving Companies: Joint-stock Politics in Victorian England*, (Routledge), 1998, pp. 87-143, examines the development of joint-stock and deposit banking from 1826.

[15] Horsefield, J. K., 'The Origins of the Bank Charter Act, 1844', *Economica*, Vol. 11, (1944), pp. 180-189. See also, Torrens, Robert, *The Principles and Practical Operation of Sir Robert Peel 's Act of 1844*, (Longmans), 1857.

By the 1860s and 1870s, the City of London had become the centre of a global monetary system, with a particularly important group of 'merchant banks' specialising in financing foreign trade and funding foreign government loans.[17] Prominent merchant bankers Baring and Rothschild, together with others such as Goshen and Hambros, were generally based around the businesses of émigré merchants and bankers and often continued with their merchant businesses alongside their banking activities.[18] The merchants and merchant bankers of the City formed a tightly integrated group with numerous overlapping business activities: they joined together to syndicate loans and to run the major dock, canal and insurance companies and dominated the board of the Bank of England. This City group was united through bonds of business, kinship and friendship and its cohesion was increased by the frequency and informality in the exchanges, coffee-houses and other meeting-places within the square mile itself.[19]

A propertied elite

In the eighteenth century, the distinction between landlords and capitalist farm tenants had been sharpened by the continuing process of agricultural improvement.[20] By 1850, the enclosure movement was all but completed

---

[16] Ackrill, Margaret, and Hannah, Leslie, *Barclays: the business of banking, 1690-1996,* (Cambridge University Press), 2001.

[17] Kynaston, David, (ed.), *The Bank of England: money, power and influence 1694-1994,* (Oxford University Press), 1995, and Cottrell, P. L., 'The Bank of England in transition, 1836-1860', in Bosbach, Franz, and Pohl, Hans, (eds.), *Das Kreditwesen in der Neuzei, Banking System in Modern History,* (K.G. Saur), 1997.

[18] See, for instance, Burk, Kathleen, *Morgan Grenfell, 1838-1988: the biography of a merchant bank,* (Oxford University Press), 1989.

[19] Collins, Michael, 'English banks and business cycles, 1848-1880', in Cottrell, P. L., and Moggridge, D. E., (eds.), *Money and power: essays in honour of L. S. Pressnell,* (Macmillan), 1988, pp. 1-40, Capie, F. H., and Collins, Michael, 'Banks, industry and finance, 1880-1914', *Business History,* Vol. 41, (1999), pp. 37-62, and 'Industrial lending by English commercial banks, 1860s-1914: why did banks refuse loans?', *Business History,* Vol. 38, (1996), pp. 26-44, Cottrell, P. L., 'The domestic commercial banks and the City of London, 1870-1939', in Cassis, Youssef, (ed.), *Finance and financiers in European history, 1880-1960,* (Cambridge University Press), 1992, pp. 39-62.

[20] Thompson, F. L. M., *English Landed Society in the Nineteenth Century,* (Routledge), 1963, is still an important work. Stone, L., and Stone, J. C. Fautier, *An Open Elite? England 1540-1880,* (Oxford University Press), 1984, Mingay, G. E., *The Gentry,* (Longman), 1976, and Beckett, J. C., *The Aristocracy in England 1660-1914,* (Basil Blackwell), 1986, second edition, 1989, cover broader periods. These should now be supplemented by Carradine, D., *The Decline and Fall of the British Aristocracy,* (Yale University Press), 1990, and

and agricultural wage labourers had been created. The three classes of landlord, tenant farmer and labourer characterised Victorian rural society and formed the basis of contemporary images of the rural world.[21]

Landlords were foremost in wealth, power and prestige while tenant farmers were under increasing economic pressure and their social status had fallen below manufacturers and merchants.[22] In 1850, rentier landowners held about 75 per cent of the land in England and a considerably higher proportion in Scotland and Wales. Running a great landed estate was a matter of efficient economic management.[23] The estate was treated as a unit of capital and was administered through procedures similar to those used in the larger mines and ironworks. In landed estates, there was a partial separation of ownership from control. General supervision of the affairs of the estate remained with the landowner while day-to-day administration was delegated to agents and stewards who collected rents, kept accounts and supervised the tenants. Large estates employed both a resident land agent with delegated authority but often also a chief agent with a subordinate staff to handle specialised tasks such as timber, minerals and so on.[24] Where land was let out to tenants, strategic control was shared between the landowner and the tenant. The landowner and his agents exercised supervision over tenants and made decisions over the renewal of tenancies as well as contributing to the capital requirements of the farms. The relationship between landowner and tenant was cemented in their financial arrangements with tenants receiving the profits from their farming activity and using it to pay his rent to the landowner.[25]

Aspects of Aristocracy: Grandeur and Decline in Modern Britain, (Yale University Press), 1994. General views, with sociological emphasis, can be found in Powis, J., *Aristocracy*, (Basil Blackwell), 1984, and Scott, J., *The Upper-classes*, (Macmillan), 1980.

[21] Lindert, Peter H., 'Who owned Victorian England?: the debate over landed wealth and inequality ', *Agricultural History*, Vol. 61, (1987), pp. 25-51.

[22] See, Moore, D. C., 'The Landed Aristocracy', in ibid., Mingay, G. E., (ed.), *The Victorian countryside*, Vol. 2, pp. 367-382.

[23] Spring, David, *The English landed estate in the 19th century: its administration*, (John Hopkins Press), 1963.

[24] See, for instance, Richards, E., 'The Land Agent', in Mingay, G. E., (ed.), *The Victorian countryside*, (Routledge), 1981, Vol. 2, pp. 439-456, Webster, Sarah A., 'Estate Improvement and the Professionalisation of Land Agents on the Egremont Estates in Sussex and Yorkshire, 1770-1835', *Rural History*, Vol. 18, (2007), pp. 47-70, and Colyer, Richard J., 'The land agent in nineteenth-century Wales', *Welsh History Review*, Vol. 8, (1977), pp. 401-425.

[25] See, Moore, D. C., 'The gentry', in ibid., Mingay, G. E., (ed.), *The Victorian countryside*, Vol. 2, pp. 383-398, and Rothery, Mark, 'The wealth of the English landed gentry, 1870-1935', *Agricultural History Review*, Vol. 55, (2007), pp. 251-268.

Family strategy was an important mechanism in economic life helping to maintain the traditional family life-style and the family estate. During the nineteenth century, farming offered a relatively poor return compared to the investment opportunities available in industry. Some landowners after 1874–when Lord Randolph Churchill (1849-1895) married the first known 'Dollar Princess', Jennie Jerome (1854-1921)– until 1905 young American heiresses married into the often impoverished British peerage bringing with them enormous dowries.[26] Other landowners diversified into investments in minerals, in urban property, in railways and docks and in overseas mining concerns to supplement their largely static agricultural earnings.[27] The Duke of Sutherland (1828-1892), the Marquess of Bute (1847-1900) and the Earl of Dudley (1817-1885) were prominent as mineral developers.[28] Many landowners began to develop those parts of their estates that were well-sited for urban growth.[29] Until 1850, apart from London, these were relatively small and localised, but the pace of development soon increased. In London the major landowners included the Duke of Portland (1800-1879), the Duke of Westminster (1825-1899) in Pimlico, Belgravia and Mayfair and the Duke of Bedford in Bloomsbury and Covent Garden.[30] In smaller cities and towns, prominent landowners included the Duke of Norfolk (1819-1891) and Earl Fitzwilliam (1815-1902) in Sheffield, the Marquess of Salisbury (1830-1903) and the Earls of Derby and Sefton (1835-1897) in Liverpool, the Marquess of Bute in Cardiff and Baron Calthorpe (1829-1910) in Birmingham. As fashion shifted from the spa towns to seaside resorts in the 1880s and 1890s, landowners such as the Duke of Devonshire (1833-1908) profited from the growth of centres such as Eastbourne, Brighton, Hastings and Scarborough. In 1886, 69 of the 261 provincial towns were largely owned by great landowners and a further 34 were owned by smaller landowners.

Rugby's headmaster Thomas Arnold (1795-1842) saw railways as

[26] De Courcy, Anne, *The Husband Hunters: Social Climbing in London and New York*, (Weidenfeld & Nicolson), 2016
[27] See, for instance, Ward, J. T., 'West Riding Landowners and Mining in the Nineteenth Century', *Bulletin of Economic Research*, Vol. 15, (1), (1963), pp. 61-74.
[28] Davies, John, *Cardiff and the Marquesses of Bute*, (University of Wales Press), 1981, Richards, Eric, *The Leviathan of Wealth: the Sutherland fortune in the Industrial Revolution*, (Routledge & Kegan Paul), 1973.
[29] Cannadine, David, *Lords and Landlords: The Aristocracy and the Towns 1774-1967*, (Leicester University Press), 1980, and Cannadine, David, (ed.), *Patricians, power, and politics in nineteenth-century towns*, (Leicester University Press), 1982.
[30] See, for instance, Sheppard, F. H. W., 'The Grosvenor estate, 1677-1977', *History Today*, Vol. 27, (1977), pp. 726-733.

heralding the downfall of the aristocracy and initially for many landowners they were interference with their territorial rights and strenuously opposed their construction. However, railways offered opportunities not only through investment but through the sale of land to railway companies and through compensation:

'There is nobody so violent against railroads as George...he organised the whole of our division against the Marham line!' 'I rather counter on his', said Lord de Mowbray, 'to assist me in resisting this joint branch here; but I was surprised to learn he had consented.' 'Not until the compensation was settled', innocently remarked Lady Marney; 'George never opposes them after that. He gave up his opposition to the Marham line when they agreed to his terms'.[31]

In 1850, Bradshaw's *General Railway Directory* listed only 24 peers and 25 sons of peers as railway directors and during the last twenty-five years of the century the number of directors in the House of Lords did not rise above fifty-one at any one time. Where landowners did invest heavily in railways, this tended not to be in main-line companies but in the secondary lines that connected their mineral interests to the main arteries of the railway network. In this way, landowners saw railway investment as a way of improving the income from the agricultural and mineral resources of their own estates.[32] As his rents fell in the depression, the Earl of Leicester (1822-1909) invested £170,000 in railways between 1870 and 1891, about half of his non-landed investment.

Landowners balanced their estate business with interests in industrial and commercial ventures, a diversification eased by close business links with City financiers. Railways were giant enterprises whose capital requirements outweighed those of all other businesses together. London bankers, especially Glyn, Mills acted as active promoters for railway companies and brought together the masses of 'anonymous' investors, many from the professions and 'widows and orphans', who provided much of the railway capital.[33] By the 1850s, over 200 railway companies, both domestic and foreign, banked with Glyn, Mills, and Co. The railway boom in the 1840s resulted in the 15 largest companies controlling 75 per cent of railway revenue and by the boom of the 1860s the top four companies had 44 per cent of revenue.[34] As a result, from the 1860s, many landowners began to take portfolio investments in the big main-line companies, a move

[31] Ibid., Disraeli, Benjamin, *Sybil: or The two nations*, p. 106.
[32] Ward, J. T., 'West Riding Landowners and the Railways', *Journal of Transport History*, Vol. 4, (1960), pp. 242-251.
[33] Gore-Browne, Eric, *The History of the House of Glyn, Mills and Co.*, (Privately Printed), 1933
[34] Irving, R. J., 'The capitalisation of Britain's railways, 1830-1914', *Journal of Transport History*, third series, Vol. 5, (1984), pp. 1-24.

away from their previous commitment only to local lines. The railway booms brought together some of the interests of the financial community and the landowners.

The development of railways had an indirect impact on industrial funding. Limited liability had rarely been thought necessary by industrial entrepreneurs but, as capital requirements of some industries increased, trusts and partnerships gave way to the joint-stock company.[35] This enabled manufacturers to draw on a wider pool of capital and to provide for the various members of their families by issuing shares to them.[36] For instance, the Pease family held several firms in the North of England including Joseph Pease & Partners, coal-owners, J. W. Pease & Co. that dealt in iron and limestone and the banking business was carried by J & J. W. Pease. Extensive woollen mills were run under the name of Henry Pease & Co. The headquarters of all these firms was in Northgate, Darlington. By the mid-1860s, a thousand new joint-stock companies were being registered annually, though the majority were still run as partnerships. The spread of railway shareholding encouraged the growth of the London and provincial stock exchanges and made it easier for expanding industrial enterprises to raise capital and for landowners to invest.

The move towards joint stock capital was linked to an increase in the levels of economic concentration.[37] In the 1880s, the hundred largest industrial firms accounted for less than 10 per cent of the total market. However, a spate of company amalgamation led to greater concentration in the 1890s as merger activity outpaced the growth of the market. Companies were floated on the Stock Exchange and might then grow by taking over their competitors or rival firms might combine to float a common holding company. Families whose firms were floated or merged at this time often retained ordinary, voting shares for themselves and allowed debentures and non-voting shares to be sold to the wider public.

---

[35] See, Bryer, R. A., 'The Mercantile Laws Commission of 1854 and the political economy of limited liability', *Economic History Review*, Vol. 50, (1997), pp. 37-56, and Loftus, Donna, 'Limited Liability, Market Democracy, and the Social Organization of Production in Mid-Nineteenth-Century Britain', in Henry, Nancy, and Schmitt, Cannon, (eds.), *Victorian investments: new perspectives on finance and culture*, (Indiana University Press), 2009, pp. 79-97.

[36] Rose, Mary B., 'The family firm in British business 1780-1914', in Kirby, M. W., and Rose, Mary B., (eds.), *Business enterprise in modern Britain: from the eighteenth to the twentieth century*, (Routledge), 1994, pp. 61-87, and Nenadic, Stana, 'The Small Family Firm in Victorian Britain', in Jones, Geoffrey, and Rose, Mary B., (eds.), *Family Capitalism*, (Routledge), 1993, pp. 86-114, provide the context.

[37] Johnson, Paul, *Making the Market: Victorian Origins of Corporate Capitalism*, (Cambridge University Press), 2010.

Family control could be maintained through relatively small capital investment. The flotation of firms allowed capital to be raised from outside the family circle while the joint-stock firm allowed family wealth to be diversified and made more secure. Large amalgamation of family firms occurred in a rapid burst between 1898 and 1900, but the rate of flotation and merger remained high until 1914.

As a result, some family firms continued to prosper. In 1848, for instance, Thomas Barlow (1825-1897) founded Barlow & Co. in Manchester, manufacturing and trading in textiles in Britain. From the mid-1850s, the firm started importing cotton from America and began exporting textiles to India and the Far East. In 1864, he founded Thomas Barlow & Bro. and during the 1870s and 1880s established his own trade agencies in Calcutta, Shanghai and Singapore to export goods from Britain, to import tea and coffee, and to acquire his own plantations in these regions. During the last two decades of the nineteenth century, Thomas's eldest son Sir John Emmott Barlow, 1st Baronet (1857-1932) steered the family firm away from textiles to develop its interests in agency work, in the export of iron and steel and in tea and coffee, which led to the acquisition of a bonded tea warehouse in London. In 1891, the Barlows took over the ailing textile importers Scott & Co. in Singapore and began to extend their business to coffee estates. When the crop failed in the late 1890s, business was diversified into planting rubber trees. In 1906, a number of estates combined to form the Highlands and Lowlands Para Rubber Co., with Barlow & Co. as its agents in Singapore and Kuala Lumpur, while Thomas Barlow & Bro. acted as Secretaries in England. Diversification was one route to family success. But, in the case of W. D. (1797-1865) & H. O. Wills (1761-1826) in the tobacco industry, family control was maintained through a combination of technical innovation and organisational change in the 1890s. This strengthened the firm and did not lead to a haemorrhage of capital and ability from the organisation into landownership and politics.[38]

Because of family loyalties and priorities, those larger companies that succeeded in adopting a more centralised structure were generally either those in which one constituent firm was considerably larger than the others or those in which a particular family managed to subordinate its fellows in the struggle for control. The families who lost in the struggle for control in the amalgamated firms were faced with the choice of either retiring into land or politics or moving into new business ventures. Families that wished to leave business often decided to sell out to a company promoter prior to the Stock Exchange flotation. These families sometimes retained a stake in the firm but were not involved in active control.[39] Promoters

---

[38] Alford, B. W.E., *W. D. & H. O. Wills and the Development of the UK Tobacco Industry, 1786-1965*, (Taylor & Francis), 2006, pp. 304-306.

were often keen to recruit peers to the board of companies that they had floated, feeling that a 'lord on the board' would help the sale of shares.[40] The number of the aristocracy on the board of the Great Western Railway rose from eight of the forty-nine directors between 1856 and 1875 to thirteen out of thirty-six between 1896 and 1915. From the 1870s, landowners joined the boards of joint-stock companies and by 1896, a quarter of all peers had directorship. Many of these men were invited on to boards to provide kudos but landowners found that their directorships provided a significant supplement to their income. Companies may also have benefited from the 'managerial' expertise of the landowners since the managerial problems of large firms and the need for delegated administration were often similar to those faced on their estates.

The declining returns from agriculture within the economy as a whole was aggravated by the agricultural depression of 1873-1896.[41] Smaller landowners were hit more severely than larger landowners who were able to diversify into non-agricultural activities. This exacerbated growing awareness and criticism of the accumulation of wealth in land, commerce and industry.[42] The result of this controversy and criticism was the establishment of an official investigation to scotch the claim that 30,000 people owned land. This backfired when the investigation found that the land was owned by a much smaller number of people. The results of the survey for 1873 were published in the *Returns of Owners of Land* (the 'New Domesday Book') and, although there is some confusion in the various summaries of the *Returns*, certain conclusions about ownership of land are clear.[43] 80 per cent of land was owned by 7,000 people, of whom 4,200 in England and Wales and 800 in Scotland held 1,000 acres or more. Of these, 363 held 10,000 acres or more and 44 had 100,000 acres or more. The largest estates were in Scotland with 35 estates over 100,000 acres, of which 25 accounted for a quarter of the Scottish land. In total,

[39] Casson, Mark, 'The economics of the family firm', *Scandinavian Economic History Review*, Vol. 47, (1999), pp. 10-23.
[40] Jeremy, David, J., 'Anatomy of the British Business Elite, 1860-1980', *Business History*, Vol. 26, (1), (1984), pp. 3-23, Channon, G., 'The recruitment of directors to the board of the Great Western Railway', manchesteruniversitypress.co.uk/uploads/docs/200001.pdf
[41] See, Channing, Francis Allston, *The Truth about Agricultural Depression: an economic study of the evidence of the Royal Commission*, (Longman, Green and Co.), 1897, pp. 29-52, on evidence for successful farming.
[42] Burrows, A. J., *The agricultural depression and how to meet it; hints to landowners and tenant farmers: By Alfred J. Burrows ...Reprinted, with considerable additions, from 'The Journal of Forestry and Estate Management'*, (William Rider & Son), 1882, was one, of several, self-help books.
[43] See Bateman, John, *The Great Landowners of Great Britain and Ireland*, (Harrison and Sons), 1879, fourth edition, (Harrison and Sons), 1883.

large landowners held about 24 per cent of the land, smaller rentiers held about 55 per cent and owner-occupiers held a further 10 per cent with the Church of England and the Crown holding a similar amount. Finally, this national picture was repeated at local level: for instance, 350 people owned 55 per cent of the agricultural land in Norfolk, Suffolk and Cambridgeshire.

2,500 people had annual rental incomes of £3,000 or more in 1873 with 866 with incomes of £10,000 or more and 76 over £50,000. Sixteen people received a rental income in excess of £100,000, the largest incomes held by the Duke of Norfolk (1847-1917) and Buccleuch (1831-1914) and the Marquess of Bute. There was not a perfect correlation between income and acreage. Only 7 people had both 100,000 acres and £100,000 annual income: the Dukes of Buccleuch, Devonshire, Northumberland (1810-1899), Portland and Sutherland, the Marquess of Bute and the Earl Fitzwilliam. The survey did not extend to the rental income derived from urban rents and the wealth of men such as the Duke of Westminster was underestimated.[44] To identify Britain's richest landowners more closely it is necessary to include the Dukes of Norfolk and Westminster, who had large incomes from relatively small estates and six men with massive estates with less than £100,000 rental: the Duke of Richmond (1818-1903), the Earl of Breadalbane (1851-1922), Earl of Fife (1814-1879) and Earl of Seafield (1817-1888), Sir Alexander Matheson (1805-1886) and Sir James Matheson (1796-1878). These fifteen people were the core of the British landed class and the continuing overlap between the rich and the peerage is obvious. Of the 363 people with both £10,000 income and 10,000 acres, together holding almost a quarter of Britain's land, 246 were members of the peerage; and a further 350 peers had smaller estates.

The number of landed millionaires fell between the first and second half of the century in relation to wealthy merchants and industrialists.[45] Perkin estimated that there were, in 1850, 2,000 businessmen with profits of £3,000 or more; 338 of these people received £10,000 or more and 26 £50,000 or more.[46] In 1867, the wealthiest 0.5 per cent of the population received 26.3 per cent of the total income. By 1880, the number of businessmen with Schedule D profits of £3,000 or more had risen to 5,000 of whom 987 received £10,000 or more and 77 £50,000 or more.

Landed wealth-holders 1809-1899			
	1809-1858	1858-1879	1880-1899
Millionaires	75	33	32
Half-millionaires	126	50	n/a
Total	222	83	–

[44] Ibid., Rubinstein, W. D., *Men of Property: The Very Wealth in Britain since the Industrial Revolution*, pp. 193-226, provides analysis based on the *Returns of Owners of Land*; see especially Table 7.1, pp. 194-195.

[45] Spring, David, and Spring, Eileen, 'Debt and the English aristocracy', *Canadian Journal of History*, Vol. 31, (1996), pp. 377-394.

[46] Ibid., Perkin, H., *The Origins of Modern English Society 1780-1880*, pp. 414-420.

By 1880, the commercial and manufacturing classes had overtaken the landed classes in economic terms. The financial sector consistently accounted for between 20 and 40 per cent of all non-landed millionaires. The main industries of the industrial revolution were well-represented among millionaires. Textiles accounted for about 10 per cent, a slight increase from earlier in the century while metals accounted for the same percentage in both of the earlier periods and then fell away.

Top British wealth-holders outside land 1809-1914				
	1809-58	1858-79	1880-99	1900-14
Millionaires	9	30	59	75
Half-millionaires	47	102	158	181
Total	56	132	217	256

In the later periods, the food, drink and tobacco industries together accounted for about a fifth of all non-landed millionaires, and from 1858 the distributive trades accounted for one-tenth. The wealthy men of land, commerce and manufacturing drew closer together during the Victorian period, though landowners still tended to disparage merchants and manufacturers as 'middle-class' and concerned with 'trade'.[47] This status exclusion was eased by the existence of a vast number of clerks, shopkeepers and tradesmen who were oriented towards the commercial and manufacturing classes and appeared to form a continuous social class with them. In fact, the economic gulf between them was immense.

The notion of 'the leisured or leisure classes' can be traced back to the 1840s and may well have existed earlier.[48] In 1868, Anthony Trollope (1815-1882) was confident that England possessed:

...the largest and wealthiest leisure class that any country, ancient or modern, ever boasted.[49]

Thorstein Veblen (1859-1929) subjected them to trenchant analysis in his 1899 *The Theory of the Leisure Class*. arguing[50]

---

[47] See, Spring, Eileen, 'Business men and landowners re-engaged', *Historical Research*, Vol. 72, (1999), pp. 77-91.

[48] Cunningham, Hugh, *Time, work and leisure: Life changes in England since 1700*, (Manchester University Press), 2014, pp. 155-177, considers the 'leisured class' from 1840 to 1970.

[49] Trollope, A., (ed.), *British Sports and Pastimes*, (Virtue & Co.), 1868, p. 18.

[50] Tilman, Rick, *Thorstein Veblen and His Critics, 1891-1963: Conservative, Liberal, and Radical Perspectives*, (Princeton University Press), 1992, is a good critique of Veblen's ideas.

The fundamental reason for the development of a leisure class was that only in conspicuous leisure and in conspicuous consumption could the wealthy achieve the status they sought.[51]

The critical words are 'conspicuous' and 'status.[52] Leisure for the leisure classes demanded that it be seen both by fellow members of the class and by an envious or admiring excluded public providing a social status to be emulated. Display was fundamental to its social position and it is difficult to determine whether there was any separation of work and leisure within the class. Nationally, the leisure class was readily observed in the London Season and until the 1880s, this was a political as well as a social occasion. The London Season was particularly busy from April to the end of June, but events were held throughout the winter starting when Parliament returned in late January and included military reviews, dinner parties, and charity events and went on to the end of July. In the limited political world, the numbers involved were relatively small, perhaps 500 families compared to the 4,000 families who participated in the more social London Season of the late-nineteenth century. Until then entry to London 'Society' was carefully guarded and its social functions mostly private. From the seventeenth century, young women of noble birth were formally presented to the king and queen at court. *Debrett's* states this tradition was strengthened in the late-eighteenth century under George III (1738-1820) with the charity interests of his queen, Charlotte (1744-1818). Their fundraising balls became the high point of the social season, giving young women of high birth an even greater opportunity to 'come out' as ready to marry and socialise.[53] It was expected that debutantes from the aristocracy would be presented at court during their coming out season but daughters of the clergy, of military and naval officers, of physicians and of barristers were also eligible for this honour.

From the 1880s it became easier to buy one's way into 'Society'.[54] This reflected a change in the nature of the leisure class and it became more difficult to identify a class whose members patently did not work. By

---

[51] Veblen, Thorstein, *The Theory of the Leisure Class*, (Macmillan), 1889, p. 218, cit., in Cunningham, H., 'Leisure and culture', in ibid., Thompson, F. M. L., (ed.), *The Cambridge Social History of Britain, 1750-1950*, Vol. 2, p. 290.
[52] Ibid., Cunningham, Hugh, *Time, Work and Leisure: Life Changes in England since 1700*, pp. 155-177, on the leisured class 1840-1970.
[53] Debutantes have not been presented at court since Elizabeth II stopped the practice in 1958, but the annual Queen Charlotte's Ball continues as an elite charity event for young women between the ages of 17 and 20 who come from wealthy families.
[54] On this see Pullar, Philippa, *Gilded Butterflies: The Rise and Fall of the London Season*, (Hamish Hamilton), 1978, and Davidoff, L., *The Best Circles: Society, Etiquette and the Season*, (Taylor & Francis), 1973.

contrast, public attention began to focus on the plutocracy whose male members worked, but so successfully that they could spend their fortunes in their leisure. The London Season formed one clearly demarcated phase in the annual life of the leisure class; the remainder of the year was centred on country houses in a mixture of activities some of which were thoroughly exclusive while others entailed a carefully calculated patronage of more popular occasions.[55] Shooting was the most exclusive of sports while foxhunting was, in ideology at least, open to peer and peasant. In the late-nineteenth century, the plutocracy began to supplant the aristocracy as its leaders.

From the mid-eighteenth century the London Season had its provincial counterparts. In the larger provincial towns, particularly in southern England the 'urban gentry' provided the lower and more modest ranks of the leisure class. After 1830, such people living on income from capital tended to gravitate towards the spas and more select seaside resorts. They were disproportionately female and old. In contrast to the national leisure class, there was neither firm structure to their year nor any flamboyance in their leisure. They maintained their status by careful observance of formalities that helped to distinguish them from those who had to work for a living. In the late-nineteenth century a new category, the retired, began to fuse with this older, modest, provincial leisure class, to form a substantial proportion of the population of the southern and coastal towns in which they congregated.

Being a gentleman

The involvement of landowners on boards of manufacturing and commercial companies was balanced by the movement of industrial and commercial wealth into land and an increase in intermarriage between the classes. By 1830, London bankers and merchants such as Lloyd, Baring, Drummond and the Rothschilds, brewers such as Barclay, Hanbury and Whitbread had bought into land, as did wealthy lawyers. Entry into land through purchase or through marriage continued after 1830 at the same rate as in the previous century. Later in the century industrialists such as Tennant, Armstrong, Coats and Wills also bought into land reflecting the continued status land brought since alternative and more profitable investment outlets were available. How typical these industrial magnates were is questionable since entry into the landed elite remained remarkably

---

[55] Mandler, Peter, *The fall and rise of the stately home*, (Yale University Press), 1997, Sykes, Christopher Simon, *The big house: the story of a country house and its family*, (HarperCollins), 2004, Gardiner, Juliet, *The Edwardian country house*, (Channel 4 Books), 2002, and Wilson, Richard, and Mackley, Alan, *Creating paradise: the building of the English country house 1660-1880*, (Hambledon), 2000.

restricted. Most sons of manufacturers inherited the family firm not a country mansion.[56]

The cultural blending of the privileged social classes was marked by a reassertion of the status of the 'gentleman' with its associated life-style.[57] Alexis de Tocqueville (1805-1859) had noted this process in the 1850s:

> ...if we follow the mutation of time and place of the English word 'gentleman...we find its connotation being steadily widened in England as the classes draw nearer to each other and intermingle. In each successive century we find it being applied to men a little lower in the social scale...[58]

What characterised a 'gentleman' was instinctively known and defined through its very elusiveness.[59] Although duelling in Britain went into sharp decline after 1840 and in 1844 the amended articles of war stated that any officer who fought a duel would be cashiered—the last recorded fatal duel took place in 1852 between two French exiles— defending one's honour was regarded as an important facet of being a gentleman.[60] This vague notion had long marked a fundamental status divide in society and, as the number of manufacturers and merchants increased so it took increasing significance in social control. Members of the aristocracy were gentlemen by right of birth—although paradoxically birth alone could not make a man a gentleman. The new industrial and mercantile elites, in the face of opposition from the aristocracy, sought to have themselves designated as gentlemen as a natural consequence of their growing wealth and influence. The small size of the peerage meant that even the admission into the peerage of the most wealthy manufacturers could only operate as a mechanism of social control if the peerage continued to be associated with the more informal and flexible concept of the gentleman. Acceptance as a gentleman by those who were already recognised as gentlemen defined a person as someone who mattered

---

[56] Speck, W. A., *A Concise History of Britain, 1707-1975*, (Cambridge University Press), (1993), pp. 59-60.

[57] In this see, Mason, P., *The English gentleman*, (André Deutsch), 1982, and Raven, S. A. N., *The English gentleman: an essay in attitudes*, (A. Blond), 1961.

[58] Tocqueville, Alexis de, *The Old Regime and the French Revolution*, (Harper & Brothers), 1856, p. 108, (Doubleday), 1955, pp. 82-83.

[59] For the evasiveness of the Victorians in defining 'gentleman' see, Osborne, Hugh, 'Hooked on Classics: Discourses of Allusion in the Mid-Victorian Novel', in Ellis, Roger, and Oakley-Brown, Liz, (eds.), *Translation and nation: towards a cultural politics of Englishness*, (Multilingula Matters), 2001, especially pp. 144-149.

[60] Banks, Stephen, *A Polite Exchange of Bullets: The Duel and the English Gentleman, 1750-1850*, (Boydell), 2010, Sharpe, James, *A Fiery & Furious People: A History of Violence in England*, (Penguin), 2015, pp. 255-282.

socially and politically. That status could be given or withdrawn without justification by influential social circles made it a subtle and effective mechanism of social control. By the 1880s it was almost universally accepted that the recipient of a traditional liberal education at one of the elite public schools would be recognised as a gentleman, no matter what his origins had been.

The life-style of the gentleman was then accommodated to the practices of the manufacturing and commercial classes. The round of visiting the great country houses, the meetings of the Quarter Sessions and rural pursuits such as fox-hunting and racing were already integrated into the London-based 'Season' of activities in which all members of 'Society' participated. After 1830, this became more formalised and acquired a new authority over those who regarded themselves as gentlemen. Davidoff is correct when she states:

> Society can be seen as a system of quasi-kinship relationships that was used to 'place' mobile individuals during the period of structural differentiation fostered by industrialisation and urbanisation.[61]

Gentlemen's clubs took over part of the role occupied by coffee houses in the eighteenth century and reached their peak at the end of the nineteenth.[62] White's, Brooks' and Boodle's were the first clubs that were aristocratic in tone providing a milieu for gambling that was illegal outside of members-only establishments. The explosion in the popularity of clubs after 1820 and especially in the last quarter of the century saw over 400 clubs in London. Each of the three Reform Acts in 1832, 1867 and 1885 corresponded with a further expansion of clubs, something evident in the extension of the franchise in 1918. Existing clubs with strict limits on membership numbers and long waiting lists were generally cautious of these potential members and so these people began forming their own clubs. Many of these new, more 'inclusive' clubs proved just as reluctant as their forebears to admit new members when the franchise was further extended. Most gentlemen had only one club, which closely corresponded with their trade or social and political identity but a few people belonged to several. For instance, the United Services Club was founded in 1815 'for officers of not less rank than Major in the Army and Captain in the Navy', the Travellers' Club, founded in 1819, 'for gentlemen who had travelled out of the British Isles to a distance of at least five hundred miles

---

[61] Davidoff, L., *The Best Circles*, (Croom Helm), 1973, p. 15.

[62] Lejeune, Anthony, *The Gentlemen's Clubs of London*, (Stacey International), 2012, Milne-Smith, Amy, *London Clubland: A Cultural History of Gender and Class in late-Victorian Britain*, (Palgrave Macmillan), 2011, Hoare, Stephen, *Palaces of Power: The Birth and Evolution of London's Clubland*, (The History Press), 2nd ed., 2021.

from London in a direct line'[63] while the Union Club for merchants, lawyers, MPs and 'gentlemen at large' was built in Trafalgar Square in 1822. The Garrick was founded in 1831 by the writer and art collector Francis Mills (1793-1854) as a 'society in which actors and men of education and refinement might meet on equal terms'.[64] Gentleman's clubs were private places where men could relax and create friendships with other men and were regarded as a central part of elite men's lives.[65] When an anxious new member of White's asked Wheeler, the genial long-serving barman, if the bar was still open, he replied, 'Bless my soul, sir, it has been open for 200 years'.

Gentlemen's clubs were not confined to London and in the early 1800s there were many clubs in Glasgow, mostly informal drinking or luncheon clubs. In January 1825, a group of 33 gentlemen, consisting of prominent local businessmen and several MPs, met in Walker's Hotel in Buchanan Street to establish a Glasgow club similar to those they had seen in London and the recently established New Club in Edinburgh.[66] A founding committee was established and on 21 January decided that the club would be known as the Western Club and would have a membership elected by ballot not exceeding 130.[67] During the nineteenth century, its membership rose reaching 300 by 1837 and 600 by 1870 and the club moved to larger premises. The Western Club was considered to be an elitist institution:

> ...from all accounts it's easier to manoeuvre an OBE for yourself than to gain entry as a member of the Western Club.[68]

In this period 'Society' was rapidly growing in size and directories listing the families of gentlemen found a growing market. In 1833, John Burke (1786-1848) published the first edition of his genealogical directory of county families: initially called *Burke's Commoners*, it was subsequently given the more acceptable title of *Burke's Landed Gentry*. The 1833 volume listed 400 county families, the qualification for inclusion being possession of at least 2,000 acres of land. The 1906 volume had grown to 5,000 families, of whom 1,000 were of industrial background. *Burke's General Armory* was published in various editions from 1842 and listed all those families claiming the right to bear heraldic arms. Most of the 60,000

---

[63] Fitzroy, Almeric William, *History of the Travellers' Club*, (Travellers' Club), 1927.

[64] Fitzgerald, Percy, *The Garrick Club*, (E. Stock), 1904.

[65] Timbs, John, *Club Life in London*, 2 Vols. (Richard Bentley), 1866.

[66] Cockburn, Harry Archibald, *A History of the New Club, Edinburgh, 1787-1937*, (London & Edinburgh), 1938.

[67] Foreman, Carol, *The History of the Western Club: 1825-200*, (Carol Foreman), 2000.

[68] *Glasgow Evening News*, 20 October 1924.

families included in the definitive 1844 edition owned little or no land.

Presentation at court was regarded as crucial to the lives of gentlemen and their families. By 1850, it was the essential entrée into Society and the needs of the newcomers were met by the publication of manuals of instruction and by Certificates of Presentation.[69] The London Season, together with such events as yachting at Cowes and grouse-shooting on the Scottish moors, were central features of the life-style of the gentleman. It was, however, the Victorian public school that forged a cultural unity between the landed classes and the newcomers. The educational changes initiated by Thomas Arnold at Rugby were intended to produce 'Christian Gentlemen,' blending traditional ideas of the gentleman with evangelical Christianity. The public school reforms of the 1860s led to the formation of the 'Headmasters' Conference' as the central forum through which the major schools could exert control and influence over the lesser schools. The rise of new men aspiring to social leadership, the expansion of the number of suitable posts in government service and the increasing use of competitive examinations for recruitment, all reinforced the benefits of a public school education. By the 1870s, the route to top positions via public school and Oxbridge had been established.

The code of gentlemanly behaviour defined what was 'done' and what was 'not done'. The gentleman had definite duties and obligations towards other members of society who had a corresponding obligation to defer to his 'natural' superiority. In part, this marked a restoration of the 'bonds of dependency' that had existed in the eighteenth century but within an industrial and urban context as well as agrarian one. Deferential behaviour was expected of subordinates as a sign of the legitimacy of the prevailing patterns of inequality. The public school ethos was, in part, a response to the reforms of recruitment and promotion in the civil service, the law and the army but it ran counter to the rationality, efficiency and functionality of trade and industry. In some respects, the ethos of public schools represented a balance between the rationalised organisation of economic change and traditional power, a compromise between landed and entrepreneurial ideals.

The dominance of the values of the gentleman and the cult of amateurism are important in arguments about entrepreneurial decline after 1870.[70] A. J. P. Taylor explained Britain's decline:

---

[69] Ellenberger, N. W., 'The transformation of London "society" at the end of Victoria's reign: evidence from the court presentation records', *Albion*, Vol. 22, (1990), pp. 633-653.
[70] Rubinstein, W. D., *Capitalism, culture and decline in Britain 1750-1990*, (Routledge), 1993, pp. 102-139, examines education, the 'gentleman' and British entrepreneurship. See also, Thompson, F. M. L., *Gentrification and the Enterprise Culture: Britain 1780-1980*, (Oxford University Press), 2001, pp. 122-

The simplest answer, which remains true to the present day, was the public schools. They taught the classics when they should have been teaching sciences.[71]

The view that 'gentlemanly' culture was privileged over science and technology and that middle-class entrepreneurship was diluted by mirroring the values and lifestyle of landed society is central to this interpretation of decline. The constant flow of successful businessmen from the ungentlemanly field of trade and industry to the more acceptable fields of politics and the land is held to have resulted in a haemorrhage of talent. In fact, the attendance by the children of businessmen at public schools did not produce a drift from business life and many manufacturers saw the creation of a successful family business as the first step in a longer-term strategy of establishing a landed family. Once they had accumulated sufficient wealth, successful businessmen would become 'gentlemen', with country seats, perhaps even a knighthood or peerage, seats in Parliament for themselves or their Oxbridge educated sons. They ceased to be 'players' in the entrepreneurial field and became 'gentlemen'. The major problem with this view is that the aristocracy had emerged from the world of business and had never rejected the idea that making money through capital investment and commerce was a good thing. Some of the commercial elite were 'gentrified' during the second half of the nineteenth century but they were primarily London financiers and bankers whose entrepreneurial performance remained confident well into the twentieth century. The cultural attack on entrepreneurial attitudes in late-Victorian Britain is far from convincing especially when British attitude to business life and entrepreneurialism was far less hostile than in the rest of Europe and there is little evidence that, despite the importance they attached to the classics, public schools were opposed to the teaching of science.[72]

Victorian society was characterised by a move towards unity among the privileged social classes, but there was never complete integration. Landowners and the City had come closer together but manufacturers and provincial merchants remained apart. By the 1870s, autonomous and assertive industrial dynasties were entrenched in Glasgow, Manchester, Liverpool, Birmingham, Newcastle and Cardiff. It was at this provincial level that manufacturers and merchants came closer together. The distinction between three privileged classes that had been self-evident in the 1800s was far less clear by 1914.[73] Although each class was based

---

142.
[71] Taylor, A. J. P., *Essays in English History*, (Pelican), 1976, p. 37.
[72] Ibid., Rubinstein, W. D., *Capitalism, culture and decline in Britain 1750-1990*, p. 49.
[73] Collins. Marcus, 'The Fall of the English Gentleman: The National Character

round a particular kind of property, they entered into ever more extensive business and personal relationships with each other. Each class also included people who were not active participants in the control and use of property, but who drew their income from this and had family links with the core of their class. Such people were to be found in politics, the professions and the intelligentsia and these occupations constituted major areas of overlap between the fringes of the three privileged groups.

Political norms

It was in politics that new patterns of class alignment were at their clearest. Between 1780 and 1850, the national political rulers were drawn exclusively from the landed classes and the City faction of the commercial class, with the manufacturers and provincial merchants pursuing their interests in the towns and cities.[74] From mid-century, this patrician approach to national politics was gradually diluted by the changing balance of power between the privileged classes and saw changes in the makeup of the political leadership.[75]

The policy of the ruling Tory elite that dominated politics between the 1780s and 1830 was based on a negative protection of the established social order: no Parliamentary reform and no concessions to working-class or middle-class radicalism. The changing balance of power between the landed and manufacturing classes led government to bolster agriculture. In 1813 and 1814, the state finally abandoned regulation of wages and apprenticeship freeing up the labour market but in 1815, it introduced the Corn Laws to support arable farmers.[76] More economic controls were dismantled in the 1820s but the pace of economic change was not as rapid as many manufacturers demanded.[77] It was not until the Whigs came to power in late 1830 that this changed. They faced tensions between

in Decline, c. 1918–1970', *Historical Research*, Vol. 75, no. 187, (2002): 90-111.

[74] Boyd Hilton, R., *A Mad, Bad, and Dangerous People? England 1783-1846*, (Oxford University Press), 2006, and Derry J. W., *Politics in the Age of Fox, Pitt and Liverpool: Continuity and Transformation*, (Macmillan), 1990, provides an overview.

[75] Hoppen, K. Theodore, *The Mid-Victorian Generation, 1846-1886*, (Oxford University Press), 1998, and Searle, G. R., *A New England?: peace and war 1886-1918*, (Oxford University Press), 2004.

[76] Fay, C. R., *The Corn Law and Social England*, (Cambridge University Press), 1932, remains the most valuable discussion of the nature of the Corn Laws while Barnes, Donald Grove, *A History of The English Corn Laws from 1660-1846*, (George Routledge & Sons, Ltd.), 1930, takes a broader approach. See also, Kadish, Alan, (ed.), *The Corn Laws: the formation of popular economics in Britain*, 6 Vols. (William Pickering), 1996.

[77] Boyd Hilton, R., *Corn, Cash, Commerce: the economic policies of the Tory governments 1815-1830*, (Oxford University Press), 1977.

retaining the political supremacy of the landed class and satisfying the demands of their commercial and manufacturing supporters. They moved towards a regulatory state and succeeded in passing a conservative measure of Parliamentary reform in 1832. But the major area of political activity for the middle-classes was at local level. Local politics was seen as more important than national politics and the Municipal Corporations Act 1835 more important than 1832. The major line of division was not between town and country—there had always been a strong connection between the two—but within towns.[78] Already established merchants and manufacturers, generally Anglican and Tory, supported by local gentry competed with newer manufacturers, often Nonconformists and Whig, for control of the council and the magistracy and to determine the choice of MPs.[79] In Oldham, there was a separation between the cotton manufacturers who looked to the merchant dynasties of Manchester and older capitalists, especially colliery-owners who identified with local landowners.[80]

The landed classes saw themselves as the natural rulers of society and as having the right to exercise such power and to speak on behalf of those who were not possess the property that entitled them to participate in the exercise of political power. This aristocratic elite was dominant nationally leaving the gentry to control local politics but this was challenged from the 1840s by the emergence of 'electoral' politics. MPs were elected by those who wished to have their interests represented in the 'public sphere', where public opinion could be formed and decisions reached. This led to the development of central organisations for the Conservative and Whig parties that handled electoral registration, selection of candidates and liaised between local and national leadership. In addition, pressure group

---

[78] Ibid., Roberts, Matthew, *Political movements in urban England, 1832-1914*, and Miskell, Louise, 'Urban Power, Industrialisation and Political Reform: Swansea Elites in the Town and Region, 1780-1850', in Roth, Ralf, and Beachy, Robert, (eds.), *Who ran the cities?: city elites and urban power structures in Europe and North America, 1750-1940*, (Ashgate), 2007, pp. 21-36.

[79] See, for instance, Garrard, John Adrian, 'The middle classes and nineteenth century national and local politics', in ibid., Garrard, John Adrian, Jary, David, Goldsmith, Michael, and Oldfield, Adrian, (eds.), *The middle class in politics*, pp. 35-66, Taylor, Peter, 'A divided middle class: Bolton, 1790-1850', *Manchester Region History Review*, Vol. 6, (1992), pp. 3-15, and Morris, R. J., *Class, Sect and Party: The making of the British middle class: Leeds, 1820-1850*, (Manchester University Press), 1990, pp. 108-136.

[80] Price, Sarah, 'Governing the community: the rise of popular radicalism in Oldham, Lancashire, 1790-1837', *Family & Community History*, Vol. 4, (2001), pp. 125-137, Winstanley, Michael J., 'Oldham radicalism and the origins of popular Liberalism, 1830-1852', *Historical Journal*, Vol. 36, (1993), pp. 619-643, and Gadian, D. S., 'Class consciousness in Oldham and other north-west industrial towns', *Historical Journal*, Vol. 21, (1978), pp. 161-172.

politics, whether by 'societies', 'leagues' or 'unions' became crucial to metropolitan and provincial politics and the political interests of business were expressed in the Chambers of Commerce[81] that were formed in the larger cities and spread more widely in the 1840s and 1850s.[82] At the heart of this system of representation was the notion of deference but this could not easily be transferred to an expanding urban context and could not be relied on to provide an effective guarantee for the continuing political rule of the landed class. Elitist politics came under increasing strain as urban influences grew. Between 1840 and 1870, there was a period of confrontation between elitist and electoral politics.[83] Yet, the outcome was not simply the replacement of elitist by electoral politics but a compromise between the landed and manufacturing classes.

Reform in 1832 opened up the system a little, but elitist patterns of representation based on property qualifications remained unaltered. Of the 13 Cabinets formed between 1830 and 1868, peers and commoners were each dominant in six and the two Houses balanced in one.[84] Those Cabinets in which the Lords had a majority were short-lived Conservative administrations in the 1850s suggesting that the Commons was the more important institution. To some extent this is true, but those who entered the Commons were not socially different from those in the Lords. There were 217 MPs in the Parliament of 1833 who were sons of peers or who were themselves baronets.[85] By 1880, the number had only fallen to 170. Of the 103 men holding Cabinet office between 1830 and 1868, 68 were major landowners, 21 merchant bankers and 14 from the legal and medical professions.

Not only were there close links between the Commons and Lords but the landowners who were active in Parliament were drawn heavily from those who had diversified into other economic activities. The 815

---

[81] Bennett, Robert J., *Local Business Voice: The History of Chambers of Commerce in Britain, Ireland and Revolutionary America, 1780-2011*, (Oxford University Press), 2011, pp. 12-45.

[82] Taylor, Miles, 'Interests, parties and the state: the urban electorate in England, *c.*1820-72', and Lawrence, Jon, 'The dynamics of urban politics, 1867-1914' in Lawrence, Jon, and Taylor, Miles, (eds.), *Party, state and society: electoral behaviour in Britain since 1820*, (Scolar), 1997, pp. 50-78, 79-105. See also, Mitchell, Jeremy C., *The Organization of Opinion: Open voting in England, 1832-68*, (Palgrave), 2008, and Machin, Ian, *The rise of democracy in Britain, 1830-1918*, (Macmillan), 2001.

[83] Hoppen, K. Theodore, 'The franchise and electoral politics in England and Ireland 1832-1885', *History*, Vol. 70, (1985), pp. 202-217.

[84] Laski, Harold, 'The personnel of the English cabinet, 1801-1924', *American Political Science Review*, Vol. 22, (1928), pp. 12-31.

[85] See Woolley, S. F., 'The personnel of the Parliament of 1833', *English Historical Review*, Vol. 54, (1938), pp. 240-262.

MPs who held seats at some time between 1841 and 1847 included 234 non-peerage landowners.[86] The 166 heads of landowning families in Parliament included 26 who had active business interests and many more who held directorships in railways, insurance and joint-stock banks. Most of those with active business interests were private or merchant bankers, only 6 were manufacturers. This elitist pattern of representation was not confined to central government or Parliament and pervaded local government and played a central role in the military. The pattern of recruitment into the officer corps meant that the structure of authority in the army mirrored the wider society and created a pool of suitable recruits for political careers.[87] Military service was an important part of the experience of a large proportion of the landed class and was proportionately more important in the higher ranks of the peerage. Conservatives and Whigs competed for the support of the privileged classes.[88] Conservatives depended on landowners and farmers, together with the support of the colonial and shipping interest and those attached to the Church of England. The Whigs, or Liberals as they became in the late-1850s, were also drawn from the landed class, but attempted to express the interests of the manufacturing and commercial classes.[89] During the 1840s, Peelite Conservatives began to broaden their support amongst commercial and manufacturing classes but the repeal of the Corn Laws in 1846 led to this group splitting-off from the rest of the party.

Patronage had always played a major role in enabling governments to manage their support. However, by the 1830s, the decline of the 'influence of the Crown' and especially its capacity to use sinecure offices to gain

---

[86] Aydelotte, W. O., 'A statistical analysis of the Parliament of 1841: some problems of method', *Bulletin of the Institute of Historical Research*, Vol. 27, (1954), pp. 141-155, and 'The business interests of the gentry in the Parliament of 1841-7', in ibid., Clark, G. Kitson, *The making of Victorian England*, pp. 290-305, McLean, Iain, 'Interests and ideology in the United Kingdom Parliament of 1841-7: an analysis of roll call voting', in Lovenduski, Joni, & Stanyer, Jeffrey, (eds.), *Contemporary Political Studies 1995*, 3 Vols. (Political Studies Association of the United Kingdom), 1995, Vol. 1, pp. 1-20, and Schonhardt-Bailey, Cheryl, 'Ideology, Party and Interests in the British Parliament of 1841-47', *British Journal of Political Science*, Vol. 33, (2003), pp. 581-605.
[87] Clayton, Anthony, *The British Officer: Leading the army from 1660 to the present*, (Pearson Longman), 2006, pp. 92-160.
[88] On the emergence of political parties see Evans, E. J., *Political Parties in Britain 1783-1867*, (Methuen), 1985, O'Gorman, F., *The Emergence of the British Two-Party System 1760-1832*, (Edward Arnold), 1982, and Hill, B.W., *British Parliamentary Parties 1742-1832*, (Allen and Unwin), 1985. See, for the later period, Jenkins, T. A., *Parliament, party and politics in Victorian Britain*, (Manchester University Press), 1996, and Hawkins, Angus, *British party politics, 1852-1886*, (Macmillan), 1998.
[89] Jenkins, T. A., *The Liberal Ascendancy, 1830-1886*, (Macmillan), 1994.

support for its government made the management of Parliament and especially the House of Commons more problematic. This combined with an absence of effective party discipline often made it difficult for governments to control their supporters, though there is ample evidence to show that most MPs either supported one party or the other or voted accordingly.[90] The resurgence of a Conservative Party during the 1850s and the final emergence of a Liberal Party by 1860 reflected a redefinition of 'party' as an effective electoral machine for achieving political power. This was reflected in the recognition by both parties that electoral politics was now central to the political system and led to the creation of national Registration Associations by both parties to replace the more informal services provided by the political clubs.[91] The emergence of a national party system–in which party discipline played an important role–reinforced government control over Parliament and restored a degree of political stability that had been lacking in the 1850s. With the increase in the franchise in 1867 and 1884, getting their supporters out to vote became central for both parties and represented the beginnings of genuinely 'popular' politics. The creation of a National Liberal Federation in Birmingham in 1877 by a caucus of local activists was important in furthering the process by which parties, as electoral machines, became the dominant feature of political representation.[92]

The gradual build-up of electoral organisations, the introduction of the secret ballot in 1872 and legislation on corrupt practices a decade later,[93] the influence of the press on public opinion, the movement from property qualifications in 1884-1885 and its replacement with one man, one vote and the advent of major political campaigns broke the elitist system of

---

[90] See, Jenkins, T. S., 'The whips in the early-Victorian House of Commons', *Parliamentary History*, Vol. 19, (2000), pp. 259-286, and Sainty, John Christopher, and Cox, Gary W., 'The identification of government whips in the House of Commons, 1830-1905', *Parliamentary History*, Vol. 16, (1997), 339-358.

[91] Jaggard, Edwin, 'Managers and Agents: Conservative Party Organisation in the 1850s', *Parliamentary History*, Vol. 27, (2008), pp. 7-18, and Rix, Kathryn, 'Hidden workers of the party: The professional Liberal agents, 1885-1910', *Journal of Liberal History*, Vol. 52, (2006), pp. 4-13 and her *Parties, Agents and Electoral Culture in England, 1880-1910*, (Boydell), 2016.

[92] Watson, R. S., *The National Liberal Federation: from its commencement to the general election of 1906*, (T. Fisher Unwin), 1907, Herrick, Francis H., 'The Origins of the National Liberal Federation', *Journal of Modern History*, Vol. 17, (2), (1945), pp. 116-129, and ibid., Hanham, H. J. *Elections and Party Management: Politics in the time of Disraeli and Gladstone*.

[93] Rix, Kathryn, '"The Elimination of Corrupt Practices in British Elections"? Reassessing the Impact of the 1883 Corrupt Practices Act', *English Historical Review*, Vol. 123, (2008), pp. 65-97.

representation.[94] The elitist pattern was modified not destroyed and the landed class remained an important social and political force. The result, in the last third of the century, was the emergence of an 'Establishment' as the newly prominent manufacturers and their party machines were admitted to the sphere of informality and personal connections that characterised the landed classes. In return for accepting the power of the values and life-style of the landed class, the most prominent manufacturers were admitted as full members of the status group of 'gentlemen'. Public schools, the professions and the Church became essential supports for the Establishment that now dominated British public life. Between the 1880s and 1914, there was a fundamental restructuring of party politics as the Conservatives became the true party of the Establishment.[95] As the Liberals became more identified with intervention and reform, the Conservative party was a safe haven for those who feared the idea of the increasing political power of the working-classes.[96] In 1886, the old Whigs and the Liberal Unionists split from the official Liberals over Irish Home Rule, made an electoral pact with the Conservatives and in 1912 they merged. The Conservatives and Unionists became the Imperial party, the party of Queen and Empire, 'social justice' and 'social reform'. They gained the support of the traditional landed and agrarian interests, the commercial and financial sectors and eventually the manufacturers and the middle stratum of clerks, shopkeepers and from sections of the working-classes whom Disraeli referred to as the 'angels in the marble'.

The Establishment dominated all aspects of the state. After 1868, new wealth gained greater representation in Parliament. In 1885, 16 per cent of MPs were landowners, 12 per cent from the military but 32 per cent were from the law and other professions and 38 per cent from industry and commerce. Between 1868 and 1886, 27 out of the 49 men holding Cabinet office were landowners, but between 1886 and 1914 the

---

[94] Lawrence, Jon, *Speaking for the people: party, language, and popular politics in England, 1867-1914*, (Cambridge University Press), 1998, and Lawrence, Jon, *Electing Our Masters: The Hustings in British Politics from Hogarth to Blair*, (Oxford University Press), 2009.

[95] Shannon, Richard, *History of the Conservative Party, Vol. 3: The age of Salisbury, 1881-1902, unionism and empire*, (Longman), 1996, Ramsden, John, *History of the Conservative Party, Vol. 4: The age of Balfour and Baldwin, 1902-1940*, (Longman), 1978, Green, E. H. H., *The Crisis of Conservatism: The Politics, Economics and Ideology of the British Conservative Party, 1880-1914*, (Routledge), 1996, and Smith, Jeremy, *The taming of democracy: the Conservative Party, 1880-1924*, (University of Wales Press), 1997.

[96] See, for instance, Roberts, Matthew, '"Villa Toryism" and popular conservatism in Leeds, 1885-1902', *Historical Journal*, Vol. 49, (2006), pp. 217-246, and Lynch, Patricia C., *The Liberal Party in rural England 1885-1910: radicalism and community*, (Oxford University Press), 2003.

proportion fell slightly to 49 out of 101. The fall in the representation of landowners was not simply a fall in the number of landowning MPs but also a fall in the average size of their estates. There was also a declining number of hereditary titles represented in Parliament but the number of knights remained constant until 1918 when the numbers increased. Businessmen were increasingly given knighthoods and baronetcies rather than full peerages.[97] It was Queen Victoria who regarded the baronetcy as appropriate for the middle-classes who might find difficulty in coping with the expense and responsibility of a peerage. In 1895, there were 31 millionaire MPs and by 1906 only 22 were linked to the decreasing importance of land as a source of millionaires.[98] The establishment still monopolised the most important national and local political positions as well as recruitment to the army and to the important professions of the church and law. But even here there is evidence of change. By 1900, there were 60 bishops but only 30 per cent of the 26 with seats in the Lords were recruited from the landed classes. Half the bishops had wives who came from the landed classes and 90 per cent of bishops were educated at Oxford or Cambridge.[99] Similarly, three-quarters of all judges between 1876 and 1920 came from the landed or business classes.[100]

At the heart of the establishment was the peerage. No longer allocated only through political patronage, peerage gradually came to be seen as indicators of achievement in politics and public service. Thus, the accommodation between the landowners and the manufacturing and commercial classes was reflected in the awarding of peerage and other titles to non-landowners. Of the 463 people awarded peerages between 1837 and 1911, 125 were neither magnates nor gentry. These men made up 10 per cent of the new peerage at the beginning and 43 per cent at the end. The annual rate of peerage creation increased rapidly from the 1860s with new entrants drawn from the politically active elements of the new commercial and manufacturing classes. Only after 1885, when the brewers Allsopp, Guinness and Bass and the railway contractor Brassey entered the Lords, did businessmen enter the peerage in any numbers. Between 1880 and 1914, 200 new peers were created: a quarter from the land, a third from industry and a third from professions such as the army and the law. Between 1875 and 1904, 162 peerage and 300 baronetcies were

---

[97] Smith, E. A., *The House of Lords in British politics and society, 1815-1911*, (Longman), 1992.

[98] Rush, Michael, *The role of the Member of Parliament since 1868: from gentlemen to players*, (Oxford University Press), 2001.

[99] Beeson, Trevor, *The Bishops*, (SCM Press), 2002, provides a valuable collective biography since 1800.

[100] See, Duman, Daniel, 'A social and occupational analysis of the English judiciary, 1770-1790 and 1855-1875', *American Journal of Legal History*, Vol. 17, (1973), pp. 353-364.

created. 2,659 knighthoods were granted in the same period and new orders of knighthoods were created for diplomatic and Indian services, the Royal Victorian Order for special public services and the grade of knight bachelor was expanded. The mixture of 'old' and 'new' in the Establishment is evident in that between 1880 and 1914, more than a half of all knights had fathers who were peers, baronets, knights or landowners.

The 'Establishment' was a tight knit group of intermarried families that formed the political rulers of Britain and that monopolised recruitment to all the major social positions. The new party organisations were a part of this h, with the party headquarters and Parliamentary leadership being drawn into the pattern of exclusivity of the London gentleman's club where the ethos and values of the public schools were carried into adult life. In economic terms, however, the privileged classes remained distinct and a unified propertied class had not been created by 1914.

Away from land

Vita Sackville-West (1892-1962), an aristocratic English novelist, remembered an upper-class world of 'warmth and security, leisure and continuity': the Edwardian country house was the heart of that world.[101] For them, the pre-war age of 'innocence' stood in stark contrast to the decline and decay that followed 1918. Between 1914 and 1945, the pace of change for the upper-classes accelerated though on lines that were already evident before the War. Duties on inheriting property had existed in one form or another since 1694 with Estate Duties, a form of death duty, being introduced in 1894 and strengthened in 1908 while a new tax on any increase in land values due to the state rather than to landowners' own efforts was proposed by Lloyd George in his 'People's Budget' in 1909.[102] A direct political attack on the rights of the landed aristocracy, it prompted those concerned at the direction of Liberal land policies to sell.[103] There were 25 aristocracy residences in London in 1914, but only 8 were left by 1936. The Great War furthered the break-up of estates. Casualties among junior officers on the Western Front were especially high with one-

---

[101] Sackville-West, Victoria, *The Edwardians*, (The Hogarth Press), 1931, p. 40.

[102] Daunton, Martin, *Trusting Leviathan. The Politics of Taxation in Britain 1799-1914*, (Cambridge University Press), 2001, pp. 218-250, on death duties, and Hoppit, Julian, *The Dreadful Monster and its Poor Relations: Taxing, Spending and the United Kingdom, 1707-2021*, (Allen Lane), 2021. See also, Green, D. R. and Owens, A., 'Geographies of wealth: real estate and personal property ownership in England and Wales, 1870–1902', *Economic History Review*, Vol. 66, (3), (2013), pp. 848-872.

[103] Short, Brian, *Land and Society in Edwardian England*, (Cambridge University Press), 1997, and Packer, I., *Lloyd George, Liberalism and the land: The Land issue and party politics in England, 1906-1914*, (Boydell), 2001.

tenth of titled families losing their heirs in the trenches. Estates often passed to relatives with no local ties who were vulnerable to death duties that were raised to up 40 per cent on estates over £2 million and over in 1919.

During and after the First World War, rising taxation and the dwindling profitability of agriculture led to the sale and break-up of many landed estates. The relative hardship experienced by Britain's aristocracy began during the First World War when conscription led to shortages in the domestic labour needed to maintain their large stately homes. There were also growing shortages of food and fuel, although the landed gentry were able to grow fruit and vegetables, and raise poultry and livestock on their country estates, unlike the mass of the population. After 1918, land ceased to be the main source of income for the landed classes. Peers, for instance, were quick to find themselves directorships on the boards of industries, banks, and commercial firms. By 1923, 272 peers held directorships in over seven hundred public companies. It was a relative hardship of course and it cannot begin to compare with the deprivations suffered by the country's working-class during Britain's industrialisation and the decades that followed. The financial decline of Britain's aristocracy was in sharp contrast to what they had enjoyed during the pre-war years, when their pleasures included house parties, the copious consumption of alcohol, dancing, gambling and the field sports of hunting and shooting. During the war--something repeated after 1939--several stately homes were turned into military hospitals and convalescent homes, with family members dutifully stepping forward to treat injured men evacuated from the front. For instance, the riding school and indoor tennis courts at Woburn were converted into a 100-bed hospital, with the Abbey's gardeners, domestic servants and chauffeurs taking on the duties of orderlies and stretcher bearers.

By 1914, the upper middle-classes displaced the landed elite as the most powerful force in British society. Yet their ascendency as social and political leaders proved short-lived and after 1945 they collapsed under pressure from economic competition, rising taxation and the challenge posed by the post-war politics of Labour. They were separated from the lower middle-classes by scale of income, inherited wealth and extent of education and their access to positions of power and authority. They brought together older gentry families and a new political class from urban and industrial backgrounds that was linked by marriage and financial interests to business and to London 'high society'. They were marked out by their exercise of power over others whether as employers, senior civil servants, colonial administrators or as employers of servants or local tradesmen. In many respects this represented an extension of nineteenth century notions of deference and paternalism combined with the idea of *noblesse oblige* that wealth and status carried a duty to act responsibly towards those under their authority. This call to duty and public service ethos informed much upper middle-class behaviour in government, business, the professions and charity. Gesture politics called for inequalities of power. For instance, the Courtaulds may not have recognised trade unions until the late 1930s but it kept its workforce employed at mills in Halifax during the slump in the 1930s at considerable financial cost. Small businessmen in the 1920s and 1930s did not have the resources to follow suit and their workers saw their wages and jobs cut.

The war was a catalyst for major upheaval within the upper-classes and ushered in a struggle between those who embraced a changing world and those with a desire to retain past values and traditions. Antiquity of family lines had no relevance to their position during the inter-war decades and members of the old dynasties struggled to identify themselves alongside new members of the House of Lords who were financiers like Lord Rothschild (1910-1990) and Lord Swaythling (1869-1927); captains of industry such as Lord Leverhulme (1888-1949) and Lord Pirie; magnates like Lord Vestey (1882-1954) and Lord Inverchapel (1882-1951) of the P & O Combine; and finally newspaper proprietors like Lords Beaverbrook (1879-1964) and Rothermere (1898-1978) and Viscount Northcliffe (1865-1922) who left a £5.2 million estate on his death in 1922. Released from the strains of war, the upper-classes began to plan again for world travel, refitting their yachts, re-opening country houses, acting as if nothing had changed.[104] Professional cricket was revived, the regatta was held at Henley, opera and ballet enjoyed a great season in 1919 and there was always social gatherings that the upper-classes turned out for. Taylor gives a detailed account of the hedonism and excesses of alcoholism and addiction of an elite mix of aristocratic socialites, bohemian party givers and a coterie of glittering artistic and literary talent. His main argument is that beneath the veneer of such glitter, a post-World War I generation of 'Bright Young People' was tormented by an irreconcilable combination of guilt and glamour.[105]

Landowners attempted to cling to whatever vestiges of their identity that they could. Often, this included shutting up the majority of large houses to save money on servants, heating bills and electricity and limiting weekend partygoers to a small number of rooms. Despite possessing tapestries, expensive works of art, multiple dinner services and lavish living areas,

...[family members] never used the room when [they] were to [themselves],

---

[104] Graves, Robert, and Hodge, Alan, *The Long Weekend*, (W. W. Norton and Co.), 1940, pp. 12-14.
[105] Taylor, D. J., *Bright Young Things: The Lost Generation of London's Jazz Age*, (Farrar Strauss & Giroux), 2009.

for patches of blue mold had spoilt the wallpaper, and one always shivered there. But nobody must think of [them] as anything but drawing-room folk.[106]

In May 1918, George Herbert realised he had little choice but to sell much of the furniture at his home in Bretby, Derbyshire.[107] A few years later Maud Alice Burke took the equally painful measure of selling her jewels and replacing them with costume pieces. But George was not an unemployed miner or factory worker facing destitution and Maud was not an impoverished middle-class widow; they were Lord Carnarvon (1866-1923) and Lady Cunard (1872-1948), members of Britain's titled aristocracy. Their severely reduced circumstances--a combination of the cost of war, death duties, crippling taxes and declining farm rentals--reflected those of many upper-class families in the years after 1918. Overall the burden of direct taxation on country estates, including land tax, rates and income tax rose from 9 to 30 per cent of income. For instance, on the Earl of Pembroke's (1880-1960) Wilton estate, income tax took more than a quarter of the estate's income from rents in 1919 compared to just 4 per cent in 1914.

Several of their contemporaries were forced to sell not just their treasured belongings to make ends meet but their stately homes. In 1918, Sir Francis Astley-Corbett (1859-1939) sold his entire 4,500-acre Everleigh Manor house and estate in Wiltshire. The previous year Lord Pembroke had sold one of his estates in the same county and went on to dispose of 8,400 acres of the Wilton estate also in Wiltshire, with many of his tenant farmers taking the opportunity to buy their holdings. The buyers were not only those who had previously been tenant farmers on the land, but also the 'nouveaux riches'--the businessmen who had profited from the war and sought to acquire the social status that accompanied ownership of extensive tracts of British countryside. Some houses were torn down--between 1918 and 1930 more than 180 country houses were demolished--others were abandoned. Some took on new roles. For instance, Nottingham Council bought the Elizabethan Wollaton Hall and opened it as a museum in 1925 after it had been vacant for over forty years and Claremont House in Surrey became a girls' school in 1930. The Wall Street Crash of 1929 had a dramatic impact on those in the aristocracy who had invested heavily in the stock market in the hope of maintaining their privileged lifestyle following the war. Sir Arthur (1866-1936) and

---

[106] Nicolson, Victoria, *Among the Bohemians: Experiments in Living 1900-1939*, (Viking), 2002, p. 104.
[107] Horn, Pamela, *Country House Society: The private lives of England's upper class after the First World War*, (Amberley), 2015, Tinniswood, Adrian, *The Long Weekend: Life in the English Country House, 1918-1939*, (Jonathan Cape), 2016.

Lady Sybil Colefax (1874-1950) lost their life savings--she reinvented herself as a fashionable interior designer in partnership with Peggy Ward, the Countess Munster (1905-1982)–while the wealthy heiress Mabelle Wichfeld (1878-1933), who had once employed 80 servants at Blair Castle in Perthshire, was so short of cash on her death in 1933 that her funeral at Savoy Chapel, next to London's Savoy Hotel, was paid for by friends.

The inter-war years have been seen as an 'Indian summer' for landed society that was simply awaiting the death knell of the Second World War. By the early 1920s there was a decrease in the creation of new members of the aristocracy. In 1923, there were 708 lay peers, of whom 198 owed their titles to creations in Queen Victoria's reign, 46 to creations of Edward VII, 176 to creations by George V, since 1910. Between 1917 and 1921, four marquisates, eight earldoms, 22 viscounties and 64 baronies were created. Between 1923 and 1930, it was one marquis, five earls, 14 viscounts and 59 barons. In 1911, the top one per cent in society owned 69 per cent of national wealth; in 1936 it was only 55 per cent. The gentry, under pressure as the price for land went sharply down before the war, could not afford to keep their second city homes in London.

The real losers in this process were the landed gentry, a group whose fortunes had been in decline since the agricultural depression of the late nineteenth century. Without the spread of resources and means to diversify of the larger landowners, the inter-war years took a heavy toll of smaller, long established families.[108]

This pessimistic scenario has obscured a world of energy, invention and change. Wartime rents had not grown as fast as prices and in 1919 and 1920 farmers were eager to purchase land that sold at half the cost in 1914. The *Estates Gazette* estimated in late 1921 that as much as a quarter of England must have changed hands in the previous four years while *The Times* in 1922 published an article entitled 'England Changing Hands'. In 1927, owner occupiers held 36 per cent of English and Welsh agricultural land compared to 11 per cent in 1914. A census of farm land in 1941 revealed that the proportion of owner occupiers was changed from 1927, a consequence of the fall in land values from 134 in 1920 to a nadir of 82 in 1929 before recovering to 100 between 1937 and 1939. The loosening bonds between family, mansion and local community meant the country house was changing, but it was not dying. In 1919, there were still 332 people with fortunes over £1 million. New owners—often Americans—brought new aesthetics, new social structures and new meanings to the country house scene. The 'week-end' entered common usage as expanding rail networks and especially the motor car meant that people could dash to

---

[108] Stevenson, John, *British Society 1914-45*, (Penguin), 1990, p. 334.

the country on Friday and return on Monday.

Only a fraction of all country houses, mansions and estates was destroyed. And new ones were built. Philip Sassoon (1888-1939), a Conservative politician, built Port Lympne in Kent as a 'fairy palace'—a theatrical Cape Dutch-style red-brick mansion overlooking Romney Marsh towards the English Channel. To its architect Sir Herbert Baker (1862-1946), it was a statement that a new aesthetic had emerged with new cultural aspirations. There were modernist novelties, too—Crowsteps near Newbury built in 1920-1930, Joldwynds in Surrey designed by Oliver Hill (1887-1968) and completed in 1932—shocking the public with their shiny white walls, flat roofs and angular façades.[109] These were exceptions and most design was retrospective as aristocrats and nouveaux-riches sought stability and refuge embarking on a frenzy of castle restorations. For those entrenched in their traditions, the drive to retain former glory and to return to the Golden Age of power and prestige was, despite the changing circumstances, strong and saw some actively flirt with fascism in the 1930s. Class war, socialism and fascism may have been un-English ideas but the upper-classes intent on finding ways to regain the power that had been steadily declining for half a century, looked abroad to Germany and Italy for inspiration.[110] When war came in 1939, the idea returned that the world was lost, symbolised, to many people, by the disappearance of domestic service. Contrary to some alarmist inter-war accounts, the supply of servants had remained buoyant for much of the preceding two decades. In the 1950s, a flood of houses passed into the hands of the National Trust and the English country house became the object of nostalgia.

What had been a major controversy in the decade before the outbreak of war in 1914, fragmented in the inter-war period into a series of separate but related political issues that transformed the ways in which land reform was understood. In the face of foreign competition, farming continued to decline while rapid and unregulated urban development especially in the suburbs combined with changing patterns of landownership put further pressure on agriculture. This contributed to the declining economic and social fortunes of the traditional landed elite and especially the remaining gentry. After 1930, the demise of the Liberal Party saw the eclipse of related policies of free trade and taxation of land values. Radical opposition to the landed elite was no longer central to socialist thinking that now focussed on the development and control of land-use and the protection of agriculture and the landscape from urban incursions.

The Labour Party's previous promise of land nationalisation was

---

[109] Powers, Alan, *Modern: The Modern Movement in Britain*, (Merrell), 2005.
[110] Urbach, Katrina, (ed.), *European Aristocracies and the Radical Right 1918-1959*, (Oxford University Press), 2007, p. 55.

significantly diluted by the experience of the war.[111] In 1942, the Uthwatt Report, established at the height of the Blitz in the light of growing public concern about property speculation, recommended the control and taxation of land use and development, but specifically rejected land nationalisation as too controversial. The Dower Report on National Parks in England and Wales in 1945 proposed the establishment of a National Parks Commission. Before 1939 a combination of electoral calculation and Labour's slender interest in rural areas created a policy vacuum, while during the war the sheer scale of the enterprise of 260,000 farmers, the enormous financial cost involved, and potential opposition from agricultural interests at a time when their co-operation was required to increase food production, led the Party to drop its historical commitment to land nationalisation.[112]

Conclusions

The Second World War did more to transform Britain's class structures than any other event in the twentieth century. This was evident in Labour's victory over Churchill's Conservatives in the 1945 General Election. The consequences of a more meritocratic social and political order was present across all classes with the creation of the National Health Service and social security for all. For the upper-classes, taxation impacted on earned and unearned income with the rate of income tax on those with annual incomes of between £700 to £2,000 rose from 9.3 per cent in 1938 to 22.7 per cent in 1947 while on the 'supertax' on the very rich increased from 6d. in the £ in 1909 to 47½d in the £ in 1945. The Second World War was a watershed that marked a reordering of the world, seeing the decline of the old European colonial powers left financially-crippled by the conflict and struggling to find relevancy in the emerging bi-polar international system of the Cold War. The end of Empire and Britain's effective subordination to the United States were made inescapable by the enormous costs of defeating Germany and Japan. Britain did not 'win' the war; it merely, and barely, survived it. American Secretary of State Dean Acheson's (1893-1971) much cited comment in a speech at West Point in 1962 that 'Great Britain has lost an Empire and has not yet found a role' was both poignant and, in the aftermath of decision to leave the EU, true.

---

[111] Tichelar, Michael, 'The Labour Party, agricultural policy and the retreat from rural land nationalisation during the Second World War', *Agricultural History Review*, Vol. 51, (2), (2003), pp. 209-225.

[112] Chase, M., 'Nothing less than a revolution? Labour's agricultural policy', in Fryth, J., (ed.), *Labour's High Noon. The government and the economy, 1945-51*, (Lawrence & Wishart), 1993, pp. 79-95.

Further Reading

The bibliography provides a general guide to relevant books. More detailed references can be found in the footnotes. Many of the references to primary sources are available on Google Books or Internet Archive either to be read or downloaded.

Brown, Callum G., and Fraser, W. Hamish, *Britain since 1707*, (Longman), 2010 provides a synopsis of developments. Hilton, Boyd, *A Mad, Bad & Dangerous People? England 1783-1846*, (Oxford University Press), 2005, Hoppen, K. Theodore, *The Mid-Victorian Generation 1846-1886*, (Oxford University Press), 1998, and Searle, G. R., *A New England? Peace and War, 1886-1918*, (Oxford University Press), 2005, are more detailed. Other general surveys include McCord, N., *British History 1815-1906*, (Oxford University Press), 1999, 2007, Rubinstein, W. D., *Britain's Century: A Political and Social History, 1815-1905*, (Edward Arnold), 1998, Cannadine, David, *Victorious Century: The United Kingdom 1800-1906*, (Allen Lane), 2017, and Pugh, M. D., *State and Society: British political and social history since 1870*, (Bloomsbury), 2017.

Daunton, M. J., *Progress and Poverty: An Economic and Social History of Britain 1700-1850*, (Oxford University Press), 1995, and *Wealth and welfare: an economic and social history of Britain, 1851-1951*, (Oxford University Press), 2007, Mokyr, Joel, *The Enlightened Economy: An Economic History of Britain 1700-1850*, (Yale University Press), 2009, and Floud, Roderick, Humphries, Jane, and Johnson, Paul A., (eds.), *The Cambridge economic history of modern Britain, Volume 1: industrialisation, 1700-1870*, (Cambridge University Press), 2014, and *The Cambridge economic history of modern Britain, Volume 2: Growth and Decline, 1870 to the Present*, (Cambridge University Press), 2014, are the most up-to-date studies. Thompson, F. M. L., (ed.), *The Cambridge Social History of Britain 1750-1950*, 3 Vols., (Cambridge University Press), 1990, adopts a thematic approach to social developments.

Cannon, John, *A Dictionary of British History*, 2nd ed., (Oxford University Press), 2009, Connolly, S. J., (ed.), *The Oxford Companion to Irish History*, 2nd ed., (Oxford University Press), 2007, and Cook, Chris, *The Routledge Companion to Britain in the Nineteenth Century, 1815-1914*, (Routledge), 2005, provide important references. Langton, J., and Morris, R. J., *Atlas of Industrialising Britain 1780-1914*, (Methuen), 1986, and Pope, R., (ed.), *Atlas of British Social and Economic History since c.1700*, (Routledge), 1989, give a valuable spatial dimension.

Aspinall, A., and Smith, E. A., (eds.), *English Historical Documents, Volume XI, 1783-1832*, (Eyre and Spottiswoode), 1959, Young, G. M., and Handcock, W. D., (eds.), *English Historical Documents, Volume XII, (1), 1832-1874*, (Eyre and Spottiswoode), 1956, Handcock, W. D., (ed.), *English Historical Documents, Volume XII, (2), 1874-1914*, (Eyre and Spottiswoode),

1977, and Hanham, H. J., *The Nineteenth Century Constitution 1815-1914: documents and commentary*, (Cambridge University Press), 1969.

Morris, R. J., *Class and Class Consciousness in the Industrial Revolution*, (Macmillan), 1980, and Reid, Alastair J., *Social Classes and Social Relations in Britain 1850-1914*, (Macmillan), 1992, provide aa introduction to this complex issue. For the working-classes see, Rule, J., *The Labouring Classes in Early Industrial England 1750-1850*, (Longman), 1986, Benson, J., *The Working-class in Britain 1850-1939*, (Longman), 1989, August, Andrew, *The British Working Class, 1832-1940*, (Longman), 2007, and Savage, M., and Miles, A., *The remaking of the British working class, 1840-1940*, (Routledge), 1994. James, Lawrence, *The middle class: a history*, (Little, Brown), 2006, is a detailed study. Wahrman, Dror, *Imagining the Middle Class. The Political Representation of Class in Britain c.1780-1840*, (Cambridge University Press), 1995, analyses the emergence of middle-class consciousness. Beckett, J. C., *The Aristocracy in England 1660-1914*, (Basil Blackwell), 1986, second edition, 1989, and Carradine, D., *The Decline and Fall of the British Aristocracy*, (Yale University Press), 1990, and Carradine, D., *Aspects of Aristocracy: Grandeur and Decline in Modern Britain*, (Yale University Press), 1994, examine the upper-classes. Chalus, Elaine, (eds.), *Women's History: Britain, 1700-1850*, (Routledge), 2005, and Purvis, June, (ed.), *Women's History: Britain 1850-1945*, (UCL), 1995, are collections of essays. Honeyman, Karina, *Women, Gender and Industrialisation in England, 1700-1870*, (Macmillan), 2000, Gleadle, Kathryn, *British Women in the Nineteenth Century*, (Palgrave), 2001, and Brown, Richard, *The Women Question: Sex, Work and Politics: Women in Britain, 1780-1945*, (Authoring History), 2021, are good introductions to the subject.

Index

equal pay, 69, 83, 84
governess, 176
leisure industries, 193–94
nursing, 177, 179, 180, 181, 182,
  183, 184, 186, 190, 192, 196
office work, 79, 80, 179
sexual division of labour, 175
shop work, 81
teaching, 177, 179, 194, 196, 197
textile, 85
women's manual work, 128
women's work, 70, 75, 79, 177, 246
Women's Army Auxiliary Corps,
  188
Women's Forage Corps, 189
Women's Forestry Corps, 190
Women's Freedom League, 187
Women's Hospital Corps, 192
Women's Industrial Council, 84,
  85
Women's Institutes, 239
Women's Land Army, 130, 189
Women's Legion, 188
women's movement, 175, 183, 220
Women's rights, 208
Women's Trade Union
  Association, 85
Women's Trade Union League,
  84, 85
Women's Volunteer Reserve, 188
Women's magazines, 133, 168,
  247, 248
Woollen industry, 28

Workhouse, 208
Working conditions, 33, 34, 54, 72,
  73, 82
Working hours, 22, 100, 107
Working-classes, 12, 14, 16, 18, 19,
  21, 28, 35, 37, 39, 48, 49, 55, 57,
  59, 60, 67, 73, 82, 92, 93, 98, 99,
  108, 109, 110, 112, 117, 134,
  135, 136, 137, 143, 145, 147,
  161, 164, 165, 227, 228, 229,
  231, 234, 240, 244, 250, 276,
  277
apprenticeship, 26, 27, 55, 70, 169,
  271
aristocracy of labour, 46, 48
artisan, 48, 100, 101
casual workers, 29, 30, 33, 57, 58,
  59
factory workers, 33, 59, 67
semi-skilled labour, 19, 20, 52, 54
skilled labour, 12, 14, 18, 25, 26, 27,
  29, 32, 33, 41, 46, 47, 49, 50, 51,
  52, 53, 54, 56, 57, 58, 60, 61, 70,
  73, 77, 78, 82, 110, 112, 134,
  135, 136, 138, 145, 163, 178,
  240, 241, 243, 250
unskilled labour, 12, 18, 19, 20, 29,
  33, 54, 56, 57, 73, 77, 135
Workplace, 4, 29, 33, 40, 47, 48,
  49, 53, 54, 70, 73, 85, 86, 101,
  118, 128, 135, 136, 164
Yorkshire, 25, 28, 50, 71, 99, 152,
  243, 254, 256
West Riding, 28

About the Author

Richard Brown is a Fellow of the Royal Historical Society and the Historical Association. He has published sixty-six print and Kindle books, over fifty articles and papers on nineteenth century history and countless reviews. He is the author of a successful blog, Looking at History, which has a wide audience among students and researchers.

Recent publications

The Woman Question: Sex, Work and Politics 1780-1945, (Authoring History), 2021, hardback revised edition.
Canada's Wars of Religion? (Authoring History), 2020.
The Woman Question: Sex, Work and Politics 1780-1945, (Authoring History), 2020. Also available in a Kindle edition.
Radicalism and Chartism 1790-1860, (*Reconsidering Chartism*, Authoring History), 2018. Also available in a Kindle edition.
Disrupting the British World, 1600-1980, 2nd ed., (*Rebellion Quartet*, Authoring History), 2017. Also available in a Kindle version.
Famine, Fenians and Freedom, 1830-1882, 2nd ed., (*Rebellion Quartet*, Authoring History), 2017. Also available in a Kindle version.
Three Rebellions: Canada, South Wales and Australia, (*Rebellion Quartet*, Authoring History), 2nd ed., 2016. Also available in a Kindle version.
Roger of Sicily: Portrait of a Ruler, (Authoring History), 2016. Also available in a Kindle version.
Robert Guiscard: Portrait of a Warlord, (Authoring History), 2016. Also available in a Kindle version.
Abbot Suger, The Life of Louis VI 'the Fat', (Authoring History), 2016. Also available in a Kindle version.
Chartism: A Global History and other essays, (*Reconsidering Chartism*, Authoring History), 2016. Also available in a Kindle version.
The Chartists, Regions and Economies, (*Reconsidering Chartism*, Authoring History), 2016. Also available in a Kindle version.
Chartism: Rise and Demise, (*Reconsidering Chartism*, Authoring History), 2014
Before Chartism: Exclusion and Resistance, (*Reconsidering Chartism*, Authoring History), 2014.

Printed in Great Britain
by Amazon